The ultimate
**Mediterranean Diet**
Cookbook:

# 600

easy, super tasty recipes
to start and maintain a healthy lifestyle

*Anna Martin*

© Copyright 2020 - All rights reserved.

The content contained within this book may not be reproduced, duplicated or transmitted without direct written permission from the author or the publisher. Under no circumstances will any blame or legal responsibility be held against the publisher, or author, for any damages, reparation, or monetary loss due to the information contained within this book. Either directly or indirectly.

Legal Notice:
This book is copyright protected. This book is only for personal use. You cannot amend, distribute, sell, use, quote or paraphrase any part, or the content within this book, without the consent of the author or publisher.

Disclaimer Notice:
Please note the information contained within this document is for educational and entertainment purposes only. All effort has been executed to present accurate, up to date, and reliable, complete information. No warranties of any kind are declared or implied. Readers acknowledge that the author is not engaging in the rendering of legal, financial, medical or professional advice. The content within this book has been derived from various sources. Please consult a licensed professional before attempting any techniques outlined in this book. By reading this document, the reader agrees that under no circumstances is the author responsible for any losses, direct or indirect, which are incurred as a result of the use of information contained within this document, including, but not limited to, — errors, omissions, or inaccuracies.

# Contents

| | | |
|---|---|---|
| **4** | INTRODUCTION | |
| **5** | CHAPTER 1 | The Mediterranean Diet |
| **8** | CHAPTER 2 | History of the Mediterranean Diet |
| **10** | CHAPTER 3 | Health Benefits of the Mediterranean Way of Eating |
| **13** | CHAPTER 4 | Diseases the Mediterranean Diet Prevents |
| **17** | CHAPTER 5 | What to Eat and Avoid in the Mediterranean Diet |
| **19** | CHAPTER 6 | The Mediterranean Way of Life |
| **22** | CHAPTER 7 | The 8 Basic Guiding Principles of the Mediterranean Diet |
| **26** | CHAPTER 8 | Reasons Why the Mediterranean Diet Is Good For You |
| **29** | CHAPTER 9 | Mediterranean Diet FAQs |
| **32** | CHAPTER 10 | How to get started with the Mediterranean diet |
| **36** | CHAPTER 11 | Mindset for Success in the Mediterranean Diet |
| **39** | CHAPTER 12 | Being Keen on a Mediterranean Diet |
| **43** | CHAPTER 13 | Breakfast |
| **71** | CHAPTER 14 | Small dishes |
| **89** | CHAPTER 15 | Salads |
| **101** | CHAPTER 16 | Snacks |
| **133** | CHAPTER 17 | Poultry |
| **183** | CHAPTER 18 | Meat |
| **207** | CHAPTER 19 | Vegetable dishes |
| **235** | CHAPTER 20 | Desserts |
| **297** | CHAPTER 21 | Eggs |
| **301** | CHAPTER 22 | Seafood |
| **337** | CHAPTER 23 | Beans |
| **391** | CHAPTER 24 | Soups |
| **407** | CHAPTER 25 | Rice and Grains |
| **435** | CHAPTER 26 | Pasta and Pizza |
| **447** | CHAPTER 27 | 7-Days Meal Plan |
| **455** | CHAPTER 28 | Conversion Tables |
| **458** | CHAPTER 29 | The Food Pyramid |
| **461** | CONCLUSION | |

# Introduction

Over the last decades, the Mediterranean diet saw a slow rise in the Western world. Many countries of the west were slow to pick it up, but once they did, they realized that they had discovered the key to the Elixir of Life.

The Mediterranean diet not only helped people rely on a wholesome and healthy diet, but it helped them lose weight, power up their immune systems, improved their vitality, and even contributed to healthy skin.

In other words, the Mediterranean diet helped people feel good and look good.

The combination of benefits changed people's perception of what they should be having and question their eating habits.

For example, many people often skip breakfast because they feel that having a meal in the morning adds more weight to their bodies. However, the Mediterranean diet does not skip breakfast. On the contrary, it considers breakfast the most important meal of the day.

The importance of breakfast has not only been communicated by dietitians, but by doctors and health advisors as well. and it is done for a reason. Even science backs up the importance of breakfast in our everyday lives. According to one study (Kahleova, Lloren, Mashchak, Hill & Fraser, 2017), having a proper breakfast contributed to the reduction in BMI, or Body Mass Index, of people. The study was conducted on 50,000 Americans, and the population included in the study featured people who had breakfast and those who skipped breakfast entirely.

Another study was conducted on overweight and obese women who were made to have the same calorie content for 12 weeks (Jakubowicz, Barnea, Wainstein & Froy, 2013). The women were split into two groups and both were given an ideal calorie content of 1,400 calories per day. However, the difference was in the way those calories were split. In one group, the women were given 700 calories during breakfast, 500 during lunch, and the remaining 200 during dinner for the other group, the order was reversed, where the women had 200 calories for breakfast, 500 for lunch, and 700 for dinner. Let's call the group having a heavy breakfast as Group A while the other group with a large dinner as Group B.

At the end of the experiment, the researchers noticed something remarkable, and their observations are summarized in the points below:

Group A experienced an 11% decrease in their body weight, while Group B showed a decrease of just 4%.

The BMI of Group A dropped by about 10%, while the BMI of Group B reduced by 5%.

The waist circumference of Group A dropped by 7.9%, and that of Group B reduced by just 3.5%.

Triglyceride is a type of fat cells that are present in people with overweight problems. At the end of the 12 weeks, the levels of triglyceride reduced by nearly 33% in Group A, whereas Group B only showed a reduction in triglyceride by just 14%.

The countries that relied on the Mediterranean diet saw its benefits way before any scientific research was conducted. They didn't have any research conducted to guide them toward a particular eating pattern or food content. They relied on habits and suggestions dropped down from one generation to another, dating back to ancient Rome and Greece. Even those ancient civilizations took inspiration from cultures that preceded them. After all, the Roman civilization began around 753 BC, but olive oil was first produced around 2,500 BC., and guess where the oil was first created? You are right. In the Mediterranean region.

Essentially, the diet has been refined over millennia, as newer methods of cooking were introduced. But the adherence to a healthy form of dithe et remained, no matter how old the diet grew.

Just how did the Mediterranean diet evolve to what it is today while still maintaining its component?

It all comes down to what we eat, when we eat it, and in what quantities.

The Mediterranean diet plan would depend on the initial foods that people used to take in countries like Italy and Greece back in 1960. Experts discovered that these people were exceptionally healthful compared to People in America and experienced a minimal risk of many means of life diseases.

The Mediterranean diet plan is among the hottest diets on the planet because it's built on whole grains along with other simple (but delicious) foods that may lower blood circulation pressure and cholesterol—a win for the heart as well as your waistline.

This is a diet plan whereby it is possible to lose excess weight by consuming the healthy Components mentioned inside this book. Be sure you consume smaller food portion sizes if you want to lose weight. Moreover, it usually includes essential everyday exercise to help keep a wholesome heart.

# 1 The Mediterranean Diet

The Mediterranean eating regimen is in excess of an eating regimen. It is a way of life. It's a method of eating so as to carry on with a full and solid life. When following along these lines of eating you'll get in shape, yet you'll likewise reinforce your heart and give your body all the best possible supplements important to carry on with a long and profitable life. Individuals following the Mediterranean eating regimen have been connected to a lower danger of Alzheimer's malady and malignancy, better generally speaking cardiovascular wellbeing, and an all-inclusive life expectancy.

This eating routine incorporates expending heaps of vegetables and grains, organic products, rice, and pasta while constraining fats, supplanting salt with herbs and flavors, and eating fish and poultry rather than red meat. The Mediterranean eating regimen doesn't contain a ton of red meat. Nuts are a piece of a solid piece of this eating routine. Be that as it may, one should restrain themselves to a bunch or so a day. Nuts have a high measure of fat, however a high level of the fat isn't immersed. Nuts are additionally high in calories so cautiously screen the sum you eat. You'll need to stay away from salted nuts and nectar simmered or sugar coated nuts.

It might even incorporate a glass of red wine every day, and normal physical exercises to completely amplify the wonderful medical advantages. The Mediterranean eating routine reflects different dietary patterns of the nations close to the Mediterranean Sea, for the most part Southern Italy, Greece, Morocco, France, and Spain. Because of their one of a kind territory, the atmosphere bolsters new organic products, vegetables, and a portion of the world's best fish.

This eating regimen isn't centered around constraining your complete utilization of fat, rather, it centers around settling on more brilliant decisions about the sorts of fat you devour. This eating routine debilitates individuals from eating trans-fats and soaked fats, the two of which have been connected to coronary illness.

Grains utilized in the Mediterranean eating regimen are ideally entire grain, which by and large contains next to no in the method of undesirable trans-fat. Bread is a significant piece of the Mediterranean way of life; be that as it may, bread ought not be canvassed in margarine or spread. Rather, the bread is eaten either dunked in olive oil or eaten plain. This chops down altogether on various Trans and soaked fats ordinarily connected with eating bread.

Wine assumes an enormous job in the Mediterranean eating regimen. A glass of wine is regularly included with each night feast.

This implies 5 ounces or less of wine for anybody beyond 65 years old for individuals under 65 close to 10 ounces every day. On the off chance that you have any history of liquor reliance or misuse, I propose avoiding inside and out expending liquor as a major aspect of your eating routine. The equivalent goes on the off chance that you as of now have liver or coronary illness. Olive oil is the essential wellspring of fat in this sort of diet. It really gives monounsaturated fat, which is the sort of fat that decreases the degrees of LDL cholesterol when used rather than Trans or immersed fats. The "Additional virgin" and "virgin" olive oils are considered to have experienced the least handling. They additionally happen to contain the biggest degrees of defensive plant mixes liable for giving cancer prevention agent impacts.

What is LDL?

Cholesterol is a compound having a place with the sterol or steroid liquor subgroup of natural atoms. It is delegated a waxy steroid of fat. It is a basic segment of cell layers and an antecedent to the creation of fat-solvent nutrients, for example, nutrient D.

There are two primary kinds of cholesterol; HDL (high-thickness lipoproteins) and LDL (low-thickness lipoproteins). Despite the fact that this isn't completely precise. HDL and LDL are lipoproteins. They are the vehicle components for cholesterol particles. They are made out of proteins and fats.

LDL particles transport cholesterols from the liver to the cells of the body.

HDLs gather any that are found in the tissues or created by different organs and convey it back to the liver for reprocessing.

This is the reason HDLs are in some cases alluded to as "great" cholesterol since they get any that are dropped in the circulation system before it can stick to the dividers of the courses. LDL is known as terrible cholesterol. In spite of the fact that it is fundamental forever, a lot of cholesterol in the circulation system may build an individual's danger of coronary illness, for the most part atherosclerosis. This is the reason balance in HDL/LDL particles is so significant, and a lopsidedness can be perilous.

Feature on Trans-fats

Trans-fats are recorded as hydrogenated or incompletely hydrogenated oils. The oils might be soy, canola or just recorded as in part hydrogenated "vegetable" il. This sort of fat is the most exceedingly terrible kind you can eat.

As indicated by the Mayo Clinic, trans-fats raise LDL levels and bring down HDL levels. It is a man-made fat that is found in prepared merchandise and other bundled nourishments. Notwithstanding causing HDL/LDL irregularity, it raises complete blood triglycerides (fats that typically course in the circulation system) and advances plaque development on blood vessel dividers. Like stoutness, trans-fat likewise adds to ceaseless irritation.

Another significant part of the Mediterranean eating regimen is greasy fish.

This incorporates lake trout, salmon, sardines, herring, mackerel, and alb.acore fish. They have a lot of omega-3 unsaturated fats.

This sort of unsaturated fat assists with diminishing blood coagulating and bring down our triglyceride levels. High triglyceride levels (in excess of 150 mg) can cause heart illnesses. Omega-3 unsaturated fats are likewise connected with assisting with directing circulatory strain, decline the danger of unexpected coronary episode, and improve the general strength of our veins.

**Significant Features of a Mediterranean Diet:**

1. The essential wellspring of your fat in this eating routine is olive oil.
2. Dinner regularly incorporates a glass of red wine.
3. Vegetables and occasional new organic products are a significant piece of each dinner.
4. Whole grain pasta and bread are served with no kind of conciliatory sentiment,
5. Meat is devoured in littler segments, and red meat is essentially stayed away from through and through.
6. Popular flavors incorporate garlic, basil, oregano, lemon, rosemary, and mint.

# 2 History of the Mediterranean Diet

Just like it sounds, the Mediterranean diet comes from the dietary traditions of the people of the Mediterranean isle region such as the Romans and Greeks. The people of these regions had a rich diet full of fruits, bread, wine, olive oil, nuts, and seafood. Despite the fatty elements in their diet, the people of this region tended to live longer and overall healthy lives with relatively less cardiovascular heart issues. This phenomenon was noticed by American scientist Ancel Keys in the 1950s.

Keys was an academic researcher at the University of Minnesota in the 1950s who researched healthy eating habits and how to reverse the decline in American cardiovascular health. He found in his research that poor people in the Mediterranean region of the world were healthier compared to the rich American population which had seen a recent rise in cardiovascular heart issues and obesity. Compared to wealthy New Yorkers, the lower class in the Mediterranean lived well into their 90s and tended to be physically active in their senior years. Keys and his team of scientists decided to travel the world and study the link between the region's diet and the health of the people who lived there. In 1957, he traveled and studied the lifestyles, nutrition, exercise, and diet of the United States, Italy, Holland, Greece, Japan, Finland, and Yugoslavia. Keys' research found that the dietary choices of the people from the Mediterranean region allowed them to live a longer lifespan and one that kept them more physically active compared to other world populations. The people of Greece, in particular, ate a diet that consisted of healthy fats like seafood, nuts, olive oil, and fatty fish. Despite the amount of fat in these sources, their cardiovascular health stayed consistent without the risk factors for a heart attack or stroke. His study became a guideline for the United States to set its own nutritional standards, and he became known as the father of nutritional science. With Keys' work leading the way, further research and clinical trials have been conducted on the Mediterranean diet which gives evidence for its health-improving properties. Not only will you lose weight, but you could lower your LDL "bad" cholesterol, lower your blood pressure, and decrease and stabilize blood sugar levels. With a decrease in these signs of cardiovascular heart disease, you can greatly reduce your risk of suffering from heart attack, stroke, or premature death.It's important to point out that the Mediterranean diet cannot alone bring about these changes to someone's health. It will depend on a variety of other factors in their lifestyle such as genetics, physical exercise, smoking, obesity, drug use, etc. Part of the combination of the Mediterranean diet is incorporating physical exercise into your life. That's how it goes from the Mediterranean "diet" to a Mediterranean "lifestyle" that truly mimics the people of that region. The people of Greece tend to live an active lifestyle with some sort of daily physical activity they partake in. Whether that is walking, sailing, rowing, swimming, or hiking, coupling that physical exercise that with a healthy plant-based diet is what can bring about beneficial health results. In our current environment, physical activity could mean a session at the gym or even just a walk around the block. It doesn't have to highly intensive, but the important part is incorporating some sort of physical activity in your day, so you can truly gain the benefits of following this diet. Before we begin listing a rudimentary list of what you can and cannot eat, it's important to highlight that the Mediterranean region consists of many countries with their own unique dietary choices. With this diversity comes many varieties of recipes that you can incorporate into your dishes as long as you are still following the healthy tenets of the Mediterranean diet. This gives a basic outline of which foods you should include on your shopping list and then you can look for recipes from there!

What does the basic Mediterranean diet look like?
- Your diet should consist heavily of whole grain bread, extra virgin olive oil, fresh fruits and vegetables, herbs and spices, nuts and seeds, fish and seafood.
- You should moderately eat: poultry, cheese, eggs.
- You should try to rarely eat red meat.
- You should avoid processed snacks, refined oils and refined grains (white bread), sugary drinks.

# 3 Health Benefits of the Mediterranean Way of Eating

- **Boosts Your Brain Health:** Preserve memory and prevent cognitive decline by following the Mediterranean diet that will limit processed foods, refined bread, and red meats. Have a glass wine versus hard liquor.

- **Improves Poor Eyesight:** Older individuals suffer from poor eyesight, but in many cases, the Mediterranean diet has provided noted improvement. An Australian Center for Eye Research discovered that the individuals who consumed a minimum of 100 ml (0.42 cup) of olive oil weekly, were almost 50% less likely to develop macular degeneration versus those who ate less than one ml each week.

- **Helps to Reduce the Risk of Heart Disease:** Evidence was provided by The New England Journal of Medicine in 2013 from a randomized clinical trial. The trial was implemented in Spain, whereas individuals did not have cardiovascular disease at enrollment but were in the 'high risk' category. The incidence of major cardiovascular events was reduced by the Mediterranean diet that was supplemented with extra-virgin olive oil or nuts. In one study, men who consumed fish in this manner reduced the risk by 23% of death from heart disease.

- **The Risk of Alzheimer's disease is reduced:** In 2018, the journal Neurology studied 70 brain scans of individuals who had no signs of dementia at the onset. They followed the eating patterns in a two-year study resulting in individuals who were on the Med diet had a lesser increase of the depots and reduction of energy use - potentially signaling risk for Alzheimer's.

- **Helps Reduce the Risk of Some Types of Cancer:** According to the results of a group study, the diet is associated with a compelling lessened risk of stomach cancer (gastric adenocarcinoma).

- **Decreases Risks for Type-2 Diabetes:** It can help stabilize blood sugar while protecting against type 2 diabetes with its low-carb elements. The Med diet maintains a richness in fiber, which will digest slowly while preventing variances in your blood sugar. It also can help you maintain a healthier weight, which is another trigger for diabetes.

- **It Suggests Improvement for Those with Parkinson's disease:** By consuming foods on the Mediterranean diet, you are adding high levels of antioxidants that can prevent your body from undergoing oxidative stress, which is a damaging process that will attack your cells. The menu plan can reduce your risk factors in half.

- **It May Reduce the Risk of Strokes In Women:** A study provided in 2018 composed of 23,232 men and women stated the diet did not observe the same results in men. The United Kingdom research indicated women following the diet plan reduced changes in the health issue by 20% using women and men from 40 to 77 years.

- **Helps Keep You Agile:** You may reduce your risks of developing signs of frailty, including muscle weakness, by about 70% by indulging in the plan to gain valuable nutrients.

- **Can Fight Inflammation:** The Mediterranean diet uses fatty fish (high in omega-3s), including salmon, mackerel, and tuna. Enjoy them boiled or baked and resist the urge to salt, dry, or fry them.

- **Can Help Strengthen Your Skin:** Omega 3 fatty acids, once again, will provide you with nutrients for elastic and healthier skin cells.

- **Rheumatoid Arthritis Improvements:** The diet plan offered using the Mediterranean diet has provided rheumatoid patients with an increase in physical function and improved vitality with the reduction of inflammatory activity.

- **Can Help With Depression & Anxiety:** By consuming the menu offered by the Mediterranean eating patterns, you are absorbing essential nutrients linked to depression prevention, including fish, legumes, cereals, nuts, fruits, and veggies.

- **Promotes Healthy Weight Management:** Your body has no choice when you boost your health with the cuisine offered, including whole grains, veggies, healthful fats, fruits, and much more.

- **Is Excellent for Your Gut:** The diet plan was studied in a study at the University Medical Center in the Netherlands and concluded that healthy fats and omega-3s were fabulous for boosting good bacteria in your gut; therefore, reducing inflammation.

- **May Reduce Risk of Old Age Frailty:** Nutrition is considered a vital role in the complex pathogenesis of frailty. Strengthened bones may help to prevent osteoporosis. The studies were mixed and inclusive at this time, but the diet plan provides you with abundant plant foods that are essential for healthier bones.

- **Is Excellent for Postmenopausal Women:** Studies have been provided that women who adhered strictly to the Mediterranean diet, had higher muscle mass and bone density, versus those who didn't. This led to the possibility of how the diet can be useful in the prevention of osteoporosis and fractures in postmenopausal women.

- **May Help Ease Pain:** Olive oil is a compound composed of oleocanthal, which may have a similar effect to NSAIDs. The oleocanthal has an anti-inflammatory and antioxidant component, which is contained in aspirin and ibuprofen.

- **The Mediterranean Diet Plan Is Linked to Longevity:** You receive significant improvement (overall at 9%) in your health when you adhere to the Mediterranean dietary pattern. Incidents of Alzheimer's as well as Parkinson's disease have lowered the overall mortality rates by 13%, mortality from cancer at 6%, and cardiovascular mortality decreased by 9%.

- **Reduction in Dental Disease:** You will soon discover that the foods in the pyramid of the Mediterranean diet are linked to healthier, stronger teeth and have also been found to lower the risk of gum and other related dental diseases. The British Journal of Cancer provided links between the Mediterranean diet and oral health, whereas the diet reduced the risk of the development of mouth cancer.

# 4 Diseases the Mediterranean Diet Prevents

It is true to say that most diets, in fact, all of them, target curing and preventing diseases. Researchers put it that, among the numerous numbers of diets available across the globe, the Mediterranean diet has the largest number of diseases it caters for. PREDIMED, which means prevention with the Mediterranean diet, is the largest group to ever carry out a study on the med diet. It revealed that the diet's components, especially, olive oil, nuts, and almonds, reduces the chances of being diagnosed with cardiovascular diseases by a bigger margin, 30% to be precise.

Below is a list of some of the diseases that the Mediterranean diet prevents and helps treat.

- Heart diseases
- Chronic diseases
- Circulatory diseases
- Blindness diseases
- Allergies
- Asthma
- Cancer
- Depression
- Diabetes
- Metabolic syndrome

**Heart disease**

The heart is one of the most crucial and sensitive parts of the body. The heart performs a lot of critical functions in the body; it is right to say that it performs 80% of the entire body's functions. It does so through pumping and circulating blood in the body. Now that you are enlightened on this fact, I suppose you dread on ever contracting any of the heart diseases. For most people, they would prefer having an alert bell that signals when the diseases try to creep in their body. That is just a mere fantasy. The reality in preventing these deadly diseases is following the Mediterranean diet to its finest details. The fact that the diet is rich in healthy nutrients drawn from fruits, vegetables, legumes, and whole grains, makes the diet the ultimate remedy for the diseases.

Common types of heart diseases include:
- Cardiac arrest
- High blood pressure
- Coronary artery disease

Signs and symptoms of heart diseases:

1. *Chest pain*: Chest pain is mostly caused by the coronary artery. Chest pain is known to bring a lot of discomforts in the body especially when you are coughing. Chest pain may switch to other areas such as the neck if the coughing continues for long.
2. *Profuse sweating*: You will wake up late at night and find your bed wet, especially on your head section. This means you have been sweating all night long. Other people sweat all over the body making it very difficult to enjoy a nap.
3. *Weak body:* Maybe you are used to handling your house chores in a jiffy, but this time around, you find yourself unusually weak. You are not even able to attend to easy tasks or even run a simple errand, that's a sign of heart disease.
4. *Increased heartbeat rate:* When you are suffering from any heart disease, the body seems to spot danger. Naturally, the only way to cope with the situation is for the body to increase its heartbeat rate in an effort to supply enough blood and oxygen.
5. *Fainting:* The heart takes care of the rest of the body, and when it experiences just a little mishap, it triggers the body to break down. Scientifically, the break down is called fainting. Fainting is common when you have symptoms of arrhythmia disease. Also, if you are just about to experience heart failure, you have a lot of fainting episodes.

**Chronic Diseases**

Did you know that some diseases are based on the age and sex of an individual? Well, now you know. According to researches, most of the chronic diseases affect mostly the old people in the community and women when it comes to gender. Going by the CDC reports, chronic diseases are top in the list in killing adults who are 65 years and above. In 2014 alone, the diseases killed

489,722 people. A forum known as Federal Interagency showed that 26% of women who were pregnant and those who were breastfeeding were killed by the diseases.

Signs and symptoms of chronic diseases:

1. *Memory loss*: Memory loss is a very common symptom of chronic diseases. If you occasionally find yourself forgetting people and things, then you are all set for a chronic disease. Don't fret and get scared of this fact, there are remedies for the memory loss condition. Avoid prescription medicine, they are known to do more harm other than solving the situation. Sleep adequately and get rid of poisonous substances in your house. Eat organic foods only, especially Paleo foods. Use spices on meals instead of sodium. It is also prudent to seek professional home therapy.

2. *Sore throats:* Sore throats will make you lose appetite for food. There is that painful wince that cuts across your throat every time you intend to swallow food. Due to this discomfort, you will give up on eating food. Sometimes, you will sense no taste in food, especially foods with a sweet sensation. Sore throats tend to destroy the tasting sensory organ.

**Circulatory Diseases**

They are also called cardiovascular diseases. They include:

- Atherosclerosis
- Heart attack
- Mitral valve prolapse
- Mitral valve regurgitation
- Mitral stenosis
- Angina pectoris
- Dysrhythmia
- Arrhythmia
- Heart failure
- High cholesterol
- Hypertension
- Cardiac Ischemia
- Stroke
- Aortic aneurysms
- Peripheral artery disease
- Venous thromboembolism

**Blindness Disease**

The truth is that nobody would ever want to be blind, even for one second. You can imagine all that pressure of not being able to see someone or something for your entire life. Blindness affects the mental status of an individual. They are used to seeing things, and now, they are faced with the bitter truth that they'll never see again. Their self-esteem drops to zero, some even lose hope in life and end up committing suicide. The virgin olive oil and nuts are very important in a diet as they help in reducing the chances of blindness to almost nil.

Signs and symptoms:

Blindness is caused by many factors including cataract, head injury, diabetes among others. Blindness can be temporary or permanent depending on the cause and how deep the cause has on the head.

1. *Flushes on the eye*
2. *Hazy eyes*
3. *Double vision*
4. *Pain in the eyes*

**Allergies**

This is the irritating result that occurs when the body reacts to the environment or certain foods. You may end up disliking the foods even for a lifetime. Allergies are detrimental because they come with a lot of restrictions on good foods. In most cases, the doctor would go ahead and write new prescriptions of foods that you are expected to eat and offer helpful advice on the same foods. The Mediterranean diet is based on traditional organic foods and seldom do they have side effects that may cause allergies.

Signs and symptoms:

1. *Sneezing*: Sneezing is the most common symptom when it comes to allergy. This can be because of some foods or even the common one, dust.

2. *Red eyes*: Allergy also causes red and fatigued eyes. The redness of the eyes may lead to conjunctivitis. Prolonged red eyes can signal glaucoma.

**Asthma Attacks**

This is a condition in which the body produces extra mucus that often blocks the windpipes and causes breathing problems. Doctors introduced plastic asthma to help breathers that are readily available in the health units. The Mediterranean diet has been proven to prevent these attacks. The diet ensures that the body is fed with appropriate foods that have the right nutrients.

Signs and symptoms:

There are three main signs of Asthma attacks:

1. *Trouble with sleep:* Statistically, in the usual eight hours of sleep, you will only sleep for three hours. You will experience severe and continuous coughing. Incidentally, you develop chest pains and have watery eyes; all these are signs of an asthma attack.
2. *Short on breath:* You will experience multiple bouts of cut breathe, especially at night. Of course, you will struggle with sleeping, sound sleep will be far-fetched.
3. *Fast heartbeat:* The heart will beat twice the rate it is used to. You will find it hard to breathe and occasionally gasp for air. It becomes difficult for you to take a short walk or a light jog. Your exercise life will be slowed down since you'll tire up quickly.

**Cancer**

There are very many forms of cancer, and almost all of them are deadly. Chances of surviving cancers are very minimal. This is because, cancer, unlike many other diseases exposes its symptoms when it is too late. Research doctors re-affirm that the hopes of surviving cancer are very slim or next to none.

The following is a list of some common types of cancers.

- Lung cancer
- Bladder cancer
- Prostate cancer
- Breast cancer
- Melanoma

# 5 What to Eat and Avoid in the Mediterranean Diet

Here is a breakdown of foods that you can eat when using the Mediterranean diet. Of course, it's not a complete list, but this will help you to make a basic shopping plan so that you can get started easily and know what foods you'll be working with.

- Fruits: Pears, Grapes, Figs, Peaches, Bananas, Melons, Dates, Oranges, Apples, Strawberries, Raspberries, Blueberries, Blackberries. Aim for seasonal, local vegetables and create recipes based on what's readily available in the greengrocery
- Vegetables: Spinach, Broccoli, Kale, Onions, Tomatoes, Carrots, Cauliflower, Cucumbers, Brussels Sprouts, Arugula
- Beans and Legumes: Chickpeas, Beans, Lentils, Peas, Peanuts
- Nuts & Seeds: Almonds, Sunflower Seeds, Hazelnuts, Pumpkin Seeds, Cashews, Walnuts
- Whole Grains: Whole Oats, Corn, Barley, Brown Rice, Buckwheat, Whole Wheat, Pasta, Rye,
- Eggs: Quail, Chicken & Duck
- Poultry: Duck, Chicken, Turkey
- Fish & Seafood: Sardines, Tuna, Shrimp, Trout, Crab, Clams, Mussels, Oysters, Mackerel, Flounder.
- Tubers: Sweet Potatoes, Potatoes, Yams, Turnips
- Dairy: Greek Yogurt, Cheese, Yogurt. You can enjoy dairy as long as it is full-fat and preferably organic.
- Healthy Fats: Avocados, Olives, Avocado Oil, Olive Oil
- Herbs & Spices: Fresh herbs and dried spices are an important part of the Mediterranean diet. Fresh parsley, cilantro/coriander, thyme, rosemary, oregano, mint, fresh chili, dried chili, paprika, cinnamon, cumin...any, and all spices!

When learning any new diet, it's also important to learn the foods that should NOT be included. Another important factor is to read the labels on everything. It is the only way to be completely aware of what goes into the food you eat. Here's a quick guide for inspiration:

**Processed foods.** If a food item has been processed, packaged, and has a list of unfamiliar ingredients on the back? Put it back! The idea is to stick with foods that are close to the source, and close to their original state, without too many added factors. Avoid pre-made sauces, junk food, fast food, and supermarket snack foods.

**Processed Meats.** Avoid heavily processed meats like sausages, hot dogs, and bacon.

**Refined sugar and sugary treats.** Sugary chocolate, candy, ice cream, cakes, cookies...it's all a no-go. These foods have been highly processed and contain lots of refined sugar that will spike your blood sugar, mess with your hormones, and cause all kinds of long-term issues such as diabetes and obesity when eaten without regulation. But hey, a little treat here and there won't harm you, so don't freak out if you eat some birthday cake at a party or enjoy dessert on a special night out! Just make sure that your daily diet and your home is sugary treat-free.

**Low-fat dairy.** When eating dairies such as milk and yogurt, stick with full-fat dairy and avoid anything that states "fat-free" or "low fat" on the label. Fat-free and low-fat dairy products have been put through processing, and often have a higher sugar content than full-fat dairy.

**Trans or Saturated Fats.** *Butter, margarine, etc.*

**Refined Grains.** Whole grains are allowed in the Mediterranean diet, but all refined grains are excluded. This includes white bread, refined pasta (aka the normal kind), refined bagels, cereal, etc.

**Refined Oils.** Oils like soybean oil, vegetable oil, and cottonseed oil are not to be used. Stick with olive oil and healthy oils instead!

# 6 The Mediterranean Way of Life

The healthy Mediterranean way of life is all about eating balanced foods rich in vitamins, minerals, antioxidants, and healthy fatty acids. However, the Mediterranean diet is just one aspect of it. The Mediterranean way of life calls for regular physical exercise, plenty of rest, healthy social interaction, and fun. Balancing all these aspects was the secret of good health of the Mediterranean folk back in the day. However, only the Mediterranean diet is the primary focus of this book, and we will spend most of our time talking about just that.

### Eat Healthy Fats

The Mediterranean diet is by no means a low-fat diet, but the fat that is included in this diet is considered healthy for the body, and the heart in particular. Remember: not all fats are created equal. Certain kinds of fats are healthy, while others do more harm than good. Monosaturated fats and polyunsaturated omega-3 fatty acids, for example, are considered healthy. Omega-6 polyunsaturated fatty acids and saturated fats are unhealthy, and these unhealthy fats are the ones primarily present in most of the common food worldwide. The United States, for example, absolutely loves saturated fats. According to a survey, saturated fats constitute 11% of the total calories of an average American, which is a very high number compared to an average Mediterranean resident, who consumes less than 8% of his/her calories through saturated fat. So, if you wish to switch to the healthy Mediterranean way of life, the first thing to do is change the oils you consume. Eliminating fats like butter and lard in favour of healthier oils like olive oil would be the place to start.

### Consume Dairy in Moderation

We all love cheese. Dairy products are delicious, nutritious, and great sources of calcium, and should be consumed in moderation if you're following the Mediterranean diet. It is usually a good idea to consume two to three servings of full-fat dairy products in a single day, where one serving can mean an 8-ounce glass of milk, or 8 ounces of yogurt, or an ounce of cheese.

### Consume Tons of Plant-Based Foods

As we saw in the pyramid, fruits, vegetables, legumes, and whole grains form the basis of the Mediterranean diet. So, it is a good idea to eat five to ten servings of these in a single day, depending on your appetite. Basically, eat as much of these as you want, but don't overeat. Plant based foods are naturally low in calories, and high in fiber and nutrients. Fresh unprocessed plants are best, so always be on the lookout for the best sources of these around you!

Spice Things Up with Fresh Herbs and Spices
Fresh herbs and Spices are what make most of the recipes insanely delicious, while also providing health benefits. If you already use these in your daily cooking, more power to you! If not, we got you covered!

### Consume Seafood Weekly

As we've talked before, one benefit of living close to the sea is easy access to seafood. However, seafood holds a lower priority than plant-based foods in the Mediterranean diet, and should be consumed in moderation. If you're a vegetarian, consider taking fish oil supplements to get those omega-3 fatty acids into your system. Better yet, considering shunning your vegetarianism, and eating seafood to get the vital nourishment only seafood can provide.

### Consume Meat Monthly

Red meat used to be a luxury for the Mediterranean people back in the day. Although not completely off-limits, you should try and reduce your red-meat intake as much as possible. If you absolutely love red meat, consider consuming it no more than two times per month. And even when you do eat it, make sure the serving size of the meat in the dish is small (two to three ounce serving). The main reason to limit meat intake is to limit the amount of unhealthy fats going into your system. As we talked before, saturated fats and omega-6 fatty acids are not good for health, but unfortunately, red meat contains significant quantities of these. As a beef lover myself, I eat a two-ounce serving of it per month, and when I do eat it, I make sure there are lots of vegetables on the side to satiate my hunger.

**Drink Wine!**
Love wine? Well, it is your lucky day. Having a glass of wine with dinner is a common practice in the Mediterranean regions. Red wine is especially good for the heart and it is a good idea to consume a glass of red wine twice a week. Excess of everything is bad, and wine is no exception so keep it in check. Also, if you're already suffering from health conditions, it is a good idea to check with your doctor before introducing wine to your daily diet.

**Work Your Body**
Now you don't have to hit the gym like a maniac to work your body. Walking to your destination instead of driving, taking the stairs instead of the lift, or kneading your own dough can all get the job done. So, be creative and work your body when you can. Better yet, play a sport or just hit the gym like a maniac. You don't have to, as I said at the start, but it will help… a lot.

**Enjoy a Big Lunch**
Lunch was usually the meal of the day when the Mediterranean residents sat with their families and took their time enjoying a big meal. This strengthens social bonds, and relaxes the mind during the most stressful time of the day, when you're just half done with your work, probably.

**Have Fun with Friends and Family**
Just spending a few minutes per day doing something fun with your loved ones is great for de-stressing. Today, we don't understand the importance of this, and people feel lonely, and in some cases, even depressed. Just doing this one thing has the power to solve a huge chunk of the problems our modern society faces.

**Be Passionate**
The Mediterranean people are passionate folk. Living on or close to sun-kissed coasts, their passion for life is naturally high. Being passionate about something in life can take you a long way towards health and wellness.

# 7 The 8 Basic Guiding Principles of the Mediterranean Diet

1. **Consume Lots of Fruits**

There isn't any limit in regards to the selection of fruits to include inside the MD. However, since culmination includes nutrients and nutrients in special quantities, it is always higher to go along with darkish-colored end result, which nutritionists claim to supply a more-normal dietary punch. Dark-colored fruits particularly the darkish crimson and orange ones, and even veggies provide anti-oxidants and phyto- nutrients. Variety is likewise a vital aspect in choosing fruits for the MD.

- The following fruits are usually grown within the Mediterranean: Figs, grapes, lemons, mandarin oranges, olives, persimmons, and pomegranates. Other important culmination inside the MD are blackberries, blueberries, cranberries, plums, red grapes, and crimson raspberries.

MD experts also recommend succulent or those containing lots of fiber and water, such as: apples, oranges, peaches, and watermelons. The idea behind more water and fiber in the diet is to help weight watchers experience glad longer and to aid in the digestive process.

2. **Consume Lots of Vegetables**

All vegetables can be included in the MD, however people need to attempt to restrict their intake of corn and white potatoes because of their high starch content, which in turn contribute to extra calories. The following greens are commonly grown inside the Mediterranean: artichokes, asparagus, broccoli, broccoli rabe, cabbage, eggplant, green beans, garlic, onions, and tomatoes. Dark-colored vegetables along with beets, carrots, purple peppers, and sweet potatoes are super sources of anti-oxidants and phyto-nutrients. Likewise, eat masses of inexperienced, leafy veggies aside from broccoli due to the fact these also are powerhouses of nutrients: bok choy, cauliflower, collards, kale, lettuce, mustard, romaine, spinach, summer time and wintry weather squash, turnip vegetables and zucchini.

Collard is also referred to as non-heading cabbage or tree-cabbage Collard is also called non-heading cabbage or tree-cabbage

Adults need to consume at the least cups of veggies in the MD. Vegetables can be eaten raw, cooked or using them as elements to different dishes. For those who would love to strive the MD however are hesitating due to the fact they don't want to eat loads of vegetables might be glad to recognize that vegetable serving sizes do now not need to be large. The following common vegetable consumption requirements can also serve as your manual in getting ready food the Mediterranean way. The good information is, it conforms to the dietary pointers of health and nutrition authorities:

At least 1 ½ cups of orange-colored greens in keeping with week At least 2 cups according to week of darkish inexperienced greens

At least 5 ½ cups in line with week of other vegetables For the ones trying the MD for healthy eating, at least 2 ½ cups in keeping with week of starchy veggies, however the ones doing the MD for weight loss must refrain from or limit intake of starch-rich veggies to a maximum of one cup in a week.

3. **Consume Legumes**

Legumes are complete within the macronutrients carbohydrates, proteins, and fats and oils, whereas end result and vegetables do now not have fat and oils. Legumes are also wealthy in vitamins B1, B3, B6, and B9 and in minerals inclusive of calcium, magnesium, and molybdenum. The following legumes are usually grown within the Mediterranean: chickpeas, lentils, and peas. However, legumes for inclusion within the MD are infinite and may also encompass black beans, black-eyed peas, fantastic northern beans, kidney beans, and cut up beans.

4. **Include Nuts and Seeds for your Diet**

Nuts and seeds are a staple in Mediterranean cuisine, both as the principle element in a snack recipe or to add fantastic flavor to food. The following nuts typically grown in the Mediterranean are: almonds, hazelnuts, pine nuts, and walnuts. Other healthy nuts and seeds which are indispensable in the MD are: Brazil nuts, cashew nuts, chia seeds, flaxseeds or linseeds, macadamia nuts, peanuts (even though peanuts are certainly legumes), pecan nuts, pistachio nuts, pumpkin seeds, sesame seeds, and sunflower seeds. Quinoa (absolutely now not a true cereal but a pseudocereal) may be taken into consideration a seed.

With all the remarkable advantages which may be derived from nuts and seeds especially healthy fat, those food items also incorporate calories. Those who are looking their weight or are following the MD weight-reduction plan for weight loss need to control their intake of nuts and seeds.

Here are approximate numbers of a few nuts that normally include an ounce - the everyday serving size of nuts:

Almonds: 20 to 25

Brazil nuts: 6 to 8

Cashew nuts: 16 to 18

Hazel nuts: 10 to 12

Peanuts: 28

Pecan nuts: 15 halves Pine nuts: 50 to 157

Pistachios: forty five to 47

Walnuts: 14 halves

A caveat approximately nuts: Brazil nuts, cashew nuts and peanuts have higher content material of unhealthy fats. The high quality nuts are almonds and walnuts because of their Omega 3 content and their splendid taste. Nuts are satisfactory when they're raw, but if you virtually needed to cook them then go for toasted nuts. Also ensure that they may be unsalted and uncoated, and with no brought sugar and fat. Also, the claims about chia seeds have not but been scientifically proven, so they should be eaten up in mild servings of one ounce at the most.

## 5. Eat entire grains, in particular whole grain bread

Technically, the term whole grain refers back to the grain or method grain products wherein the caryopsis such as the anatomical components bran, germ and endosperm are intact whether they're ground, cracked, or flaked. Whole grains are necessary to the MD as they contain excessive quantities of fiber and impart natural goodness to food. Among the entire grain produce commonplace within the Mediterranean region are: barley, corn, rice, and wheat. If you like bread, select dense, heavy chewy breads baked from while wheat, barley, and oats. If you love pasta, pick out complete grain pasta products from the grocery store.

There are many motives for deciding on entire grain foods no longer simplest for his or her health blessings but additionally for that feeling of fullness you want for your each day routines. MD experts additionally endorse steel-cut, entire-grain oatmeal and multi-grain hot cereals. The good information with MD is that it lets in humans a wide preference for whole grains. Even people who love rice can enjoy ingesting rice so long as they chose brown rice. Couscous and polenta are also amazing entire grain choices.

Whole grains are a critical a part of the Mediterranean diet.

Whole grains are a fundamental a part of the Mediterranean weight-reduction plan.

## 6. Use Olive Oil in Cooking and in Salads

Olive oil is the main fat supply used within the MD. Thus, the consumption of olive oil in Mediterranean international locations is excessive even of other less expensive oils are becoming famous. With the cutting-edge interest in MD, even non-Mediterranean international locations together with Germany, Japan, UK and US have increasing consumption of olive oil. Olive oil defines the distinctive taste of the MD and is therefore of precise significance within the average context of the MD.

Olive oil now not most effective increases the palatability of foods however also improves the feel and complements the taste. In Greece, the very famous lathera dish consists of veggies cooked in an olive oil-based totally sauce, tomatoes, and garlic. Leading government at the MD believes that without the use of olive oil within the instruction of Mediterranean dishes, it might be practically impossible for humans in Greece and inside the surrounding international locations inside the area to consume high quantities of greens and legumes.

Olive oil is used inside the Mediterranean weight-reduction plan no longer most effective for cooking however additionally for the following functions among others:

Raw olive oil is used in aiolli and other dips; Vegetable marinades;

Flavoring for soups and stews by using long, slow cooking, especially in pistou; For batter, dough, and numerous pastries;

Bread with oil, which is taken into consideration as elemental Mediterranean cuisine, which includes the Catalan dish pa amb oli.

Mediterranean people very not often use butter in their cuisine and they do no longer omit it because olive oil has its simple appeal for his or her dishes. In activities in which olive oil does no longer suit a particular recipe, canola oil is used instead. Extra virgin olive oil, mainly the lighter model is the nice preference for salad dressings, for use in meals eaten raw, and in baking. However, for cooking, everyday extra virgin oil from the supermarket is just fine. One should no longer hesitate to put together foods the Mediterranean way due to the price of olive oil because it will replace butter and margarine. The small fee delivered in the use of olive is nothing as compared to its health advantages.

## 7. Include Moderate Amounts of Low Fat Dairy or If Possible, Non-Fat Dairy

In the Mediterranean, goat and sheep milk are extra desired than cow's milk. However, as long as you select low-fat or non-fat milk, it's miles good sufficient for inclusion within the MD. Rather than the standard Western cheese, yogurt is a very crucial constituent of the MD, collectively with some difficult and soft forms of cheese. Greek yogurt has a rich silky texture and is widely available in many supermarkets within the US. It is a better desire because it has two times the protein content of regular commercial yogurt however expenses the same as the name-brand ordinary yogurt.

There is even fat-unfastened Greek yogurt for weight-watchers which is already available within the US. Even Starbucks has jumped into the Greek yogurt bandwagon and is teaming up with a Greek yogurt manufacturer. By subsequent year, Americans established with the healthful Mediterranean weight loss program can buy ready- to-consume Greek yogurt parfaits from the multi-chain international espresso store.

Meanwhile, the MD isn't always acknowledged for its heavy use of cheese. Rather, cheese is used extra as a flavoring to decorate the taste of food, however now not necessarily to crush it. Cheese is also utilized in MD in combination with dessert. If you want cheese, make certain that it is also the low-fats variety and consume dairy products in moderation.

## 8. Eat Fish and Shellfish

Influenced by way of geography, the Mediterranean weight loss program includes seafood as one in every of its crucial components. Moreover, the selection of fish inside the traditional eating regimen is largely responsible for the coronary heart-healthy popularity of the MD weight loss program. Fish like cod, haddock, mackerel, red mullet, salmon, and sardines, which can be cold-water fish varieties, are rich in Omega 3 and different unsaturated fats. Squid and octopus also are staple seafood inside the MD. Consuming fish with high Omega three rather than animal meats guarantees that the body's arteries are not clogged and are protected from coronary diseases.

Other fish now not essential from the Mediterranean which might be rich in Omega 3 and unsaturated fats are Albacore tuna, anchovies, Arctic char or iwana, Atlantic mackerel, sablefish or black cod, Pacific halibut, rainbow trout, shad, smelt, and wild salmon. Shellfish are also welcome in the MD. Among the healthiest are clams, crab, lobster, mussels, oysters, scallops, and shrimps.

# 8 Reasons Why the Mediterranean Diet Is Good for You

## Low in Saturated Fat

Worldwide, physicians and nutritionists believe that a diet high in saturated fat can have very negative effects on a person's health and wellness. Yes, a diet high in saturated fat can lead to a person suffering from heart disease, may lead to cancer, and can trigger a whole variety of other health issues and concerns.

## High in Whole Grains and Fiber

A contribution to the Mediterranean diet is seen in the fact that the occurrence of certain types of cancer reduces. Another explanation the Mediterranean diet reduces cancer risk is because the diet is high in whole grains and dietary fiber. All whole grain and fiber have been shown to decrease cancer incidence like colorectal cancer.

## High in Anti-Oxidants

Mediterranean diet has a strong antioxidant quality. Anti-oxidants play an important role in keeping the body in top condition— like liver, muscles, and skin. It is known that a diet high in anti-oxidants can ensure a person lives a longer, healthier life.

## Low in Red Meat

The diet plan works to reduce the level of "bad cholesterol" because the Mediterranean diet is minimal in red meat. A diet reduced in "bad cholesterol" decreases the risk of cardiovascular disease, obesity, and stroke.

## High in Lean Meats

The Mediterranean diet contains fairly portioned lean meats. The reasonable amount of lean meats— like beef and some shrimp and vegetables— provides an individual with a good source of protein and energy.

## Low in Dairy

In dairy products, the Mediterranean diet is poor. In reality, a true adherence to the Mediterranean diet is almost without dairy products. Every food that falls into the diet is poor in fat or non-fat. Because the diet is low in dairy products, particularly fatty dairy products, the diet allows

an individual to get an ideal weight or maintain it. The diet frequently helps to lower cholesterol, which aims to prevent heart disease.

## Prevents Diseases

When described above, one of the reasons the Mediterranean diet is good for you is because the diet plan seems to reduce the incidence of certain diseases, including:

Heart and cardiovascular disease

Cancer

Diabetes

Hypertension

Diabetes

Longevity

The background of the Mediterranean people shows that the Mediterranean diet helps to prolong the life of a person. However, though helping to prolong a person's life, this diet program often aims to guarantee that a person's long life is also safe.

## A Convenient Diet Program

Ultimately, the Mediterranean diet is good for you, because it is a food system for comfort. For adopting the Mediterranean diet, you don't need to purchase any special products or devise a complex diet plan that's difficult to manage. It is a good method to shed weight while remaining healthy if used with moderate exercise.

## 8 Reasons to Love the Mediterranean Diet

1. *Surprise! No Calorie Counting*

For that meal plan, you won't need a calculator. You trade bad fats for heart-healthy ones, instead of adding up amounts. Instead of butter, go for olive oil. Consider seafood or poultry instead of red meat. Love the fresh fruit and miss the trendy, sugar desserts.

Eat your veggies and beans full of flavor. Nuts are good, so stick to a couple of them a day. Bread and wine can be eaten but in moderate amounts.

2. *The Food Is Really Fresh*
You are not going to have to walk the frozen food lane or visit a fast-food drive-thru. The emphasis is on seasonal food which is processed in clear, mouthwatering ways. Build a savory spinach salad, cucumbers, and tomatoes. Attach traditional Greek ingredients such as black olives, and feta cheese with a recipe for Fast Light Greek Salad. You can also whip up a fun bowl of Grilled Tomato Gazpacho, packed with vegetables.

3. *You Can Have Wine*
In many Mediterranean countries, a glass with meals is popular, where eating is often leisurely and social. Several studies suggest that up to one glass a day can be good for your heart for some individuals, for women and two for men. Red wine is actually safer than normal. Check with your doctor to see if you think this is a good idea.

4. *You Won't Be Hungry*
You will have the opportunity to eat rich-tasting foods such as roasted sweet potatoes, hummus, and even this Lima Bean Salad. You gradually eat them, so that you feel full longer. Hunger isn't a concern when you can munch on low-fat cheese chips, olives, or bites when a hunger hits. Feta and halloumi are lower in fat than cheddar but still fatty and tasty.

5. *You Can Lose Weight*
If you are eating nuts, chocolate, and fats, you would think it would take a miracle to lose any pounds. But those Mediterranean basics (and the slower eating style) help you to feel satisfied and whole. And this helps you stay on with a diet. Regular exercise often forms an important part of a lifestyle.

6. *Your Heart Will Thank You*
Quick everything that's good for your heart in this diet. Olive oil and nuts help to bring down "evil" cholesterol. Fruits, vegetables, and beans help to clear arteries. Fish helps lower blood pressure and triglycerides. Even a glass of wine per day can be good for your heart! If you've

never eaten seafood, consider this Mediterranean-inspired Grilled Whole Trout with Lemon-Tarragon Bean Salad recipe.

7. *You'll Stay Sharper Longer*
Always good for your brain is the same goods that protect your skin. You don't eat bad fats and processed foods, which can result in inflammation. Alternatively, foods rich in antioxidants render the eating style a brain-friendly alternative.

8. *A Convenient Course in Health Eating*
The Mediterranean diet is essentially quite easy. The diet consists of very simple, quick to prepare food items. Furthermore, the Mediterranean diet includes various relatively inexpensive food items. So you can choose to adopt the Mediterranean diet and not disrupt the routine or break the bank in the process.

# 9 Mediterranean Diet FAQs

- **What's The Main Idea behind the Mediterranean Diet?** The main concept behind this diet is a simple one. The idea is to model the diet after the people of the Mediterranean who eat simple, natural foods. Their dietary habits have been shown to increase lifespan, lose weight, lower the rates of heart disease and cancer, along with a bevy of other diseases like lowering the odds of Alzheimer's or Parkinson's.

- **Who Should I Consult Before I Start On The Mediterranean Diet?** You should always consult a doctor, physician, or a dietitian before starting any new type of meal plan or diet. You want someone who can give you the right information based on what is right for your specific set of needs.

- **Do I Need To Drink Wine On This Diet? What Is The Recommended Amount I Should Have Daily?** Women should consume approximately 2.5% of calories from wine on this diet. Men should consume approximately 5% of calories from wine. That being said, wine is a completely optional part of this diet and is not necessary for it to be effective.

- **What Is An Aromatic Olive Oil?** Aromatic olive oil has been made in Greece for as long as it can be remembered. This type of oil has herbs and spices added to it. Aromatic olive oil is known throughout the world for its antioxidant, astringent, and medicinal properties. Herbs supply the antioxidant properties to the olive oil and prevent oxidation. It also helps to improve the flavor which is a nice added bonus. The different ingredients of aromatic olive oil are: *Spices*: Cardamom, Cedar Fruit, Coriander, Cumin Seed, Nutmeg, Aniseed, Ginger, Guinea Grains, Cinnamon, Pepper, and Fennel Seed. *Herbs and Aromatic Plants*: Lay, Marjoram, Oregano, Basil, Mint, Spearmint, Sage, Rosemary, Thyme, Tarragon, Savory, Parsley, Fresh Fennel, Dill, and Coriander. *Vegetables*: Garlic, Red Hot Peppers, Sun-Dried Tomatoes, Red Sweet Peppers, Capers, Truffles, and Chinese Mushrooms.

- **What Health Benefits Are Directly Associated With the Mediterranean Diet?** Studies have shown that the Mediterranean diet is associated with prolonged longevity, overall greater health, lower rates of cancers (particularly breast, colon, uterus, and prostate), and a lower rate of cardiovascular disease. These benefits are attributed to the diet composition and the active Mediterranean lifestyle.

- **What Type of Effect Does the Mediterranean Diet Have in Lowering One's Chance of Heart Disease?** Studies have shown this diet plays an important role in lowering heart disease. This is due to the fact that the Mediterranean diet promotes a more holistic approach to eating and staying healthy. Another factor is the inclusion of red wine as part of the diet. Red wine has been shown to lower the odds of heart disease when consumed in moderate amounts.

- **What Role Does Exercise Play In The Mediterranean Diet?** The Mediterranean diet was developed in the 1960's. During this time physical activity and exercise was a regular part of the culture in the region of the Mediterranean. This is one of the main reasons why the Mediterranean diet emphasizes the importance of having a regular exercise routine to attain better health. I like to go on daily walks and I try to swim a few times each week. Make your exercise fun and you won't have a problem incorporating it into your daily routine.

- **What Is The Difference Between A Low-Carb Diet And The Mediterranean Diet?** The main difference between these types of diet is protein. Generally, the Mediterranean diet has lower protein content. On the Mediterranean diet, you only get approximately 15% of your daily calories from the protein. On low-carb diets, the majority of your daily calories comes in the form of protein.

- **What Is The Mediterranean Diet's View On The Fattening Foods It Recommends We Eat?** The Mediterranean diet promotes consuming foods like bread, pasta, nuts, and rice. All of these foods have been traditionally perceived as being fattening. While these foods do contain higher fat content than other types of food the Mediterranean diet preaches having them in moderation. These types of food are bulkier in nature and will make you feel more satisfied than foods that are refined or processed. Add in some vegetables and fruits to go along with these fattening foods and you'll feel satisfied quicker and for a longer period of time. Always be aware of what and how much you're putting in your body. The sooner you get good at this important step the better off you'll be.

- **What Is The Mediterranean Diet's View On Fats?** The Mediterranean diet focuses on the types of fats you consume. Unsaturated fats like olive oil are much healthier for you than trans or saturated fats (such as margarine, cream, and butter). For that reason, unsaturated fats, in moderation, are encouraged while the less healthy types of fats are frowned upon and should be avoided whenever possible.

- **What Is The Mediterranean Diet's View On Consuming Fish?** The Mediterranean diet promotes eating fish in moderation (between 2 to 3 times a week), as they provide a wonderful source of omega-3 fatty acids and protein. If you don't like fish you'll need to supplement your diet with more beans, lentils, and peas to get the necessary amounts of protein needed. Poultry is only allowed a few times per week and red meat is to be avoided so I would not suggest trying to supplement your diet by adding more of those types of foods to your diet.

- **How Hard Is It To Follow The Mediterranean Diet?** This type of lifestyle is completely doable. Entire countries have followed the basic tenets of this diet for centuries. While some people have a hard time giving up red meat, this diet allows you to still indulge in any foods you want, only not as often and in smaller portions. Once you've gotten to the recipes section of this book you'll see all the amazing options available and realize that it might not be as difficult as you're building it up to be. As with every diet, this one does take a period of time to adjust to. However, once you get past the first few weeks and realize how much better you're feeling overall, you'll quickly fall into your new routine.

- **How Effective Is The Mediterranean Diet For People With Diabetes?** This is a question I hear often. The answer is it is great for people with diabetes. You may need to tweak a few items here and there but overall the Mediterranean diet consists of eating plenty of veggies and whole grain foods while cutting down on red meat, sugar, and unhealthy fats. Research has shown that this diet helps to regulate our blood sugar, which is ideal for people with diabetes.

- **How Effective Is The Mediterranean Diet For Obese People?** The Mediterranean diet is a great tool to help you lose weight. It practices quality over quantity, natural unprocessed foods, and promotes eating healthier alternatives to the average person's normal diet. Eating a reduced amount of animal fat content helps to reduce weight while eating more veggies and low calories foods still leave you feeling full and satisfied. If you start this diet to lose weight, be sure to keep track of how much olive oil, nuts, and other high-calorie food you consume on a daily basis. While those foods are all good for you and an important part of the Mediterranean diet they're high in calories and should only be had in moderation.

# 10 How to get started with the Mediterranean Diet

**Your goals**
Before you get started with this diet, spend some time and come up with the goals you wish to achieve. Your goals will determine your level of motivation whenever you decide to follow a diet. Perhaps you want to lose weight, or maybe want to improve your overall health. Regardless of your goals, it is quintessential that you know what you wish to achieve from the diet. If you don't have any goals, it becomes difficult to stay on track in the long run.

**Pick a date**
Once you know your goal, you should work on setting a timeline. Select a date you want to start this diet. Don't be in a rush, and don't think that you can get started with this diet right this instance. It takes a while to prepare your mind and body for the diet you wish to follow. The Mediterranean diet doesn't require any drastic dietary changes. However, if your diet is rich in processed foods and sugars, your body will take time adjusting to the new diet. Therefore, pick a date and ensure you start your diet on that particular date. Don't make any excuses, and don't try to put it off until a later date. If you keep telling yourself that you can start this diet tomorrow, then tomorrow will never come. Take a calendar, mark the date, and get started.

**Take the first step**
Once you have made up your mind about this diet, then it is time to get started. Don't get scared of the diet, instead think of it as a stepping-stone towards better health. If you get scared, remind yourself of the goals you wish to achieve from this diet. It will make it easier to keep going.

**Clean your pantry**
Before you start this diet, it is time to clean your pantry. Go through the Mediterranean diet shopping list given in the next section and make a list of all the ingredients you will require. Once you have this list, it's time to go shopping for groceries. Simultaneously, you're also supposed to get rid of any other items that don't fit the Mediterranean diet eating protocols. So, it is time to get rid of all processed foods, unhealthy carbs, and sugary treats. Think of it as spring-cleaning for your kitchen. It is quintessential that you do this because if you're surrounded by temptations all the time, the chances of giving in to your urges to eat unhealthy foods will increase. Out of sight, out of mind, is the best approach when it comes to junk food.

**Make the transition**
Once you follow the steps mentioned up until now, it is time to make the transition. As mentioned in the previous point, if your diet is predominantly rich in processed foods and sugars, it might be a little tricky to shift to any other diet. You might not know this, but a diet rich in sugars is quite addictive to your body. Therefore, there are two ways in which you can change your diet. You can either go cold turkey or make a slow transition to the new diet. Slowly start eliminating all unhealthy foods from your diet while incorporating Mediterranean diet-friendly foods. This way, you are conditioning your mind and body to get used to the new diet. Give yourself at least two to three weeks before you come to any conclusions about this diet.

**Support system**
You must have a support system in place if you want to stick to this diet in the long run. Let go of the "I will just wing it" attitude. There will be days when you have little to no motivation. This is where your support system comes into the picture. Whenever you feel like you don't have the motivation to keep going, you can depend on your support system. Your support system can include your partner, loved ones, friends, or anyone else you want. Talk to them about your reasons for following the diet and tell them what you wish to achieve. By doing this, you are making yourself accountable to someone else. This, in turn, increases your motivation to stick to this diet. You can always get online and get in touch with

those who are following the same diet as you.

**Be patient**

A common mistake a lot of dieters make is that they are always in a hurry. Making any sort of dietary change is not easy, and it takes time. Not just time, but consistency as well. Don't think that you'll be able to shed all those extra pounds overnight. After all, you didn't gain all that extra weight within a day or two. Therefore, you can't expect yourself to get rid of it quickly. Whenever you make a dietary change, you might notice certain fluctuations in your energy levels. This happens because your body is trying to get used to the new diet. So, don't be upset with yourself if you can exercise as vigorously as you used to. Within two to three weeks, your energy levels will stabilize, your body will get used to the new diet, and you will be able to exercise the way you want. Until then, be patient and don't weigh yourself daily. It might be quite tempting to see whether you've lost any weight daily, but it is not practical. There will be days when the scale doesn't fluctuate like you want to. Make it a point to weigh yourself every week. It will help keep track of your progress.

**Shopping List**

Use this basic shopping list whenever you shop for groceries. Ensure that you stock your pantry with all these ingredients and get rid of any other item, which is not suitable for your diet.

Your shopping list must include:

- Veggies like kale, garlic, spinach, arugula, onions, carrots
- Fruits like grapes, oranges, apples and bananas
- Berries like blueberries, strawberries, raspberries
- Frozen veggies
- Grains like whole-grain pasta, whole-grain breads
- Legumes like beans, lentils, chickpeas
- Nuts like walnuts, cashews, almonds
- Seeds like pumpkin seeds and sunflower seeds
- Condiments like turmeric, cinnamon, salt, pepper
- Shrimp and shellfish
- Fish like mackerel, trout, tuna, salmon and sardines
- Cheese
- Yogurt and Greek yogurt
- Potatoes and sweet potatoes
- Chicken
- Eggs
- Olives
- Olive oil and avocado oil

If you buy healthy and adequate ingredients, you will most certainly eat the right foods and you will definitely stay on your diet.

**Tricks and tips that will make things easier**

- Keeping in mind that you cannot eat red meat, you can replace it with salmon. It will satisfy your cravings, but it will allow you to stay on your diet.
- Make sure you always have olive oil at hand. You have to forget about using butter if you are on the Mediterranean diet, but you can replace it with the extra virgin olive oil.
- Give up consuming sodas and replace them with some red wine. Cut out the sweet drinks from your diet and try one glass of red wine instead.
- Replace white rice with brown rice. The Mediterranean diet allows you to continue to eat rice but make sure you replace the white rice with brown one. Consume whole grains like buckwheat, corn and quinoa.
- Your snacks should mainly contain fruits. Consume more citrus, melons, berries or grapes. You can also try seeds as a Mediterranean diet snack, but fruits would be a better option.
- Exercise a lot and drink plenty of water. This is the main principle to follow if you are on a Mediterranean diet. It will help you look better and feel amazing. That's a fact!

- Another great idea to keep in mind when you are on such a diet is to make a great shopping list. It will help you buy the right ingredients. Choose organic products if you can.

- You must keep your body hydrated. Regardless of the dietary changes you make, the one thing you must always concentrate on is proper hydration. When your body is hydrated, all the toxins present within will be flushed out. Not just this, but it also helps improve the health of your skin. You must consume at least eight glasses of water daily. Also, when you're transitioning to this diet or making any dietary changes, hunger pangs are quite common. To keep hunger pangs at bay, ensure that your body is thoroughly hydrated.

## Three Reasons You Are Not Losing Weight in The Mediterranean Diet

*You're overestimating just how many calories you're burning.*
If you don't spend your entire day performing physical labour or are a dynamic athlete, you almost certainly won't lose weight eating 2,000 calories each day unless you're incorporating exercise into the routine. Likewise, simply walking up several flights of stairs to attain your workplace won't burn enough calories to qualify as a good work out. "Many people overestimate the calories they burn per day normally by as much as 25%. Keep track and make use of a journal or an app.

*You're concentrating on diet and ignoring exercise.*
The Mediterranean diet is approximately more than simply your grocery list. To be able to reap the weight loss, great things about this manner of consuming, you can't just forget about staying active.
"Though it is achievable to lose excess weight by modifying diet alone, though it is difficult. Adding regular physical exercise to any weight loss regimen increases your likelihood of burning more calories than you consume, causing you to slim down even more consistently." All weight loss plans reap the benefits of a committed action to exercise and burning up calories. To make the

Mediterranean a highly effective weight loss strategy, make sure to keep the body moving.

*You're eating prematurely rather than savoring your meal.*
Enjoy your meal by taking enough time to look for fresh ingredients, spend some time cooking with friends or family, and linger in the table.
To be sure you're not overcooking it, pre-portion your nut products in plastic bags or reusable containers to be sure you can enjoy the health advantages without accidentally consuming more than you designed to.

# 11 Mindset for Success in the Mediterranean Diet

If you're motivated at this point to begin the Mediterranean diet and see the results for yourself, we are here to give you tips for success!

The more informed you are about what to expect and what changes to make, the more success you will see as you adjust your life to this new diet.

- **Start using the right fats.** For the Mediterranean diet, you need to make the switch to a choice of healthy oil like extra virgin olive oil. This oil is high in anti-inflammatory properties which help the body. This means making the switch in your diet and removing the unhealthy oils such as canola oil, vegetable oil, margarine or butter. Olive oil should be your go-to for all your cooking needs. Avocado oil is a good substitute as well to keep on hand. Remind yourself that "less is more," and focus on minimizing your quantity of the oil but focusing on its healthy qualities.

- **Get rid of what you can't eat.** You want to get rid of those items to ensure you are not tempted. That means getting rid of the unhealthy oils, processed foods and meats, sugary snacks and juices, fast food, and junk food. Get used to having fresh ingredients on hand and allowing yourself to meal plan and prep so you have a delicious meal waiting for you. If you had a favorite dish you enjoyed, like lamb chops or fried chicken, see if you can find a Mediterranean diet alternative which is healthier for you.

- **Get used to seafood.** Your main source of protein on the Mediterranean diet will be fish and seafood. If you're already a seafood lover, this is a great time to incorporate it more into your week where you would have eaten red meat. Remember, seafood is more than just fish - there's clams, shrimp, crab, lobsters, and so many other choices! It's a great addition in so many recipes whether it's served with rice, in tortillas, on top of a salad, or grilled. Not to mention the dozens of varieties of fish you can try from your local grocery store or specialized fish market store. The more variety you incorporate into your diet, the more you will be able to explore new recipes and find favorites.

- **Try other sources of protein instead of red meat.** If you often had red meat throughout the week, it can be tough adjusting to other sources of protein. But it's a necessary switch and one you have to stick to, especially if you're hoping to fight symptoms of cardiovascular heart disease. Ease back on the red meat you include in your diet so you have it only sparingly. Get used to fish, seafood, chicken, beans, and legumes as a source of protein. These are low in carbs and much healthier for you. Keep meat as your "cheat meal," if you wish!

- **Make vegetables the star of your meals.** You want to have a variety of vegetables on hand to incorporate it into your meals, or even as the main dish! Whether it's a healthy salad full of many vegetables, or a sautéed side of veggies with fish, it's important you are including veggies in your meals as often as you can. Fiber, vitamins and minerals which keep us full in between meals are primarily sourced through vegetables. It also ensures that your blood sugar levels stay stable. The Mediterranean diet is all about choosing plant-based ingredients so you should try and experiment with more veggies and different ways to eat them.

- **Use herbs and spices to season your food.** High sodium intake can cause health concerns and increase the risk of heart disease. Most of us are consuming too much salt and don't even realize it! Since the Mediterranean diet is all about heart health, try and experiment with a variety of spices or herbs to add flavor to your meals rather than salt.

- **You can choose to have wine but remember the limits you should follow.** Some people love the red wine aspect of the Mediterranean diet, but it's important to remember that moderation is the key. For women, that means no more than 1 glass. 2 glasses is the maximum for men. Remember, this is only for red wine and you cannot substitute other varieties of alcohol or hard liquor.

- **Make fruit your choice of dessert.** We are so used to thinking of dessert as something like cake or chocolate that we don't realize the effect that has on our health. But in the Mediterranean region of the world and many others, fresh fruit is considered a dessert and is often served at the end of a meal. Whether it's ripe melons, juicy orange slices, or sweet pears, these fruits and the natural sugars they contain are much better for your health and blood sugar levels than refined or artificial sugar. Get used to having fresh fruit on hand and treating it like the dessert platter in your house. It's delicious and healthy!

- **Get moving!** To truly gain the benefits of the Mediterranean people, you should try and incorporate physical activity into your routine as well. If you don't like the atmosphere of a gym, that means making voluntary choices to be more active in your day like walking, biking, swimming, hiking, performing more housework or chores around the house, etc. Whatever activity you prefer, get moving and gain the health benefits that exercise offers!

- **Plan your meals.** As we mentioned before, excessive snacking can be your downfall when it comes to any diet! Even though the Mediterranean does encourage healthy snacking, the more calories you consume, the harder it will be ultimately to lose weight. It's more important to have a filling and healthy meal that will tide you over until the next mealtime! To do this, planning your meals is a great way to ensure your success. This allows you to plan, grocery shop, and prep your meals for the week. This reduces the temptation of grabbing fast food or going for something unhealthy because you know you have a meal waiting for you. Maybe use a day on the weekend to cut your veggies, marinate your fish fillets, and prepare some beans or lentils so you have them for a couple of days in advance. It helps reduce food waste, and keeps you motivated to eat what you've prepared!

- **Try and share your mealtimes with people when you can.** Another wonderful thing about the Mediterranean region is their cultural tradition of eating meals together. In the West, it seems more common to have a quick "grab and go" meals alone at work or even at home. Everyone on is a different schedule and people eat when it's most convenient for them. But many believe that some of the benefits of this diet could be associated with their ritual of eating together.

- **Be flexible and embrace the possibilities!** The Mediterranean diet appeals to so many because of the flexibility it gives. You don't have to count calories, count macronutrients, or drastically cut the portions of your meals. There are so many varieties of foods you can eat from fish, legumes, beans, vegetables, fruit, whole grains, poultry, dairy, and seafood. This gives you such variety in your meals so that you can experiment with new recipes and new cuisines. Don't allow yourself to get bored when there are so many options available and new combinations you can try.

# 12 Being Keen on a Mediterranean Diet

*There are no counting calories!*

This is one of those positives that people love about the Mediterranean diet. So many new diets restrict people on a calorie basis which can be quite frustrating and often detrimental to your health if you require a greater caloric intake for your physical and health needs. If you're required to count calories, you have to be very careful to remember every little thing you're eating as a snack, or even adding on your dishes like dressing or cheese. The Mediterranean diet offers a great amount of flexibility regarding this because it's shifting you away from unhealthy food choices to healthier ones. Of course, you should be aware of your dietary choices and avoid overeating, but you also have the freedom to decide on your portion sizes which means you can take an extra few veggies if you'd like, or you can skip having a snack if you're not feeling hungry. The idea is to eat more filling meals that will ensure you aren't feeling hungry other than at mealtimes. By cutting out the sugar, junk food, and fast food from your diet and loading up on fiber from fruits, vegetables, and whole grains, you're eating healthier without having to worry about every item's calorie count.

*You can have wine!*

If you're someone who already enjoys a glass of wine to unwind after a long day, this is going to be an aspect you love about the Mediterranean diet. You get to have that glass of wine and feel good that it is allowed on your diet and can have heart-healthy properties. Recent research on red wine has found that it is high in antioxidants that may prevent cardiovascular heart disease. The people of the Mediterranean also enjoyed having red wine with a meal so it could tentatively be linked to their excellent cardiovascular health. But it's important to note many warnings regarding alcohol consumption. The Mediterranean diet encourages "moderate consumption," which means there are limits in place. Healthy men can drink 2 glasses a day. Healthy women may have up to 1 glass a day. Also, these possible health benefits are only associated with red wine - not other alcoholic beverages or hard liquor. If you're an avid drinker of those and hoping to substitute that for wine in your Mediterranean diet, that won't work! Before incorporating alcohol into your diet, you should speak to your doctor to ensure it does not interfere with your health, family history, if you're pregnant or breastfeeding, or any medication you may be taking. You don't have to be drinking wine to gain the benefits of the diet, but if you are a drinker, then you're going to love this diet even more!

*The Mediterranean diet is full of fiber-rich foods so you will feel full for longer.*

Some diets will often restrict the amount of carbohydrates, fruit or vegetable that you can eat due to worries about too much glucose production from carbs, or natural sugars contained in fruit. Thankfully, the Mediterranean diet does no such thing! And that's a good thing because it allows you to have a diet full of fibrous foods. Beans, whole grains, lentils, and fresh vegetables are rich in fiber which is great for your body. Fiber keeps you feeling full for a longer period of time which means you are less likely to snack in between meals. That means fewer calories and more weight loss! Not only that, some diets can truly have a damaging effect on your digestive system causing constipation or diarrhea due to changes in your regular fiber intake. With the Mediterranean diet, having this high intake of fiber will keep your digestive tract functioning smoothly and keep your bowel movements regular. That means less chance of gastrointestinal or rectal problems. Fiber also gives you energy which is why many people will try and have whole grains for breakfast, such as whole grain cereal, whole wheat bread, or whole grain oatmeal.

*This diet will improve your mental alertness.*

The Mediterranean diet removes all the processed and unhealthy substances from your diet such as refined grains, soda, fast food, trans fats, and junk food. That can be tough to do, but the results it brings are very beneficial for your body and mind. All these sugary treats would cause spikes in your blood sugar and cause a rush of insulin throughout the body. That brings around symptoms like mood swings, false hunger pants, irritability, fatigue, and weakness. Instead of keeping you mentally alert, those foods slow you down and distract you from working at your best potential. When following the Mediterranean diet, you are replacing the processed sugars with fresh vegetables and fruits that are full of healthy minerals like vitamin B, folic acid, potassium, vitamin D, omega 3 fatty acids, and more! This keeps the body functioning in top mental and cognitive functioning which gives you more alertness, focus, memory recall, and concentration.

*You can have fruit which is great to satisfy your sweet tooth!*
Many diets forbid you from eating fruit because of their natural sugars and the net carbs that they could add to your daily caloric intake. This can be quite tough, especially if you're already giving up artificial and refined sugar. Sometimes, your sweet tooth just needs to be satisfied! The more you have to give up, often the more tempting it will be to reach for those same ingredients! With the Mediterranean diet, you're encouraged to make fruit a healthy dessert option. Instead of unhealthy sugary snacks, fruit should be your go-to. Whether it's juicy watermelon, a ripe banana, or sweet berries, these natural sugars are much less harmful to your body than artificial ones. Portion size is important so you don't want to go overboard, but many people are happy to have this option as a sweet treat!

*It's very easy to adjust if you're eating outside of your home.*
One of the worries when you're dieting is feeling constrained if you're ever outside the comfort of your own home at mealtimes. Especially if your diet requires specialized ingredients without a lot of freedom in making meal choices at restaurants or at a friend's house. You may be panicking and wondering how to adjust. With the Mediterranean diet, it's very easy to do just that! Let's say you're out at dinner with friends. What can you order that would fit the requirements of the Mediterranean diet? Most places will offer a seafood option so you can have your choice of fish, lobster, shrimp, or crab! If there isn't a seafood choice, you can pick a poultry option - just be sure to avoid red meat! You can also pick a side of fresh vegetables or a small salad. When it comes to dessert, be sure to go for the most natural and organic option instead of a baked good full of refined sugar. You can ask for fresh fruit, or maybe an organic smoothie. The ease and flexibility that the Mediterranean diet allows even when you are outside of the home and away from your prepared meals is what makes it such a favorite among its followers. There's no panic about breaking your diet or making an unhealthy food choice.

*There's so much delicious variety to choose from in the Mediterranean diet.*
This is not a diet you will get bored of easily or feel like the food choice is restricting. There is so much that you can eat and so many foods and recipes you can try. Remember, the Mediterranean region includes countries like Greece, Turkey, Spain, Italy, Morocco and many more! So there are always new recipes and ethnic foods that you can include in your menu. Maybe by experimenting, you'll find a new favorite! Not only that, there are great varieties of protein that you can incorporate in your dishes, as well as vegetables, whole grains, poultry, and the occasional meal of red meat. You're also encouraged to use spices, fresh herbs, and olive oil to add flavor to your meal which gives it another depth of flavor. With many avenues of exploration, you will not feel constrained by this diet or feel like you're running out of things to eat. Of course, there are clear items you should avoid like trans fats, sugar, and processed foods, but focusing on what you can eat will allow you to enjoy your meals so much more and be excited for the next one!

*There will be no harmful side effects that often occur when you reduce your intake of carbohydrates.*

Many diets lately have been embracing the concept of low carbohydrate intake believing it causes blood sugar spikes and wanting to guide the body through a different fat-burning process called ketosis. The keto diet and other low carb diets drastically reduce the number of carbohydrates you're consuming a day. This can be a quick method to reduce weight, but it actually can bring a tough adjustment period for the body which includes symptoms like weakness, fatigue, diarrhea, muscle cramps, nausea, and other things that could interfere with your health and daily life. These are temporary, but they could still last a matter of weeks as your body adjusts. That's because carbohydrates tend to make up more than half of our diet. Cutting it down to something very minimal like 5% of your daily intake can be tough on your body! The Mediterranean diet embraces the concept of whole grains because they are healthier for you than refined carbohydrates. They're full of fiber and vitamin B12 and keep you feeling full. Whole grains tend to be lower on the glycemic index compared to refined grains. That means they will not cause blood sugar spikes. This allows you to have a more natural place for whole grains in your diet and still feel confident that you are gaining the health benefits they provide. Cutting something completely from your diet, especially something you will encounter all the time in your food choices, can be very tough and make them seem more tempting!

*You don't have to become a gym rat!*
One of the things that people also love about the Mediterranean diet is that it doesn't require intense exercise that some diets will encourage. This makes it appealing to people of all health levels and physical fitness. It simply encourages you to incorporate more physical activity into your routine, whether that's a walk around the block, a swim session at the pool, or jogging or biking. You don't have to join an array of gym classes or feel like you're not doing enough to burn calories. The people of the Mediterranean very naturally fit exercise into their daily life and activities. They didn't end up dreading it or getting burned out which can often happen if you're following a diet where you have to devote too much time at the gym. Instead, try and make the choices to be more active voluntarily, such as taking the stairs instead of the elevator, or parking your car a few blocks away and enjoying the walk to work. This way, you're still burning calories which means you're keeping yourself healthy and losing weight at the same time!

# 13 Breakfast

Preparation: 10 min   Cooking: 1 hour and 10 min   Servings: 8

## 1. BANANA AND QUINOA CASSEROLE

### INGREDIENTS

- 3 cups bananas, peeled and mashed
- ¼ cup pure maple syrup
- ¼ cup molasses
- 1 tablespoon cinnamon powder
- 2 teaspoons vanilla extract
- 1 teaspoon cloves, ground
- 1 teaspoon ginger, ground
- ½ teaspoon allspice, ground
- 1 cup quinoa
- ¼ cup almonds, chopped
- 2 and ½ cups almond milk

### DIRECTIONS

1. In a baking dish, combine the bananas with the maple syrup, molasses and the rest of the ingredients.
2. Bake at 350 degrees F for 1 hour and 10 minutes.
3. Divide the mix between plates and serve for breakfast.

CALORIES: 213 Kcal   FAT: 4.1 g   FIBER: 4 g   PROTEIN: 4.5 g   CARBOHYDRATES: 41 g

*Preparation: 10 min*     *Cooking: 40 min*     *Servings: 8*

## 2. STUFFED SWEET POTATOES

### INGREDIENTS

- 8 sweet potatoes, pierced with a fork
- 14 ounces canned chickpeas, drained and rinsed
- 1 small red bell pepper, chopped
- 1 tablespoon lemon zest, grated
- 2 tablespoons lemon juice
- 3 tablespoons olive oil
- 1 teaspoon garlic, minced
- 1 tablespoon oregano, chopped
- 2 tablespoons parsley, chopped
- A pinch of salt and black pepper
- 1 avocado, peeled, pitted and mashed
- ¼ cup water
- ¼ cup tahini paste

### DIRECTIONS

1. Arrange the potatoes on a baking sheet lined with parchment paper, bake them at 400 degrees F for 40 minutes, cool them down and cut a slit down the middle in each.
2. In a bowl, combine the chickpeas with the bell pepper, lemon zest, half of the lemon juice, half of the oil, half of the garlic, oregano, half of the parsley, salt and pepper, toss and stuff the potatoes with this mix.
3. In another bowl, mix the avocado with the water, tahini, the rest of the lemon juice, oil, garlic and parsley, whisk well and spread over the potatoes.
4. Serve cold for breakfast.

CALORIES: 308 Kcal     FAT: 2 g     FIBER: 8 g     PROTEIN: 7 g     CARBOHYDRATES: 38 g

---

*Preparation: 10 min*     *Cooking: 15 min*     *Servings: 6*

## 3. HAM MUFFINS

### INGREDIENTS

- 9 ham slices
- 5 eggs, whisked
- 1/3 cup spinach, chopped
- ¼ cup feta cheese, crumbled
- ½ cup roasted red peppers, chopped
- A pinch of salt and black pepper
- 1 and ½ tablespoons basil pesto
- Cooking spray

### DIRECTIONS

1. Grease a muffin tin with cooking spray and line each muffin mould with 1 and ½ ham slices.
2. Divide the peppers and the rest of the ingredients except the eggs, pesto, salt and pepper into the ham cups.
3. In a bowl, mix the eggs with the pesto, salt and pepper, whisk and pour over the peppers mix.
4. Bake the muffins in the oven at 400 degrees F for 15 minutes and serve for breakfast.

CALORIES: 109 Kcal     FAT: 6.7 g     FIBER: 1.8 g     PROTEIN: 9.3 g     CARBOHYDRATES: 1.8 g

Preparation: 5 min         Cooking: 0 min/ Freezing: 4 hours         Servings: 4

## 4. CHEESY YOGURT

### INGREDIENTS

- 1 cup Greek yogurt
- 1 tablespoon honey
- ½ cup feta cheese, crumbled
- 1 cup raspberries
- ½ lemon

### DIRECTIONS

1. In a blender, combine the yogurt with the honey and the cheese and pulse well.
2. Divide into bowls and freeze for 4 hours.
3. Add raspberries and lemon zests before serving for breakfast.

CALORIES: 161 Kcal     FAT: 11.5 g     FIBER: 9.6 g     PROTEIN: 15.4 g     CARBOHYDRATES: 36.6 g

*Preparation: 10 min*  *Cooking: 50 min*  *Servings: 4*

# 5. CAULIFLOWER FRITTERS

## INGREDIENTS

- 30 ounces canned chickpeas, drained and rinsed
- 2 and ½ tablespoons olive oil
- 1 small yellow onion, chopped
- 2 cups cauliflower florets chopped
- 2 tablespoons garlic, minced
- A pinch of salt and black pepper

## DIRECTIONS

1. Spread half of the chickpeas on a baking sheet lined with parchment pepper, add 1 tablespoon oil, season with salt and pepper, toss and bake at 400 degrees F for 30 minutes.
2. Transfer the chickpeas to a food processor, pulse well and put the mix into a bowl.
3. Heat up a pan with the ½ tablespoon oil over medium-high heat, add the garlic and the onion and sauté for 3 minutes.
4. Add the cauliflower, cook for 6 minutes more, transfer this to a blender, add the rest of the chickpeas, pulse, pour over the crispy chickpeas mix from the bowl, stir and shape medium fritters out of this mix.
5. Heat up a pan with the rest of the oil over medium-high heat, add the fritters, cook them for 3 minutes on each side and serve for breakfast.

CALORIES: 333 Kcal    FAT: 12.6 g    FIBER: 12.8 g    PROTEIN: 13.6 g    CARBOHYDRATES: 44.7 g

---

*Preparation: 20 min*  *Cooking: 20 min*  *Servings: 2*

# 6. AVOCADO CHICKPEA PIZZA

## INGREDIENTS

- 1 and ¼ cups chickpea flour
- A pinch of salt and black pepper
- 1 and ¼ cups water
- 2 tablespoons olive oil
- 1 teaspoon onion powder
- 1 teaspoon garlic, minced
- 1 tomato, sliced
- 1 avocado, peeled, pitted and sliced
- 2 ounces gouda, sliced
- ¼ cup tomato sauce
- 2 tablespoons green onions, chopped

## DIRECTIONS

1. In a bowl, mix the chickpea flour with salt, pepper, water, the oil, onion powder and the garlic, stir well until you obtain a dough, knead a bit, put in a bowl, cover and leave aside for 20 minutes.
2. Transfer the dough to a working surface, shape a bit circle, transfer it to a baking sheet lined with parchment paper and bake at 425 degrees F for 10 minutes.
3. Spread the tomato sauce over the pizza, also spread the rest of the ingredients and bake at 400 degrees F for 10 minutes more.
4. Cut and serve for breakfast.

CALORIES: 416 Kcal    FAT: 24.5 g    FIBER: 9.6 g    PROTEIN: 15.4 g    CARBOHYDRATES: 36.6 g

Preparation: 5 min    Cooking: 0 min    Servings: 4

## 7. AVOCADO SPREAD

### INGREDIENTS

- 2 avocados, peeled, pitted and roughly chopped
- 1 tablespoon sun-dried tomatoes, chopped
- 2 tablespoons lemon juice
- 3 tablespoons cherry tomatoes, chopped
- ¼ cup red onion, chopped
- 1 teaspoon oregano, dried
- 2 tablespoons parsley, chopped
- 4 kalamata olives, pitted and chopped
- A pinch of salt and black pepper
- 8 bread slices

### DIRECTIONS

1. Put the avocados in a bowl and mash with a fork.
2. Add the rest of the ingredients, stir to combine.
3. Place the mixture over the bread slices and serve as a morning spread.

CALORIES: 110 Kcal    FAT: 10.5 g    FIBER: 3.6 g    PROTEIN: 1.4 g    CARBOHYDRATES: 5.6 g

*Preparation: 10 min*  *Cooking: 0 min*  *Servings: 2*

# 8. TUNA SALAD

## INGREDIENTS

- 12 ounces canned tuna in water, drained and flaked
- ¼ cup roasted red peppers, chopped
- 2 tablespoons capers, drained
- 8 kalamata olives, pitted and sliced
- 2 tablespoons olive oil
- 1 tablespoon parsley, chopped
- 1 tablespoon lemon juice
- A pinch of salt and black pepper

## DIRECTIONS

1. In a bowl, combine the tuna with roasted peppers and the rest of the ingredients and toss.
2. Divide between plates and serve for breakfast.

CALORIES: 250 Kcal  FAT: 17.5 g  FIBER: 0.6 g  PROTEIN: 10.4 g  CARBOHYDRATES: 2.6 g

---

*Preparation: 10 min*  *Cooking: 8 min*  *Servings: 1*

# 9. ARTICHOKES AND CHEESE OMELET

## INGREDIENTS

- 1 teaspoon avocado oil
- 1 tablespoon almond milk
- 2 eggs, whisked
- A pinch of salt and black pepper
- 2 tablespoons tomato, cubed
- 2 tablespoons kalamata olives, pitted and sliced
- 1 artichoke heart, chopped
- 1 tablespoon tomato sauce
- 1 tablespoon feta cheese, crumbled

## DIRECTIONS

1. In a bowl, combine the eggs with the milk, salt, pepper and the rest of the ingredients except the avocado oil and whisk well.
2. Heat up a pan with the avocado oil over medium-high heat
3. Add the omelet mix, spread into the pan, cook for 4 minutes, flip, cook for 4 minutes more, transfer to a plate and serve.

CALORIES: 303 Kcal  FAT: 17.5 g  FIBER: 9.6 g  PROTEIN: 15.4 g  CARBOHYDRATES: 6.6 g

Preparation: 10 min     Cooking: 10 min     Servings: 2

# 10. WALNUT POACHED EGGS

## INGREDIENTS

- 2 slices whole grain bread toasted
- 1 oz sun-dried tomato, sliced
- 1 tablespoon cream cheese
- 1/3 teaspoon minced garlic
- 2 slices prosciutto
- 2 eggs
- 1 tablespoon walnuts
- ½ cup fresh basil
- 1 oz Parmesan, grated
- 3 tablespoons olive oil
- ¼ teaspoon ground black pepper
- 1 cup water, for cooking

## DIRECTIONS

1. Pour water in the saucepan and bring it to boil.
2. Then crack eggs in the boiling water and cook them for 3-4 minutes or until the egg whites are white.
3. Meanwhile, churn together minced garlic and cream cheese.
4. Spread the bread slices with the cream cheese mixture.
5. Top them with the sun-dried tomatoes.
6. Make the pesto sauce: Blend together ground black pepper, Parmesan, olive oil, and basil. When the mixture is homogenous, pesto is cooked.
7. Carefully transfer the poached eggs over the sun-dried tomatoes and sprinkle with pesto sauce.
8. The poached eggs should be hot while serving.

CALORIES: 317 Kcal     FAT: 36.5 g     FIBER: 3.6 g     PROTEIN: 17.4 g     CARBOHYDRATES: 17.6 g

*Preparation: 10 min*     Cooking: 10 min     *Servings: 4*

# 11. CORN AND SHRIMP SALAD

## INGREDIENTS

- 4 ears of sweet corn, husked
- 1 avocado, peeled, pitted and chopped
- ½ cup basil, chopped
- A pinch of salt and black pepper
- 1 pound shrimp, peeled and deveined
- 1 and ½ cups cherry tomatoes, halved
- ¼ cup olive oil

## DIRECTIONS

1. Put the corn in a pot, add water to cover, bring to a boil over medium heat, cook for 6 minutes, drain, cool down, cut corn from the cob and put it in a bowl.
2. Thread the shrimp onto skewers and brush with some of the oil.
3. Place the skewers on the preheated grill, cook over medium heat for 2 minutes on each side, remove from skewers and add over the corn.
4. Add the rest of the ingredients to the bowl, toss, divide between plates and serve for breakfast.

CALORIES: 316 Kcal     FAT: 22.5 g     FIBER: 5.6 g     PROTEIN: 15.4 g     CARBOHYDRATES: 23.6 g

---

*Preparation: 5 min*     Cooking: 0 min     *Servings: 4*

# 12. QUINOA AND EGGS SALAD

## INGREDIENTS

- 4 eggs, soft boiled, peeled and cut into wedges
- 2 cups baby arugula
- 2 cups cherry tomatoes, halved
- 1 cucumber, sliced
- 1 cup quinoa, cooked
- 1 cup almonds, chopped
- 1 avocado, peeled, pitted and sliced
- 1 tablespoon olive oil
- ½ cup mixed dill and mint, chopped
- A pinch of salt and black pepper
- Juice of 1 lemon

## DIRECTIONS

1. In a large salad bowl, combine the eggs with the arugula and the rest of the ingredients and toss.
2. Divide between plates and serve for breakfast.

CALORIES: 519 Kcal     FAT: 32.5 g     FIBER: 11.6 g     PROTEIN: 19.4 g     CARBOHYDRATES: 43.6 g

*Preparation: 10 min*  *Cooking: 2 min*  *Servings: 3*

## 13. HUMMUS AND TOMATO SANDWICH

### INGREDIENTS

- 6 whole grain bread slices
- 1 tomato
- 3 Cheddar cheese slices
- ½ teaspoon dried oregano
- 1 teaspoon green chili paste
- ½ red onion, sliced
- 1 teaspoon lemon juice
- 1 tablespoon hummus
- 3 lettuce leaves

### DIRECTIONS

1. Slice tomato into 6 slices.
2. In the shallow bowl mix up together dried oregano, green chili paste, lemon juice, and hummus.
3. Spread 3 bread slices with the chili paste mixture.
4. After this, place the sliced tomatoes on them.
5. Add sliced onion, Cheddar cheese, and lettuce leaves.
6. Cover the lettuce leaves with the remaining bread slices to get the sandwiches.
7. Preheat the grill to 365F.
8. Grill the sandwiches for 2 minutes.

CALORIES: 269 Kcal   FAT: 12.5 g   FIBER: 9.6 g   PROTEIN: 13.4 g   CARBOHYDRATES: 25.6 g

*Preparation: 10 min*      *Cooking: 0 min*      *Servings: 4*

# 14. GARBANZO BEAN SALAD

## INGREDIENTS

- 1 and ½ cups cucumber, cubed
- 15 ounces canned garbanzo beans, drained and rinsed
- 3 ounces black olives, pitted and sliced
- 1 tomato, chopped
- ¼ cup red onion, chopped
- 5 cups salad greens
- A pinch of salt and black pepper
- ½ cup feta cheese, crumbled
- 3 tablespoons olive oil
- 1 tablespoon lemon juice
- ¼ cup parsley, chopped

## DIRECTIONS

1. In a salad bowl, combine the garbanzo beans with the cucumber, tomato and the rest of the ingredients except the cheese and toss.
2. Divide the mix into small bowls, sprinkle the cheese on top and serve for breakfast.

CALORIES: 268 Kcal    FAT: 16.5 g    FIBER: 7.6 g    PROTEIN: 9.4 g    CARBOHYDRATES: 36.6 g

---

*Preparation: 10 min*      *Cooking: 30 min*      *Servings: 4*

# 15. SPICED CHICKPEAS BOWLS

## INGREDIENTS

- 15 ounces canned chickpeas, drained and rinsed
- ¼ teaspoon cardamom, ground
- ½ teaspoon cinnamon powder
- 1 and ½ teaspoons turmeric powder
- 1 teaspoon coriander, ground
- 1 tablespoon olive oil
- A pinch of salt and black pepper
- ¾ cup Greek yogurt
- ½ cup green olives, pitted and halved
- ½ cup cherry tomatoes, halved
- 1 cucumber, sliced

## DIRECTIONS

1. Spread the chickpeas on a lined baking sheet, add the cardamom, cinnamon, turmeric, coriander, the oil, salt and pepper, toss and bake at 375 degrees F for 30 minutes.
2. In a bowl, combine the roasted chickpeas with the rest of the ingredients, toss and serve for breakfast.

CALORIES: 519 Kcal    FAT: 34.5 g    FIBER: 13.6 g    PROTEIN: 11.4 g    CARBOHYDRATES: 36.6 g

*Preparation: 10 min*  *Cooking: 10 min*  *Servings: 5*

# 16. BUTTERY PANCAKES

## INGREDIENTS

- 1 cup wheat flour, whole-grain
- 1 teaspoon baking powder
- 1 teaspoon lemon juice
- 3 eggs, beaten
- ¼ cup Splenda
- 1 teaspoon vanilla extract
- ⅓ cup blueberries
- 1 tablespoon olive oil
- 1 teaspoon butter
- ⅓ cup milk

## DIRECTIONS

1. In the mixer bowl, combine together baking powder, wheat flour, lemon juice, eggs, Splenda, vanilla extract, milk, and olive oil.
2. Blend the liquid until it is smooth and homogenous.
3. After this, toss the butter in the skillet and melt it.
4. With the help of the ladle pour the pancake batter in the hot skillet and flatten it in the shape of the pancake.
5. Sprinkle the pancake with the blueberries gently and cook for 1.5 minutes over the medium heat.
6. Then flip the pancake onto another side and cook it for 30 seconds more.
7. Repeat the same steps with all remaining batter and blueberries.
8. Transfer the cooked pancakes in the serving plate.

CALORIES: 152 Kcal  FAT: 7.5 g  FIBER: 3.6 g  PROTEIN: 7.4 g  CARBOHYDRATES: 30.6 g

*Preparation: 10 min*     Cooking: 35 min     Servings: 4

## 17. TOMATO AND LENTILS SALAD

### INGREDIENTS

- 2 yellow onions, chopped
- 4 garlic cloves, minced
- 2 cups brown lentils
- 1 tablespoon olive oil
- A pinch of salt and black pepper
- ½ teaspoon sweet paprika
- ½ teaspoon ginger, grated
- 3 cups water
- ¼ cup lemon juice
- ¾ cup Greek yogurt
- 3 tablespoons tomato paste

### DIRECTIONS

1. Heat up a pot with the oil over medium-high heat, add the onions and sauté for 2 minutes.
2. Add the garlic and the lentils, stir and cook for 1 minute more.
3. Add the water, bring to a simmer and cook covered for 30 minutes.
4. Add the lemon juice and the remaining ingredients except the yogurt. Toss, divide the mix into bowls, top with the yogurt and serve.

CALORIES: 294 Kcal     FAT: 3.5 g     FIBER: 9.6 g     PROTEIN: 15.4 g     CARBOHYDRATES: 26.6 g

---

*Preparation: 15 min*     Cooking: 20 min     Servings: 4

## 18. EGG AND ARUGULA SALAD

### INGREDIENTS

- 3 tomatoes
- 1 cucumber
- 4 eggs, boiled, peeled
- ½ cup black olives, pitted
- ¼ red onion, peeled
- ½ cup arugula
- 1/3 cup Plain yogurt
- 1 teaspoon lemon juice
- ¼ teaspoon paprika
- 1/3 teaspoon Sea salt
- ½ teaspoon dried oregano

### DIRECTIONS

1. Chop tomatoes and cucumber into the medium cubes and transfer in the salad bowl.
2. Then tear arugula and add it in the salad bowl.
3. In the shallow bowl whisk together Plain yogurt, lemon juice, paprika, sea salt, and dried oregano.
4. Chop the boiled eggs roughly and add in the salad.
5. Add black olives (slice them if desired).
6. Then add red onion.
7. Shake the salad well.
8. Pour Plain yogurt dressing over the salad and stir it only before serving.

CALORIES: 169 Kcal     FAT: 6.5 g     FIBER: 2.6 g     PROTEIN: 9.4 g     CARBOHYDRATES: 10.6 g

*Preparation: 6 min*  *Cooking: 7 min*  *Servings: 2*

## 19. HERBED FRIED EGGS

### INGREDIENTS

- 4 eggs
- 1 tablespoon butter
- ½ teaspoon chives, chopped
- ½ teaspoon fresh parsley, chopped
- 1/3 teaspoon fresh dill, chopped
- ¾ teaspoon sea salt

### DIRECTIONS

1. Toss butter in the skillet and bring it to boil.
2. Then crack the eggs in the coiled butter and sprinkle with sea salt.
3. Cook the eggs with the closed lid for 2 minutes over the medium heat.
4. Then open the lid and sprinkle them with parsley, dill, and chives.
5. Cook the eggs for 3 minutes more over the medium heat.
6. Carefully transfer the cooked meal in the plate. Use the wooden spatula for this step.

CALORIES: 177 Kcal    FAT: 14.5 g    FIBER: 0.6 g    PROTEIN: 11.4 g    CARBOHYDRATES: 0.6 g

*Preparation: 10 min*     *Cooking: 2 hours*     *Servings: 4*

## 20. ALMOND CREAM CHEESE BAKE

**INGREDIENTS**

- 1 cup cream cheese
- 4 tablespoons honey
- 1 oz almonds, chopped
- ½ teaspoon vanilla extract
- 3 eggs, beaten
- 1 tablespoon semolina

**DIRECTIONS**

1. Put beaten eggs in the mixing bowl.
2. Add cream cheese, semolina, and vanilla extract.
3. Blend the mixture with the help of the hand mixer until it is fluffy.
4. After this, add chopped almonds and mix up the mass well.
5. Transfer the cream cheese mash in the non-sticky baking mold.
6. Flatten the surface of the cream cheese mash well.
7. Preheat the oven to 325F.
8. Cook the breakfast for 2 hours.
9. The meal is cooked when the surface of the mash is light brown.
10. Chill the cream cheese mash little and sprinkle with honey.

CALORIES: 352 Kcal     FAT: 22.5 g     FIBER: 1.6 g     PROTEIN: 10.4 g     CARBOHYDRATES: 7.6 g

---

*Preparation: 15 min*     *Cooking: 15 min*     *Servings: 4*

## 21. CHILI EGG CUPS

**INGREDIENTS**

- 1 teaspoon chives, chopped
- 4 eggs
- 1 teaspoon tomato paste
- 1 tablespoon Plain yogurt
- ½ teaspoon butter, softened
- ¼ teaspoon chili flakes
- ½ oz Cheddar cheese, shredded

**DIRECTIONS**

1. Preheat the oven to 365F.
2. Brush the muffin molds with the softened butter from inside.
3. Then mix up together Plain yogurt with chili flakes and tomato paste.
4. Crack the eggs in the muffin molds.
5. After this, carefully place the tomato paste mixture over the eggs and top with Cheddar cheese.
6. Sprinkle the eggs with chili flakes and place in the preheated oven.
7. Cook the egg cups for 15 minutes.
8. Then check if the eggs are solid and remove them from the oven.
9. Chill the egg cups till the room temperature and gently remove from the muffin molds.

CALORIES: 85 Kcal     FAT: 6.5 g     FIBER: 0.6 g     PROTEIN: 6.4 g     CARBOHYDRATES: 0.6 g

*Preparation: 10 min*     Cooking: 0 min     *Servings: 2*

## 22. BANANA OATS

### INGREDIENTS

- 1 banana, peeled and sliced
- 1¾ cup almond milk
- 4 almonds
- ½ cup cold brewed coffee
- 2 dates, pitted
- 2 tablespoons cocoa powder
- 1 cup rolled oats
- 1 and ½ tablespoons chia seeds

### DIRECTIONS

1. In a blender, combine the banana with the milk and the rest of the ingredients, then pulse.
2. Divide the mixture into bowls and serve for breakfast.

CALORIES: 451 Kcal    FAT: 25.1 g    FIBER: 9.9 g    PROTEIN: 9.3 g    CARBOHYDRATES: 55.4 g

*Preparation: 10 min*  *Cooking: 15 min*  *Servings: 2*

## 23. DILL EGGS MIX

### INGREDIENTS

- 2 eggs
- 2 oz Feta cheese
- 1 teaspoon fresh dill, chopped
- 1 teaspoon butter
- ½ teaspoon olive oil
- ¼ teaspoon onion powder
- ¼ teaspoon chili flakes

### DIRECTIONS

1. Toss butter in the skillet.
2. Add olive oil and bring to boil.
3. After this, crack the eggs in the skillet.
4. Sprinkle them with chili flakes and onion powder.
5. Preheat the oven to 360F.
6. Transfer the skillet with eggs in the oven and cook for 10 minutes.
7. Then crumble Feta cheese and sprinkle it over the eggs.
8. Bake the eggs for 2 minutes more.

CALORIES: 185 Kcal   FAT: 13.5 g   FIBER: 0.6 g   PROTEIN: 15.4 g   CARBOHYDRATES: 2.6 g

---

*Preparation: 15 min*  *Cooking: 20 min*  *Servings: 6*

## 24. CREAM OLIVE MUFFINS

### INGREDIENTS

- ½ cup quinoa, cooked
- 2 oz Feta cheese, crumbled
- 2 eggs, beaten
- 3 kalamata olives, chopped
- ¾ cup heavy cream
- 1 tomato, chopped
- 1 teaspoon butter, softened
- 1 tablespoon wheat flour, whole grain
- ½ teaspoon salt

### DIRECTIONS

1. In the mixing bowl whisk eggs and add Feta cheese.
2. Then add chopped tomato and heavy cream.
3. After this, add wheat flour, salt, and quinoa.
4. Then add kalamata olives and mix up the ingredients with the help of the spoon.
5. Brush the muffin molds with the butter from inside.
6. Transfer quinoa mixture in the muffin molds and flatten it with the help of the spatula or spoon if needed.
7. Cook the muffins in the preheated to 355F oven for 20 minutes.

CALORIES: 165 Kcal   FAT: 10.5 g   FIBER: 1.6 g   PROTEIN: 5.4 g   CARBOHYDRATES: 11.6 g

*Preparation: 10 min*     Cooking: 5 min     Servings: 4

# 25. VEGETARIAN BOWL

## INGREDIENTS

- 1 tablespoon olive oil
- 1 pound asparagus, trimmed and roughly chopped
- 3 cups kale, shredded
- 3 cups Brussels sprouts, shredded
- 1 cup pecorino cheese
- ½ cup hummus
- 1 avocado, peeled, pitted and sliced
- 4 eggs, soft boiled, peeled and sliced

**For the dressing:**
- 2 tablespoons lemon juice
- 1 garlic clove, minced
- 2 teaspoons Dijon mustard
- 2 tablespoons olive oil
- Salt and black pepper to the taste

## DIRECTIONS

1. Heat up a pan with 2 tablespoons oil over medium-high heat, add the asparagus and sauté for 5 minutes stirring often.
2. In a bowl, combine the other 2 tablespoons oil with the lemon juice, garlic, mustard, salt and pepper and whisk well.
3. In a salad bowl, combine the asparagus with the kale, sprouts, hummus, avocado and the eggs and toss gently.
4. Add the dressing and the pecorino cheese, toss and serve.

CALORIES: 323 Kcal     FAT: 21 g     FIBER: 10.9 g     PROTEIN: 14 g     CARBOHYDRATES: 24.8 g

*Preparation: 15 min*  *Cooking: 15 min*  *Servings: 4*

## 26. CHILI SCRAMBLE

### INGREDIENTS

- 3 tomatoes
- 4 eggs
- ¼ teaspoon of sea salt
- ½ chili pepper, chopped
- 1 tablespoon butter
- 1 cup water, for cooking

### DIRECTIONS

1. Pour water in the saucepan and bring it to boil.
2. Then remove water from the heat and add tomatoes.
3. Let the tomatoes stay in the hot water for 2-3 minutes.
4. After this, remove the tomatoes from water and peel them.
5. Place butter in the pan and melt it.
6. Add chopped chili pepper and fry it for 3 minutes over the medium heat.
7. Then chop the peeled tomatoes and add into the chili peppers.
8. Cook the vegetables for 5 minutes over the medium heat. Stir them from time to time.
9. After this, add sea salt and crack the eggs
10. Stir (scramble) the eggs well with the help of the fork and cook them for 3 minutes over the medium heat.

CALORIES: 177 Kcal    FAT: 7.5 g    FIBER: 1.6 g    PROTEIN: 6.4 g    CARBOHYDRATES: 4.6 g

---

*Preparation: 10 min*  *Cooking: 6 min*  *Servings: 4*

## 27. COUSCOUS AND CHICKPEAS BOWL

### INGREDIENTS

- ¾ cup whole wheat couscous
- 1 yellow onion, chopped
- 1 tablespoon olive oil
- 1 cup water
- 2 garlic cloves, minced
- 15 ounces canned chickpeas, drained and rinsed
- A pinch of salt and black pepper
- 15 ounces canned tomatoes, chopped
- 14 ounces canned artichokes, drained and chopped
- ½ cup Greek olives, pitted and chopped
- ½ teaspoon oregano, dried
- 1 tablespoon lemon juice

### DIRECTIONS

1. Put the water in a pot, bring to a boil over medium heat, add the couscous, stir, take off the heat, cover the pan, leave aside for 10 minutes and fluff with a fork.
2. Heat up a pan with the oil over medium-high heat, add the onion and sauté for 2 minutes.
3. Add the rest of the ingredients, toss and cook for 4 minutes more.
4. Add the couscous, toss, divide into bowls and serve for breakfast.

CALORIES: 540 Kcal    FAT: 10.5 g    FIBER: 9.6 g    PROTEIN: 11.4 g    CARBOHYDRATES: 51.6 g

*Preparation: 5 min*        *Cooking: 0 min*        *Servings: 2*

# 28. AVOCADO AND APPLE SMOOTHIE

## INGREDIENTS

- 3 cups spinach
- 1 green apple, cored and chopped
- 1 avocado, peeled, pitted and chopped
- 3 tablespoons chia seeds
- 1 teaspoon honey
- 1 banana, frozen and peeled
- 2 cups coconut water

## DIRECTIONS

1. In your blender, combine the spinach with the apple and the rest of the ingredients, then pulse.
2. If you have any other green vegetable or fruit, you can try to add it to the mixture.
3. Divide into glasses and serve.

CALORIES: 168 Kcal     FAT: 8.1 g     FIBER: 6 g     PROTEIN: 2.1 g     CARBOHYDRATES: 21 g

*Preparation: 10 min*  *Cooking: 11 min*  Servings: 2

## 29. EGGS WITH ZUCCHINI NOODLES

### INGREDIENTS

- 2 tablespoons extra-virgin olive oil
- 3 zucchinis, cut with a spiralizer
- 4 eggs
- Salt and black pepper to the taste
- A pinch of red pepper flakes
- Cooking spray
- 1 tablespoon basil, chopped

### DIRECTIONS

1. In a bowl, combine the zucchini noodles with salt, pepper and the olive oil and toss well.
2. Grease a baking sheet with cooking spray and divide the zucchini noodles into 4 nests on it.
3. Crack an egg on top of each nest, sprinkle salt, pepper and the pepper flakes on top and bake at 350 degrees F for 11 minutes.
4. Divide the mix between plates, sprinkle the basil on top and serve.

CALORIES: 296 Kcal   FAT: 23.6 g   FIBER: 3.3 g   PROTEIN: 14.7 g   CARBOHYDRATES: 10.6 g

---

*Preparation: 10 min*  *Cooking: 3 hours*  Servings: 6

## 30. SLOW-COOKED PEPPERS FRITTATA

### INGREDIENTS

- ½ cup almond milk
- 8 eggs, whisked
- Salt and black pepper to the taste
- 1 teaspoon oregano, dried
- 1 and ½ cups roasted peppers, chopped
- ½ cup red onion, chopped
- 4 cups baby arugula
- 1 cup goat cheese, crumbled
- Cooking spray

### DIRECTIONS

1. In a bowl, combine the eggs with salt, pepper and the oregano and whisk.
2. Grease your slow cooker with the cooking spray, arrange the peppers and the remaining ingredients inside and pour the eggs mixture over them.
3. Put the lid on and cook on Low for 3 hours.
4. Divide the frittata between plates and serve.

CALORIES: 259 Kcal   FAT: 20.2 g   FIBER: 1 g   PROTEIN: 16.3 g   CARBOHYDRATES: 4.4 g

*Preparation: 10 min* — Cooking: 3 min — Servings: 2

## 31. AVOCADO TOAST

### INGREDIENTS

- 1 tablespoon goat cheese, crumbled
- 1 avocado, peeled, pitted and mashed
- A pinch of salt and black pepper
- 2 whole wheat bread slices, toasted
- ½ teaspoon lime juice
- 1 persimmon, thinly sliced
- 1 fennel bulb, thinly sliced
- 2 teaspoons honey
- 1 teaspoon chia seeds

### DIRECTIONS

1. In a bowl, combine the avocado flesh with salt, pepper, lime juice and the cheese and whisk.
2. Toast the bread slices for 3 minutes.
3. Spread the mixture onto toasted bread slices, top each slice with the remaining ingredients and serve for breakfast.

CALORIES: 348 Kcal   FAT: 20.8 g   FIBER: 12.3 g   PROTEIN: 7.1 g   CARBOHYDRATES: 38.7 g

*Preparation: 5 min*     *Cooking: 15 min*     *Servings: 8*

## 32. MINI FRITTATAS

### INGREDIENTS

- 1 yellow onion, chopped
- 1 cup parmesan, grated
- 1 yellow bell pepper, chopped
- 1 red bell pepper, chopped
- 1 zucchini, chopped
- Salt and black pepper to the taste
- 8 eggs, whisked
- A drizzle of olive oil
- 2 tablespoons chives, chopped

### DIRECTIONS

1. Heat up a pan with the oil over medium-high heat, add the onion, the zucchini and the rest of the ingredients except the eggs and chives and sauté for 5 minutes stirring often.
2. Divide this mix on the bottom of a muffin pan, pour the eggs mixture on top, sprinkle salt, pepper and the chives and bake at 350 degrees F for 10 minutes.
3. Serve the mini frittatas for breakfast right away.

CALORIES: 55 Kcal     FAT: 3 g     FIBER: 0.7 g     PROTEIN: 4.2 g     CARBOHYDRATES: 3.2 g

---

*Preparation: 10 min*     *Cooking: 25 min*     *Servings: 4*

## 33. SUN-DRIED TOMATOES OATMEAL

### INGREDIENTS

- 3 cups water
- 1 cup almond milk
- 1 tablespoon olive oil
- 1 cup steel-cut oats
- ¼ cup sun-dried tomatoes, chopped
- A pinch of red pepper flakes

### DIRECTIONS

1. In a pan, mix the water with the milk, bring to a boil over medium heat.
2. Meanwhile, heat up a pan with the oil over medium-high heat, add the oats, cook them for about 2 minutes and transfer m to the pan with the milk.
3. Stir the oats, add the tomatoes and simmer over medium heat for 23 minutes.
4. Divide the mix into bowls, sprinkle the red pepper flakes on top and serve for breakfast.

CALORIES: 170 Kcal     FAT: 17.8 g     FIBER: 1.5 g     PROTEIN: 1.5 g     CARBOHYDRATES: 3.8 g

*Preparation:* 5 min   *Cooking:* 0 min   *Servings:* 2

## 34. BERRY OATS

### INGREDIENTS

- ½ cup rolled oats
- 1 cup almond milk
- ¼ cup chia seeds
- A pinch of cinnamon powder
- 2 teaspoons honey
- 1 cup berries, pureed
- 1 tablespoon yogurt

### DIRECTIONS

1. In a bowl, combine the oats with the milk and the rest of the ingredients except the yogurt, toss and divide into bowls.
2. Top with the yogurt and serve cold for breakfast.

CALORIES: 420 Kcal   FAT: 30.3 g   FIBER: 7.2 g   PROTEIN: 6.4 g   CARBOHYDRATES: 35.3 g

*Preparation: 10 min*  *Cooking: 30 min*  *Servings: 8*

## 35. QUINOA MUFFINS

**INGREDIENTS**

- 1 cup quinoa, cooked
- 6 eggs, whisked
- Salt and black pepper to the taste
- 1 cup Swiss cheese, grated
- 1 small yellow onion, chopped
- 1 cup white mushrooms, sliced
- ½ cup sun-dried tomatoes, chopped

**DIRECTIONS**

1. In a bowl, combine the eggs with salt, pepper and the rest of the ingredients and whisk well.
2. Divide this into a silicone muffin pan, bake at 350 degrees F for 30 minutes, then serve for breakfast.

CALORIES: 123 Kcal    FAT: 5.6 g    FIBER: 1.3 g    PROTEIN: 7.5 g    CARBOHYDRATES: 10.8 g

---

*Preparation: 10 min*  *Cooking: 23 min*  *Servings: 4*

## 36. QUINOA AND EGGS PAN

**INGREDIENTS**

- 4 bacon slices, cooked and crumbled
- A drizzle of olive oil
- 1 small red onion, chopped
- 1 red bell pepper, chopped
- 1 sweet potato, grated
- 1 green bell pepper, chopped
- 2 garlic cloves, minced
- 1 cup white mushrooms, sliced
- ½ cup quinoa
- 1 cup chicken stock
- 4 eggs, fried
- Salt and black pepper to the taste

**DIRECTIONS**

1. Heat up a pan with the oil over medium-low heat, add the onion, garlic, bell peppers, sweet potato and the mushrooms, toss and sauté for 5 minutes.
2. Add the quinoa, toss and cook for 1 more minute.
3. Add the stock, salt and pepper, stir and cook for 15 minutes.
4. Divide the mix between plates, top each serving with a fried egg, sprinkle some salt, pepper and crumbled bacon and serve for breakfast.

CALORIES: 304 Kcal    FAT: 14 g    FIBER: 3.8 g    PROTEIN: 17.8 g    CARBOHYDRATES: 27.5 g

Preparation: 10 min        Cooking: 10 min        Servings: 2

# 37. SCRAMBLED EGGS

## INGREDIENTS

- 1 yellow bell pepper, chopped
- 8 cherry tomatoes, cubed
- 2 spring onions, chopped
- 1 tablespoon olive oil
- 1 tablespoon capers, drained
- 2 tablespoons black olives, pitted and sliced
- 4 eggs
- A pinch of salt and black pepper
- ¼ teaspoon oregano, dried
- 1 tablespoon parsley, chopped
- 2 bread slices

## DIRECTIONS

1. Heat up a pan with the oil over medium-high heat, add the bell pepper and spring onions and sauté for 3 minutes.
2. Add the tomatoes, capers and the olives and sauté for 2 minutes more.
3. Crack the eggs into the pan, add salt, pepper and the oregano and scramble for 5 minutes more.
4. Divide the scramble between plates, placing it over the bread.
5. Sprinkle the parsley on top and serve.

CALORIES: 249 Kcal    FAT: 17 g    FIBER: 3.2 g    PROTEIN: 13.5 g    CARBOHYDRATES: 13.3 g

*Preparation: 10 min*  *Cooking: 15 min*  *Servings: 4*

## 38. STUFFED TOMATOES

### INGREDIENTS

- 2 tablespoons olive oil
- 8 tomatoes, insides scooped
- ¼ cup almond milk
- 8 eggs
- ¼ cup parmesan, grated
- Salt and black pepper to the taste
- 4 tablespoons rosemary, chopped

### DIRECTIONS

1. Grease a pan with the oil and arrange the tomatoes inside.
2. Crack an egg in each tomato, divide the milk and the rest of the ingredients, introduce the pan in the oven and bake at 375 degrees F for 15 minutes.
3. Serve for breakfast right away.

CALORIES: 276 Kcal    FAT: 20.3 g    FIBER: 4.7 g    PROTEIN: 13.7 g    CARBOHYDRATES: 13.2 g

---

*Preparation: 10 min*  *Cooking: 0 min*  *Servings: 4*

## 39. WATERMELON "PIZZA"

### INGREDIENTS

- 1 watermelon slice cut 1-inch thick and then from the center cut into 4 wedges resembling pizza slices
- 6 kalamata olives, pitted and sliced
- 1 ounce feta cheese, crumbled
- ½ tablespoon balsamic vinegar
- 1 teaspoon mint, chopped

### DIRECTIONS

1. Arrange the watermelon slice on a plate, sprinkle the olives and the rest of the ingredients on each slice.
2. Serve cold for breakfast.

CALORIES: 90 Kcal    FAT: 3 g    FIBER: 1 g    PROTEIN: 2 g    CARBOHYDRATES: 14 g

*Preparation: 10 min*  *Cooking: 45 min*  *Servings: 8*

## 40. BAKED OMELET MIX

### INGREDIENTS

- 12 eggs, whisked
- 8 ounces spinach, chopped
- 2 cups almond milk
- 12 ounces canned artichokes, chopped
- 2 garlic cloves, minced
- 5 ounces feta cheese, crumbled
- 1 tablespoon dill, chopped
- 1 teaspoon oregano, dried
- 1 teaspoon lemon pepper
- A pinch of salt
- 4 teaspoons olive oil

### DIRECTIONS

1. Heat up a pan with the oil over medium-high heat, add the garlic and the spinach and sauté for 3 minutes.
2. In a baking dish, combine the eggs with the artichokes and the rest of the ingredients.
3. Add the spinach mix as well, toss a bit, bake the mix at 375 degrees F for 40 minutes.
4. Divide between plates and serve for breakfast.

**CALORIES:** 186 Kcal   **FAT:** 13 g   **FIBER:** 1 g   **PROTEIN:** 10 g   **CARBOHYDRATES:** 5 g

# 14 Small Dishes

*Preparation: 30 min*  *Cooking: 30 min*  *Servings: 4*

# 41. ROASTED BROCCOLI SALAD

## INGREDIENTS

- 1 lb. Broccoli, Cut into Florets & Stem Sliced
- 3 Tablespoons Olive Oil, Divided
- 1 Pint Cherry Tomatoes
- 1 ½ Teaspoons Honey, Raw & Divided
- 3 Cups Cubed Bread
- 1 Tablespoon Balsamic Vinegar
- ½ Teaspoon Black Pepper
- ¼ Teaspoon Sea Salt, Fine
- Grated Parmesan for Serving

## DIRECTIONS

1. Start by heating your oven to 450, and then get out a rimmed baking sheet. Place it in the oven to heat up.
2. Drizzle your broccoli with a tablespoon of oil, and toss to coat.
3. Remove the baking sheet form the oven, and spoon the broccoli on it. Leave oil in the bottom of the bowl and add in your tomatoes, toss to coat, and then toss your tomatoes with a tablespoon of honey. Pour them on the same baking sheet as your broccoli.
4. Roast for fifteen minutes, and stir halfway through your cooking time.
5. Add in your bread, and then roast for three more minutes.
6. Whisk two tablespoons of oil, vinegar, and remaining honey. Season with salt and pepper. Pour this over your broccoli mix to serve.

CALORIES: 226 Kcal    FAT: 12 g    PROTEIN: 7 g    CARBOHYDRATES: 26 g

*Preparation: 10 min*  *Cooking: 20 min*  *Servings: 6*

## 42. MELON SALAD

### INGREDIENTS

- ¼ Teaspoon Sea Salt
- ¼ Teaspoon Black Pepper
- 1 Tablespoon Balsamic Vinegar
- 1 Cantaloupe, Quartered & Seeded
- 12 Watermelon, Small & Seedless
- 2 Cups Mozzarella Balls, Fresh
- 1/3 Cup Basil, Fresh & Torn
- 2 Tablespoons Olive Oil

### DIRECTIONS

1. Get out a melon baller and scoop out balls of cantaloupe, and the put them in a colander over a serving bowl.
2. Use your melon baller to cut the watermelon as well, and then put them in with your cantaloupe.
3. Allow your fruit to drain for ten minutes, and then refrigerate the juice for another recipe. It can even be added to smoothies.
4. Wipe the bowl dry, and then place your fruit in it.
5. Add in your basil, oil, vinegar, mozzarella and tomatoes before seasoning with salt and pepper.
6. Gently mix and serve immediately or chilled.

CALORIES: 218 Kcal  FAT: 13 g  PROTEIN: 10 g  CARBOHYDRATES: 17 g

---

*Preparation: 5 min*  *Cooking: 0 min*  *Servings: 6*

## 43. ORANGE CELERY SALAD

### INGREDIENTS

- 1 Tablespoon Lemon Juice, Fresh
- ¼ Teaspoon Sea Salt, Fine
- ¼ Teaspoon Black Pepper
- 1 Tablespoon Olive Brine
- 1 Tablespoon Olive Oil
- ¼ Cup Red Onion, Sliced
- ½ Cup Green Olives
- 2 Oranges, Peeled & Sliced
- 3 Celery Stalks, Sliced Diagonally in ½ Inch Slices

### DIRECTIONS

1. Put your oranges, olives, onion and celery in a shallow bowl.
2. In a different bowl whisk your oil, olive brine and lemon juice, pour this over your salad.
3. Season with salt and pepper before serving.

CALORIES: 62 Kcal  FAT: 0 g  PROTEIN: 2 g  CARBOHYDRATES: 9 g

Preparation: 5 min  Cooking: 0 min  Servings: 4

## 44. TOMATO SALAD

### INGREDIENTS

- 1 Cucumber, Sliced
- ¼ Cup Sun Dried Tomatoes, Chopped
- 1 lb. Tomatoes, Cubed
- ½ Cup Black Olives
- 1 Red Onion, Sliced
- 1 Tablespoons Balsamic Vinegar
- ¼ Cup Parsley, Fresh & Chopped
- 2 Tablespoons Olive Oil
- Sea Salt & Black Pepper to Taste

### DIRECTIONS

1. In a bowl, combine all of your vegetables together.
2. Make your dressing mixing all your seasoning, olive oil and vinegar.
3. Toss with your salad and serve fresh.

CALORIES: 126 Kcal  FAT: 0 g  PROTEIN: 2.1 g  CARBOHYDRATES: 11.5 g

*Preparation: 5 min*     *Cooking: 0 min*     *Servings: 4*

## 45. FETA BEET SALAD

### INGREDIENTS

- 6 Red Beets, Cooked & Peeled
- 3 Ounces Feta Cheese, Cubed
- 2 Tablespoons Olive Oil
- 2 Tablespoons Balsamic Vinegar

### DIRECTIONS

1. Combine every ingredient in a bowl.
2. Season with olive oil and balsamic vinegar, then serve.

CALORIES: 230 Kcal     FAT: 12 g     PROTEIN: 7.3 g     CARBOHYDRATES: 26.3 g

---

*Preparation: 5 min*     *Cooking: 0 min*     *Servings: 4*

## 46. CAULIFLOWER & TOMATO SALAD

### INGREDIENTS

- 1 Head Cauliflower, Chopped
- 2 Tablespoons Parsley, Fresh & chopped
- 2 Cups Cherry Tomatoes, Halved
- 2 Tablespoons Lemon Juice, Fresh
- 2 Tablespoons Pine Nuts
- Sea Salt & Black Pepper to Taste

### DIRECTIONS

1. Mix your lemon juice, cherry tomatoes, cauliflower and parsley together, and then season.
2. Top with pine nuts, mix well before serving.

CALORIES: 64 Kcal     FAT: 3.3 g     PROTEIN: 2.8 g     CARBOHYDRATES: 7.9 g

Preparation: 10 min     Cooking: 30 min     Servings: 4

## 47. PILAF WITH CREAM CHEESE

### INGREDIENTS

- 2 Cups Yellow Long Grain Rice, Parboiled
- 1 Cup Onion
- 4 Green Onions
- 3 Tablespoons Butter
- 3 Tablespoons Vegetable Broth
- 2 Teaspoons Cayenne Pepper
- 1 Teaspoons Paprika
- ½ Teaspoon Cloves, Minced
- 2 Tablespoons Mint Leaves, Fresh & Chopped
- 1 Bunch Fresh Mint Leaves to Garnish
- 1 Tablespoons Olive Oil
- Sea Salt & Black Pepper to Taste
- 3 Tablespoons Olive Oil
- Sea Salt & Black Pepper to Taste
- 9 Ounces Cream Cheese

### DIRECTIONS

1. Start by heating your oven to 360, and then get out a pan. Heat your butter and olive oil together and cook your onions and spring onions for two minutes.
2. Add in your salt, pepper, paprika, cloves, vegetable broth, rice and remaining seasoning. S
3. Sauté for three minutes.
4. Cover with foil, and bake for another half hour. Allow it to cool.
5. Mix in the cream cheese, cheese, olive oil, salt and pepper. Serve your pilaf garnished with fresh mint leaves.

CALORIES: 364 Kcal     FAT: 30 g     PROTEIN: 5 g     CARBOHYDRATES: 30 g

*Preparation: 5 min*     *Cooking: 5 min*     Servings: 4

# 48. TAHINI SPINACH

## INGREDIENTS

- 10 Spinach, Chopped
- ½ Cup Water
- 1 Tablespoon Tahini
- 2 Cloves Garlic, Minced
- ¼ Teaspoon Cumin
- ¼ Teaspoon Paprika
- ¼ Teaspoon Cayenne Pepper
- 1/3 Cup Red Wine Vinegar
- Sea Salt & Black Pepper to Taste

## DIRECTIONS

1. Add your spinach and water to the saucepan, and then boil it on high heat. Once boiling reduce to low, and cover. Allow it to cook on simmer for five minutes.
2. Add in your garlic, cumin, cayenne, red wine vinegar, paprika and tahini. Whisk well, and season with salt and pepper.
3. Drain your spinach and top with tahini sauce to serve.

**CALORIES: 69 Kcal**     **FAT: 3 g**     **PROTEIN: 5 g**     **CARBOHYDRATES: 8 g**

---

*Preparation: 15 min*     *Cooking: 25 min*     Servings: 4

# 49. EASY SPAGHETTI SQUASH

## INGREDIENTS

- 2 Spring Onions, Chopped Fine
- 3 Cloves Garlic, Minced
- 1 Zucchini, Diced 1 Red Bell Pepper, Diced
- 1 Tablespoon Italian Seasoning
- 1 Tomato, Small & Chopped Fine
- 1 Tablespoons Parsley, Fresh & Chopped
- Pinch Lemon Pepper
- Dash Sea Salt, Fine
- 4 Ounces Feta Cheese, Crumbled
- 3 Italian Sausage Links, Casing Removed
- 2 Tablespoons Olive Oil
- 2 Cups Tomato Sauce

## DIRECTIONS

1. Start by heating your oven to 350, and get out a large baking sheet. Coat it with cooking spray, and then put your squash on it with the cut side down.
2. Bake at 350 for forty-five minutes. It should be tender.
3. Turn the squash over, and bake for five more minutes. Scrape the strands into a larger bowl. Heat up a tablespoon of olive oil in a skillet, and then add in tomato sauce. Cook eight minutes before removing it and placing it in a bowl.
4. Add another tablespoon of olive oil to the skillet and cook your garlic and onions until softened. This will take five minutes. Throw in your Italian seasoning, red peppers and zucchini. Cook for another five minutes. Your vegetables should be softened.
5. Mix in your feta cheese and squash, cooking until the cheese has melted. Stir in your sausage, and then season with lemon pepper and salt. Serve with parsley and tomato.

**CALORIES: 423 Kcal**     **FAT: 30 g**     **PROTEIN: 18 g**     **CARBOHYDRATES: 22 g**

Preparation: 5 min    Cooking: 20 min    Servings: 6

## 50. ROASTED VEGGIES

### INGREDIENTS

- 6 Cloves Garlic
- 6 Tablespoons Olive Oil
- 2 Carrots
- 1 Fennel Bulb, cut into slices
- 2 Zucchini, cut into slices
- 2 Red Bell Peppers, cut into slices
- 2 Teaspoons Sea Salt
- ½ Cup Balsamic Vinegar
- ¼ Cup Rosemary, Chopped & Fresh
- 2 Teaspoons Vegetable Bouillon Powder

### DIRECTIONS

1. Start by heating your oven to 400.
2. Get out a baking dish and place your carrots, zucchini, peppers, garlic and fennel on a baking dish, drizzling with olive oil. Sprinkle with salt, bouillon powder, and rosemary. Mix well, and then bake at 450 for thirty to forty minutes. Mix your vinegar into the vegetables before serving.

CALORIES: 225 Kcal    FAT: 6 g    PROTEIN: 13 g    CARBOHYDRATES: 40 g

*Preparation: 15 min*  *Cooking: 40 min*  *Servings: 6*

## 51. ROASTED EGGPLANT SALAD

**INGREDIENTS**

- 1 Red Onion, Sliced
- 2 Tablespoons Parsley, Fresh & Chopped
- 1 Teaspoon Thyme
- 2 Cups Cherry Tomatoes, Halved
- Sea Salt & Black Pepper to Taste
- 1 Teaspoon Oregano
- 3 Tablespoons Olive Oil
- 1 Teaspoon Basil
- 3 Eggplants, Peeled & Cubed

**DIRECTIONS**

1. Start by heating your oven to 350.
2. Season your eggplant with basil, salt, pepper, oregano, thyme and olive oil.
3. Spread it on a baking tray, and bake for a half hour.
4. Toss with your remaining ingredients before serving.

CALORIES: 148 Kcal   FAT: 4.7 g   PROTEIN: 3.5 g   CARBOHYDRATES: 20.5 g

---

*Preparation: 10 min*  *Cooking: 20 min*  *Servings: 8*

## 52. PENNE WITH TAHINI SAUCE

**INGREDIENTS**

- ⅓ Cup Water
- 1 Cup Yogurt, Plain
- ⅛ Cup Lemon Juice
- 3 Tablespoons Tahini
- 3 Cloves Garlic
- 1 Onion, Chopped
- ¼ Cup Olive Oil
- 2 Portobello Mushrooms, Large & Sliced
- ½ Red Bell Pepper, Diced
- 16 Ounces Penne Pasta
- ½ Cup Parsley, Fresh & Chopped
- Black Pepper to Taste

**DIRECTIONS**

1. Start by getting out a pot and bring a pot of salted water to a boil. Cook your pasta al dente per package instructions.
2. Mix your lemon juice and tahini together, and then place it tin a food processor. Process with garlic, water and yogurt. It should be smooth.
3. Get out a saucepan, and place it over medium heat. Heat up your oil, and cook your onions until soft.
4. Add in your mushroom and continue to cook until softened.
5. Add in your bell pepper, and cook until crispy.
6. Drain your pasta, and then toss with your tahini sauce, top with parsley and pepper and serve with vegetables.

CALORIES: 332 Kcal   FAT: 12 g   PROTEIN: 11 g   CARBOHYDRATES: 48 g

Preparation: 10 min Cooking: 20 min Servings: 6

## 53. FETA & SPINACH PITA BAKE

### INGREDIENTS

- 2 Roma Tomatoes, Chopped
- 6 Whole Wheat Pita Bread
- 1 Jar Sun Dried Tomato Pesto
- 4 Mushrooms, Fresh & Sliced
- 1 Bunch Spinach, Rinsed & Chopped
- 2 Tablespoons Parmesan Cheese, Grated
- 3 Tablespoons Olive Oil
- ½ Cup Feta Cheese, Crumbled
- Dash Black Pepper

### DIRECTIONS

1. Start by heating the oven to 350, and get to your pita bread. Spread the tomato pesto on the side of each one. Put them in a baking pan with the tomato side up.
2. Top with tomatoes, spinach, mushrooms, parmesan and feta. Drizzle with olive oil and season with pepper.
3. Bake for twelve minutes, and then serve cut into quarters.

CALORIES: 350 Kcal FAT: 17 g PROTEIN: 12 g CARBOHYDRATES: 42 g

*Preparation: 15 min*     *Cooking: 30 min*     *Servings: 6*

# 54. PARMESAN BARLEY RISOTTO

## INGREDIENTS

- 1 Cup yellow Onion, Chopped
- 1 Tablespoon Olive Oil
- 4 Cups Vegetable Broth, Low Sodium
- 2 Cups Pearl Barley, Uncooked
- ½ Cup Dry White Wine
- 1 Cup Parmesan Cheese, Grated Fine & Divided
- Sea Salt & Black Pepper to Taste
- Fresh Chives, Chopped for Serving
- Lemon Wedges for Serving

## DIRECTIONS

1. Add your broth into a saucepan and bring it to a simmer over medium-high heat.
2. Get out a stock pot and put it over medium-high heat as well. Heat up your oil before adding in your onion. Cook for eight minutes and stir occasionally. Add in your barley and cook for two minutes more. Stir in your barley, cooking until it's toasted.
3. Pour in the wine, cooking for a minute more. Most of the liquid should have evaporated before adding in a cup of warm broth. Cook and stir for two minutes. Your liquid should be absorbed. Add in the remaining broth by the cup, and cook until ach cup is absorbed fore adding more. It should take about two minutes each time. It will take a little longer for the last cup to be absorbed.
4. Remove from heat, and stir in a half a cup of cheese, and top with remaining cheese chives and lemon wedges.

CALORIES: 346 Kcal     FAT: 7 g     PROTEIN: 14 g     CARBOHYDRATES: 56 g

---

*Preparation: 15 min*     *Cooking: 30 min*     *Servings: 4*

# 55. ZUCCHINI PASTA

## INGREDIENTS

- 3 Tablespoons Olive Oil
- 2 Cloves Garlic, Minced
- 3 Zucchini, Large & Diced
- Sea Salt & Black Pepper to Taste
- ½ Cup Milk, 2%
- ¼ Teaspoon Nutmeg
- 1 Tablespoon Lemon Juice, Fresh
- ½ Cup Parmesan, Grated
- 8 Ounces Farfalle Pasta

## DIRECTIONS

1. Get out a skillet and place it over medium heat, and then heat up the oil. Add in your garlic and cook for a minute. Stir often so that it doesn't burn. Add in your salt, pepper and zucchini. Stir well, and cook covered for fifteen minutes. During this time, you'll want to stir the mixture twice.
2. Get out a microwave safe bowl, and heat the milk for thirty seconds. Stir in your nutmeg, and then pour it into the skillet. Cook uncovered for five minutes. Stir occasionally to keep from burning.
3. Get out a stockpot and cook your pasta per package instructions. Drain the pasta, and then save two tablespoons of pasta water.
4. Stir everything together, and add in the cheese and lemon juice and pasta water.

CALORIES: 410 Kcal     FAT: 17 g     PROTEIN: 15 g     CARBOHYDRATES: 45 g

*Preparation: 15 min*  *Cooking: 25 min*  Servings: 4

# 56. VEGETABLES SANDWICH

## INGREDIENTS

- 2 Tablespoons Olive Oil, Divided
- ¼ Cup Onion, Diced
- 1 Cup Zucchini, Diced
- 1 ½ Cups Broccoli, Diced
- ¼ Teaspoon Oregano
- Sea Salt & Black Pepper to Taste
- 12 Ounces Jar Roasted Red Peppers, Drained & Chopped Fine
- 2 Tablespoons Parmesan Cheese, Grated
- 1 Cup Mozzarella, Fresh & Sliced
- 2-Foot-Long Whole Grain Italian Loaf, Cut into 4 Pieces

## DIRECTIONS

1. Heat your oven to 450, and then get out a baking sheet. Heat the oven with your baking sheet inside.
2. Get out a bowl and mix your broccoli, zucchini, oregano, pepper, onion and salt with a tablespoon of olive oil.
3. Remove your baking sheet from the oven and coat it in a nonstick cooking spray. Spread the vegetable mixture over it to roast for five minutes. Stir halfway through.
4. Remove it from the oven, and add your red pepper, and sprinkle with parmesan cheese. Mix everything together.
5. Get out a panini maker or grill pan, placing it over medium-high heat. Heat up a tablespoon of oil.
6. Spread the bread horizontally on it, but don't cut it all the way through. Fill with the vegetable mix, and then a slice of mozzarella cheese on top. Close the sandwich and cook like you would a normal panini. With a press it should grill for five minutes. For a grill pan cook for two and a half minutes per side. Repeat for the remaining sandwiches.

CALORIES: 352 Kcal   FAT: 15 g   PROTEIN: 16 g   CARBOHYDRATES: 45 g

*Preparation: 10 min*     *Cooking: 25 min*     *Servings: 6*

## 57. ASPARAGUS PASTA

### INGREDIENTS

- 8 Ounces Farfalle Pasta, Uncooked
- 1 ½ Cups Asparagus, Fresh, Trimmed & Chopped into 1 Inch Pieces
- 1 Pint Grape Tomatoes, Halved
- 2 Tablespoons Olive Oil
- Sea Salt & Black Pepper to Taste
- 2 Cups Mozzarella, Fresh & Drained
- 1/3 Cup Basil Leaves, Fresh & Torn
- 2 Tablespoons Balsamic Vinegar

### DIRECTIONS

1. Start by heating the oven to 400, and then get out a stockpot. Cook your pasta per package instructions, and reserve ¼ cup of pasta water.
2. Get out a bowl and toss the tomatoes, oil, asparagus, and season with salt and pepper. Spread this mixture on a baking sheet, and bake for fifteen minutes. Stir twice in this time.
3. Remove your vegetables from the oven, and then add the cooked pasta to your baking sheet. Mix with a few tablespoons of pasta water so that your sauce becomes smoother.
4. Mix in your basil and mozzarella, drizzling with balsamic vinegar. Serve warm.

CALORIES: 307 Kcal     FAT: 14 g     PROTEIN: 18 g     CARBOHYDRATES: 60 g

---

*Preparation: 10 min*     *Cooking: 0 min*     *Servings: 6*

## 58. PISTACHIO ARUGULA SALAD

### INGREDIENTS

- 6 Cups Kale, Chopped
- ¼ Cup Olive Oil
- 2 Tablespoons Lemon Juice, Fresh
- ½ Teaspoon Smoked Paprika
- 2 Cups Arugula
- 1/3 Cup Pistachios, Unsalted & Shelled
- 6 Tablespoons Parmesan Cheese, Grated

### DIRECTIONS

1. Take salad bowl and combine your oil, lemon, smoked paprika and kale. Gently massage the leaves for half a minute.
2. Coat the kale as well.
3. Gently mix your arugula and pistachios when ready to serve.

CALORIES: 150 Kcal     FAT: 12 g     PROTEIN: 5 g     CARBOHYDRATES: 8 g

Preparation: 7 min  Cooking: 25 min  Servings: 2

## 59. ROASTED BEETROOT AND GARLIC

### INGREDIENTS

- 2 slices Whole grain bread
- Salt and pepper to taste
- 1 tablespoon of finely chopped basil
- 4 cloves of garlic
- Extra virgin oil
- 2 large beetroots

### DIRECTIONS

1. Preheat your oven to 400 degrees F.
2. Use the olive oil to brush the bottom of a baking dish. Set aside.
3. Slice the beetroots into some pieces.
4. Lay the pieces of beetroots and the garlic cloves into the baking dish that you had prepared earlier. Sprinkle some basil and garlic on top of the beetroots, season with pepper and salt to taste.
5. Drizzle with olive oil and then place the baking dish into the oven. Bake for about 20-25 minutes.
6. Remove from the oven, give it a few seconds to cool down and then serve and enjoy.
7. *The beetroots juice and olive oil at the bottom of the pan can be used as a dipping sauce. If you want, you can put it into a small bowl and enjoy it with warm whole grain bread.

CALORIES: 142 Kcal    FAT: 1 g    PROTEIN: 8 g    CARBOHYDRATES: 25 g

*Preparation: 15 min*     *Cooking: 30 min*     *Servings: 6*

# 60. ASPARAGUS COUSCOUS

## INGREDIENTS

- 1 Cup Goat Cheese, Garlic & Herb Flavored
- 1 ½ lbs. Asparagus, Trimmed & Chopped into 1 Inch Pieces
- 1 Tablespoon Olive Oil
- 1 Clove Garlic, Minced
- ¼ Teaspoon Black Pepper
- 1 ¾ Cup Water
- 8 Ounces Whole Wheat Couscous, Uncooked
- ¼ Teaspoon Sea Salt, Fine

## DIRECTIONS

1. Start by heating your oven to 425, and then put your goat cheese on the counter. It needs to come to room temperature.
2. Get out a bowl and mix your oil, pepper, garlic and asparagus. Spread the asparagus on a baking sheet and roast for ten minutes. Make sure to stir at least once.
3. Remove it from the pan, and place your asparagus in a serving bowl.
4. Get out a medium saucepan, and bring your water to a boil. Add in your salt and couscous. Reduce the heat to medium-low, and then cover your saucepan. Cook for twelve minutes. All your water should be absorbed.
5. Pour the couscous in a bowl with asparagus, and ad din your goat cheese. Stir until melted, and serve warm.

CALORIES: 263 Kcal     FAT: 9 g     PROTEIN: 11 g     CARBOHYDRATES: 36 g

---

*Preparation: 10 min*     *Cooking: 0 min*     *Servings: 4*

# 61. EASY SALAD WRAPS

## INGREDIENTS

- 1 ½ Cups Cucumber, Seedless, Peeled & Chopped
- 1 Cup Tomato, Chopped
- ½ Cup Mint, Fresh & Chopped Fine
- Ounce Can Black Olives, Sliced & Drained
- ¼ Cup Red Onion, Diced
- 2 Tablespoons olive Oil
- Sea Salt & Black Pepper to Taste
- 1 Tablespoon Red Wine Vinegar
- ½ Cup Goat Cheese, Crumbled
- 4 Flatbread Wraps, Whole Wheat

## DIRECTIONS

1. Get out a bowl and mix your tomato, mint, cucumber, onion and olives together.
2. Get out another bowl and whisk your vinegar, oil, pepper and salt. Drizzle this over your salad, and mix well.
3. Spread your goat cheese over the four wraps, and then spoon your salad filling in each one. Fold up to serve.

CALORIES: 262 Kcal     FAT: 15 g     PROTEIN: 7 g     CARBOHYDRATES: 23 g

Preparation: 20 min  Cooking: 0 min / Freezing: 2 hours  Servings: 8

## 62. CUCUMBER AND NUTS SALAD

### INGREDIENTS

- ½ cup (2 ounce) of crumbled feta cheese
- ⅓ cup of toasted walnuts
- 1 chili pepper
- ½ teaspoon of salt
- 1 tablespoon of grated lemon peel
- ⅓ cup of chopped fresh mint leaves
- ⅓ cup of chopped parsley
- ½ cup of dried cranberries
- ½ cup of chopped red onion
- ½ medium cucumber, unpeeled, seeded and chopped
- 2 tablespoons of olive oil
- ¼ cup of lemon juice
- 1 cup of boiling water
- 1 cup of uncooked bulgur
- 1 tablespoon poppy seeds

### DIRECTIONS

1. Start by placing the bulgur in a large heatproof bowl. Pour in some hot boiling water into the heatproof bowl and give the mixture a stir. Let the bulgur sit for about 1 hour or until the water has been absorbed.
2. Add in a chopped chili pepper, mint, parsley, cranberries, onion, cucumber, salt, oil and lemon juice and toss well. Cover the large bowl and refrigerate it for 2-3 hours or until the mixture is chilled.
3. Remove the mixture from the fridge and lightly sprinkle the mixture with cheese, walnuts and poppy seeds. Serve and enjoy.

CALORIES: 252 Kcal  FAT: 10 g  PROTEIN: 16 g  CARBOHYDRATES: 35 g

*Preparation: 5 min*  *Cooking: 35 min*  *Servings: 4*

## 63. CHILI OREGANO BAKED CHEESE

### INGREDIENTS

- 8 oz. feta cheese
- 4 oz. mozzarella, crumbled
- 1 chili pepper, sliced
- 1 teaspoon dried oregano
- 2 tablespoons olive oil

### DIRECTIONS

1. Place the feta cheese in a small deep-dish baking pan.
2. Top with the mozzarella then season with pepper slices and oregano.
3. Cover the pan with aluminum foil and cook in the preheated oven at 350F for 20 minutes.
4. Serve the cheese right away.

CALORIES: 292 Kcal   FAT: 24.2 g   PROTEIN: 16.2 g   CARBOHYDRATES: 3.7 g

---

*Preparation: 5 min*  *Cooking: 15 min*  *Servings: 4*

## 64. UNUSUAL MARGHERITA SLICES

### INGREDIENTS

- 1 Tomato, Cut into 8 Slices
- 1 Clove Garlic, Halved
- 1 Tablespoon Olive Oil
- ¼ Teaspoon Oregano
- 1 Cup Mozzarella, Fresh & Sliced
- ¼ Cup Basil Leaves, Fresh, Tron & Lightly Packed
- Sea Salt & Black Pepper to Taste
- 2 Hoagie Rolls, 6 Inches Each

### DIRECTIONS

1. Start by heating your oven broiler to high. Your rack should be four inches under the heating element.
2. Place the sliced bread on a rimmed baking sheet. Broil for a minute. Your bread should be toasted lightly. Brush each one down with oil and rub your garlic over each half.
3. Place the bread back on your baking sheet. Distribute the tomato slices on each one, and then sprinkle with oregano and cheese.
4. Bake for one to two minutes, but check it after a minute. Your cheese should be melted.
5. Top with basil and pepper before serving.

CALORIES: 297 Kcal   FAT: 11 g   PROTEIN: 12 g   CARBOHYDRATES: 38 g

*Preparation: 7 min*  *Cooking: 25 min*  *Servings: 6*

## 65. HUMMUS FILLED ROASTED VEGGIES

**INGREDIENTS**

- 6 pitted kalamata olives quartered
- ½ cup (2ounce) of feta cheese
- 1 cup of hummus
- 2 tablespoons of olive oil
- 1 medium red bell pepper
- 1 small zucchini (6 inch)

**DIRECTIONS**

1. Heat a closed medium sized contact grill at 375 degrees Fahrenheit for about 5 minutes.
2. Cut the summer squash and zucchini into half lengthwise. Use a spoon to scoop out the seeds from the two vegetables and discard the seeds. Cut the red bell pepper around the stem and remove the stem and the seeds; cut them into quarters and set aside.
3. Use olive oil to brush the bell pepper, squash and zucchini pieces. Once done, place them on the grill. Do not close the grill. Cook them for 4-6 minutes and turn only once. The vegetables should be tender by the end of the sixth minute. Remove from the grill and let them cool for 2 minutes. Cut the vegetables into 1-inch pieces.
4. Use a spoon to scoop 2 tablespoons of humus onto each piece of vegetable. Light drizzle the vegetables with cheese and top it with one piece of olive. Serve cold or warm.

CALORIES: 342 Kcal   FAT: 15 g   PROTEIN: 10 g   CARBOHYDRATES: 35 g

---

*Preparation: 10 min*  *Cooking: 0 min*  *Servings: 4*

## 66. GOAT CHEESE STUFFED TOMATOES

**INGREDIENTS**

- 6-8 arugula leaves
- 3 ounces crumbled feta cheese
- 2 medium ripe tomatoes
- Extra-virgin olive oil to drizzle
- Balsamic vinegar to drizzle
- 1 red onion, very thinly sliced for garnish
- Fresh chopped parsley for garnish
- Salt and freshly ground pepper to taste

**DIRECTIONS**

1. Arrange the arugula leaves in the center of a plate.
2. Remove the tops and the core of the tomatoes. Ideally, you should remove the top first and scoop out the core.
3. Fill the tomatoes with feta cheese. Add salt and pepper, to taste
4. Drizzle with olive oil and balsamic vinegar.
5. Garnish with chopped parsley and red onion.
6. Serve at room temperature.

CALORIES: 142 Kcal   FAT: 13.1 g   PROTEIN: 7 g   CARBOHYDRATES: 7 g

# 15 Salads

Preparation: 10 min  Cooking: 0 min  Servings: 4

# 67. TOMATO, CUCUMBER AND FETA SALAD

## INGREDIENTS

- 3 tablespoons extra-virgin olive oil
- ½ teaspoon Dijon mustard
- 4 medium Persian cucumbers, thinly sliced crosswise
- 1 teaspoon chopped fresh oregano, plus extra for garnish
- 1 ½ tablespoons red-wine vinegar
- 1 cup (8 ounces) tomatoes, cut into wedges
- ¼ teaspoon salt
- 1 ½ ounces feta cheese, crumbled
- 25 g black olive, sliced
- 1 medium onion, sliced

## DIRECTIONS

1. Take out a medium bowl and combine oregano, vinegar, mustard, and salt.
2. Drizzle the oil on top. Add tomatoes, cucumbers, feta, olives and onion.
3. Mix them well and serve with oregano leaves toppings, if you prefer.
4. Refrigerate if you are planning to serve later.

CALORIES: 153 Kcal  FAT: 13.1 g  PROTEIN: 3 g  CARBOHYDRATES: 6.1 g

*Preparation: 15 min*  *Cooking: 0 min*  *Servings: 4*

# 68. COURGETTE, FENNEL, AND ORANGE SALAD

## INGREDIENTS

- 1 orange
- 2 small courgettes (green or yellow)
- 2 small fennel bulbs
- 2 teaspoon sherry vinegar
- 4 tablespoon olive oil
- 1 Baby Gem lettuce, washed and leaves separated
- Juice ½ lemon

## DIRECTIONS

1. Cut the peel off the orange. Remove any pith. Slice the orange and halve each slice. Ideally, you should be cutting the orange on a plate or the chopping board since we are going to collect the juice left over from the cutting.
2. Take the fennel and remove any outer leaves that are tough. Cut the cores into halves and then slice them as thinly as you can.
3. Remove the ends of the courgettes and shave thin and long slices using a vegetable peeler. You can toss away the watery and seedy centers.
4. Take a small bowl and mix together olive oil, vinegar, and the orange juice left over on the plate or chopping board.
5. Take out another bowl and mix the courgette, fennel, orange slices, and lettuce leaves.
6. Serve the fennel mixture and top it with the orange juice dressing.

CALORIES: 130 Kcal   FAT: 2 g   PROTEIN: 3 g   CARBOHYDRATES: 10 g

---

*Preparation: 10 min*  *Cooking: 6 min*  *Servings: 4*

# 69. POTATO SALAD

## INGREDIENTS

- 1 small onion, thinly sliced
- 1 tablespoon olive oil
- 1 garlic clove, crushed
- 100 g roasted red pepper sliced
- 25 g black olive, sliced
- 1 teaspoon fresh oregano
- 200 g canned cherry tomatoes
- 300 g new potato, halved if large
- Handful basil leaves, torn

## DIRECTIONS

1. Take out a saucepan and place it over medium heat. Pour the olive oil into it and allow it to heat. Add the onions and cook for about 10 minutes, or until the onions have become soft.
2. Add oregano and garlic. Cook for another 1 minute.
3. Add the peppers and tomato. Let the mixture simmer for about 10 minutes.
4. Use a pan and place it over medium-high heat. Bring it to a boil and then add the potatoes into the water. Cook the potatoes for about 15 minutes, or until they turn tender. Drain the potatoes.
5. Take out a small bowl and add the pepper and tomato sauce into it. Toss in the potatoes and mix well.
6. Serve your salad with a sprinkle of basil and olives.

CALORIES: 250 Kcal   FAT: 4 g   PROTEIN: 3 g   CARBOHYDRATES: 80 g

*Preparation: 10 min* — *Cooking: 0 min* — *Servings: 4*

# 70. MEDITERRANEAN GREENS

## INGREDIENTS

- 6 cups assorted fresh mixed greens (such as radicchio, arugula, watercress, baby spinach, and romaine)
- 1 small red onion, thinly sliced
- 20 cherry tomatoes, halved
- ¼ cup dried cranberries
- ¼ cup chopped walnuts
- Crumbled feta cheese
- Freshly ground pepper to taste
- 2 tablespoons balsamic vinegar
- 2 cloves fresh garlic, finely minced
- 4 tablespoons extra-virgin olive oil
- 1 tablespoon water
- ½ teaspoon crushed dried oregano

## DIRECTIONS

1. Take out a large salad bowl, combine walnuts, greens, tomatoes, onion, and cranberries. Gently toss.
2. For the dressing, combine water, vinegar, oregano, olive oil, and garlic. Mix the ingredients well. Pour over the salad and lightly toss.
3. Add feta cheese as garnish, if preferred.
4. Add pepper to taste.

CALORIES: 140 Kcal — FAT: 12 g — PROTEIN: 2 g — CARBOHYDRATES: 6 g

Preparation: 10 min  Cooking: 0 min  Servings: 4

## 71. TUNA SALAD

### INGREDIENTS

- 10 cherry tomatoes, quartered
- 4 scallions, trimmed and sliced
- 2 tablespoons extra-virgin olive oil
- 2 6-ounce cans chunk light tuna, drained
- 2 tablespoons lemon juice
- One 15-ounce can cannellini white beans, rinsed
- ¼ teaspoon salt, to taste
- Freshly ground pepper, to taste

### DIRECTIONS

1. Take out a medium bowl and combine tomatoes, tuna, beans, lemon juice, scallions, oil, salt and pepper.
2. Mix them well and serve.
3. Refrigerate if you are planning to serve later.

CALORIES: 199 Kcal   FAT: 8.8 g   PROTEIN: 16.5 g   CARBOHYDRATES: 19.8 g

---

Preparation: 10 min  Cooking: 10 min  Servings: 4

## 72. CLASSIC TABBOULEH

### INGREDIENTS

- ¾ cup bulgur
- 2 cups freshly chopped parsley
- 1½ cups water
- ½ cup fresh lemon juice
- ½ cup extra-virgin olive oil
- ½ red bell pepper, diced
- 3 ripe plum tomatoes, diced
- 1 large cucumber, peeled, seeded, and diced
- ¾ cup chopped scallions, white and green parts
- ½ green bell pepper, diced
- ½ cup finely chopped fresh mint
- Handful of greens for serving
- Seasoned pita wedges
- Sea salt and pepper to taste

### DIRECTIONS

1. Preheat the oven to around 375° F.
2. Take a medium-sized bowl and add the asparagus with 2 tablespoons of salt and olive oil.
3. Take out a baking dish and add the asparagus. Place the tray in the oven and roast for about 10 minutes, or until the asparagus becomes tender.
4. Take out the asparagus and set aside.
5. Use another medium-sized bowl and add garlic, lime juice, orange juice, and remaining 2 tablespoons of olive oil. Whisk all the ingredients together. Add salt and pepper to taste.
6. Take the lettuce and split it into 6 plates. Take out the asparagus and place it on top of the lettuce.
7. Pour the dressing over the asparagus and lettuce salad. Top the salad with basil and pine nuts. Add a small amount of Romano cheese for garnish, if you prefer.
8. Add the nuts to the salad as a topping.

CALORIES: 177 Kcal   FAT: 11 g   PROTEIN: 12 g   CARBOHYDRATES: 28 g

Preparation: 15 min    Cooking: 0 min    Servings: 6

## 73. CLASSIC GREEK SALAD

### INGREDIENTS

- 6 large firm tomatoes, quartered
- 20 Greek black olives
- ½ pound Greek feta cheese, cut into small cubes
- ½ head of escarole, shredded
- 3 tablespoons red wine vinegar
- ¼ cup extra-virgin olive oil
- 1 tablespoon dried oregano
- ½ English cucumber, peeled, seeded, and thinly sliced
- 2 cloves fresh garlic, finely minced
- ½ red onion, sliced
- 1 medium red bell pepper, seeded and sliced
- ¼ cup freshly chopped Italian parsley
- Salt and freshly ground pepper to taste

### DIRECTIONS

1. Take out a large bowl and add vinegar, oregano, olive oil, and garlic. Add salt and pepper to taste. Set aside the bowl.
2. In another large bowl, add onion, tomatoes, escarole, cucumber, bell pepper, and cheese and mix them well.
3. Take the vinegar mixture and pour it over the salad in the second bowl.
4. Top the salad with olives and parsley.

CALORIES: 268 Kcal    FAT: 17 g    PROTEIN: 23 g    CARBOHYDRATES: 20 g

*Preparation: 10 min*  *Cooking: 0 min*  *Servings: 4*

## 74. NORTH AFRICAN ZUCCHINI SALAD

### INGREDIENTS

- 1 pound firm green zucchini, thinly sliced
- ½ teaspoon ground cumin
- 2 cloves fresh garlic, finely minced
- Juice from 1 large lemon
- 1 tablespoon extra-virgin olive oil
- 1½ tablespoons plain low-fat yogurt
- Crumbled feta cheese
- Finely chopped parsley for garnish
- Salt and freshly ground pepper to taste

### DIRECTIONS

1. Add the zucchini into a large saucepan and steam it for about 2-5 minutes, or until it becomes tender and crispy. Place the zucchini under cold water and drain well.
2. Take out a large bowl and mix cumin, olive oil, lemon juice, garlic, and yogurt. Add salt and pepper to taste.
3. Add the zucchini into the mixture in the bowl and toss gently.
4. Serve with feta cheese and parsley as garnish.

CALORIES: 000 Kcal    FAT: 000 g    PROTEIN: 000 g    CARBOHYDRATES: 000 g

---

*Preparation: 15 min*  *Cooking: 0 min*  *Servings: 6*

## 75. TUNISIAN STYLE CARROT SALAD

### INGREDIENTS

- 10 medium carrots, peeled and sliced
- 1 cup crumbled feta cheese, divided
- 2 teaspoons caraway seed
- ¼ cup extra-virgin olive oil
- 6 tablespoons apple cider vinegar
- 5 teaspoons freshly minced garlic
- 1 tablespoon Harissa paste (choose the level of heat based on your preference)
- 20 pitted Kalamata olives, reserving some for garnish
- Salt to taste

### DIRECTIONS

1. Take out a medium saucepan and place it on medium heat. Fill it with water and add the carrots. Cook carrots until tender. Drain and cool the carrots under cold water. Drain again to remove any excess water.
2. Place the carrots in a large bowl, then take out a mortar and combine salt, garlic, and caraway seeds. Grind them until they form a paste. Another option would be to toss the ingredients into a blender and pulse them.
3. Add vinegar and Harissa into the bowl with the carrots and mix them well.
4. Use a large spoon and mash the carrots. Add the garlic mixture into the carrot and mix again until they have all blended well. Add the olive oil and mix again.
5. Add about ½ the feta cheese and all the olives and mix well.
6. Place the salad in a bowl and top with the remaining feta cheese.

CALORIES: 138 Kcal    FAT: 6 g    PROTEIN: 7 g    CARBOHYDRATES: 13 g

*Preparation: 5 min* — Cooking: 0 min — Servings: 4

# 76. CASEAR SALAD

## INGREDIENTS

- 1-2 bunches romaine lettuce, cleaned and torn in pieces
- 2 teaspoons lemon juice
- 2½ teaspoons balsamic vinegar
- ½ cup grated parmesan cheese
- ½ cup nonfat plain yogurt
- ½ teaspoon anchovy paste
- 2 cloves freshly minced garlic
- 8 thin flat bread slices
- *2 crispy bacon slices, chopped

## DIRECTIONS

1. Take out a large bowl and place romaine lettuce in it.
2. Take out your blended and add mix lemon juice, yogurt, garlic, anchovy paste, vinegar and ¼ cup parmesan cheese. Mix all the ingredients well until they are smooth.
3. Pour the yogurt mixture over the lettuce and toss lightly.
4. Top the salad with the remaining parmesan cheese and serve with 2 oiled flat bread slices.
5. *If you like a twist, try to garnish the salad with some chopped crispy bacon. Everything will change!

CALORIES: 142 Kcal — FAT: 5 g — PROTEIN: 4 g — CARBOHYDRATES: 4 g

Preparation: 10 min  Cooking: 0 min  Servings: 6

## 77. SPANISH SALAD

### INGREDIENTS

- 2 bunches romaine lettuce, cleaned and trimmed
- 1 large sweet onion, thinly sliced
- 3 medium ripe tomatoes, chopped
- 3 tablespoons balsamic vinegar
- ¼ cup extra-virgin olive oil
- 1 red bell pepper, seeded and thinly sliced
- 1 green bell pepper, seeded and thinly sliced
- ¼ cup chopped and pitted black olives
- ¼ cup chopped and pitted marinated green olives
- Salt and pepper to taste

### DIRECTIONS

1. Take out 6 plates and place romaine lettuce on them to form a base.
2. Add peppers, tomatoes, onion, and olives on top of each of the lettuce bases.
3. In a small bowl, combine olive oil and vinegar together. Add the dressing over the salad.
4. Add salt and pepper to taste, if preferred.

CALORIES: 107 Kcal  FAT: 9 g  PROTEIN: 2 g  CARBOHYDRATES: 6 g

---

Preparation: 15min/ Rest: 2 hours  Cooking: 0 min  Servings: 4

## 78. PARSLEY COUSCOUS SALAD

### INGREDIENTS

- ¼ cup couscous
- 2 teaspoons extra-virgin olive oil
- ¼ cup water
- 2 teaspoons lemon zest
- 1 medium ripe tomato, peeled, seeded, and diced
- 2 tablespoons pine nuts
- 2 tablespoons fresh lemon juice
- ¼ cup finely chopped fresh flat parsley leaves
- 2 tablespoons finely chopped fresh mint leaves
- 2 heads Belgian endive, leaves for scooping
- Whole wheat pita rounds
- Salt and pepper to taste

### DIRECTIONS

1. Take out a medium bowl and then combine lemon juice and water. All the mixture to stand for about 1 hour.
2. After the hour, add mint, parsley, lemon zest, olive oil, and pine nuts. Mix the ingredients well.
3. Add in the couscous to the mixture. Allow it to stand for about 1 hour. After 1 hour, add salt and pepper to taste.
4. Place couscous mixture in the center of a plate and top it with tomato. You can surround the couscous salad with toasted pita wedges and endive leaves, which makes for a wonderful presentation.
5. Refrigerator overnight so that you can have it the next day.

CALORIES: 120 Kcal  FAT: 2 g  PROTEIN: 5 g  CARBOHYDRATES: 18 g

*Preparation:* 10 min    *Cooking:* 0 min    *Servings:* 2

## 79. AVOCADO SALAD

### INGREDIENTS

- 1 small onion, finely chopped
- 1 cup valerian or lettuce
- 1 large ripe avocado, pitted and peeled
- 2 tablespoons chopped fresh parsley
- 2 teaspoons fresh lime juice
- ½ small hot pepper, finely chopped (optional)
- 1 cup halved cherry tomatoes
- Salt and freshly ground pepper to taste
- ½ cup ricotta cheese
- 4 slices whole grain bread

### DIRECTIONS

1. Start with the avocado and cut it into bite-sized pieces.
2. Add parsley, lime juice, tomatoes, onion, and hot pepper if you like it.
3. Mix all the ingredients well. Add salt and pepper to taste.
4. Add the avocado and the valerian into the mixture and mix well.
5. Serve with some ricotta cheese and whole grain bread.

CALORIES: 130 Kcal    FAT: 10 g    PROTEIN: 2 g    CARBOHYDRATES: 10 g

*Preparation: 15 min*     *Cooking: 0 min*     *Servings: 4*

# 80. CRESS AND TANGERINE SALAD

## INGREDIENTS

- 4 large sweet tangerines
- ¼ cup extra-virgin olive oil
- 2 large bunches watercress, washed and stems removed
- Juice from 1 fresh lemon
- 10 cherry tomatoes, halved
- 16 pitted Kalamata olives
- Sea salt and freshly ground pepper to taste

## DIRECTIONS

1. Take the tangerines and peel them into a medium-sized bowl. Make sure that you remove any pits and squeeze the sections. You should have around ¼ cup of tangerine juice. Set sections aside.
2. Take a large bowl and add lemon juice, tangerine juice, and olive oil. Mix them together and add salt and pepper for flavor, if you prefer.
3. Use paper towels to pat the cress dry. Add watercress, tomatoes, and olives to the bowl containing the tangerine sections (not to be confused with the bowl containing tangerine juice). Toss them lightly.
4. Pour the tangerine juice mixture on top. Mix well and serve.

CALORIES: 195 Kcal     FAT: 16 g     PROTEIN: 3 g     CARBOHYDRATES: 14 g

---

*Preparation: 10 min*     *Cooking: 0 min*     *Servings: 4*

# 81. PROSCIUTTO AND FIGS SALAD

## INGREDIENTS

- One 10-12-ounce package fresh baby spinach
- 1 small hot red chili pepper, finely diced
- 1 carton figs, stems removed and quartered
- ½ cup walnuts, coarsely chopped
- 1 tablespoon fresh orange juice
- 1 tablespoon honey
- 4 slices prosciutto, cut into strips
- Shaved parmesan cheese for garnish

## DIRECTIONS

1. Take your spinach and divide them into 4 equal portions. Each portion should be on a separate plate and will act as a base. Add quartered prosciutto, figs, and walnuts on each spinach as toppings.
2. For the dressing, take a small bowl and add honey, orange juice, and diced pepper. Add the mixture over the salad.
3. Finally, toss the salad lightly and use parmesan cheese for the garnish.

CALORIES: 190 Kcal     FAT: 9 g     PROTEIN: 26 g     CARBOHYDRATES: 17 g

Preparation: 10 min  Cooking: 0 min  Servings: 4

## 82. GARDEN VEGETABLES AND CHICKPEAS SALAD

### INGREDIENTS

- 2 tablespoons freshly squeezed lemon juice
- ⅛ Teaspoon freshly ground pepper
- 1 cup cubed part-skim mozzarella cheese
- 1 tablespoon fresh basil leaf, snipped
- 1 (15-ounce) can chickpeas, rinsed and well drained
- 2 cups coarsely chopped fresh broccoli
- 2 cloves fresh garlic, finely minced
- ½ cup sliced fresh carrots
- 1 7½-ounce can diced tomatoes, undrained

### DIRECTIONS

1. Use a large bowl and add garlic, basil, lemon juice, and ground pepper. Mix them well.
2. Add the chickpeas, carrots, tomatoes with juice, broccoli, and mozzarella cheese. Toos all the ingredients well.
3. You can serve immediately, or you can keep it refrigerated overnight.

CALORIES: 195 Kcal  FAT: 7 g  PROTEIN: 16 g  CARBOHYDRATES: 24 g

---

Preparation: 5 min  Cooking: 0 min  Servings: 4

## 83. PEPPERED WATERCRESS SALAD

### INGREDIENTS

- 2 teaspoons champagne vinegar
- 2 bunches (about 8 cups) watercress, rinsed and rough stems removed
- 2 tablespoons extra-virgin olive oil
- Salt and freshly ground pepper to taste

### DIRECTIONS

1. Drain the watercress properly.
2. Take out a small bowl and then add salt, pepper, vinegar, and olive oil. Mix them well together.
3. Transfer the watercress to a bowl. Add the vinegar mixture into it and toss well.
4. Serve immediately.

CALORIES: 67 Kcal  FAT: 7 g  PROTEIN: 4 g  CARBOHYDRATES: 1 g

# 16 Snacks

*Preparation: 10 min*  *Cooking: 25 min*  *Servings: 4*

## 84. CRUNCHY ROASTED CHICKPEAS

### INGREDIENTS

- 15 oz can chickpeas, drained, rinsed and pat dry
- ¼ teaspoon paprika
- 1 tablespoon olive oil
- ¼ teaspoon pepper
- Pinch of salt

### DIRECTIONS

1. Preheat the oven to 450 F.
2. Spray a baking tray with cooking spray and set aside.
3. In a large bowl, toss chickpeas with olive oil and spread chickpeas onto the prepared baking tray.
4. Roast chickpeas in preheated oven for 25 minutes. Shake after every 10 minutes.
5. Once chickpeas are done then immediately toss with paprika, pepper, and salt.
6. Serve and enjoy.

CALORIES: 157 Kcal    FAT: 4.7 g    PROTEIN: 5.3 g    CARBOHYDRATES: 24.2 g

*Preparation: 10 min*     *Cooking: 10 min*     *Servings: 8*

# 85. HEALTHY COCONUT BLUEBERRY BALLS

## INGREDIENTS

- ¼ cup flaked coconut
- ¼ cup blueberries
- ½ teaspoon vanilla
- ¼ cup honey
- ½ cup creamy almond butter
- ¼ teaspoon cinnamon
- 1 ½ tablespoon chia seeds
- ¼ cup flaxseed meal
- 1 cup rolled oats, gluten-free

## DIRECTIONS

1. In a large bowl, add oats, cinnamon, chia seeds, and flaxseed meal and mix well.
2. Add almond butter in microwave-safe bowl and microwave for 30 seconds. Stir until smooth.
3. Add vanilla and honey in melted almond butter and stir well.
4. Pour almond butter mixture over oat mixture and stir to combine.
5. Add coconut and blueberries and stir well.
6. Make small balls from oat mixture and place onto the baking tray and place in the refrigerator for 1 hour.
7. Serve and enjoy.

**CALORIES:** 129 Kcal     **FAT:** 7.4 g     **PROTEIN:** 4 g     **CARBOHYDRATES:** 14.1 g

---

*Preparation: 10 min*     *Cooking: 15 min*     *Servings: 6*

# 86. TASTY ZUCCHINI CHIPS

## INGREDIENTS

- 2 medium zucchini, sliced 4mm thick
- ½ teaspoon paprika
- ¼ teaspoon garlic powder
- ¾ cup parmesan cheese, grated
- 4 tablespoon olive oil
- ¼ teaspoon pepper
- Pinch of salt

## DIRECTIONS

1. Preheat the oven to 375 F.
2. Spray a baking tray with cooking spray and set aside.
3. In a bowl, combine the oil, garlic powder, paprika, pepper, and salt.
4. Add sliced zucchini and toss to coat.
5. Arrange zucchini slices onto the prepared baking tray and sprinkle grated cheese on top.
6. Bake in preheated oven for 15 minutes or until lightly golden brown.
7. Serve and enjoy.

**CALORIES:** 110 Kcal     **FAT:** 1.8 g     **PROTEIN:** 4.4 g     **CARBOHYDRATES:** 2.2 g

Preparation: 10 min      Cooking: 20 min      Servings: 8

## 87. ROASTED ALMONDS

### INGREDIENTS

- 2 ½ cups almonds
- ¼ teaspoon cayenne
- ¼ teaspoon ground coriander
- ¼ teaspoon cumin
- ¼ teaspoon chili powder
- 1 tablespoon fresh rosemary, chopped
- 1 tablespoon olive oil
- 2 ½ tablespoon maple syrup
- Pinch of salt

### DIRECTIONS

1. Preheat the oven to 325 F.
2. Spray a baking tray with cooking spray and set aside.
3. In a mixing bowl, whisk together oil, cayenne, coriander, cumin, chili powder, rosemary, maple syrup, and salt.
4. Add almond and stir to coat.
5. Spread almonds onto the prepared baking tray.
6. Roast almonds in preheated oven for 20 minutes. Stir halfway through.
7. Serve and enjoy.

CALORIES: 137 Kcal      FAT: 11.2 g      PROTEIN: 4.2 g      CARBOHYDRATES: 7.3 g

*Preparation: 10 min*  *Cooking: 15 min*  *Servings: 4*

## 88. ROASTED GREEN BEANS

**INGREDIENTS**

- 1 lb green beans
- 4 tablespoon parmesan cheese
- 2 tablespoon olive oil
- ¼ teaspoon garlic powder
- Pinch of salt

**DIRECTIONS**

1. Preheat the oven to 400 F.
2. Add green beans in a large bowl.
3. Add remaining ingredients on top of green beans and toss to coat.
4. Spread green beans onto the baking tray and roast in preheated oven for 15 minutes. Stir halfway through.
5. Serve and enjoy.

CALORIES: 101 Kcal   FAT: 0.5 g   PROTEIN: 2.6 g   CARBOHYDRATES: 8.3 g

---

*Preparation: 10 min*  *Cooking: 0 min*  *Servings: 8*

## 89. SAVORY PISTACHIO BALLS

**INGREDIENTS**

- ½ cup pistachios, unsalted
- 1 cup dates, pitted
- ½ teaspoon ground fennel seeds
- ½ cup raisins
- Pinch of pepper

**DIRECTIONS**

1. Add all ingredients into the food processor and process until well combined.
2. Make small balls and place onto the baking tray.
3. Serve and enjoy.

CALORIES: 55 Kcal   FAT: 0.9 g   PROTEIN: 0.8 g   CARBOHYDRATES: 12.5 g

Preparation: 5 min     Cooking: 0 min / Freezing: 4 hours     Servings: 6

## 90. BANANA CHERRY POPSICLE

### INGREDIENTS

- ½ cup Greek yogurt
- 1 banana, peeled and sliced
- 1 ¼ cup fresh cherries
- ¼ cup of water

### DIRECTIONS

1. Add all ingredients into the blender and blend until smooth.
2. Pour blended mixture into the popsicle molds and place in the refrigerator for 4 hours or until set.
3. Serve and enjoy.

CALORIES: 31 Kcal     FAT: 0 g     PROTEIN: 1.2 g     CARBOHYDRATES: 6.2 g

*Preparation: 10 min*     *Cooking: 0 min*     *Servings: 8*

# 91. CHOCOLATE MATCHA BALLS

## INGREDIENTS

- 2 tablespoon unsweetened cocoa powder
- 3 tablespoon oats, gluten-free
- ½ cup pine nuts
- ½ cup almonds
- 1 cup dates, pitted
- 2 tablespoon matcha powder

## DIRECTIONS

1. Add oats, pine nuts, almonds, and dates into a food processor and process until well combined.
2. Place matcha powder in a small dish.
3. Make small balls from mixture and coat with matcha powder.
4. Enjoy or store in refrigerator until ready to eat.

CALORIES: 88 Kcal     FAT: 4.9 g     PROTEIN: 1.9 g     CARBOHYDRATES: 11.3 g

---

*Preparation: 5 min*     *Cooking: 0 min*     *Servings: 1*

# 92. CHIA ALMOND BUTTER PUDDING

## INGREDIENTS

- ¼ cup chia seeds
- 1 cup unsweetened almond milk
- 1 ½ tablespoon maple syrup
- 2 ½ tablespoon almond butter

## DIRECTIONS

1. Add almond milk, maple syrup, and almond butter in a bowl and stir well.
2. Add chia seeds and stir to mix.
3. Pour pudding mixture into the Mason jar and place in the refrigerator for overnight.
4. Serve and enjoy.

CALORIES: 354 Kcal     FAT: 21.3 g     PROTEIN: 11.2 g     CARBOHYDRATES: 31.2 g

Preparation: 10 min  Cooking: 0 min / Freezing: 2 hours  Servings: 4

## 93. DARK CHOCOLATE MOUSSE

### INGREDIENTS

- 3.5 oz unsweetened dark chocolate, grated
- ½ teaspoon vanilla
- 1 tablespoon honey
- 2 cups Greek yogurt
- ¾ cup unsweetened almond milk
- 1 tablespoon pomegranate seeds

### DIRECTIONS

1. Add chocolate and almond milk in a saucepan and heat over medium heat until just chocolate melted. Do not boil.
2. Once the chocolate and almond milk combined then add vanilla and honey and stir well.
3. Add yogurt in a large mixing bowl.
4. Pour chocolate mixture on top of yogurt and mix until well combined.
5. Pour chocolate yogurt mixture into the serving bowls and place in refrigerator for 2 hours.
6. Top with pomegranate seeds and serve chilled.

CALORIES: 278 Kcal    FAT: 15.4 g    PROTEIN: 10.5 g    CARBOHYDRATES: 20 g

*Preparation: 5 min*  *Cooking: 0 min / Freezing: 4 hours*  *Servings: 6*

# 94. REFRESHING STRAWBERRY POPSICLES

## INGREDIENTS

- ½ cup almond milk
- 2 ½ cup fresh strawberries

## DIRECTIONS

1. Add strawberries and almond milk into the blender and blend until smooth.
2. Pour strawberry mixture into popsicles molds and place in the refrigerator for 4 hours or until set.
3. Serve and enjoy.

CALORIES: 49 Kcal    FAT: 3.7 g    PROTEIN: 0.6 g    CARBOHYDRATES: 4.3 g

---

*Preparation: 10 min*  *Cooking: 25 min*  *Servings: 4*

# 95. WARM & SOFT BAKED PEARS

## INGREDIENTS

- 4 pears, cut in half and core
- ½ teaspoon vanilla
- ¼ teaspoon cinnamon
- ½ cup maple syrup

## DIRECTIONS

1. Preheat the oven to 375 F.
2. Spray a baking tray with cooking spray.
3. Arrange pears, cut side up on a prepared baking tray and sprinkle with cinnamon.
4. In a small bowl, whisk vanilla and maple syrup and drizzle over pears.
5. Bake pears in preheated oven for 25 minutes.
6. Serve and enjoy.

CALORIES: 226 Kcal    FAT: 0.4 g    PROTEIN: 0.8 g    CARBOHYDRATES: 58.4 g

Preparation: 10 min  Cooking: 30 min  Servings: 4

# 96. CHICKEN WINGS PLATTER

## INGREDIENTS

- 2 pounds chicken wings
- ½ cup tomato sauce
- A pinch of salt and black pepper
- 1 teaspoon smoked paprika
- 1 tablespoon cilantro, chopped
- 1 tablespoon chives, chopped

## DIRECTIONS

1. In your instant pot, combine the chicken wings with the sauce and the rest of the ingredients, stir, put the lid on and cook on High for 20 minutes.
2. Release the pressure naturally for 10 minutes.
3. Arrange the chicken wings on a platter and serve as an appetizer.

CALORIES: 203 Kcal   FAT: 13 g   FAT: 15 g   CARBOHYDRATES: 5 g

*Preparation: 10 min*  *Cooking: 0 min / Freezing: 1 hour*  *Servings: 8*

# 97. HEALTHY & QUICK ENERGY BITES

## INGREDIENTS

- 2 cups cashew nuts
- ¼ teaspoon cinnamon
- 1 teaspoon lemon zest
- 4 tablespoon dates, chopped
- 1/3 cup unsweetened shredded coconut
- ¾ cup dried apricots

## DIRECTIONS

1. Line baking tray with parchment paper and set aside.
2. Add all ingredients in a food processor and process until the mixture is crumbly and well combined.
3. Make small balls from mixture and place on a prepared baking tray.
4. Place in refrigerator for 1 hour.
5. Serve and enjoy.

CALORIES: 100 Kcal  FAT: 7.5 g  PROTEIN: 2.4 g  CARBOHYDRATES: 7.2 g

---

*Preparation: 10 min*  *Cooking: 0 min*  *Servings: 4*

# 98. CREAMY YOGURT BANANA BOWLS

## INGREDIENTS

- 2 bananas, sliced
- ½ teaspoon ground nutmeg
- 3 tablespoon flaxseed meal
- ¼ cup creamy peanut butter
- 4 cups Greek yogurt

## DIRECTIONS

1. Divide Greek yogurt between 4 serving bowls and top with sliced bananas.
2. Add peanut butter in microwave-safe bowl and microwave for 30 seconds.
3. Drizzle 1 tablespoon of melted peanut butter on each bowl on top of the sliced bananas.
4. Sprinkle cinnamon and flax meal on top and serve.

CALORIES: 351 Kcal  FAT: 13.1 g  PROTEIN: 19.6 g  CARBOHYDRATES: 35.6 g

Preparation: 10 min · Cooking: 6 min · Servings: 4

## 99. CHOCOLATE MOUSSE

### INGREDIENTS

- 4 egg yolks
- ½ teaspoon vanilla
- ½ cup unsweetened almond milk
- 1 cup whipping cream
- ¼ cup cocoa powder
- ¼ cup water
- ½ cup Swerve
- 1/8 teaspoon salt

### DIRECTIONS

1. Add egg yolks to a large bowl and whisk until well beaten.
2. In a saucepan, add swerve, cocoa powder, and water and whisk until well combined.
3. Add almond milk and cream to the saucepan and whisk well. Once saucepan mixtures are heated up then turn off the heat.
4. Add vanilla and salt and stir well.
5. Add a tablespoon of chocolate mixture into the eggs and whisk until well combined.
6. Slowly pour remaining chocolate to the eggs and whisk until well combined, then pour batter into the ramekins.
7. Pour 1 ½ cups of water into the instant pot then place a trivet in the pot, then place ramekins on a trivet.
8. Seal pot with lid and set timer for 6 minutes.
9. Release pressure using quick release method than open the lid.
10. Carefully remove ramekins from the instant pot and let them cool completely, then serve.

CALORIES: 128 Kcal · FAT: 11.9 g · PROTEIN: 3.6 g · CARBOHYDRATES: 4 g

*Preparation: 10 min*  *Cooking: 20 min*  *Servings: 4*

## 100. CARROT SPREAD

### INGREDIENTS

- ¼ cup veggie stock
- A pinch of salt and black pepper
- 1 teaspoon onion powder
- ½ teaspoon garlic powder
- ½ teaspoon oregano, dried
- 1 pound carrots, sliced
- ½ cup coconut cream

### DIRECTIONS

1. In your instant pot, combine all the ingredients except the cream, put the lid on and cook on High for 10 minutes.
2. Release the pressure naturally for 10 minutes, transfer the carrots mix to food processor, add the cream, pulse well, divide into bowls and serve cold.

CALORIES: 124 Kcal    FAT: 1 g    PROTEIN: 8 g    CARBOHYDRATES: 5 g

---

*Preparation: 10 min*  *Cooking: 10 min*  *Servings: 4*

## 101. VEGGIE FRITTERS

### INGREDIENTS

- 2 garlic cloves, minced
- 2 yellow onions, chopped
- 4 scallions, chopped
- 2 carrots, grated
- 2 teaspoons cumin, ground
- ½ teaspoon turmeric powder
- Salt and black pepper to the taste
- ¼ teaspoon coriander, ground
- 2 tablespoons parsley, chopped
- ¼ teaspoon lemon juice
- ½ cup almond flour
- 2 beets, peeled and grated
- 2 eggs, whisked
- ¼ cup tapioca flour
- 3 tablespoons olive oil

### DIRECTIONS

1. In a bowl, combine the garlic with the onions, scallions and the rest of the ingredients except the oil, stir well and shape medium fritters out of this mix.
2. Heat up a pan with the oil over medium-high heat, add the fritters, cook for 5 minutes on each side, arrange on a plate and serve.

CALORIES: 209 Kcal    FAT: 11.2 g    PROTEIN: 4.8 g    CARBOHYDRATES: 4.4 g

*Preparation: 10 min*     *Cooking: 15 min*     *Servings: 6*

## 102. BULGUR LAMB MEATBALLS

### INGREDIENTS

- 1 and ½ cups Greek yogurt
- ½ teaspoon cumin, ground
- 1 cup cucumber, shredded
- ½ teaspoon garlic, minced
- A pinch of salt and black pepper
- 1 cup bulgur
- 2 cups water
- 1 pound lamb, ground
- ¼ cup parsley, chopped
- ¼ cup shallots, chopped
- ½ teaspoon allspice, ground
- ½ teaspoon cinnamon powder
- 1 tablespoon olive oil

### DIRECTIONS

1. In a bowl, combine the bulgur with the water, cover the bowl, leave aside for 10 minutes, drain and transfer to a bowl.
2. Add the meat, the yogurt and the rest of the ingredients except the oil, stir well and shape medium meatballs out of this mix.
3. Heat up a pan with the oil over medium-high heat, add the meatballs, cook them for 7 minutes on each side.
4. Arrange them all on a platter and serve as an appetizer.

CALORIES: 300 Kcal     FAT: 9.6 g     PROTEIN: 6.6 g     CARBOHYDRATES: 22.6 g

*Preparation: 10 min*     *Cooking: 0 min*     *Servings: 4*

## 103. WHITE BEAN DIP

**INGREDIENTS**

- 15 ounces canned white beans, drained and rinsed
- 6 ounces canned artichoke hearts, drained and quartered
- 4 garlic cloves, minced
- 1 tablespoon basil, chopped
- 2 tablespoons olive oil
- Juice of ½ lemon
- Zest of ½ lemon, grated
- Salt and black pepper to the taste

**DIRECTIONS**

1. In your food processor, combine the beans with the artichokes and the rest of the ingredients except the oil and pulse well.
2. Add the oil gradually, pulse the mix again, divide into cups and serve as a party dip.

**CALORIES:** 274 Kcal     **FAT:** 11.7 g     **PROTEIN:** 16.5 g     **CARBOHYDRATES:** 18.5 g

---

*Preparation: 10 min*     *Cooking: 40 min*     *Servings: 4*

## 104. EGGPLANT DIP

**INGREDIENTS**

- 1 eggplant, poked with a fork
- 2 tablespoons tahini paste
- 2 tablespoons lemon juice
- 2 garlic cloves, minced
- 1 tablespoon olive oil
- Salt and black pepper to the taste
- 1 tablespoon parsley, chopped

**DIRECTIONS**

1. Put the eggplant in a roasting pan, bake at 400° F for 40 minutes, cool down, peel and transfer to your food processor.
2. Add the rest of the ingredients except the parsley and pulse well.
3. Divide into small bowls and serve as an appetizer with the parsley sprinkled on top.

**CALORIES:** 121 Kcal     **FAT:** 4.3 g     **PROTEIN:** 4.3 g     **CARBOHYDRATES:** 1.4 g

*Preparation: 5 min* — *Cooking: 10 min* — *Servings: 6*

## 105. ONION SALSA

### INGREDIENTS

- 1 garlic clove, minced
- 4 tablespoons olive oil
- 5 onions, chopped
- 1 tablespoon balsamic vinegar
- ¼ cup basil, chopped
- 1 tablespoon parsley, chopped
- 1 tablespoon chives, chopped
- Salt and black pepper to the taste
- Pita chips for serving

### DIRECTIONS

1. In a bowl, mix the onion with the garlic and the rest of the ingredients except the pita chips, then stir.
2. Cook the mixture for 10 minutes, then let it cool.
3. Divide into small cups and serve with the pita chips.

CALORIES: 160 Kcal — FAT: 13.7 g — PROTEIN: 2.2 g — CARBOHYDRATES: 10.1 g

*Preparation: 10 min*     *Cooking: 0 min*     *Servings: 8*

## 106. CUCUMBER BITES

### INGREDIENTS

- 1 English cucumber, sliced into 32 rounds
- 10 ounces hummus
- 16 cherry tomatoes, halved
- 1 tablespoon parsley, chopped
- 1 ounce feta cheese, crumbled

### DIRECTIONS

1. Spread the hummus on each cucumber round.
2. Divide the tomatoes in half, sprinkle the cheese and parsley all over.
3. Serve as an appetizer.

CALORIES: 162 Kcal     FAT: 3.4 g     PROTEIN: 2.4 g     CARBOHYDRATES: 6.4 g

---

*Preparation: 10 min*     *Cooking: 0 min*     *Servings: 2*

## 107. STUFFED AVOCADO

### INGREDIENTS

- 1 avocado, halved and pitted
- 10 ounces canned tuna, drained
- 2 tablespoons sun-dried tomatoes, chopped
- 1 and ½ tablespoon basil pesto
- 2 tablespoons black olives, pitted and chopped
- Salt and black pepper to the taste
- 2 teaspoons pine nuts, toasted and chopped
- 1 tablespoon basil, chopped

### DIRECTIONS

1. In a bowl, combine the tuna with the sun-dried tomatoes and the rest of the ingredients except the avocado and stir.
2. Stuff the avocado halves with the tuna mix and serve as an appetizer.

CALORIES: 233 Kcal     FAT: 9 g     PROTEIN: 5.6 g     CARBOHYDRATES: 11.4 g

# 108. CREAMY SPINACH AND SHALLOTS DIP

## INGREDIENTS

- 1 pound spinach, roughly chopped
- 2 shallots, chopped
- 2 tablespoons mint, chopped
- ¾ cup cream cheese, soft
- Salt and black pepper to the taste
- 1 tomato, chopped
- 1 tablespoon lime juice
- 1 tablespoon parsley, chopped

## DIRECTIONS

1. In a blender, combine the spinach with the shallots and the rest of the ingredients, and pulse well.
2. Divide into small bowls and serve as a party dip.

*Preparation: 10 min*  *Cooking: 0 min*  *Servings: 4*

CALORIES: 204 Kcal   FAT: 11.5 g   PROTEIN: 5.9 g   CARBOHYDRATES: 4.2 g

*Preparation: 10 min*  *Cooking: 15 min*  *Servings: 8*

## 109. HUMMUS WITH GROUND LAMB

**INGREDIENTS**

- 10 ounces hummus
- 12 ounces lamb meat, ground
- ½ cup pomegranate seeds
- ¼ cup parsley, chopped
- 1 tablespoon olive oil
- Pita chips for serving

**DIRECTIONS**

1. Heat up a pan with the oil over medium-high heat, add the meat, and brown for 15 minutes stirring often.
2. Spread the hummus on a platter, spread the ground lamb all over, also spread the pomegranate seeds and the parsley.
3. Serve with pita chips as a snack.

CALORIES: 133 Kcal  FAT: 9.7 g  PROTEIN: 5 g  CARBOHYDRATES: 6.4 g

---

*Preparation: 5 min*  *Cooking: 0 min*  *Servings: 4*

## 110. WRAPPED PLUMS

**INGREDIENTS**

- 2 ounces prosciutto, cut into 16 pieces
- 4 plums, quartered
- 1 tablespoon chives, chopped
- A pinch of red pepper flakes, crushed

**DIRECTIONS**

1. Wrap each plum quarter in a prosciutto slice.
2. Arrange them all on a platter, sprinkle the chives and pepper flakes all over and serve.

CALORIES: 30 Kcal  FAT: 1 g  PROTEIN: 2 g  CARBOHYDRATES: 4 g

Preparation: 10 min  Cooking: 30 min  Servings: 8

## 111. FETA ARTICHOKE DIP

### INGREDIENTS

- 8 ounces artichoke hearts, drained and quartered
- ¾ cup basil, chopped
- ¾ cup green olives, pitted and chopped
- 1 cup parmesan cheese, grated
- 5 ounces feta cheese, crumbled
- 4 carrots, sliced

### DIRECTIONS

1. In your food processor, mix the artichokes with the basil and the rest of the ingredients, pulse well, and transfer to a baking dish.
2. Introduce in the oven, bake at 375° F for 30 minutes.
3. Serve as a dip for the sliced carrots.

CALORIES: 186 Kcal  FAT: 12.4 g  PROTEIN: 1.5 g  CARBOHYDRATES: 2.6 g

*Preparation: 5 min*     *Cooking: 0 min*     *Servings: 8*

# 112. CUCUMBER SANDWICH BITES

## INGREDIENTS

- 1 cucumber, sliced
- 8 slices whole wheat bread
- 2 tablespoons cream cheese, soft
- 1 tablespoon chives, chopped
- ¼ cup avocado, peeled, pitted and mashed
- 1 teaspoon mustard
- Salt and black pepper to the taste

## DIRECTIONS

1. Spread the mashed avocado on each bread slice, also spread the rest of the ingredients except the cucumber slices.
2. Divide the cucumber slices on the bread slices, cut each slice in thirds, arrange on a platter and serve as an appetizer.

CALORIES: 187 Kcal     FAT: 12.4 g     PROTEIN: 8.2 g     CARBOHYDRATES: 4.5 g

---

*Preparation: 5 min*     *Cooking: 0 min*     *Servings: 6*

# 113. CUCUMBER ROLLS

## INGREDIENTS

- 1 big cucumber, sliced lengthwise
- 1 tablespoon parsley, chopped
- 8 ounces canned tuna, drained and mashed
- Salt and black pepper to the taste
- 1 teaspoon lime juice

## DIRECTIONS

1. Arrange cucumber slices on a working surface, divide the rest of the ingredients, and roll.
2. Arrange all the rolls on a platter and serve as an appetizer.

CALORIES: 200 Kcal     FAT: 6 g     PROTEIN: 3.5 g     CARBOHYDRATES: 7.6 g

Preparation: 000 min    Cooking: 1 hour and 10 min    Servings: 6

## 114. CINNAMON BABY BACK RIBS PLATTER

### INGREDIENTS

- 1 rack baby back ribs
- 2 teaspoons smoked paprika
- 2 teaspoon chili powder
- A pinch of salt and black pepper
- 1 teaspoon garlic powder
- 1 teaspoon onion powder
- 1 teaspoon cinnamon powder
- ½ teaspoon cumin seeds
- A pinch of cayenne pepper
- 1 cup tomato sauce
- 3 garlic cloves, minced

### DIRECTIONS

1. In your instant pot, combine the baby back ribs with the rest of the ingredients, put the lid on and cook on High for 30 minutes.
2. Release the pressure naturally for 10 minutes, arrange the ribs on a platter and serve as an appetizer.

CALORIES: 222 Kcal    FAT: 12 g    PROTEIN: 14 g    CARBOHYDRATES: 6 g

*Preparation: 10 min*  *Cooking: 0 min*  Servings: 8

# 115. OLIVES AND CHEESE STUFFED TOMATOES

## INGREDIENTS

- 24 cherry tomatoes, top cut off and insides scooped out
- 2 tablespoons olive oil
- ¼ teaspoon red pepper flakes
- ½ cup feta cheese, crumbled
- 2 tablespoons black olive paste
- ¼ cup mint, torn

## DIRECTIONS

1. In a bowl, mix the olives paste with the rest of the ingredients except the cherry tomatoes and whisk well.
2. Stuff the cherry tomatoes with this mix, arrange them all on a platter and serve as an appetizer.

CALORIES: 136 Kcal    FAT: 8.6 g    PROTEIN: 5.1 g    CARBOHYDRATES: 5.6 g

---

Preparation: 5 min    Cooking: 0 min    Servings: 8

# 116. CHILI MANGO AND WATERMELON SALSA

## INGREDIENTS

- 1 red tomato, chopped
- Salt and black pepper to the taste
- 1 cup watermelon, seedless, peeled and cubed
- 1 red onion, chopped
- 2 mangos, peeled and chopped
- 2 chili peppers, chopped
- ¼ cup cilantro, chopped
- 3 tablespoons lime juice
- Pita chips for serving

## DIRECTIONS

1. In a bowl, mix the tomato with the watermelon, the onion and the rest of the ingredients except the pita chips and toss well.
2. Divide the mix into small cups and serve with pita chips on the side.

CALORIES: 62 Kcal    FAT: 1 g    PROTEIN: 2.3 g    CARBOHYDRATES: 3.9 g

Preparation: 10 min — Cooking: 10 min — Servings: 4

## 117. COOKED OLIVES

### INGREDIENTS

- A pinch of salt and black pepper
- 1 and ½ cups black olives, pitted
- 1 and ½ cups green olives, pitted
- ½ tablespoon Cajun seasoning
- 2 garlic cloves, minced
- 1 red chili pepper, chopped
- ¼ cup veggie stock
- 1 tablespoon parsley, chopped
- 1 lemon slice
- 4 orange slices

### DIRECTIONS

1. In your instant pot, combine the all the olives and the rest of the ingredients, put the lid on and cook on High 10 minutes.
2. Release the pressure fast for 5 minutes, divide the mix into small bowls and serve as an appetizer.

CALORIES: 105 Kcal — FAT: 1 g — PROTEIN: 7 g — CARBOHYDRATES: 4 g

Preparation: 5 min  Cooking: 0 min  Servings: 8

## 118. AVOCADO DIP

**INGREDIENTS**

- ½ cup heavy cream
- 1 green chili pepper, chopped
- Salt and pepper to the taste
- 4 avocados, pitted, peeled and chopped
- 1 cup cilantro, chopped
- ¼ cup lime juice

**DIRECTIONS**

1. In a blender, combine the cream with the avocados and the rest of the ingredients and pulse well.
2. Divide the mix into bowls and serve cold as a party dip.

CALORIES: 200 Kcal  FAT: 14.5 g  PROTEIN: 7.6 g  CARBOHYDRATES: 8.1 g

---

Preparation: 10 min  Cooking: 0 min  Servings: 4

## 119. GOAT CHEESE AND CHIVES SPREAD

**INGREDIENTS**

- 2 ounces goat cheese, crumbled
- ¾ cup sour cream
- 2 tablespoons chives, chopped
- 1 tablespoon lemon juice
- Salt and black pepper to the taste
- 2 tablespoons extra virgin olive oil

**DIRECTIONS**

1. In a bowl, mix the goat cheese with the cream and the rest of the ingredients and whisk really well.
2. Keep in the fridge for 10 minutes and serve as a party spread.

CALORIES: 200 Kcal  FAT: 11.5 g  PROTEIN: 5.6 g  CARBOHYDRATES: 8.9 g

*Preparation: 10 min*   *Cooking: 15 min*   *Servings: 2*

## 120. HOT ASPARAGUS STICKS

### INGREDIENTS

- 1 and ½ pounds asparagus, intact
- 2 tablespoons olive oil
- 2 tablespoons cayenne pepper sauce
- A pinch of salt and black pepper
- ½ cup water
- 1 lemon, halved
- 2 garlic cloves
- 1 cup cherry tomatoes

### DIRECTIONS

1. In a bowl, mix the asparagus with the other ingredients except the water and toss.
2. Grease an oven pan with the olive oil and the water, then place the mix in the pan.
3. Bake at 400 degrees F for 15 minutes or until well cooked.
4. Arrange the asparagus on a platter and serve.

CALORIES: 70 Kcal   FAT: 1 g   PROTEIN: 4 g   CARBOHYDRATES: 4.2 g

Preparation: 000 min        Cooking: 000 min        Servings: 6

## 121. BUTTERY CARROT STICKS

### INGREDIENTS

- 1 pound carrot, cut into sticks
- 4 garlic cloves, minced
- ¼ cup chicken stock
- 1 teaspoon rosemary, chopped
- A pinch of salt and black pepper
- 2 tablespoons olive oil
- 2 tablespoons ghee, melted

### DIRECTIONS

1. Set the instant pot on Sauté mode, add the oil and the ghee, heat them up, add the garlic and brown for 1 minute.
2. Add the rest of the ingredients, put the lid on and cook on High for 14 minutes.
3. Release the pressure naturally for 10 minutes, arrange the carrot sticks on a platter and serve.

CALORIES: 142 Kcal        FAT: 4 g        PROTEIN: 7 g        CARBOHYDRATES: 5 g

---

Preparation: 10 min        Cooking: 10 min        Servings: 2

## 122. MANGO SALSA

### INGREDIENTS

- 2 mangoes, peeled and cubed
- ½ tablespoon sweet paprika
- 2 garlic cloves, minced
- 2 tablespoons cilantro, chopped
- 1 tablespoon spring onions, chopped
- 1 cup cherry tomatoes, cubed
- 1 cup avocado, peeled, pitted and cubed
- A pinch of salt and black pepper
- 1 tablespoon olive oil
- ¼ cup tomato puree
- ½ cup kalamata olives, pitted and sliced

### DIRECTIONS

1. In your instant pot, combine the mangoes with the paprika and the rest of the ingredients except the cilantro, put the lid on and cook on High for 5 minutes.
2. Release the pressure fast for 5 minutes, divide the mix into small bowls, sprinkle the cilantro on top and serve.

CALORIES: 123 Kcal        FAT: 4 g        PROTEIN: 5 g        CARBOHYDRATES: 3 g

*Preparation: 10 min*     Cooking: 5 min     Servings: 6

## 123. TOMATO BRUSCHETTA

### INGREDIENTS

- 1 baguette, sliced
- 1/3 cup basil, chopped
- 6 tomatoes, cubed
- 2 garlic cloves, minced
- A pinch of salt and black pepper
- 1 teaspoon olive oil
- 1 tablespoon balsamic vinegar
- ½ teaspoon garlic powder
- 1 mozzarella cheese, cubed
- Cooking spray

### DIRECTIONS

1. Arrange the baguette slices on a baking sheet lined with parchment paper, grease them with cooking spray and bake at 400° F for 5 minutes.
2. In a bowl, mix the tomatoes with the basil and the remaining ingredients, toss well and leave aside for 10 minutes.
3. Place the tomato mix and the mozzarella on each baguette slice, arrange them all on a platter and serve.

CALORIES: 162 Kcal     FAT: 4 g     PROTEIN: 4 g     CARBOHYDRATES: 29 g

*Preparation: 10 min*  *Cooking: 30 min*  *Servings: 4*

# 124. PORK BITES

## INGREDIENTS

- 1 pound pork roast, cubed and browned
- 1 tablespoon Italian seasoning
- 1 cup beef stock
- 2 tablespoons water
- 1 tablespoon sweet paprika
- 2 tablespoons tomato sauce
- 1 tablespoon rosemary, chopped

## DIRECTIONS

1. In your instant pot, combine the pork cubes with the seasoning and the rest of the ingredients except the rosemary.
2. Toss, put the lid on and cook on High for 30 minutes.
3. Release the pressure naturally for 10 minutes, arrange the pork cubes on a platter, sprinkle the rosemary on top and serve.

CALORIES: 242 Kcal   FAT: 12 g   PROTEIN: 14 g   CARBOHYDRATES: 6 g

---

*Preparation: 10 min*  *Cooking: 15 min*  *Servings: 4*

# 125. MEATBALL PLATTER

## INGREDIENTS

- 1 pound beef meat, ground
- ¼ cup panko breadcrumbs
- A pinch of salt and black pepper
- 3 tablespoons red onion, grated
- ¼ cup parsley, chopped
- 2 garlic cloves, minced
- 2 tablespoons lemon juice
- Zest of 1 lemon, grated
- 1 egg
- ½ teaspoon cumin, ground
- ½ teaspoon coriander, ground
- ¼ teaspoon cinnamon powder
- 2 ounces feta cheese, crumbled

## DIRECTIONS

1. In a bowl, mix the beef with the breadcrumbs, salt, pepper and the rest of the ingredients except the cooking spray, stir well and shape medium balls out of this mix.
2. Arrange the meatballs on a baking sheet lined with parchment paper, grease them with cooking spray and bake at 450°F for 15 minutes.
3. Arrange the meatballs on a platter and serve as an appetizer.

CALORIES: 300 Kcal   FAT: 15.4 g   PROTEIN: 15 g   CARBOHYDRATES: 22.4 g

*Preparation: 10 min*     *Cooking: 10 min*     Servings: 8

## 126. CORIANDER FALAFEL

### INGREDIENTS

- 1 cup canned garbanzo beans, drained and rinsed
- 1 bunch parsley leaves
- 1 yellow onion, chopped
- 5 garlic cloves, minced
- 1 teaspoon coriander, ground
- A pinch of salt and black pepper
- ¼ teaspoon cayenne pepper
- ¼ teaspoon baking soda
- ¼ teaspoon cumin powder
- 1 teaspoon lemon juice
- 3 tablespoons tapioca flour
- Olive oil for frying

### DIRECTIONS

1. In your food processor, combine the beans with the parsley, onion and the rest the ingredients except the oil and the flour and pulse well.
2. Transfer the mix to a bowl, add the flour, stir well, shape 16 balls out of this mix and flatten them a bit.
3. Heat up a pan with some oil over medium-high heat, add the falafels, cook them for 5 minutes on each side, transfer to paper towels, drain excess grease, arrange them on a platter and serve as an appetizer.

CALORIES: 112 Kcal    FAT: 6.2 g    PROTEIN: 3.1 g    CARBOHYDRATES: 12.3 g

*Preparation: 10 min*   *Cooking: 0 min*   *Servings: 6*

# 127. YOGURT DIP

## INGREDIENTS

- 2 cups Greek yogurt
- 2 tablespoons pistachios, toasted and chopped
- A pinch of salt and white pepper
- 2 tablespoons mint, chopped
- 1 tablespoon kalamata olives, pitted and chopped
- ¼ cup za'atar spice
- ¼ cup pomegranate seeds
- 1/3 cup olive oil

## DIRECTIONS

1. In a bowl, combine the yogurt with the pistachios and the rest of the ingredients and whisk well.
2. Divide into small cups and serve with pita chips on the side.

CALORIES: 294 Kcal    FAT: 18 g    PROTEIN: 10 g    CARBOHYDRATES: 21 g

---

*Preparation: 10 min*   *Cooking: 15 min*   *Servings: 4*

# 128. ARTICHOKE FLATBREAD

## INGREDIENTS

- 5 tablespoons olive oil
- 2 garlic cloves, minced
- 2 tablespoons parsley, chopped
- 2 round whole wheat flatbreads
- 4 tablespoons parmesan, grated
- ½ cup mozzarella cheese, grated
- 14 ounces canned artichokes, drained and quartered
- 1 cup baby spinach, chopped
- ½ cup cherry tomatoes, halved
- ½ teaspoon basil, dried
- Salt and black pepper to the taste

## DIRECTIONS

1. In a bowl, mix the parsley with the garlic and 4 tablespoons oil, whisk well and spread this over the flatbreads.
2. Sprinkle the mozzarella and half of the parmesan.
3. In a bowl, mix the artichokes with the spinach, tomatoes, basil, salt, pepper and the rest of the oil, toss and divide over the flatbreads as well.
4. Sprinkle the rest of the parmesan on top, arrange the flatbreads on a baking sheet lined with parchment paper and bake at 425° F for 15 minutes.
5. Serve as an appetizer.

CALORIES: 223 Kcal    FAT: 11.2 g    PROTEIN: 7.4 g    CARBOHYDRATES: 15.5 g

*Preparation: 10 min*      *Cooking: 0 min*      *Servings: 4*

## 129. RED PEPPER TAPENADE

### INGREDIENTS

- 7 ounces roasted red peppers, chopped
- ½ cup parmesan, grated
- 1/3 cup parsley, chopped
- 14 ounces canned artichokes, drained and chopped
- 3 tablespoons olive oil
- ¼ cup capers, drained
- 1 and ½ tablespoons lemon juice
- 2 garlic cloves, minced

### DIRECTIONS

1. In your blender, combine the red peppers with the parmesan and the rest of the ingredients and pulse well.
2. Divide into cups and serve as a snack.

CALORIES: 200 Kcal      FAT: 5.6 g      PROTEIN: 4.6 g      CARBOHYDRATES: 12.4 g

---

*Preparation: 10 min*      *Cooking: 0 min*      *Servings: 6*

## 130. RED PEPPER HUMMUS

### INGREDIENTS

- 6 ounces roasted red peppers, peeled and chopped
- 16 ounces canned chickpeas, drained and rinsed
- ¼ cup Greek yogurt
- 3 tablespoons tahini paste
- Juice of 1 lemon
- 3 garlic cloves, minced  1 tablespoon olive oil
- A pinch of salt and black pepper
- 1 tablespoon parsley, chopped

### DIRECTIONS

1. In your food processor, combine the red peppers with the rest of the ingredients except the oil and the parsley and pulse well.
2. Add the oil, pulse again, divide into cups, sprinkle the parsley on top and serve as a party spread.

CALORIES: 255 Kcal      FAT: 11.4 g      PROTEIN: 6.5 g      CARBOHYDRATES: 17.4 g

# 17 Poultry

*Preparation:* 25 min  |  Cooking: 1 hour and 10 min  |  Servings: 4

# 131. SICILIAN LEMON CHICKEN PASTA

## INGREDIENTS

- 2 Tablespoons Olive Oil
- 2 Chicken Breast Halves
- 8 Ounces tagliatelle pasta
- ½ Lemon, Juice & Zested
- ½ Onion, Sliced Thin
- 2 Tablespoons Parmesan Cheese
- ¼ Teaspoon Cayenne Pepper
- ½ Tablespoons Garlic, Minced
- 1 Tablespoon Black Olives
- 1 Tablespoon Pine Nuts
- 1 Bay Leaf
- 8 Ounces Tomatoes, Diced
- ¼ Teaspoon Oregano
- ½ Tablespoon Balsamic Vinegar
- 1 Tablespoon Fresh Basil
- ½ Teaspoon Sugar
- Sea Salt & Black Pepper to Taste

## DIRECTIONS

1. Heat your olive oil over medium-high heat in a saucepan, and then once it's hot add in your olives, pine nuts, garlic and onion. Season with bay leaf, cayenne and oregano. Cook for five minutes. Your onion should be softened.
2. Add in tomatoes, sugar and balsamic vinegar, seasoning with salt and pepper. Cook for 10 minutes more. Remove your basil and bay leaf, and then cover to keep warm.
3. Bring a pot of water to a boil, and then cook your pasta for about ten minutes, then drain it.
4. Heat another half tablespoon of olive oil using medium heat in a different skillet, cooking your chicken with lemon juice. Make sure it's browned on both sides, which will take roughly fifteen minutes. Allow it to rest on a plate for five more minutes.
5. Slice the chicken breast again the grain, and try to make thin slices. Divide your pasta, and then top with your chicken slices and tomato sauce. Sprinkle on your parmesan, lemon zest and before serving warm.

CALORIES: 245 Kcal  |  FAT: 8.9 g  |  PROTEIN: 8.6 g  |  CARBOHYDRATES: 31.2 g

*Preparation: 15 min*  *Cooking: 30 min*  *Servings: 4*

## 132. ARUGULA FIG CHICKEN

### INGREDIENTS

- 2 teaspoons cornstarch
- 2 clove garlic, crushed
- ¾ cup Mission figs, chopped
- ¼ cup black or green olives, chopped
- 1 bag baby arugula
- ½ cup chicken broth
- 8 skinless chicken thighs
- 2 teaspoons olive oil
- 2 teaspoons brown sugar
- ½ cup red wine vinegar
- Ground black pepper and salt, to taste

### DIRECTIONS

1. Over medium stove flame, heat the oil in a skillet or saucepan (preferably of medium size).
2. Add the chicken, sprinkle with some salt and cook until evenly brown. Set it aside.
3. Add and sauté the garlic.
4. In a mixing bowl, combine the vinegar, broth, cornstarch and sugar. Add the mixture into the pan and simmer until the sauce thickens.
5. Add the figs and olives; simmer for a few minutes. Serve warm with chopped arugula on top.

CALORIES: 364 Kcal     FAT: 14 g     PROTEIN: 31 g     CARBOHYDRATES: 29 g

---

*Preparation: 7 min*  *Cooking: 30 min*  *Servings: 2*

## 133. CHICKEN MILANO

### INGREDIENTS

- 4.5 Ounces Green Beans, Frozen
- 1/2 Teaspoon Red Pepper Flakes, Crushed
- 14 Ounces Stewed Tomatoes, Canned & Drained
- 1/2 Teaspoon Italian Style Seasoning
- 1/2 Tablespoon Vegetable Oil
- 1 Clove Garlic, Crushed
- 2 Chicken Breast Halves, Skinless & Boneless
- Sea Salt & Black Pepper to Taste

### DIRECTIONS

1. Use a large skillet over medium-high heat to heat up your vegetable oil. Once your oil is hot add your chicken, and season with red pepper flakes, salt, pepper, garlic and Italian seasoning.
2. Cook for five minutes before adding the tomatoes in. cook for an additional five minutes, and then add in your green beans. Stir well.
3. Cover, and then reduce the heat to medium-low. Allow it to simmer for twenty minutes before serving warm.

CALORIES: 165 Kcal     FAT: 5.9 g     PROTEIN: 7 g     CARBOHYDRATES: 2.2 g

*Preparation:* 20 min     *Cooking:* 1 hour and 5 min     *Servings:* 4

# 134. BRAISED CHICKEN & OLIVES

## INGREDIENTS

- 2 Small Carrots, Diced
- 1 Clove Garlic, Minced 1/2 Tablespoon Olive Oil
- 2 Chicken Legs, Skinned & Cut into Drumstick and Thighs
- 1/2 Cup Chicken Broth, Low Sodium
- 1 Tablespoon Ginger, Fresh & Chopped
- 1/2 Cup Dry White Wine
- 1/2 Cup Water
- 1/4 Cup Green Olives, Pitted & Chopped
- 3 Tablespoons Raisins
- 1/3 Cup Chickpeas, Canned, Drained & Rinsed
- 2 Sprigs Thyme, Fresh

## DIRECTIONS

1. Start by heating your oven to 350, and then get out a Dutch oven or oven safe skillet. Heat your olive oil using medium heat, and then place the chicken in the skillet. Make sure that the pan isn't overcrowded. Sauté for five minutes per side, which should make your chicken crisp. Transfer it to a plate, and place the chicken to the side for now.
2. Reduce the heat to medium-low, throwing in your garlic, ginger, onion and carrots. Sauté, and make sure to stir frequently as to not burn your onion. Your onion should soften in five minutes, and then throw in your wine, broth and water. Bring it to a boil to deglaze the pan.
3. Add your chicken back in, and then add in your thyme. Bring it up to a boil again, and then place it in the oven. Cook for forty-five minutes.
4. Take it out of the oven, and stir in your olives, raisins, and chickpeas. Return it to the oven, braising while uncovered for twenty minutes. Discard the thyme before serving.

CALORIES: 285 Kcal     FAT: 8 g     PROTEIN: 6 g     CARBOHYDRATES: 11.2 g

*Preparation: 10 min*     *Cooking: 30 min*     *Servings: 4*

## 135. PARMESAN CHICKEN GRATIN

### INGREDIENTS

- 2 chicken thighs, skinless, boneless
- 1 teaspoon paprika
- 1 tablespoon lemon juice
- ½ teaspoon chili flakes
- ¼ teaspoon garlic powder
- 3 oz Parmesan, grated
- 1/3 cup milk
- 1 onion, sliced
- 2 oz pineapple, sliced

### DIRECTIONS

1. Chop the chicken thighs roughly and sprinkle them with paprika, lemon juice, chili flakes, garlic powder, and mix up well.
2. Arrange the chopped chicken thighs in the baking dish in one layer.
3. Then place sliced onion over the chicken.
4. Add the layer of sliced pineapple.
5. Mix up together milk and Parmesan and pour the liquid over the pineapple,
6. Cover the surface of the baking dish with foil and bake gratin for 30 minutes at 355F.

CALORIES: 100 Kcal     FAT: 5.2 g     PROTEIN: 8.1 g     CARBOHYDRATES: 6.7 g

---

*Preparation: 10 min*     *Cooking: 25 min*     *Servings: 2*

## 136. CHICKEN SAUTE

### INGREDIENTS

- 4 oz chicken fillet
- 4 tomatoes, peeled
- 1 bell pepper, chopped
- 1 teaspoon olive oil
- 1 cup of water
- 1 teaspoon salt
- 1 chili pepper, chopped
- ½ teaspoon saffron

### DIRECTIONS

1. Pour water in the pan and bring it to boil.
2. Meanwhile, chop the chicken fillet.
3. Add the chicken fillet in the boiling water and cook it for 10 minutes or until the chicken is tender.
4. After this, put the chopped bell pepper and chili pepper in the skillet.
5. Add olive oil and roast the vegetables for 3 minutes.
6. Add chopped tomatoes and mix up well.
7. Cook the vegetables for 2 minutes more.
8. Then add salt and a ¾ cup of water from chicken.
9. Add chopped chicken fillet and mix up.
10. Cook the saute for 10 minutes over the medium heat.

CALORIES: 192 Kcal     FAT: 7.2 g     PROTEIN: 19.2 g     CARBOHYDRATES: 14.4 g

*Preparation: 35 min*  *Cooking: 20 min*  Servings: 6

## 137. GRILLED MARINATED CHICKEN

### INGREDIENTS

- 2-pound chicken breast, skinless, boneless
- 2 tablespoons lemon juice
- 1 teaspoon sage
- ½ teaspoon ground nutmeg
- ½ teaspoon dried oregano
- 1 teaspoon paprika
- 1 teaspoon onion powder
- 2 tablespoons olive oil
- 1 teaspoon chili flakes
- 1 teaspoon salt
- 1 teaspoon apple cider vinegar

### DIRECTIONS

1. Make the marinade: whisk together apple cider vinegar, salt, chili flakes, olive oil, onion powder, paprika, dried oregano, ground nutmeg, sage, and lemon juice.
2. Then rub the chicken with marinade carefully and leave for 25 minutes to marinate.
3. Meanwhile, preheat grill to 385F.
4. Place the marinated chicken breast in the grill and cook it for 10 minutes from each side.
5. Cut the cooked chicken on the servings.

CALORIES: 218 Kcal   FAT: 8.2 g   PROTEIN: 32.2 g   CARBOHYDRATES: 0.4 g

*Preparation: 5 min*     *Cooking: 1 hour*     *Servings: 4*

## 138. STICKY SKILLET CHICKEN

### INGREDIENTS

- 4 chicken legs
- Salt and pepper to taste
- 3 tablespoons olive oil
- 2 garlic cloves, chopped
- 2 tablespoons honey
- 2 tablespoons lemon juice
- 1 thyme sprig
- 1 rosemary sprig

### DIRECTIONS

1. Season the chicken with salt and pepper.
2. Heat the oil in a skillet and place the chicken in the hot oil.
3. Fry on each side for 10-15 minutes until golden brown.
4. Drizzle in the honey and lemon juice then place the herb sprigs on top.
5. Cover with a lid or aluminum foil and place in the preheated oven at 350F for 20 minutes.
6. Serve the chicken and the sauce right away.

CALORIES: 316 Kcal     FAT: 18 g     PROTEIN: 29.1 g     CARBOHYDRATES: 9.3 g

---

*Preparation: 10 min*     *Cooking: 35 min*     *Servings: 4*

## 139. CHICKEN LEEK SOUP

### INGREDIENTS

- 1 cup cabbage, shredded
- 6 oz leek, chopped
- ½ yellow onion, diced
- 1-pound chicken breast, skinless, boneless
- 1 tablespoon butter
- 1 teaspoon salt
- ½ teaspoon dried oregano
- ½ teaspoon dried thyme
- 1 tablespoon canola oil
- 4 cups of water

### DIRECTIONS

1. Chop the chicken breast into the cubes and place in the pan.
2. Add butter and canola oil.
3. Cook the chicken for 5 minutes. Stir it from time to time.
4. After this, add yellow onion and chopped leek.
5. Add salt, dried oregano, and thyme. Mix up the ingredients well and saute for 5 minutes.
6. Then add water and cabbage.
7. Close the lid and cook soup over the medium heat for 25 minutes.

CALORIES: 222 Kcal     FAT: 9.4 g     PROTEIN: 25.1 g     CARBOHYDRATES: 8.5 g

*Preparation: 000 min* — *Cooking: 1 hour and 10 min* — *Servings: 6*

## 140. CRISPY ITALIAN CHICKEN

### INGREDIENTS

- 4 chicken breasts
- 1 teaspoon dried basil
- 1 teaspoon dried oregano
- Salt and pepper to taste
- 3 tablespoons olive oil
- 1 tablespoon balsamic vinegar

### DIRECTIONS

1. Season the chicken with salt, pepper, basil and oregano.
2. Heat the oil in a skillet and add the chicken in the hot oil.
3. Cook on each side for 5 minutes until golden then cover the skillet with a weight – another skillet or a very heavy lid is recommended.
4. Place over medium heat and cook for 10 minutes on one side then flip the chicken repeatedly, cooking for another 10 minutes until crispy.
5. Serve the chicken right away, with a sauce presented in the "snacks" chapter if you like.

CALORIES: 262 Kcal — FAT: 13.9 g — PROTEIN: 32.6 g — CARBOHYDRATES: 0.3 g

*Preparation: 10 min*  *Cooking: 30 min*  *Servings: 2*

# 141. CHICKEN FILLETS WITH ARTICHOKE HEARTS

## INGREDIENTS

- 1 can artichoke hearts, chopped
- 12 oz chicken fillets (3 oz each fillet)
- 1 teaspoon avocado oil
- ½ teaspoon ground thyme
- ½ teaspoon white pepper
- 1/3 cup water
- 1/3 cup shallot, roughly chopped
- 1 lemon, sliced

## DIRECTIONS

1. Mix up together chicken fillets, artichoke hearts, avocado oil, ground thyme, white pepper, and shallot.
2. Line the baking tray with baking paper and place the chicken fillet mixture in it.
3. Then add sliced lemon and water.
4. Bake the meal for 30 minutes at 375F. Stir the ingredients during cooking to avoid burning.

CALORIES: 267 Kcal     FAT: 8.2 g     PROTEIN: 35.2 g     CARBOHYDRATES: 10.4 g

---

*Preparation: 10 min*  *Cooking: 40 min*  *Servings: 4*

# 142. CHICKEN LOAF

## INGREDIENTS

- 2 cups ground chicken
- 1 egg, beaten
- 1 tablespoon fresh dill, chopped
- 1 garlic clove, chopped
- ½ teaspoon salt
- 1 teaspoon chili flakes
- 1 onion, minced

## DIRECTIONS

1. In the mixing bowl combine together all ingredient and mix up until you get smooth mass.
2. Then line the loaf dish with baking paper and put the ground chicken mixture inside.
3. Flatten the surface well.
4. Bake the chicken loaf for 40 minutes at 355F.
5. Then chill the chicken loaf to the room temperature and remove from the loaf dish.
6. Slice it and serve.

CALORIES: 167 Kcal     FAT: 6.2 g     PROTEIN: 32.2 g     CARBOHYDRATES: 3.4 g

*Preparation: 10 min*  *Cooking: 20 min*  Servings: 4

## 143. TOMATO & CHICKEN SKILLET

INGREDIENTS

- 1 cup tomatoes
- 1-pound chicken breast, skinless, boneless
- 3 bell peppers, chopped
- ½ cup of water
- 1 jalapeno pepper, chopped
- ½ teaspoon salt
- 1 tablespoon olive oil
- 1 teaspoon parsley
- 1 mozzarella cheese, chopped

DIRECTIONS

1. Chop tomatoes into the tiny pieces.
2. Chop the chicken breast into the medium cubes.
3. Pour olive oil in the skillet and heat it up.
4. Add chicken breast cubes and roast them for 5 minutes.
5. After this, add chopped bell pepper and jalapeno pepper. Stir the ingredients well and cook for 5 minutes.
6. Add salt and tomatoes. Mix up well.
7. Cook the ingredients for 5 minutes and add water.
8. Stir it well, then add the mozzarella cheese and parsley.
9. Close the lid and cook the meal for 5 minutes more, then serve.

CALORIES: 197 Kcal   FAT: 6.7 g   PROTEIN: 25.4 g   CARBOHYDRATES: 8.7 g

*Preparation: 5 min* — *Cooking: 1 hour* — *Servings: 6*

## 144. CHICKEN AND CHORIZO CASSEROLE

### INGREDIENTS

- 6 chicken thighs
- 4 chorizo links, sliced
- 2 tablespoons olive oil
- 1 cup tomato juice
- 2 tablespoons tomato paste
- 1 bay leaf
- 1 teaspoon dried thyme
- Salt and pepper to taste

### DIRECTIONS

1. Heat the oil in a skillet and add the chicken. Cook on all sides until golden then transfer the chicken in a deep-dish baking pan.
2. Add the rest of the ingredients and season with salt and pepper.
3. Cook in the preheated oven at 350F for 25 minutes.
4. Serve the casserole right away.

CALORIES: 424 Kcal — FAT: 27.5 g — PROTEIN: 39.1 g — CARBOHYDRATES: 3.6 g

---

*Preparation: 10 min* — *Cooking: 10 min* — *Servings: 8*

## 145. CHICKEN MEATBALLS WITH CARROTS

### INGREDIENTS

- ⅓ cup carrots, grated
- 1 onion, diced
- 2 cups ground chicken
- 1 tablespoon semolina
- 1 egg, beaten
- ½ teaspoon salt
- 1 teaspoon dried oregano
- 1 teaspoon dried cilantro
- 1 teaspoon chili flakes
- 1 tablespoon coconut oil

### DIRECTIONS

1. In the mixing bowl combine together grated carrot, diced onion, ground chicken, semolina, egg, salt, dried oregano, cilantro, and chili flakes.
2. With the help of scooper make the meatballs.
3. Heat up the coconut oil in the skillet.
4. When it starts to shimmer, put meatballs in it.
5. Cook the meatballs for 5 minutes from each side over the medium-low heat.

CALORIES: 107 Kcal — FAT: 4.2 g — PROTEIN: 11.2 g — CARBOHYDRATES: 2.4 g

*Preparation: 15 min*     Cooking: 15 min     Servings: 4

## 146. CHICKEN BURGERS

### INGREDIENTS

- 8 oz ground chicken
- 1 cup carrots, grated
- 1 teaspoon minced onion
- ½ teaspoon salt
- 1 red bell pepper, grinded
- 1 egg, beaten
- 1 teaspoon ground black pepper
- 4 tablespoons Panko breadcrumbs

### DIRECTIONS

1. In the mixing bowl mix up together ground chicken, blended spinach, minced garlic, salt, grinded bell pepper, egg, and ground black pepper.
2. When the chicken mixture is smooth, make 4 burgers from it and coat them in Panko breadcrumbs.
3. Place the burgers in the non-sticky baking dish or line the baking tray with baking paper.
4. Bake the burgers for 15 minutes at 365F.
5. Flip the chicken burgers on another side after 7 minutes of cooking.
6. If you prefer, you can cook the burgers in the grill. In that case, the cooking time will be less, around 5 minutes each side (depending on the temperature of the grill).

CALORIES: 177 Kcal     FAT: 5.2 g     PROTEIN: 13.2 g     CARBOHYDRATES: 10.4 g

*Preparation: 15 min*     *Cooking: 10 min*     *Servings: 8*

# 147. DUCK PATTIES

## INGREDIENTS

- 1-pound duck breast, skinless, boneless
- 1 teaspoon semolina
- ½ teaspoon cayenne pepper
- 2 eggs, beaten
- 1 teaspoon salt
- 1 tablespoon fresh cilantro, chopped
- 1 tablespoon olive oil

## DIRECTIONS

1. Chop the duck breast on the tiny pieces (grind it) and combine together with semolina, cayenne pepper, salt, and cilantro. Mix up well.
2. Then add eggs and stir gently.
3. Pour olive oil in the skillet and heat it up.
4. Place the duck mixture in the oil with the help of the spoon to make the shape of small patties.
5. Roast the patties for 3 minutes from each side over the medium heat.
6. Then close the lid and cook patties for 4 minutes more over the low heat.

CALORIES: 106 Kcal     FAT: 5.2 g     PROTEIN: 13.2 g     CARBOHYDRATES: 0.4 g

---

*Preparation: 10 min*     *Cooking: 1 hour*     *Servings: 8*

# 148. ITALIAN CHICKEN BUTTERNUT POT

## INGREDIENTS

- 4 chicken breasts, cubed
- 1 tablespoon all-purpose flour
- 3 tablespoons olive oil
- 4 cups butternut squash cubes
- 1 thyme sprig
- 1 rosemary sprig
- 2 garlic cloves, minced
- 1 teaspoon dried oregano
- 1 tablespoon balsamic vinegar
- 1 cup vegetable stock
- Salt and pepper to taste

## DIRECTIONS

1. Season the chicken with salt and pepper then sprinkle it with flour.
2. Heat the oil in a pot that can go in the oven then add the chicken.
3. Cook on all sides for 10 minutes then add the rest of the ingredients.
4. Season with salt and pepper and cover with a lid.
5. Cook in the preheated oven at 350F for 35 minutes.
6. Serve the dish warm and fresh.

CALORIES: 178 Kcal     FAT: 9.1 g     PROTEIN: 15.4 g     CARBOHYDRATES: 9.4 g

*Preparation: 10 min* — *Cooking: 1 hour and 30 min* — *Servings: 8*

## 149. VEGETABLE TURKEY CASSEROLE

### INGREDIENTS

- 3 tablespoons olive oil
- 2 pounds turkey breasts, cubed
- 1 sweet onion, chopped
- 3 carrots, sliced
- 2 celery stalks, sliced
- 2 garlic cloves, chopped
- ½ teaspoon cumin powder
- ½ teaspoon dried thyme
- 2 cans diced tomatoes
- 1 cup chicken stock
- 1 bay leaf
- Salt and pepper to taste

### DIRECTIONS

1. Heat the oil in a deep heavy pot and stir in the turkey.
2. Cook for 5 minutes until golden on all sides then add the onion, carrot, celery and garlic. Cook for 5 more minutes then add the rest of the ingredients.
3. Season with salt and pepper and cook in the preheated oven at 350F for 40 minutes.
4. Serve the casserole warm and fresh.

CALORIES: 186 Kcal    FAT: 7.3 g    PROTEIN: 20.1 g    CARBOHYDRATES: 9.9 g

*Preparation: 10 min*  *Cooking: 20 min*  *Servings: 6*

# 150. CREAMY CHICKEN PATE

## INGREDIENTS

- 8 oz chicken liver
- 3 tablespoon butter
- 1 white onion, chopped
- 1 bay leaf
- 1 teaspoon salt
- ½ teaspoon ground black pepper
- ½ cup of water

## DIRECTIONS

1. Place the chicken liver in the saucepan.
2. Add onion, bay leaf, salt, ground black pepper, and water.
3. Mix up the mixture and close the lid.
4. Cook the liver mixture for 20 minutes over the medium heat.
5. Then transfer it in the blender and blend until smooth.
6. Add butter and mix up until it is melted.
7. Pour the pate mixture in the pate ramekin and serve.

CALORIES: 122 Kcal    FAT: 8.2 g    PROTEIN: 9.2 g    CARBOHYDRATES: 2.4 g

---

*Preparation: 10 min*  *Cooking: 30 min*  *Servings: 4*

# 151. CURRY CHICKEN DRUMSTICKS

## INGREDIENTS

- 4 chicken drumsticks
- 1 apple, grated
- 1 tablespoon curry paste
- 4 tablespoons milk
- 1 teaspoon coconut oil
- 1 teaspoon chili flakes
- ½ teaspoon minced ginger

## DIRECTIONS

1. Mix up together grated apple, curry paste, milk, chili flakes, and minced garlic.
2. Put coconut oil in the skillet and melt it.
3. Add apple mixture and stir well.
4. Then add chicken drumsticks and mix up well.
5. Roast the chicken for 2 minutes from each side.
6. Then preheat oven to 360F.
7. Place the skillet with chicken drumsticks in the oven and bake for 25 minutes.

CALORIES: 152 Kcal    FAT: 7.2 g    PROTEIN: 13.2 g    CARBOHYDRATES: 9.4 g

*Preparation: 000 min*  Cooking: 1 hour and 10 min  Servings: 6

## 152. CHICKEN ENCHILADAS

### INGREDIENTS

- 5 corn tortillas
- 10 oz chicken breast, boiled, shredded
- 1 teaspoon chipotle pepper
- 3 tablespoons green salsa
- ½ teaspoon minced garlic
- ½ cup cream
- ¼ cup chicken stock
- 1 cup Mozzarella, shredded
- 1 teaspoon butter, softened
- 1 tablespoon chives

### DIRECTIONS

1. Mix up together shredded chicken breast, chipotle pepper, green salsa, and minced garlic.
2. Then put the shredded chicken mixture in the center of every corn tortilla and roll them.
3. Spread the baking dish with softened butter from inside and arrange the rolled corn tortillas.
4. Then pour chicken stock and cream over the tortillas.
5. Top them with shredded Mozzarella.
6. Bake the enchiladas for 15 minutes at 365F.
7. Garnish with chives and serve.

CALORIES: 152 Kcal    FAT: 5.2 g    PROTEIN: 15.2 g    CARBOHYDRATES: 12.4 g

*Preparation: 10 min*  *Cooking: 20 min*  *Servings: 4*

# 153. CHICKEN STROGANOFF

## INGREDIENTS

- 1 cup cremini mushrooms, sliced
- 1 onion, sliced
- 1 tablespoon olive oil
- ½ teaspoon thyme
- 1 teaspoon salt
- 1 cup Plain yogurt
- 10 oz chicken fillet, chopped

## DIRECTIONS

1. Heat up olive oil in the saucepan.
2. Add mushrooms and onion.
3. Sprinkle the vegetables with thyme and salt. Mix up well and cook them for 5 minutes.
4. After this, add chopped chicken fillet and mix up well.
5. Cook the ingredients for 5 minutes more.
6. Then add plain yogurt, mix up well, and close the lid.
7. Cook chicken stroganoff for 10 minutes over the low heat.

CALORIES: 224 Kcal     FAT: 9.2 g     PROTEIN: 24.2 g     CARBOHYDRATES: 7.4 g

---

*Preparation: 10 min*  *Cooking: 25 min*  *Servings: 2*

# 154. EUROPEAN POSOLE

## INGREDIENTS

- 1 ½ cup water
- 6 oz chicken fillet
- 1 chili pepper, chopped
- 1 onion, diced
- 1 teaspoon butter
- ½ teaspoon salt
- ½ teaspoon paprika
- 1 tablespoon fresh dill, chopped

## DIRECTIONS

1. Pour water in the saucepan.
2. Add chicken fillet and salt. Boil it for 15 minutes over the medium heat.
3. Then remove the chicken fillet from water and shred it with the help of the fork.
4. Return it back in the hot water.
5. Melt butter in the skillet and add diced onion. Roast it until light brown and transfer in the shredded chicken.
6. Add paprika, dill, chili pepper, and mix up.
7. Close the lid and simmer Posole for 5 minutes.

CALORIES: 207 Kcal     FAT: 8.3 g     PROTEIN: 25.4 g     CARBOHYDRATES: 6 g

*Preparation: 15 min*  *Cooking: 15 min*  *Servings: 2*

## 155. CHICKEN FAJITAS

### INGREDIENTS

- 1 bell pepper
- ½ red onion, peeled
- 5 oz chicken fillets
- 1 garlic clove, sliced
- 1 tablespoon olive oil
- 1 teaspoon balsamic vinegar
- 1 teaspoon chili pepper
- ½ teaspoon salt
- 1 teaspoon lemon juice
- 2 flour tortillas

### DIRECTIONS

1. Cut the bell pepper and chicken fillet on the wedges.
2. Then slice the onion.
3. Pour olive oil in the skillet and heat it up.
4. Add chicken wedges and sprinkle them with chili pepper and salt.
5. Roast the chicken for 4 minutes. Stir it from time to time.
6. After this, add lemon juice and balsamic vinegar. Mix up well.
7. Add bell pepper, onion, and garlic clove.
8. Roast the mixture for 10 minutes over the medium-high heat. Stir it from time to time.
9. Put the cooked mixture on the tortillas and transfer in the serving plates.

CALORIES: 346 Kcal    FAT: 14.2 g    PROTEIN: 25.2 g    CARBOHYDRATES: 23.4 g

*Preparation: 10 min*     *Cooking: 12 min*     *Servings: 3*

## 156. MANGO CHICKEN SALAD

### INGREDIENTS

- 1 cup lettuce, chopped
- 1 cup arugula, chopped
- 1 mango, peeled, chopped
- 8 oz chicken breast, skinless, boneless
- 1 tablespoon lime juice
- 1 teaspoon sesame oil
- ½ teaspoon salt
- ½ teaspoon ground black pepper
- 1 teaspoon butter

### DIRECTIONS

1. Sprinkle the chicken breast with salt and ground black pepper.
2. Melt butter in the skillet and add chicken breast.
3. Roast it for 10 minutes over the medium heat. Flip it on another side from time to time.
4. Meanwhile, combine together lettuce, arugula, mango, and sesame oil in the salad bowl.
5. Add lime juice.
6. Chop the cooked chicken breast roughly and chill it to the room temperature.
7. Add it in the mango salad and mix up.

CALORIES: 183 Kcal     FAT: 5.2 g     PROTEIN: 17.2 g     CARBOHYDRATES: 17.4 g

---

*Preparation: 15 min*     *Cooking: 30 min*     *Servings: 2*

## 157. CHICKEN ZUCCHINI BOATS

### INGREDIENTS

- 1 zucchini
- ½ cup ground chicken
- ½ teaspoon chipotle pepper
- ½ teaspoon tomato sauce
- 1 oz Swiss cheese, shredded
- ½ teaspoon salt
- 4 tablespoons water

### DIRECTIONS

1. Trim the zucchini and cut it on 2 halves.
2. Remove the zucchini pulp.
3. In the mixing bowl mix up together ground chicken, chipotle pepper, tomato sauce, and salt.
4. Fill the zucchini with chicken mixture and top with Swiss cheese.
5. Place the zucchini boats in the tray. Add water.
6. Bake the boats for 30 minutes at 355F.

CALORIES: 134 Kcal     FAT: 6.3 g     PROTEIN: 13.4 g     CARBOHYDRATES: 6.2 g

*Preparation: 10 min*     *Cooking: 20 min*     Servings: 4

# 158. TENDER CHICKEN QUESADILLA

## INGREDIENTS

- 4 bread tortillas
- 1 teaspoon butter
- 2 teaspoons olive oil
- 1 teaspoon Taco seasoning
- 6 oz chicken breast, skinless, boneless, sliced
- 1/3 cup Cheddar cheese, shredded
- 1 bell pepper, cut on the wedges

## DIRECTIONS

1. Pour 1 teaspoon of olive oil in the skillet and add chicken.
2. Sprinkle the meat with Taco seasoning and mix up well.
3. Roast chicken for 10 minutes over the medium heat. Stir it from time to time.
4. Then transfer the cooked chicken in the plate.
5. Add remaining olive oil in the skillet.
6. Add bell pepper and roast it for 5 minutes. Stir it all the time.
7. Mix up together bell pepper with chicken.
8. Toss butter in the skillet and melt it.
9. Put 1 tortilla in the skillet.
10. Put Cheddar cheese on the tortilla and flatten it.
11. Then add chicken-pepper mixture and cover it with the second tortilla.
12. Roast the quesadilla for 2 minutes from each side.
13. Cut the cooked meal on the halves and transfer in the serving plates.

CALORIES: 167 Kcal     FAT: 8.2 g     PROTEIN: 24.2 g     CARBOHYDRATES: 16.4 g

*Preparation: 10 min*   *Cooking: 20 min*   *Servings: 2*

## 159. URBAN CHICKEN ALFREDO

### INGREDIENTS

- 1 onion, chopped
- 1 sweet red pepper, roasted, chopped
- 1 cup spinach, chopped
- ½ cup cream
- 1 teaspoon cream cheese
- 1 tablespoon olive oil
- ½ teaspoon ground black pepper
- 8 oz chicken breast, skinless, boneless, sliced

### DIRECTIONS

1. Mix up together sliced chicken breast with ground black pepper and put in the saucepan.
2. Add olive oil and mix up.
3. Roast the chicken for 5 minutes over the medium-high heat. Stir it from time to time.
4. After this, add chopped sweet pepper, onion, and cream cheese.
5. Mix up well and bring to boil.
6. Add spinach and cream. Mix up well.
7. Close the lid and cook chicken Alfredo for 10 minutes more over the medium heat.

CALORIES: 279 Kcal    FAT: 14 g    PROTEIN: 26.4 g    CARBOHYDRATES: 4.2 g

---

*Preparation: 10 min*   *Cooking: 10 min*   *Servings: 4*

## 160. LIGHT CASEAR

### INGREDIENTS

- 4 oz chicken fillet, chopped
- ¼ cup black olives, chopped
- 2 cups lettuce, chopped
- 1 tablespoon mayo sauce
- 1 teaspoon lemon juice
- ½ oz Parmesan cheese, shaved
- 1 teaspoon olive oil
- ½ teaspoon ground black pepper
- ½ teaspoon coconut oil

### DIRECTIONS

1. Sprinkle the chicken fillet with ground black pepper.
2. Heat up coconut oil and add chopped chicken fillet.
3. Roast it got 10 minutes or until it is cooked. Stir it from time to time.
4. Meanwhile, mix up together black olives, lettuce, Parmesan in the bowl.
5. Make mayo dressing: whisk together mayo sauce, olive oil, and lemon juice.
6. Add the cooked chicken in the salad and shake well.
7. Pour the mayo sauce dressing over the salad.

CALORIES: 134 Kcal    FAT: 13.3 g    PROTEIN: 9.4 g    CARBOHYDRATES: 2 g

*Preparation: 10 min*  *Cooking: 30 min*  *Servings: 4*

# 161. CHICKEN PARM

## INGREDIENTS

- 4 chicken breasts
- ½ cup crushed tomatoes
- ¼ cup fresh cilantro
- 1 garlic clove, diced
- ½ cup of water
- 1 onion, diced
- 1 teaspoon olive oil
- 6 oz Parmesan, grated
- 3 tablespoon Panko breadcrumbs
- 2 eggs, beaten
- 1 teaspoon ground black pepper

## DIRECTIONS

1. Pour olive oil in the saucepan.
2. Add garlic and onion. Roast the vegetables for 3 minutes.
3. Then add fresh cilantro, crushed tomatoes, and water.
4. Simmer the mixture for 5 minutes.
5. Meanwhile, mix up together ground black pepper and eggs.
6. Dip the chicken breasts in the egg mixture.
7. Coat them in Panko breadcrumbs and again in the egg mixture.
8. Coat the chicken in grated Parmesan.
9. Place the prepared chicken in the crushed tomato mixture.
10. Close the lid and cook chicken parm for 20 minutes. Flip the chicken breasts after 10 minutes of cooking.
11. Serve the chicken parm with crushed tomatoes sauce and the sauce made from the parmesan.

CALORIES: 354 Kcal   FAT: 21.3 g   PROTEIN: 32.4 g   CARBOHYDRATES: 12 g

*Preparation: 7 min*  *Cooking: 25 min*  *Servings: 4*

## 162. CHICKEN BOLOGNESE

### INGREDIENTS

- 1 cup ground chicken
- 2 oz Parmesan, grated
- 1 tablespoon olive oil
- 2 tablespoons fresh parsley, chopped
- 1 teaspoon chili pepper
- 1 teaspoon paprika
- ½ teaspoon dried oregano
- ¼ teaspoon garlic, minced
- ½ teaspoon dried thyme
- 1/3 cup crushed tomatoes

### DIRECTIONS

1. Heat up olive oil in the skillet.
2. Add ground chicken and sprinkle it with chili pepper, paprika, dried oregano, dried thyme, and parsley. Mix up well.
3. Cook the chicken for 5 minutes and add crushed tomatoes. Mix up well.
4. Close the lid and simmer the chicken mixture for 10 minutes over the low heat.
5. Then add grated Parmesan and mix up.
6. Cook chicken bolognese for 5 minutes more over the medium heat.

CALORIES: 154 Kcal  FAT: 9.3 g  PROTEIN: 15.4 g  CARBOHYDRATES: 3 g

---

*Preparation: 10 min*  *Cooking: 30 min*  *Servings: 2*

## 163. JERK CHICKEN

### INGREDIENTS

- 2 chicken thighs, skinless, boneless
- 1 teaspoon fresh ginger, chopped
- 1 garlic clove, chopped
- ½ spring onion, chopped
- 1 teaspoon liquid honey
- 1 teaspoon fresh parsley, chopped
- 1 teaspoon fresh coriander, chopped
- ¼ teaspoon chili flakes
- ¼ teaspoon ground black pepper
- 2 teaspoons lemon juice

### DIRECTIONS

1. Mix up together fresh ginger, garlic, onion, liquid honey, parsley, coriander, chili flakes, and ground black pepper.
2. Rub the chicken thighs with honey mixture generously.
3. Preheat the grill to 385F.
4. Place the chicken thighs in the grill and cook for 30 minutes. Flip the chicken thighs on another side after 15 minutes of cooking. The cooked jerk chicken should have a brown crust.
5. Sprinkle the cooked chicken with lemon juice.

CALORIES: 139 Kcal  FAT: 7.3 g  PROTEIN: 19.4 g  CARBOHYDRATES: 4 g

*Preparation: 7 min*  *Cooking: 20 min*  *Servings: 2*

## 164. LEMON CHICKEN

### INGREDIENTS

- ¼ Teaspoon Black Pepper
- ½ Cup white flour
- 1 Egg
- ¾ lb. Chicken Breast Halves, Skinless & Boneless (Pounded 3/4 Inch Thick & Sliced), or chicken thighs
- 1 Lemon, Cut into Wedges
- 3 Tablespoon olive oil
- 1 Teaspoon balsamic vinegar

### DIRECTIONS

1. Start by beating your eggs with your pepper.
2. Get out a skillet and heat your olive oil using medium heat. Dip the chicken into the egg mixture, spreading the flour into the chicken, shaking any lose ones off.
3. Fry chicken in the pan for about eight minutes per side so that it becomes golden.
4. Drizzle your chicken with lemon juice and balsamic vinegar, then serve.

CALORIES: 310 Kcal    FAT: 10.9 g    PROTEIN: 9.6 g    CARBOHYDRATES: 11.2 g

*Preparation: 10 min* — *Cooking: 30 min* — *Servings: 4*

## 165. CRACK CHICKEN

### INGREDIENTS

- 4 chicken thighs, skinless, boneless
- 1 teaspoon ground black pepper
- ½ teaspoon salt
- 1 teaspoon paprika
- ¼ cup Cheddar cheese, shredded
- 1 tablespoon cream cheese
- ½ teaspoon garlic powder
- 1 teaspoon fresh dill, chopped
- 1 tablespoon butter
- 1 teaspoon olive oil
- ½ teaspoon ground nutmeg

### DIRECTIONS

1. Grease the baking dish with butter.
2. Then heat up olive oil in the skillet.
3. Meanwhile, rub the chicken thighs with ground nutmeg, garlic powder, paprika, and salt. Add ground black pepper.
4. Roast the chicken thighs in the hot oil over the high heat for 2 minutes from each side.
5. Then transfer the chicken thighs in the prepared baking dish.
6. Mix up together Cheddar cheese, cream cheese, and dill.
7. Top every chicken thigh with cheese mixture and bake for 25 minutes at 365F.

CALORIES: 119 Kcal — FAT: 7.3 g — PROTEIN: 5 g — CARBOHYDRATES: 1 g

---

*Preparation: 5 min* — *Cooking: 15 min* — *Servings: 2*

## 166. SPICED TURKEY & GRAPEFRUIT RELISH

### INGREDIENTS

- 1 Grapefruit, Seedless
- 1 Small Shallot, Minced
- 1 Teaspoon Red Wine Vinegar
- 1 Teaspoon Honey, Raw
- 1/2 Small Avocado, Pitted, Peeled & Diced
- 1 Tablespoon Cilantro, Fresh & Chopped
- 2 Turkey Cutlets, 8 Ounces Each
- 1/2 Teaspoon Five Spice Powder
- 1 Tablespoon Chili Powder
- 1 Tablespoon Olive Oil
- Pinch Sea Salt, Fine

### DIRECTIONS

1. Start by peeling your grapefruit and cutting away the white pith. Cut the fruit into segments, making sure to remove the membrane.
2. Squeeze any juice that remains in a bowl, and then add in your vinegar, shallots, honey, avocado and cilantro. Toss to combine, and then set it to the side.
3. Combine the chili powder, salt and five spice powder, coating your turkey in the mixture.
4. Heat the oil in a skillet over medium-high heat, cooking your turkey for three minutes per side. It should still be pink in the middle when you remove it from the pan.
5. Divide your turkey between plates, adding your relish on the side to serve.

CALORIES: 165 Kcal — FAT: 4.9 g — PROTEIN: 6.6 g — CARBOHYDRATES: 9.2 g

Preparation: 10 min  Cooking: 30 min  Servings: 4

# 167. THE SKILLET CHICKEN

## INGREDIENTS

- 12 oz chicken breast, skinless, boneless, chopped
- 1 tablespoon taco seasoning
- 1 tablespoon nut oil
- ½ teaspoon cayenne pepper
- ½ teaspoon salt
- ½ teaspoon garlic, chopped
- ½ red onion, sliced
- 1/3 cup black beans, canned, rinsed
- 10 baby carrots

## DIRECTIONS

1. Rub the chopped chicken breast with taco seasoning, salt, and cayenne pepper.
2. Place the chicken in the skillet, add nut oil and roast it for 10 minutes over the medium heat. Mix up the chicken pieces from time to time to avoid burning.
3. After this, transfer the chicken in the plate.
4. Add sliced onion, garlic and the carrots in the skillet. Roast the vegetables for 5 minutes. Stir them constantly. Add some water and cook the ingredients for 10 minutes more.
5. Add the chopped chicken and mix up well.
6. Close the lid and cook the meal for 3 minutes, then serve.

CALORIES: 184 Kcal   FAT: 6.3 g   PROTEIN: 22.4 g   CARBOHYDRATES: 13 g

*Preparation: 10 min*     *Cooking: 10 min*     *Servings: 2*

## 168. POMEGRANATE CHICKEN THIGHS

### INGREDIENTS

- 1 tablespoon pomegranate molasses
- 8 oz chicken thighs (4 oz each chicken thigh)
- ½ teaspoon paprika
- 1 teaspoon cornstarch
- ½ teaspoon chili flakes
- ½ teaspoon ground black pepper
- 1 teaspoon olive oil
- ½ teaspoon lime juice

### DIRECTIONS

1. In the shallow bowl mix up together ground black pepper, chili flakes, paprika, and cornstarch.
2. Rub the chicken thighs with spice mixture.
3. Heat up olive oil in the skillet.
4. Add chicken thighs and roast them for 4 minutes from each side over the medium heat.
5. When the chicken thighs are light brown, sprinkle them with pomegranate molasses and roast for 1 minute from each side.

CALORIES: 347 Kcal     FAT: 21.3 g     PROTEIN: 30.4 g     CARBOHYDRATES: 9 g

*Preparation: 15 min*     *Cooking: 30 min*     *Servings: 5*

## 169. BUTTER CHICKEN

### INGREDIENTS

- 1-pound chicken fillet
- 1/3 cup butter, softened
- 1 tablespoon rosemary
- ½ teaspoon thyme
- 1 teaspoon salt
- ½ lemon

### DIRECTIONS

1. Churn together thyme, salt, and rosemary.
2. Chop the chicken fillet roughly and mix up with churned butter mixture.
3. Place the prepared chicken in the baking dish.
4. Squeeze the lemon over the chicken.
5. Chop the squeezed lemon and add in the baking dish.
6. Cover the chicken with foil and bake it for 20 minutes at 365F.
7. Then discard the foil and bake the chicken for 10 minutes more.

CALORIES: 254 Kcal     FAT: 19.3 g     PROTEIN: 36.4 g     CARBOHYDRATES: 1 g

*Preparation: 10 min*  **Cooking: 3 hour**  *Servings: 4*

## 170. FLAVORFUL LEMON CHICKEN TACOS

### INGREDIENTS

- 2 lbs chicken breasts, boneless
- 14.5 oz salsa
- 1 tablespoon taco seasoning, homemade
- 2 fresh lime juice
- ¼ cup fresh parsley, chopped
- ¼ teaspoon red chili powder
- Pepper
- Salt
- 4 tacos
- 2 peppers

### DIRECTIONS

1. Chop the chicken into pieces, than place it in the crockpot.
2. Pour the salsa, the seasonings, the peppers and the onions over the chicken.
3. Cover the crockpot and cook on low flame for 3 hours, being careful to don't let it go too high on temperature.
4. Serve directly in the tacos.

CALORIES: 235 Kcal  FAT: 8 g  PROTEIN: 30 g  CARBOHYDRATES: 5 g

*Preparation: 10 min*     *Cooking: 45 min*     *Servings: 6*

## 171. BBQ PULLED CHICKEN

### INGREDIENTS

- 1.5 pound chicken breast, skinless, boneless
- 2 tablespoons BBQ sauce
- 1 tablespoon butter
- 1 teaspoon Dijon mustard
- 1 tablespoon olive oil
- 1 teaspoon cream cheese
- 1 teaspoon salt
- 1 teaspoon cayenne pepper

### DIRECTIONS

1. Sprinkle the chicken breast with cayenne pepper, salt, and olive oil.
2. Place it in the baking tray and bake for 35 minutes at 365F. Flip it from time to time to avoid burning.
3. When the chicken breast is cooked, transfer it on the chopping board and shred with the help of the fork.
4. Put the shredded chicken in the saucepan.
5. Add butter, cream cheese, mustard, and BBQ sauce. Mix up gently and heat it up until boiling.
6. Remove the cooked meal from the heat and stir well.

CALORIES: 154 Kcal     FAT: 7.3 g     PROTEIN: 24.4 g     CARBOHYDRATES: 2 g

---

*Preparation: 10 min*     *Cooking: 4 hours*     *Servings: 6*

## 172. CRISP CHICKEN CARNITAS

### INGREDIENTS

- 2 lbs chicken breasts, skinless and boneless
- ¼ cup fresh parsley, chopped
- 1 tablespoon garlic, minced
- 2 teaspoon cumin powder
- 2 tablespoon fresh lime juice
- 1 tablespoon chili powder
- ½ teaspoon salt

### DIRECTIONS

1. Add chicken into the crockpot.
2. Pour remaining ingredients over the chicken.
3. Cover and cook on low flame for 4 hours.
4. Shred the chicken using a fork.
5. Transfer shredded chicken on a baking tray and broil for 5 minutes.
6. Serve and enjoy.

CALORIES: 225 Kcal     FAT: 8.7 g     PROTEIN: 33.2 g     CARBOHYDRATES: 2.1 g

Preparation: 10 min  Cooking: 15 min  Servings: 4

## 173. DELICIOUS CHICKEN TENDERS

### INGREDIENTS

- 1 ½ lbs chicken tenders
- 2 tablespoon BBQ sauce, homemade & sugar-free
- 1 tablespoon olive oil
- 1 teaspoon poultry seasoning
- Pepper

### DIRECTIONS

1. Add all ingredients except oil in a zip-lock bag. Seal bag and place in the fridge for 2 hours. You can skip this step if you don't have time, but the result will be worse.
2. Heat oil in a pan over medium heat.
3. Place marinated chicken tenders on the hot pan and cook until browned.
4. Serve and enjoy.
5. *if you like, you can also cook the chicken on the grill. The result will be amazing!

CALORIES: 366 Kcal  FAT: 15 g  PROTEIN: 50 g  CARBOHYDRATES: 3 g

*Preparation: 10 min*  *Cooking: 5 min*  Servings: 2

# 174. CILANTRO LIME CHICKEN SALAD

## INGREDIENTS

- 1 ½ cups cooked chicken, shredded
- 2 tablespoon fresh lime juice
- 2 tablespoon fresh cilantro, chopped
- 2 tablespoon green onion, sliced
- 1 teaspoon chili powder
- Pepper

## DIRECTIONS

1. Add all ingredients into the medium bowl and mix well.
2. Season with pepper and salt, then serve.

CALORIES: 113 Kcal   FAT: 2 g   PROTEIN: 20 g   CARBOHYDRATES: 1 g

---

*Preparation: 10 min*  *Cooking: 3 hours*  Servings: 8

# 175. SHREDDED TURKEY BREAST

## INGREDIENTS

- 4 lbs turkey breast, skinless, boneless, and halves
- 1 ½ tablespoon taco seasoning, homemade
- 12 oz chicken stock
- ½ cup butter, cubed
- Pepper
- Salt

## DIRECTIONS

1. Place turkey breast into the crockpot.
2. Pour remaining ingredients over turkey breast.
3. Cover and cook on low flame for 3 hours.
4. Shred turkey breast with a fork.
5. Serve and enjoy.

CALORIES: 327 Kcal   FAT: 15.4 g   PROTEIN: 34.3 g   CARBOHYDRATES: 11.8 g

*Preparation: 4 min*  *Cooking: 4 hours*  Servings: 8

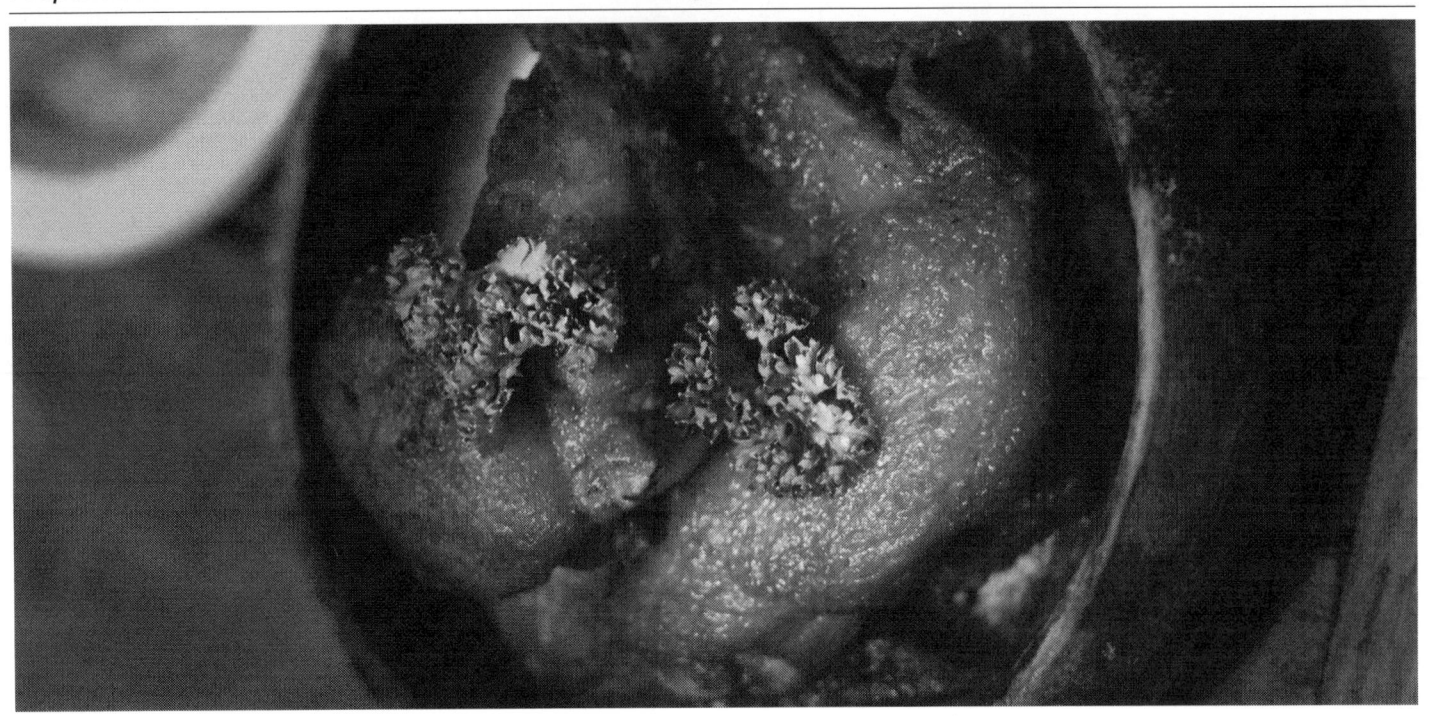

## 176. TENDER TURKEY

### INGREDIENTS

- 4 lbs turkey breast, bone-in
- ½ cup chicken stock
- 6 garlic cloves, peeled
- 3 fresh rosemary sprigs
- Pepper
- Salt

### DIRECTIONS

1. Place turkey breast into a pot. Season with pepper and salt.
2. Add stock, garlic, and rosemary on top.
3. Cover and cook on low flame for 4 hours.
4. Serve and enjoy.

CALORIES: 235 Kcal    FAT: 3.5 g    PROTEIN: 39 g    CARBOHYDRATES: 10 g

*Preparation: 10 min*  *Cooking: 30 min*  *Servings: 4*

## 177. STUFFED CHICKEN

### INGREDIENTS

- 4 chicken breasts, skinless, boneless and butterflied
- 1 ounce spring onions, chopped
- ½ pound white mushrooms, sliced
- 1 teaspoon hot paprika
- A pinch of salt and black pepper
- 1 cup tomato sauce

### DIRECTIONS

1. Flatten chicken breasts with a meat mallet and place them on a plate.
2. In a bowl, mix the spring onions with the mushrooms, paprika, salt and pepper and stir well.
3. Divide this on each chicken breast half, roll them and secure with a toothpick.
4. Add the tomato sauce in the instant pot, put the chicken rolls inside as well. put the lid on and cook on High for 30 minutes.
5. Release the pressure naturally for 10 minutes, arrange the stuffed chicken breasts on a platter and serve.

CALORIES: 221 Kcal    FAT: 12 g    PROTEIN: 11 g    CARBOHYDRATES: 6 g

---

*Preparation: 10 min*  *Cooking: 10 min*  *Servings: 6*

## 178. GRILLED PESTO CHICKEN

### INGREDIENTS

- 1 ½ lbs chicken breasts, skinless, boneless, and slice
- ¼ cup pesto
- ½ cup mozzarella cheese, shredded
- Pepper
- Salt

### DIRECTIONS

1. Place chicken into the large bowl.
2. Add pesto, pepper, and salt over chicken and coat well. Cover and place in the fridge for 2 hours.
3. Heat grill over medium-high heat.
4. Place marinated chicken on hot grill and cook until completely done.
5. Sprinkle cheese over chicken.
6. Serve and enjoy.

CALORIES: 300 Kcal    FAT: 14 g    PROTEIN: 40 g    CARBOHYDRATES: 1 g

*Preparation:* 10 min  *Cooking:* 4 hours  Servings: 4

## 179. CHICKEN CHILI

### INGREDIENTS

- 1 lb chicken breasts, skinless and boneless
- 14 oz can tomato, diced
- 2 cups of water
- 1 jalapeno pepper, chopped
- 1 poblano pepper, chopped
- 12 oz can green chilies
- ½ teaspoon paprika
- ½ teaspoon dried sage
- ½ teaspoon cumin
- 1 teaspoon dried oregano
- ½ cup dried chives
- 1 teaspoon sea salt

### DIRECTIONS

1. Add all ingredients into the crockpot and stir well.
2. Cover and cook on low for 4 hours.
3. Shred the chicken using a fork.
4. Stir well and serve, if you like, with Basmati rice.

CALORIES: 265 Kcal   FAT: 8.9 g   PROTEIN: 34.9 g   CARBOHYDRATES: 11.1 g

*Preparation: 10 min*  *Cooking: 2 hours*  *Servings: 6*

## 180. EASY & TASTY SALSA CHICKEN

**INGREDIENTS**

- 1 ½ lbs chicken tenders, skinless
- ¼ teaspoon garlic powder
- ⅛ teaspoon ground cumin
- ⅛ teaspoon oregano
- 15 oz tomato sauce
- ¼ teaspoon onion powder
- ¼ teaspoon chili powder
- Pepper
- Salt

**DIRECTIONS**

1. Place chicken tenders into the crockpot.
2. Pour the ingredients over chicken.
3. Cover and cook on high for 2 hours.
4. Shred the chicken using a fork and serve.

CALORIES: 235 Kcal  FAT: 8 g  PROTEIN: 35 g  CARBOHYDRATES: 5 g

---

*Preparation: 10 min*  *Cooking: 5 min*  *Servings: 2*

## 181. BACON CHICKEN SALAD

**INGREDIENTS**

- 2 cups cooked chicken, shredded
- 1 cup cheddar cheese, shredded
- 1 cup celery, chopped
- ½ cup sour cream
- ¼ cup mayonnaise
- ½ cup bacon, crumbles
- 3 green onions, sliced
- ¼ cup onion, chopped
- Pepper
- Salt

**DIRECTIONS**

1. Add all ingredients into the large bowl and mix until well combined.
2. Serve and enjoy.

CALORIES: 482 Kcal  FAT: 31.3 g  PROTEIN: 39.6 g  CARBOHYDRATES: 9.9 g

*Preparation: 10 min*     *Cooking: 18 min*     *Servings: 6*

## 182. CHICKEN ZUCCHINI MEATBALLS

### INGREDIENTS

- 1 lb ground chicken
- 2 tablespoon chives, chopped
- ¼ cup almond flour
- 1 ½ cups zucchini, grated & squeeze out all liquid
- 1 teaspoon Italian seasoning
- 1 egg, lightly beaten
- ½ teaspoon salt

### DIRECTIONS

1. Preheat the oven to 350 F.
2. Line baking tray with parchment paper and set aside.
3. Add all ingredients into the mixing bowl and mix until well combined.
4. Make small balls from mixture and place on parchment lined baking tray.
5. Bake for 18 minutes.
6. Serve and enjoy.

CALORIES: 189 Kcal     FAT: 8.8 g     PROTEIN: 24.2 g     CARBOHYDRATES: 2.1 g

*Preparation: 10 min*     *Cooking: 3 hours*     *Servings: 6*

## 183. GREEN SALSA CHICKEN

### INGREDIENTS

- 1 lb chicken breasts, skinless and boneless
- 15 oz green salsa
- Pepper
- Salt

### DIRECTIONS

1. Add all ingredients into the crock pot.
2. Cover and cook on high for 3 hours.
3. Shred the chicken using fork.
4. Serve and enjoy.

CALORIES: 166 Kcal     FAT: 6 g     PROTEIN: 22 g     CARBOHYDRATES: 3 g

---

*Preparation: 10 min*     *Cooking: 3 hours*     *Servings: 6*

## 184. CHEESY SALSA CHICKEN

### INGREDIENTS

- 2 lbs chicken breasts, cut into cubes
- 2 cups cheddar cheese, shredded
- 2 tablespoon taco seasoning
- 2 cups salsa
- Pepper
- Salt

### DIRECTIONS

1. Add all ingredients except cheese into a pot.
2. Cover and cook on low flame for 2 hours 30 minutes.
3. Add cheese and stir well and cook for 30 minutes more.
4. Stir and serve.

CALORIES: 463 Kcal     FAT: 23.8 g     PROTEIN: 24.5 g     CARBOHYDRATES: 5.9 g

*Preparation: 10 min*      *Cooking: 10 min*      *Servings: 6*

## 185. TASTY CHICKEN KABOBS

### INGREDIENTS

- 1 ½ lbs chicken breast, boneless & cut into 1-inch pieces
- 1 teaspoon dried oregano
- 1 tablespoon fresh lime juice
- 1 tablespoon olive oil
- ½ teaspoon pepper
- ½ teaspoon sea salt
- 3 zucchini, diced
- 3 sweet peppers, diced

### DIRECTIONS

1. Add chicken into the mixing bowl. Pour remaining ingredients over chicken and coat well and place it in the refrigerator overnight.
2. Stick with a large toothpick the pieces of chicken, zucchini and sweet peppers.
3. Heat grill over medium heat.
4. Thread marinated chicken onto the skewers.
5. Place chicken skewers onto the hot grill and cook for 8-10 minutes.
6. Serve and enjoy.

CALORIES: 228 Kcal      FAT: 7.8 g      PROTEIN: 36.2 g      CARBOHYDRATES: 1.3 g

*Preparation: 10 min*  *Cooking: 5 min*  *Servings: 4*

## 186. RANCH CHICKEN SALAD

### INGREDIENTS

- 3 cups cooked chicken, shredded
- ½ cup green onion, chopped
- ¾ cup carrots, chopped
- 1 ½ cups celery, chopped
- ½ cup mayonnaise
- ¼ sweet onion, diced
- 1 tablespoon ranch seasoning
- 4 tablespoon hot sauce
- Pepper
- Salt

### DIRECTIONS

1. In a small bowl, mix together hot sauce, ranch seasoning, and mayonnaise.
2. Add remaining ingredients into the large bowl and mix well.
3. Pour hot sauce mixture over salad and mix well.
4. Serve and enjoy.

CALORIES: 275 Kcal   FAT: 13 g   PROTEIN: 20 g   CARBOHYDRATES: 12 g

---

*Preparation: 10 min*  *Cooking: 5 min*  *Servings: 4*

## 187. ALMOND CRANBERRY CHICKEN SALAD

### INGREDIENTS

- 1 lb cooked chicken, shredded
- ¼ teaspoon garlic powder
- 1 celery stalk, chopped
- ¼ cup almonds, sliced
- ¼ cup cranberries, dried
- ¼ cup mayonnaise
- ¼ cup sour cream
- ¼ teaspoon onion powder
- ¼ teaspoon pepper
- ½ teaspoon salt

### DIRECTIONS

1. Add all ingredients into the mixing bowl and mix well.
2. Place in refrigerator for some time.
3. Serve and enjoy.

CALORIES: 175 Kcal   FAT: 12 g   PROTEIN: 8 g   CARBOHYDRATES: 6 g

*Preparation: 10 min* — Cooking: 1 hour — Servings: 4

## 188. HARISSA CHICKEN

### INGREDIENTS

- 1 lb chicken breasts, skinless and boneless
- 1 cup harissa sauce
- ¼ teaspoon garlic powder
- ½ teaspoon ground cumin
- ¼ teaspoon onion powder
- ½ teaspoon kosher salt

### DIRECTIONS

1. Season chicken with garlic powder, onion powder, cumin, and salt.
2. Place chicken into a pot. Pour harissa sauce over chicken.
3. Cover and cook on low flame for 55 minutes.
4. Uncover the pot and roast the chicken for 5 minutes at high flame.
5. Serve and enjoy.

CALORIES: 230 Kcal — FAT: 10 g — PROTEIN: 33 g — CARBOHYDRATES: 2 g

*Preparation: 10 min*  *Cooking: 33 min*  Servings: 4

## 189. ROASTED TOMATO CHICKEN CURRY

**INGREDIENTS**

- 1 ½ lbs chicken thighs, skinless and boneless
- 14 oz can roast tomatoes, diced
- 1 teaspoon ground ginger
- 1 tablespoon curry powder
- 1 tablespoon olive oil
- 14 oz coconut milk
- 1 teaspoon salt

**DIRECTIONS**

1. Add all ingredients into the instant pot and stir well.
2. Cover and cook on high pressure for 22 minutes.
3. Once done, release pressure using quick release. Open the lid.
4. Remove chicken from pot.
5. Set pot on saute mode and cook for 10 minutes.
6. Cut chicken into small pieces and return into the pot.
7. Stir well and serve.

CALORIES: 312 Kcal   FAT: 25 g   PROTEIN: 22.5 g   CARBOHYDRATES: 11.6 g

*Preparation: 10 min*  *Cooking: 2 hours*  Servings: 3

## 190. PESTO CHICKEN

**INGREDIENTS**

- 2 chicken breasts, skinless and boneless
- 1 ½ cups grape tomatoes, halved
- 2 tablespoon pesto
- 2 cups zucchini, chopped
- 2 cups green beans, chopped
- Pepper
- Salt

**DIRECTIONS**

1. Place chicken into a standard pot.
2. Pour remaining ingredients over the chicken.
3. Cover and cook on low flame for 2 hours.
4. Serve and enjoy.

CALORIES: 281 Kcal   FAT: 12 g   PROTEIN: 32.2 g   CARBOHYDRATES: 11.9 g

Preparation: 10 min  Cooking: 45 min  Servings: 6

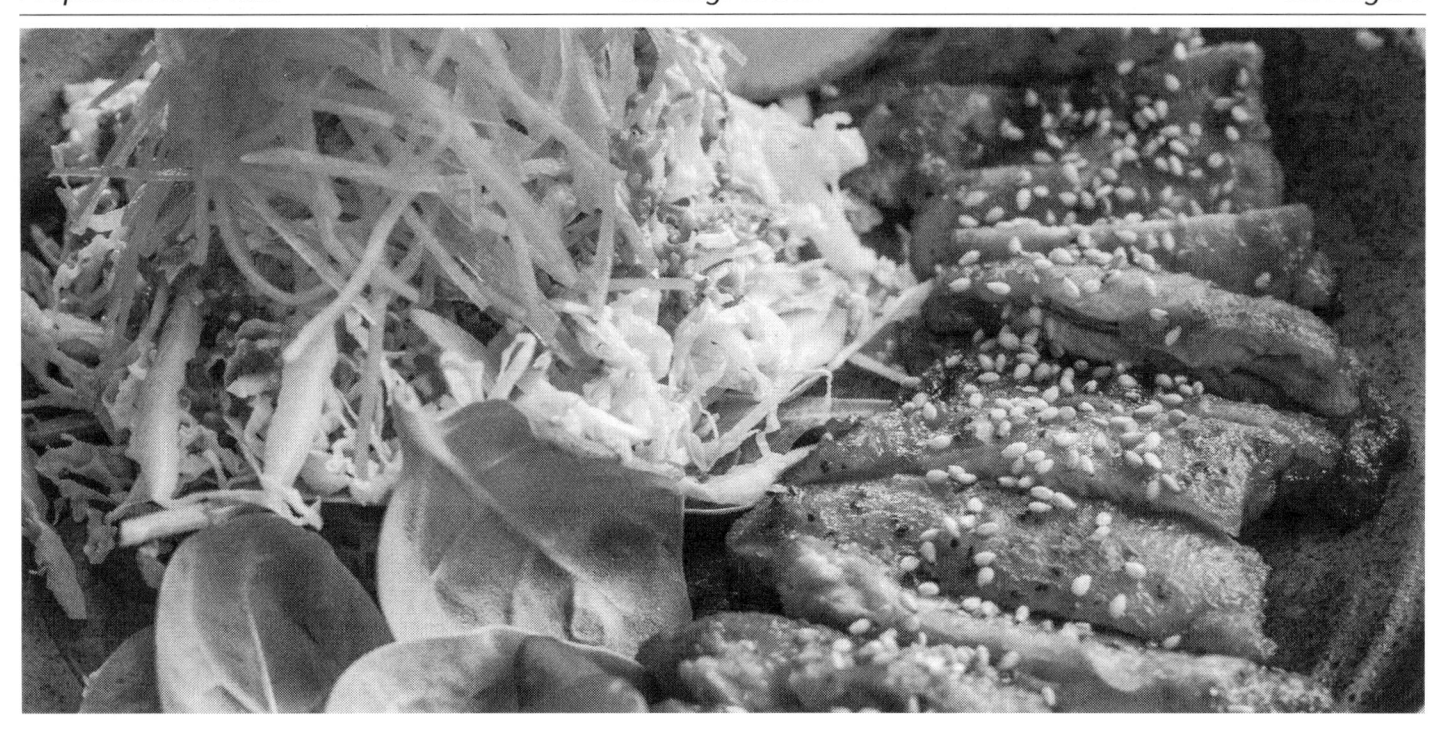

## 191. MARINATED CHICKEN BREASTS

### INGREDIENTS

- 6 chicken breasts, skinless and boneless
- ½ cup olive oil
- ¼ cup soy sauce
- 1 tablespoon oregano
- 2 tablespoon fresh lemon juice
- 1 teaspoon garlic salt
- 1 tablespoon sesame seeds

### DIRECTIONS

1. Add all ingredients into the large zip-lock bag. Seal bag and shake well and place in the fridge for 3-4 hours.
2. Preheat the oven to 350 F.
3. Place marinated chicken into a baking dish and bake for 45 minutes.
4. Serve with some vegetables and enjoy.

CALORIES: 435 Kcal  FAT: 27 g  PROTEIN: 43 g  CARBOHYDRATES: 2 g

*Preparation: 10 min*  *Cooking: 15 min*  *Servings: 1*

## 192. BAKED LEMON CHICKEN

### INGREDIENTS

- 1 chicken breast, boneless
- ½ tablespoon Italian seasoning
- 1 fresh lemon juice
- 1 fresh lemon, sliced
- Pepper
- Salt

### DIRECTIONS

1. Preheat the oven to 350 F.
2. Spray baking dish with cooking spray.
3. Season chicken with Italian seasoning, pepper and salt.
4. Place chicken into the baking dish.
5. Pour lemon juice over chicken and arrange lemon slices on top of chicken.
6. Bake for 15 minutes.
7. Serve and enjoy.

CALORIES: 139 Kcal   FAT: 4.7 g   PROTEIN: 21.4 g   CARBOHYDRATES: 1.6 g

---

*Preparation: 10 min*  *Cooking: 5 min*  *Servings: 6*

## 193. MAYO CHICKEN SALAD

### INGREDIENTS

- 2 lbs cooked chicken, shredded
- 3 celery stalks, chopped
- 1 cup mayonnaise
- ¼ teaspoon garlic powder
- ¼ teaspoon onion powder
- ¼ teaspoon pepper
- ¼ teaspoon salt

### DIRECTIONS

1. Add all ingredients into the large mixing bowl and stir to combine.
2. Serve and enjoy.

CALORIES: 445 Kcal   FAT: 24 g   PROTEIN: 45 g   CARBOHYDRATES: 9 g

*Preparation: 10 min*  *Cooking: 10 min / Refrigeration: 1 hour*  *Servings: 6*

## 194. TASTY CHICKEN BITES

### INGREDIENTS

- 1 lb chicken breasts, boneless and cut into cubes
- 2 tablespoon fresh lemon juice
- 1 tablespoon fresh oregano, chopped
- 2 tablespoon olive oil
- ⅛ teaspoon cayenne pepper
- Pepper
- Salt

### DIRECTIONS

1. Place chicken in a bowl.
2. Add reaming ingredients over chicken and toss well. Place in the fridge for 1 hour.
3. Heat grill over medium heat.
4. Spray grill with cooking spray.
5. Thread marinated chicken onto the skewers.
6. Place skewers on hot grill and cooks until chicken is cooked.
7. Serve and enjoy.

CALORIES: 560 Kcal   FAT: 31 g   PROTEIN: 65 g   CARBOHYDRATES: 2 g

Preparation: 10 min  Cooking: 4 hours  Servings: 4

## 195. DELICIOUS ITALIAN CHICKEN

### INGREDIENTS

- 4 chicken breasts, skinless and boneless
- 1 onion, chopped
- 1 tablespoon garlic, minced
- 2 tablespoon fresh lemon juice
- 2 teaspoon Italian seasoning
- 1 tablespoon olive oil
- 2 tablespoon capers
- 1 cup roasted red peppers, chopped
- 1 cup olives
- Pepper
- Salt

### DIRECTIONS

1. Season chicken with pepper and salt.
2. Heat oil in a pan over medium heat. Place chicken in the pan and cook until browned from both sides.
3. Transfer chicken into a pot.
4. Add remaining ingredients over chicken.
5. Cover and cook on low flame for 4 hours.
6. Serve and enjoy.

CALORIES: 335 Kcal  FAT: 15 g  PROTEIN: 43 g  CARBOHYDRATES: 9 g

---

Preparation: 10 min  Cooking: 1 hour  Servings: 4

## 196. ROASTED PEPPER CHICKEN

### INGREDIENTS

- 4 chicken breasts, skinless and boneless
- 1 cup roasted red peppers, chopped
- 1 tablespoon garlic, minced
- 2 tablespoon capers
- 2 tablespoon lemon juice
- ¾ cup olives, sliced
- 1 medium onion, chopped
- 3 teaspoon Italian seasoning
- Pepper
- Salt

### DIRECTIONS

1. Season chicken with pepper and salt.
2. Cook chicken in a pan until lightly browned.
3. Transfer the chicken into a pot.
4. Add remaining ingredients over chicken.
5. Cover and cook on low flame for 1 hour.
6. Serve and enjoy.

CALORIES: 327 Kcal  FAT: 13.1 g  PROTEIN: 36 g  CARBOHYDRATES: 8.2 g

*Preparation: 10 min*  *Cooking: 16 min / Refrigeration: 2 hours*  Servings: 4

## 197. CHICKEN SHAWARMA

### INGREDIENTS

- 8 chicken thighs, skinless
- 1 tablespoon cumin
- 2 garlic cloves, minced
- 3 tablespoon olive oil
- 2 tablespoon lemon juice
- ½ teaspoon cayenne pepper
- 2 teaspoon paprika
- 1 tablespoon ground cardamom
- 1 tablespoon coriander
- ¼ teaspoon pepper
- 2 teaspoon salt
- 4 pita bread
- 2 sweet peppers, sliced
- 2 red onions, sliced

### DIRECTIONS

1. Add chicken into the zip-lock bag. Pour remaining ingredients over chicken. Seal bag and shake well.
2. Place marinated chicken and vegetables in the refrigerator for 2 hours.
3. Heat grill over medium-high heat.
4. Place marinated chicken on hot grill and cook for 8 minutes on each side.
5. At the same time, place the marinated peppers and onions on the grill and cook for 10 minutes.
6. Clean the chicken from the bone and chop it.
7. Serve in the pitas and enjoy.

CALORIES: 665 Kcal    FAT: 33 g    PROTEIN: 42 g    CARBOHYDRATES: 3 g

*Preparation: 10 min*  *Cooking: 15 min*  *Servings: 4*

## 198. ARTICHOKE BASIL CHICKEN

**INGREDIENTS**

- 1 ½ lbs chicken thighs
- ½ teaspoon dried oregano
- 1 ½ cup marinated artichokes
- 2 cups cherry tomatoes
- 8 fresh basil leaves
- 3 tablespoon balsamic vinegar
- ¼ teaspoon dried thyme
- ¼ teaspoon pepper
- ½ teaspoon salt

**DIRECTIONS**

1. Spray a large pan with cooking spray and heat over medium-high heat.
2. Add chicken in a hot pan and cook for 3 minutes on each side.
3. Add tomatoes, marinated artichokes, vinegar, and seasoning and stir well.
4. Turn heat to medium. Cover and simmer for 10 minutes.
5. Turn heat to high and cook until all liquid reduced.
6. Turn chicken and cook until chicken is lightly browned or until cooked through.
7. Garnish with basil and serve.

CALORIES: 400 Kcal   FAT: 18 g   PROTEIN: 50 g   CARBOHYDRATES: 6 g

*Preparation: 10 min*  *Cooking: 12 min*  *Servings: 4*

## 199. GRILLED GREEK CHICKEN

**INGREDIENTS**

- 1 ½ lbs chicken breasts, skinless and boneless
- 1 tablespoon garlic, minced
- ¼ teaspoon cayenne pepper
- 1 teaspoon fresh thyme
- ½ teaspoon oregano
- 1 tablespoon red wine vinegar
- 3 tablespoon olive oil
- 3 tablespoon fresh lemon juice
- ½ teaspoon pepper
- ½ teaspoon salt

**DIRECTIONS**

1. Add chicken into the zip-lock bag. Pour remaining ingredients over chicken. Seal bag and shake well.
2. Place marinated chicken into the refrigerator overnight.
3. Heat grill over medium-high heat.
4. Place marinated chicken on hot grill and cook for 4-6 minutes on each side.
5. Serve and enjoy.

CALORIES: 420 Kcal   FAT: 23 g   PROTEIN: 40 g   CARBOHYDRATES: 1 g

*Preparation: 10 min*     *Cooking: 10 min*     *Servings: 3*

## 200. GUACAMOLE CHICKEN SALAD

### INGREDIENTS

- 2 chicken breasts, cooked and cubed
- 1 cup cilantro, chopped
- 1 tablespoon fresh lime juice
- 2 avocados, peeled and pitted
- 2 Serrano chili peppers, chopped
- ½ cup celery, chopped
- ½ cup onion, chopped
- 1 teaspoon kosher salt

### DIRECTIONS

1. Add avocados and lime juice into the bowl and mash using a fork.
2. Add remaining ingredients into the bowl and stir to combine.
3. Serve and enjoy.

CALORIES: 477 Kcal     FAT: 33.4 g     PROTEIN: 31.2 g     CARBOHYDRATES: 15.9 g

---

*Preparation: 10 min*     *Cooking: 5 min*     *Servings: 1*

## 201. GREEK CHICKEN SALAD

### INGREDIENTS

- 1 cup cooked chicken, shredded
- 2 teaspoon fresh basil, chopped
- ¼ cup cucumber, diced
- 1 teaspoon vinegar
- 1 tablespoon sour cream
- Pepper
- Salt

### DIRECTIONS

1. Add all ingredients into the medium bowl and mix well to combine.
2. Season with pepper and salt. Place in refrigerator for 10 minutes.
3. Serve and enjoy.

CALORIES: 243 Kcal     FAT: 6.8 g     PROTEIN: 41.2 g     CARBOHYDRATES: 1.6 g

*Preparation: 10 min*  *Cooking: 15 min*  *Servings: 4*

## 202. GREEK TURKEY BURGERS

### INGREDIENTS

- ⅓ cup feta cheese, crumbled
- 1 teaspoon dill
- 1 egg white
- 7 ounces roasted red bell peppers, sliced
- ½ cup breadcrumbs
- 4 whole-wheat buns
- ¾ cup mint, chopped
- 1 cup red onion, sliced
- 1 pound ground turkey
- 2 tablespoons lemon juice
- Canola oil as needed
- 4 Iceberg salad leaves

### DIRECTIONS

1. In a mixing bowl, beat the egg whites. Add the mint, breadcrumbs, onions, feta cheese, lemon juice, dill and turkey; combine well.
2. Form 4 patties from the mixture.
3. Over medium stove flame, heat the oil in a skillet or saucepan (preferably of medium size).
4. Add the patties and cook them until evenly brown on both sides.
5. Serve the patties in the buns topping them with roasted peppers and iceberg leaves.

CALORIES: 362 Kcal    FAT: 13 g    PROTEIN: 33 g    CARBOHYDRATES: 38 g

---

*Preparation: 25 min*  *Cooking: 30 min*  *Servings: 5*

## 203. CASHEW BROCCOLI CHICKEN

### INGREDIENTS

- ½ cup carrots, chopped
- 1/3 cup unsalted cashews
- 3 green onions, chopped
- 1 cup sugar snap peas
- 1 red bell pepper, chopped
- 2 cups broccoli florets
- 1 pound chicken breasts, cubed
- 1 tablespoon olive oil
- 3 cloves garlic, crushed
- 1 teaspoon sesame oil
- 2 tablespoons honey
- 3 tablespoons peanut butter
- 3 tablespoons water
- 1 tablespoon crushed ginger
- 4 tablespoons soy sauce

### DIRECTIONS

1. In a mixing bowl, add the sauce ingredients and mix them together.
2. Over medium stove flame, heat the oil in a skillet or saucepan (preferably of medium size).
3. Add the chicken and cook it until evenly brown; season with garlic, salt, and black pepper.
4. Add the broccoli, snap peas, bell pepper, and carrots and fry for 5-6 minutes, stirring often.
5. Add the sauce and combine well. Add in the cashews, mix and serve warm.

CALORIES: 235 Kcal    FAT: 9 g    PROTEIN: 26 g    CARBOHYDRATES: 21 g

Preparation: 35 min Cooking: 15 min Servings: 4

## 204. MEDITERRANEAN WHITE WINE CHICKEN

### INGREDIENTS

- 3 cloves garlic, minced
- ½ cup diced onion
- 3 cups tomatoes, chopped
- 2 teaspoons olive oil
- 4 skinless, boneless chicken breast halves
- ½ cup + 2 tablespoons white wine
- 1 tablespoon chopped basil
- ¼ cup chopped parsley
- 2 teaspoons chopped thyme
- Ground black pepper and salt to taste

### DIRECTIONS

1. Over medium flame, heat the oil and 2 tablespoons white wine in a skillet or saucepan (preferably of medium size).
2. Add the chicken and fry until evenly brown. Set it aside.
3. Add the garlic and sauté for 30 seconds. Add the onion and sauté for 2-3 minutes.
4. Mix in the tomatoes and bring the mixture to a simmer.
5. Reduce the heat and mix in ½ cup white wine; simmer the mix for 10 minutes and add the basil and thyme. Cook for another 5 minutes.
6. Add the chicken; combine and cook over low heat for 7-10 minutes. Add the parsley on top. Season with black pepper and salt.
7. Serve warm.

CALORIES: 239 Kcal FAT: 8 g PROTEIN: 36 g CARBOHYDRATES: 14 g

---

Preparation: 20 min Cooking: 15 min Servings: 4

## 205. MEDITERRANEAN FETA CHICKEN

### INGREDIENTS

- 2 tablespoons olive oil
- 1 cup crumbled feta cheese
- 2 (6-ounce) boneless and skinless chicken breast halves
- 1 teaspoon Greek seasoning
- ⅓ cup chopped sun-dried tomatoes

### DIRECTIONS

1. Preheat your oven to 375°F (190°C). Line a baking pan with parchment paper. Grease it with some avocado oil. (You can also use cooking spray)
2. Mix the feta cheese and tomatoes in a mixing bowl.
3. Coat the chicken with olive oil and season with the seasoning. Add the cheese mixture and roll up chicken breasts. Secure with a toothpick, pinning them.
4. Place the chicken into the pan; bake for 25-30 minutes. Remove the toothpicks and serve warm.

CALORIES: 204 Kcal FAT: 14 g PROTEIN: 19 g CARBOHYDRATES: 9 g

# 18 Meat

Preparation: 10 min    Cooking: 3 hours    Servings: 4

## 206. TENDER LAMB CHOPS

### INGREDIENTS

- 8 lamb chops
- ½ teaspoon dried thyme
- 1 onion, sliced
- 1 teaspoon dried oregano
- 2 garlic cloves, minced
- 4 baby carrots
- Pepper and salt
- 2 potatoes, cubed
- 8 small tomatoes, halved

### DIRECTIONS

1. Add the onion, carrots, tomatoes and potatoes into a pot.
2. Combine together thyme, oregano, pepper, and salt. Rub over lamb chops.
3. Place lamb chops in the pot and top with garlic.
4. Pour ¼ cup water around the lamb chops.
5. Cover and cook on low flame for around 3 hours.
6. Uncover the pot and roast at high flame for 10 minutes.
7. Serve and enjoy.

CALORIES: 210 Kcal    FAT: 4.1 g    PROTEIN: 20.4 g    CARBOHYDRATES: 7.3 g

*Preparation: 10 min*  *Cooking: 4 hours*  *Servings: 2*

## 207. BEEF STROGANOFF

### INGREDIENTS

- ½ lb beef stew meat
- 10 oz mushroom soup, homemade
- 1 medium onion, chopped
- ½ cup sour cream
- 2.5 oz mushrooms, sliced
- Pepper and salt

### DIRECTIONS

1. Add all ingredients except sour cream into a pot and mix well.
2. Cover and cook on low flame for 4 hours.
3. Add sour cream and stir well.
4. Serve and enjoy.

CALORIES: 470 Kcal    FAT: 25 g    PROTEIN: 49 g    CARBOHYDRATES: 8.6 g

---

*Preparation: 7 min*  *Cooking: 25 min*  *Servings: 2*

## 208. LAMB & COUSCOUS SALAD

### INGREDIENTS

- ½ Cup Water
- ½ Tablespoon Garlic, Minced
- 1 ¼ lb. Lamb Loin Chops, Trimmed
- ¼ Cup Couscous, Whole Wheat
- Pinch Sea Salt
- ½ Tablespoon Parsley, Fresh & Chopped Fine
- 1 Tomato, Chopped
- 1 Teaspoon Olive Oil
- 1 Small Cucumber, Chopped
- 1 ½ Tablespoons Lemon Juice, Fresh
- ¼ Cup Feta, Crumbled
- 1 Tablespoon Dill, Fresh & Chopped Fine

### DIRECTIONS

1. Get out a saucepan and bring the water to a boil.
2. Get out a bowl and mix your garlic, salt and parsley. Press this mixture into the side of each lamb chop, and then heat your oil using medium-high heat in a skillet.
3. Add the lamb, cooking for six minutes per side. Place it to the side, and cover to help keep the lamb chops warm.
4. Stir the couscous into the water once it's started to boil, returning it to a boil before reducing it to low so that it simmers.
5. Cover, then cook for about two minutes more. Remove from heat, and allow it to stand uncovered for five minutes.
6. Fluff using a fork, and then add in your tomatoes, lemon juice, feta and dill. Stir well.
7. Serve on the side of your lamb chops.

CALORIES: 232 Kcal    FAT: 7.9 g    PROTEIN: 5.6 g    CARBOHYDRATES: 31.2 g

Preparation: 10 min  Cooking: 3 hours  Servings: 6

## 209. SMOKY PORK & CABBAGE

### INGREDIENTS

- 3lb pork
- ½ cabbage head, chopped
- 1 cup water
- ⅓ cup liquid smoke
- 1 tablespoon kosher salt

### DIRECTIONS

1. Rub the pork with kosher salt and place into a pot.
2. Pour liquid smoke over the pork. Add water.
3. Cover and cook on low flame for 2 hours.
4. Remove pork from the pot and add cabbage in the bottom.
5. Place pork on top of the cabbage.
6. Cover again and cook for 1 hour more.
7. Slice the pork and serve.

CALORIES: 484 Kcal    FAT: 21.5 g    PROTEIN: 36 g    CARBOHYDRATES: 4 g

*Preparation: 10 min*      Cooking: 3 hours      Servings: 4

## 210. LEMON BEEF

### INGREDIENTS

- 1 lb beef chuck roast
- 1 fresh lime juice
- 1 garlic clove, crushed
- 1 teaspoon chili powder
- 2 cups lemon-lime soda
- ½ teaspoon salt

### DIRECTIONS

1. Place beef chuck roast into a pot.
2. Season roast with garlic, chili powder, and salt.
3. Pour lemon-lime soda over the roast.
4. Cover the pot with lid and cook on low flame for 3 hours. Shred the meat using fork.
5. Add lime juice over shredded roast and serve.

CALORIES: 355 Kcal      FAT: 16.8 g      PROTEIN: 35.5 g      CARBOHYDRATES: 14 g

---

*Preparation: 10 min*      Cooking: 2 hours      Servings: 8

## 211. HERB PORK ROAST

### INGREDIENTS

- 5 lbs pork roast, boneless or bone-in
- 1 tablespoon dry herb mix
- 4 garlic cloves, cut into slivers
- 1 tablespoon salt

### DIRECTIONS

1. Using a sharp knife make small cuts all over meat then insert garlic slivers into the cuts.
2. In a small bowl, mix together Italian herb mix and salt and rub all over pork roast.
3. Place the pork roast into a pot.
4. Cover and cook on low flame for 2 hours.
5. Uncover the pot and roast at high flame for 10 minutes.
6. Remove the meat from the pot and slice it.
7. Serve and enjoy.

CALORIES: 327 Kcal      FAT: 8 g      PROTEIN: 59 g      CARBOHYDRATES: 0.5 g

*Preparation: 10 min*     Cooking: 3 hours     *Servings: 6*

## 212. SEASONED PORK CHOPS

### INGREDIENTS

- 4 pork chops
- 2 garlic cloves, minced
- 1 cup chicken broth
- 1 tablespoon poultry seasoning
- ¼ cup olive oil
- Pepper and salt

### DIRECTIONS

1. In a bowl, whisk together olive oil, poultry seasoning, garlic, broth, pepper, and salt.
2. Pour olive oil mixture into the slow cooker then place pork chops in the pot.
3. Cover and cook on low flame for about 3 hours.
4. Uncover the pot and roast at high flame for 10 minutes.
5. Dress the pork in the cooking sauce and serve along with vegetables.

CALORIES: 386 Kcal     FAT: 32.9 g     PROTEIN: 20 g     CARBOHYDRATES: 3 g

*Preparation: 10 min*     *Cooking: 2 hours*     *Servings: 6*

## 213. GREEK BEEF ROAST

**INGREDIENTS**

- 2 lbs lean top round beef roast
- 1 tablespoon Italian seasoning
- 6 garlic cloves, minced
- 1 onion, sliced
- 2 cups beef broth
- ½ cup red wine
- 1 teaspoon red pepper flakes
- Pepper
- Salt

**DIRECTIONS**

1. Season meat with pepper and salt and place into a pot.
2. Pour remaining ingredients over meat.
3. Cover and cook on low flame for 2 hours.
4. Slice the meat, dress with cooking sauce and serve.

CALORIES: 231 Kcal     FAT: 6 g     PROTEIN: 35 g     CARBOHYDRATES: 4 g

---

*Preparation: 10 min*     *Cooking: 1 hour and 10 min*     *Servings: 4*

## 214. TOMATO PORK CHOPS

**INGREDIENTS**

- 4 pork chops, bone-in
- 1 tablespoon garlic, minced
- ½ small onion, chopped
- 6 oz can tomato paste
- 1 bell pepper, chopped
- ¼ teaspoon red pepper flakes
- 1 teaspoon Worcestershire sauce
- 1 tablespoon dried Italian seasoning
- 14.5 oz can tomatoes, diced
- 2 teaspoon olive oil
- ¼ teaspoon pepper
- 1 teaspoon kosher salt

**DIRECTIONS**

1. Heat oil in a pan over medium-high heat.
2. Season pork chops with pepper and salt.
3. Sear pork chops in pan until brown from both the sides.
4. Transfer the pork chops into a pot.
5. Add the remaining ingredients to the pot.
6. Cover and cook on low flame for 1 hour.
7. Remove the lid and roast for about 10 minutes.
8. Serve and enjoy.

CALORIES: 325 Kcal     FAT: 23.4 g     PROTEIN: 20 g     CARBOHYDRATES: 10 g

Preparation: 10 min  Cooking: 1 hour and 35 min  Servings: 6

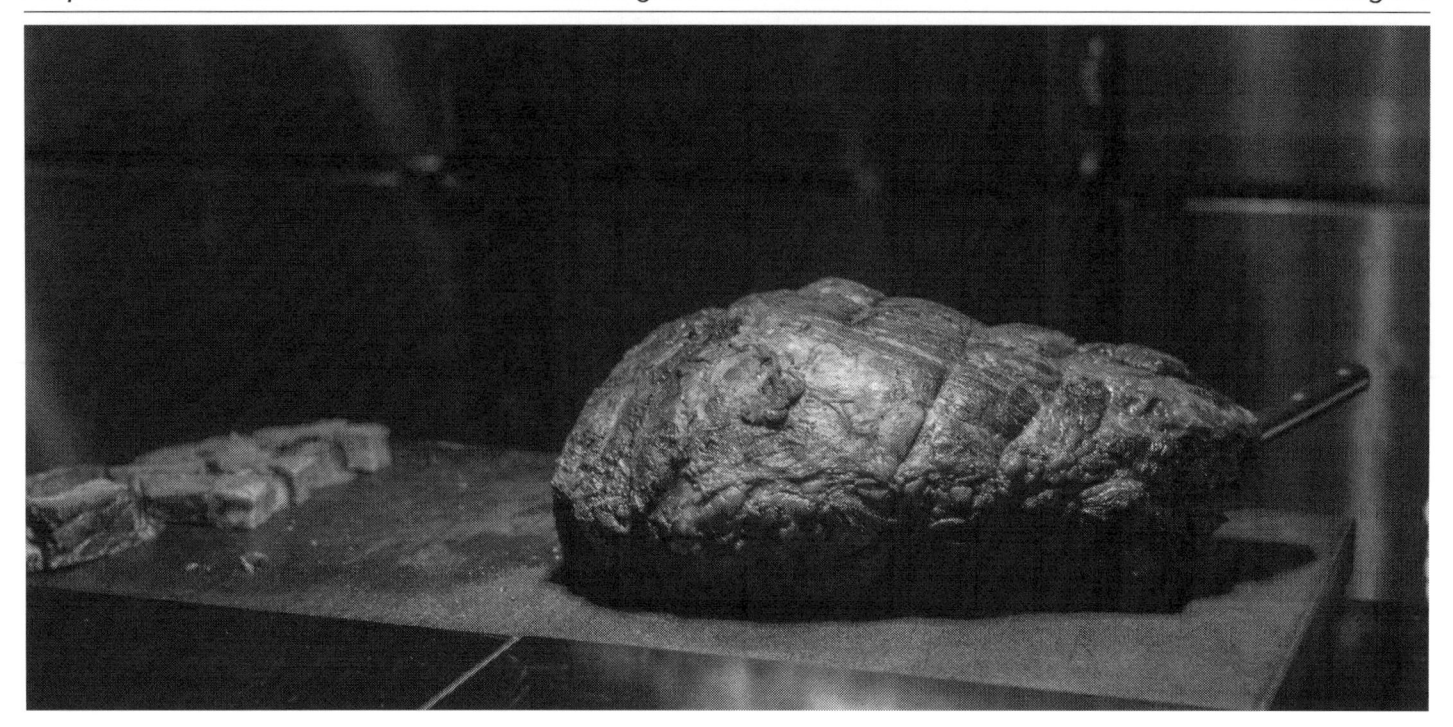

## 215. PORK ROAST

### INGREDIENTS

- 3 lbs pork roast, boneless
- 1 cup water
- 1 onion, chopped
- 3 garlic cloves, chopped
- 1 tablespoon black pepper
- 1 rosemary sprig
- 2 fresh oregano sprigs
- 2 fresh thyme sprigs
- 1 tablespoon olive oil
- 1 tablespoon kosher salt

### DIRECTIONS

1. Season pork roast with pepper and salt.
2. Heat olive oil in a stockpot and sear pork roast on each side, about 4 minutes.
3. Add onion and garlic. Pour in the water, oregano, and thyme and bring to boil for a minute.
4. Cover pot and roast in the preheated oven for 1 ½ hours.
5. Serve and enjoy.

CALORIES: 502 Kcal  FAT: 23.8 g  PROTEIN: 65 g  CARBOHYDRATES: 3 g

*Preparation: 10 min*     *Cooking: 15 min*     *Servings: 4*

# 216. GREEK PORK CHOPS

## INGREDIENTS

- 8 pork chops, boneless
- 4 teaspoon dried oregano
- 2 tablespoon Worcestershire sauce
- 3 tablespoon fresh lemon juice
- ¼ cup olive oil
- 1 teaspoon ground mustard
- 2 teaspoon garlic powder
- 2 teaspoon onion powder
- Pepper
- Salt

## DIRECTIONS

1. Whisk together oil, garlic powder, onion powder, oregano, Worcestershire sauce, lemon juice, mustard, pepper, and salt.
2. Place pork chops in a baking dish then pour marinade over pork chops and coat well. Place in refrigerator overnight.
3. Preheat the grill.
4. Place pork chops on hot grill and cook for 7-8 minutes on each side.
5. Serve and enjoy.

CALORIES: 324 Kcal     FAT: 26.5 g     PROTEIN: 18 g     CARBOHYDRATES: 2.5 g

---

*Preparation: 10 min*     *Cooking: 2 hours*     *Servings: 4*

# 217. PORK CACCIATORE

## INGREDIENTS

- 1 ½ lbs pork chops
- 1 teaspoon dried oregano
- 1 cup beef broth
- 3 tablespoon tomato paste
- 14 oz can tomatoes, diced
- 2 cups mushrooms, sliced
- 1 small onion, diced
- 1 garlic clove, minced
- 2 tablespoon olive oil
- ¼ teaspoon pepper
- ½ teaspoon salt

## DIRECTIONS

1. Heat oil in a pan over medium-high heat.
2. Add pork chops in pan and cook until brown on both the sides.
3. Transfer pork chops into a pot.
4. Pour remaining ingredients over the pork chops.
5. Cover and cook on low flame for 2 hours.
6. Serve and enjoy.

CALORIES: 440 Kcal     FAT: 33 g     PROTEIN: 28 g     CARBOHYDRATES: 6 g

Preparation: 10 min    Cooking: 10 min    Servings: 6

## 218. EASY BEEF KOFTA

### INGREDIENTS

- 2 lbs ground beef
- 4 garlic cloves, minced
- 1 onion, minced
- 2 teaspoon cumin
- 1 cup fresh parsley, chopped
- ¼ teaspoon pepper
- 1 teaspoon salt
- 1 tablespoon oil

### DIRECTIONS

1. With a knife, chop the beef very well.
2. Add all the ingredients except oil into the mixing bowl and mix until combined.
3. Roll meat mixture into mini-kabab shapes.
4. Add the oil to a pan and heat at high flame.
5. Roast the meat in the hot pan for 4-6 minutes on each side or until cooked.
6. Serve with some vegetables and a sauce if you like.

CALORIES: 223 Kcal    FAT: 7.3 g    PROTEIN: 35 g    CARBOHYDRATES: 2.5 g

*Preparation: 10 min*  *Cooking: 30 min*  *Servings: 6*

## 219. PORK WITH TOMATO & OLIVES

### INGREDIENTS

- 6 pork chops, boneless and cut into thick slices
- ⅛ teaspoon ground cinnamon
- ½ cup olives, pitted and sliced
- 8 oz can tomatoes, crushed
- ¼ cup beef broth
- 2 garlic cloves, chopped
- 1 large onion, sliced
- 1 tablespoon olive oil

### DIRECTIONS

1. Heat olive oil in a pan over medium-high heat.
2. Place pork chops in a pan and cook until lightly brown and set aside.
3. Cook garlic and onion in the same pan over medium heat, until onion is softened.
4. Add broth and bring to boil over high heat.
5. Return pork to pan and stir in crushed tomatoes and remaining ingredients.
6. Cover and simmer for 20 minutes.
7. Serve and enjoy.

CALORIES: 321 Kcal  FAT: 23 g  PROTEIN: 19 g  CARBOHYDRATES: 7 g

---

*Preparation: 10 min*  *Cooking: 8 min*  *Servings: 4*

## 220. JALAPENO LAMB PATTIES

### INGREDIENTS

- 1 lb ground lamb
- 1 jalapeno pepper, minced
- 5 basil leaves, minced
- 10 mint leaves, minced
- ¼ cup fresh parsley, chopped
- 1 cup feta cheese, crumbled
- 1 tablespoon garlic, minced
- 1 teaspoon dried oregano
- ¼ teaspoon pepper
- ½ teaspoon kosher salt

### DIRECTIONS

1. Add all ingredients into the mixing bowl and mix until well combined.
2. Preheat the grill to 450 F.
3. Spray grill with cooking spray.
4. Make four equal shape patties from meat mixture and place on hot grill and cook for 3 minutes. Turn patties to another side and cook for 4 minutes.
5. Serve and enjoy.

CALORIES: 317 Kcal  FAT: 16 g  PROTEIN: 37.5 g  CARBOHYDRATES: 3 g

Preparation: 10 min     Cooking: 25 min     Servings: 4

## 221. RED PEPPER PORK TENDERLOIN

### INGREDIENTS

- 1 lb pork tenderloin
- ¾ teaspoon red pepper
- 2 teaspoon dried oregano
- 1 tablespoon olive oil
- 3 tablespoon feta cheese, crumbled
- 3 tablespoon olive tapenade

### DIRECTIONS

1. Add pork, oil, red pepper, and oregano in a zip-lock bag and rub well and place in a refrigerator for 2 hours.
2. Remove pork from zip-lock bag. Using sharp knife make lengthwise cut through the center of the tenderloin.
3. Spread olive tapenade on half tenderloin and sprinkle with feta cheese.
4. Fold another half of meat over to the original shape of tenderloin.
5. Tie close pork tenderloin with twine at 2-inch intervals.
6. Grill the pork tenderloin for 20 minutes.
7. Cut into slices and serve with some vegetables.

CALORIES: 215 Kcal     FAT: 9.1 g     PROTEIN: 30.8 g     CARBOHYDRATES: 1 g

*Preparation: 10 min*     *Cooking: 2 hours*     *Servings: 8*

## 222. BASIL PARMESAN PORK ROAST

### INGREDIENTS

- 2 lbs lean pork roast, boneless
- 1 tablespoon parsley
- ½ cup parmesan cheese, grated
- 28 oz can tomatoes, diced
- 1 teaspoon dried oregano
- 1 teaspoon dried basil
- 1 teaspoon garlic powder
- Pepper
- Salt

### DIRECTIONS

1. Add the meat into the crock pot.
2. Mix together tomatoes, oregano, basil, garlic powder, parsley, cheese, pepper, and salt and pour over meat.
3. Cover and cook on low for 6 hours.
4. Serve and enjoy.

**CALORIES:** 294 Kcal     **FAT:** 11.6 g     **PROTEIN:** 38 g     **CARBOHYDRATES:** 5 g

---

*Preparation: 10 min*     *Cooking: 2 hours*     *Servings: 6*

## 223. SUN-DRIED TOMATO CHUCK ROAST

### INGREDIENTS

- 2 lbs beef chuck roast
- ½ cup beef broth
- ¼ cup sun-dried tomatoes, chopped
- 25 garlic cloves, peeled
- ¼ cup olives, sliced
- 1 teaspoon dried Italian seasoning, crushed
- 2 tablespoon balsamic vinegar

### DIRECTIONS

1. Place meat into a pot.
2. Pour remaining ingredients over meat.
3. Cover and cook on low flame for 2 hours.
4. Shred the meat using fork.
5. Serve and enjoy.

**CALORIES:** 582 Kcal     **FAT:** 43 g     **PROTEIN:** 40 g     **CARBOHYDRATES:** 5 g

*Preparation: 10 min*     Cooking: 3 hours     Servings: 2

## 224. LAMB STEW

### INGREDIENTS

- ½ lb lamb, boneles
- ¼ cup green olives, sliced
- 2 tablespoon lemon juice
- ½ onion, chopped
- 2 garlic cloves, minced
- 2 fresh thyme sprigs
- ¼ teaspoon turmeric
- ½ teaspoon pepper
- ¼ Teaspoon salt
- ½ teaspoon sesame seeds

### DIRECTIONS

1. Slice the lamb into thin pieces.
2. Add every ingredient into a pot and stir.
3. Cover and cook on low flame for 3 hours.
4. Stir well, garnish with sesame seeds and serve.

CALORIES: 297 Kcal     FAT: 20.3 g     PROTEIN: 21 g     CARBOHYDRATES: 5.4 g

*Preparation: 10 min*     *Cooking: 2 hours*     *Servings: 8*

## 225. LEMON LAMB LEG

### INGREDIENTS

- 4 lbs lamb leg, boneless and slice of fat
- 1 tablespoon rosemary, crushed
- ¼ cup water
- ¼ cup lemon juice
- 1 teaspoon black pepper
- ¼ teaspoon salt

### DIRECTIONS

1. Place lamb into a pot.
2. Add remaining ingredients over the lamb, into the pot.
3. Cover and cook on low flame for 2 hours.
4. Remove lamb from the pot and slice it.
5. Serve and enjoy.

CALORIES: 275 Kcal     FAT: 10.2 g     PROTEIN: 42 g     CARBOHYDRATES: 0.4 g

---

*Preparation: 10 min*     *Cooking: 20 min*     *Servings: 4*

## 226. PORK MEATBALLS

### INGREDIENTS

- 1 lb ground lamb
- 2 teaspoon fresh oregano, chopped
- 2 tablespoon fresh parsley, chopped
- 1 tablespoon garlic, minced
- 1 egg, lightly beaten
- 3 tablespoon olive oil
- ¼ teaspoon red pepper flakes
- 1 teaspoon ground cumin
- ¼ teaspoon pepper
- 1 teaspoon kosher salt

### DIRECTIONS

1. Preheat the oven to 425 F.
2. Line baking tray with parchment paper.
3. Add every ingredient except the oil in the mixing bowl and mix until well combined.
4. Make small balls from meat mixture and place on baking tray.
5. Drizzle the oil over the meatballs and bake for 20 minutes.
6. Serve and enjoy.

CALORIES: 325 Kcal     FAT: 20 g     PROTEIN: 33 g     CARBOHYDRATES: 2 g

Preparation: 10 min | Cooking: 1 hour and 30 min | Servings: 6

# 227. ITALIAN BEEF CASSEROLE

## INGREDIENTS

- 1 lb lean stew beef, cut into chunks
- 3 teaspoon paprika
- 4 oz black olives, sliced
- 7 oz can tomatoes, chopped
- 1 tablespoon tomato puree
- ¼ teaspoon garlic powder
- 2 teaspoon herb de Provence
- 2 cups beef stock
- 2 tablespoon olive oil
- ¼ cup soybean sprouts

## DIRECTIONS

1. Preheat the oven to 350 F.
2. Heat oil in a pan over medium heat.
3. Add meat to the pan and cook until brown.
4. Add stock, olives, tomatoes, tomato puree, garlic powder, herb de Provence, paprika and soybean sprouts. Stir well and bring to boil.
5. Transfer meat mixture to the casserole dish.
6. Cover and cook in preheated oven for 1 ½ hours.
7. Garnish with the cooking sauce, then serve.

CALORIES: 228 Kcal | FAT: 11.6 g | PROTEIN: 26 g | CARBOHYDRATES: 6 g

Preparation: 5 min    Cooking: 1 hour    Servings: 6

## 228. LAMB STUFFED TOMATOES WITH HERBS

### INGREDIENTS

- 6 large tomatoes
- 1-pound ground lamb
- ¼ cup white rice
- 2 shallots, chopped
- 2 garlic cloves, minced
- 1 tablespoon chopped dill
- 1 tablespoon chopped parsley
- 1 tablespoon chopped cilantro
- 1 teaspoon dried mint
- Salt and pepper to taste
- 1 tablespoon lemon juice
- 2 tablespoons olive oil
- 1 cup vegetable stock

### DIRECTIONS

1. Mix the lamb, rice, shallots, garlic, dill, parsley, cilantro and mint in a bowl. Add salt and pepper to taste.
2. Remove the top of each tomato then carefully remove the flesh, leaving the skins intact.
3. Chop the flesh finely and place it in a deep heavy saucepan. Add the lemon juice, as well as salt and pepper to taste.
4. Stuff the tomatoes with the lamb mixture and place them all in the pan.
5. Drizzle with oil then pour in the stock.
6. Cover with a lid and cook on low heat for 35 minutes.
7. Serve the tomatoes right away.

CALORIES: 248 Kcal    FAT: 10.7 g    PROTEIN: 23.7 g    CARBOHYDRATES: 14.6 g

---

Preparation: 10 min    Cooking: 2 hours 5 min    Servings: 4

## 229. FLAVORFUL BEEF STEW

### INGREDIENTS

- 2 lbs beef chuck, diced into chunks
- 3 thyme sprigs
- 2 bay leaves
- 3.5 oz olives, pitted
- 3 cups red wine
- 2 garlic cloves, chopped
- 2 tablespoon olive oil
- Pepper
- Salt

### DIRECTIONS

1. Season meat with pepper and salt.
2. Heat oil in a pan over high heat.
3. Add meat in hot oil and sear for 3-4 minutes on each side.
4. Add bay leaves, half red wine, garlic, and thyme. Bring to boil, turn heat to low and simmer for 90 minutes. Remove pan from heat.
5. Add olives and remaining red wine. Stir well.
6. Return pan on heat and simmer for 30 minutes more.
7. Serve hot and enjoy.

CALORIES: 630 Kcal    FAT: 20.3 g    PROTEIN: 69.2 g    CARBOHYDRATES: 7 g

*Preparation: 10 min* — *Cooking: 30 min* — *Servings: 6*

## 230. ROASTED SIRLOIN STEAK

### INGREDIENTS

- 2 lbs sirloin steak
- 2 garlic cloves, minced
- 3 tablespoon fresh lemon juice
- 1 teaspoon dried oregano
- ¼ cup water
- ¼ cup olive oil
- 2 cups fresh parsley, chopped
- ½ teaspoon pepper
- 1 teaspoon salt

### DIRECTIONS

1. Add all the ingredients except beef into the large bowl and mix well.
2. Pour bowl mixture into the large zip-lock bag.
3. Add beef to the bag and shake well and refrigerate for 1 hour.
4. Preheat the oven 400 F.
5. Place marinated beef on a baking tray and bake in preheated oven for 30 minutes.
6. Remove the beef from the oven, then cut it into slices.
7. Serve with some vegetables and enjoy.

CALORIES: 365 Kcal — FAT: 18.1 g — PROTEIN: 46.6 g — CARBOHYDRATES: 2 g

*Preparation: 10 min*     *Cooking: 15 min*     *Servings: 4*

## 231. HERB GROUND BEEF

**INGREDIENTS**

- 1 lb ground beef
- ½ teaspoon dried parsley
- ½ teaspoon dried basil
- ½ teaspoon dried oregano
- 1 teaspoon garlic, minced
- 1 tablespoon olive oil
- 1 teaspoon pepper
- ¼ teaspoon nutmeg
- ½ teaspoon dried thyme
- ½ teaspoon dried rosemary
- 1 teaspoon salt

**DIRECTIONS**

1. Heat oil in a pan over medium heat.
2. Add ground meat to the pan and fry until cooked.
3. Add remaining ingredients and stir well.
4. Serve and enjoy.

CALORIES: 215 Kcal     FAT: 7.2 g     PROTEIN: 34 g     CARBOHYDRATES: 1 g

---

*Preparation: 10 min*     *Cooking: 1 hour*     *Servings: 8*

## 232. OLIVE FETA BEEF

**INGREDIENTS**

- 2 lbs beef stew meat, cut into half-inch pieces
- 1 cup olives, pitted and cut in half
- 30 oz can tomatoes, diced
- ½ cup feta cheese, crumbled
- ¼ teaspoon pepper
- ½ teaspoon salt

**DIRECTIONS**

1. Add every ingredient into a pot and stir.
2. Cover and simmer for 1 hour, stirring occasionally.
3. Season with pepper and salt.
4. Stir for the last time, then serve.

CALORIES: 370 Kcal     FAT: 14 g     PROTEIN: 49.1 g     CARBOHYDRATES: 9 g

Preparation: 10 min | Cooking: 20 min / Refrigerating: 4 hours | Servings: 6

## 233. EASY PORK SKEWERS

### INGREDIENTS

- 2 lbs pork tenderloin, cut into 1-inch cubes
- 1 onion, chopped
- ½ cup olive oil
- ½ cup red wine vinegar
- 2 tablespoon fresh parsley, chopped
- 2 garlic cloves, chopped
- Pepper
- Salt
- 1 sweet pepper, cut into medium-sized pieces

### DIRECTIONS

1. In a large zip-lock bag, mix together red wine vinegar, parsley, garlic, onion, sweet pepper and oil.
2. Add meat to bag and marinate in the refrigerator for 4 hours.
3. Remove marinated pork from refrigerator and thread onto soaked wooden skewers, together with the sweet pepper. Season with pepper and salt.
4. Preheat the grill over high heat.
5. Grill the pork for 3-4 minutes on each side.
6. Serve and enjoy.

CALORIES: 375 Kcal | FAT: 22 g | PROTEIN: 40 g | CARBOHYDRATES: 2.5 g

*Preparation: 10 min* | *Cooking: 4 hours* | *Servings: 4*

# 234. TASTY MEATBALLS

## INGREDIENTS

- 1 egg
- 2 tablespoon fresh parsley, chopped
- 1 garlic clove, minced
- ½ lb ground beef
- ½ lb ground pork
- 14 oz can tomatoes, crushed
- 2 tablespoon fresh basil, chopped
- ¼ teaspoon pepper
- ½ teaspoon salt

## DIRECTIONS

1. In a mixing bowl, mix together beef, pork, egg, parsley, garlic, pepper, and salt until well combined.
2. Make small balls from meat mixture.
3. Arrange the meatballs into a pot.
4. Pour crushed tomatoes, basil, pepper, and salt over the meatballs.
5. Cover and cook on low flame for 4 hours.
6. Serve and enjoy.

CALORIES: 250 Kcal | FAT: 10 g | PROTEIN: 24 g | CARBOHYDRATES: 4 g

---

*Preparation: 10 min* | *Cooking: 15 min* | *Servings: 4*

# 235. BAKED PATTIES

## INGREDIENTS

- 1 lb ground lamb
- 1 teaspoon ground coriander
- 1 teaspoon ground cumin
- ¼ cup fresh parsley, chopped
- ¼ cup onion, minced
- ¼ teaspoon cayenne pepper
- ½ teaspoon ground allspice
- 1 teaspoon ground cinnamon
- 1 tablespoon garlic, minced
- ¼ teaspoon pepper
- 1 teaspoon kosher salt

## DIRECTIONS

1. Preheat the oven to 450 F.
2. Add all ingredients into the large bowl and mix until well combined.
3. Make small balls from meat mixture and place on a baking tray and lightly flatten the meatballs with back on spoon.
4. Bake in preheated oven for 12-15 minutes.
5. Serve and enjoy

CALORIES: 112 Kcal | FAT: 4.3 g | PROTEIN: 16 g | CARBOHYDRATES: 1.3 g

*Preparation: 10 min*     **Cooking: 3 hours**     Servings: 8

## 236. TENDER & JUICY LAMB ROAST

### INGREDIENTS

- 4 lbs lamb, boneless
- ½ teaspoon thyme
- 1 teaspoon oregano
- 4 garlic cloves, cut into slivers
- ½ teaspoon marjoram
- ¼ teaspoon pepper
- 2 teaspoon salt

### DIRECTIONS

1. Using a sharp knife make small cuts all over meat then insert garlic slivers into the cuts.
2. In a small bowl, mix together marjoram, thyme, oregano, pepper, and salt and rub all over lamb roast.
3. Place the lamb into a pot.
4. Roast for 10 minutes at high flame.
5. Cover and cook on low flame for 2 hours 50 minutes.
6. Remove the meat from the pot, slice it, then serve.

CALORIES: 605 Kcal     FAT: 48 g     PROTEIN: 36 g     CARBOHYDRATES: 0.7 g

*Preparation: 10 min*  *Cooking: 8 min*  *Servings: 4*

## 237. KETO BEEF PATTIES

### INGREDIENTS

- 1 lb ground beef
- 1 egg, lightly beaten
- 3 tablespoon almond flour
- 1 small onion, grated
- 2 tablespoon fresh parsley, chopped
- 1 teaspoon dry oregano
- 1 teaspoon dry mint
- Pepper
- Salt

### DIRECTIONS

1. Add all the ingredients into the mixing bowl and mix until combined.
2. Make small patties from the meat mixture.
3. Heat grill pan over medium-high heat.
4. Place patties in a hot pan and cook for 4-5 minutes on each side.
5. Serve and enjoy.

CALORIES: 234 Kcal    FAT: 8.6 g    PROTEIN: 28.9 g    CARBOHYDRATES: 1.7 g

---

*Preparation: 10 min*  *Cooking: 3 hours*  *Servings: 6*

## 238. BASIL CHEESE PORK ROAST

### INGREDIENTS

- 2 lbs lean pork roast, boneless
- 1 teaspoon garlic powder
- 1 tablespoon parsley
- ½ cup cheddar cheese, grated
- 30 oz can tomatoes, diced
- 1 teaspoon dried oregano
- 1 teaspoon dried basil
- Pepper
- Salt

### DIRECTIONS

1. Add the meat into a pot.
2. Mix together tomatoes, oregano, basil, garlic powder, parsley, cheese, pepper, and salt and pour over meat.
3. Roast for 10 minutes at high flame.
4. Cover and cook on low flame for 2 hours 50 minutes
5. Serve and enjoy.

CALORIES: 260 Kcal    FAT: 9 g    PROTEIN: 35 g    CARBOHYDRATES: 5.5 g

*Preparation: 10 min*  *Cooking: 12 min*  *Servings: 4*

## 239. FETA LAMB PATTIES

**INGREDIENTS**

- 1 lb ground lamb
- ½ teaspoon garlic powder
- ½ cup feta cheese, crumbled
- ¼ cup mint leaves, chopped
- ¼ cup roasted red pepper, chopped
- ¼ cup onion, chopped
- Pepper
- Salt

**DIRECTIONS**

1. Add all the ingredients into a bowl and mix until well combined.
2. Spray pan with cooking spray and heat over medium-high heat.
3. Make small patties from meat mixture and place on hot pan and cook for 6-7 minutes on each side.
4. Serve and enjoy.

**CALORIES:** 270 Kcal   **FAT:** 12 g   **PROTEIN:** 34.9 g   **CARBOHYDRATES:** 2.9 g

# 19 Vegetable Dishes

Preparation: 10 min Cooking: 25 min Servings: 4

## 240. ROASTED BRUSSELS SPROUTS AND PECANS

### INGREDIENTS

- 1 ½ pounds fresh Brussels sprouts
- 4 tablespoons olive oil
- 4 cloves of garlic, minced
- 3 tablespoons water
- Salt and pepper to taste
- ½ cup chopped pecans

### DIRECTIONS

1. Place all the ingredients in a pot.
2. Combine all ingredients well.
3. Close the lid and cook on low flame for 15 minutes.
4. Remove the lid and roast at high flame for 10 minutes.
5. Sprinkle with a dash of lemon juice if desired.

CALORIES: 161 Kcal FAT: 13.1 g PROTEIN: 4.1 g CARBOHYDRATES: 10.2 g

*Preparation: 15 min*  *Cooking: 25 min*  *Servings: 4*

# 241. RUSTIC VEGETABLE AND BROWN RICE BOWL

## INGREDIENTS

- Nonstick cooking spray
- 2 cups broccoli florets
- 2 cups cauliflower florets
- 1 (15-ounce) can chickpeas, drained and rinsed
- 1 cup carrots sliced 1 inch thick
- 2 to 3 tablespoons extra-virgin olive oil, divided
- 2 to 3 tablespoons sesame seeds
- 2 cups cooked brown rice
- 3 to 4 tablespoons tahini
- 2 tablespoons honey
- 1 lemon, juiced
- 1 garlic clove, minced
- Salt
- Freshly grounded black pepper

## DIRECTIONS

1. Preheat the oven to 400°F. Spray two baking sheets with cooking spray.
2. Cover the first baking sheet with the broccoli and cauliflower and the second with the chickpeas and carrots. Toss each sheet with half of the oil and season with salt and pepper before placing in oven.
3. Cook the carrots and chickpeas for 10 minutes, leaving the carrots still just crisp, and the broccoli and cauliflower for 20 minutes, until tender. Stir each halfway through cooking.
4. To make the dressing, in a small bowl, mix the tahini, honey, lemon juice, and garlic. Season with salt and pepper and set aside.
5. Divide the rice into individual bowls, then layer with vegetables and drizzle dressing over the dish.

CALORIES: 192 Kcal   FAT: 15.5 g   PROTEIN: 3.8 g   CARBOHYDRATES: 12.7 g

---

*Preparation: 5 min*  *Cooking: 20 min*  *Servings: 2*

# 242. YOGURT BAKED EGGPLANTS

## INGREDIENTS

- 2 eggplants
- 4 garlic cloves, minced
- 1 teaspoon dried basil
- 2 tablespoons lemon juice
- Salt and pepper to taste
- 1 cup Greek yogurt
- 2 tablespoons chopped parsley

## DIRECTIONS

1. Cut the eggplants in half and score the halves with a sharp knife.
2. Season the eggplants with salt and pepper, as well as the basil then drizzle with lemon juice and place the eggplant halves on a baking tray.
3. Spread the garlic over the eggplants and bake in the preheated oven at 350F for 20 minutes.
4. When done, place the eggplants on serving plates and top with yogurt and parsley.
5. Serve the eggplants right away.

CALORIES: 113 Kcal   FAT: 1.6 g   PROTEIN: 8.1 g   CARBOHYDRATES: 19.4 g

Preparation: 10 min     Cooking: 1 hour and 30 min     Servings: 6

## 243. GRILLED VEGETABLES FETA TART

### INGREDIENTS

- 2 cups all-purpose flour
- 1 teaspoon instant yeast
- ½ teaspoon salt
- 1 cup water
- 2 tablespoons olive oil
- 1 zucchini, sliced
- 2 tomatoes, sliced
- 1 shallot, sliced
- 1 teaspoon dried basil
- 1 teaspoon dried oregano
- 2 garlic cloves, minced
- 2 tablespoons tomato paste
- 4 oz. feta cheese, crumbled
- 2 eggs, beaten

### DIRECTIONS

1. For the crust, combine all the ingredients in a bowl and mix well. Knead for a few minutes until elastic.
2. Allow the dough to rest and rise for 20 minutes then roll it into a thin round of dough.
3. Place the dough on a baking tray.
4. Mix the garlic, basil, oregano and tomato paste in a bowl. Spread the mixture over the dough.
5. Heat a grill pan over medium flame and place the zucchini and tomatoes on the grill. Cook for a few minutes on all sides until browned.
6. Top the tart with the vegetables, the eggs and the shallot, then sprinkle the cheese on top.
7. Bake in the preheated oven at 350F for 25 minutes.
8. Serve the tart warm or fresh.

CALORIES: 198 Kcal     FAT: 7 g     PROTEIN: 6.3 g     CARBOHYDRATES: 28 g

*Preparation: 10 min*     *Cooking: 7 min*     *Servings: 2*

## 244. ROASTED VEGETABLES AND ZUCCHINI PASTA

**INGREDIENTS**

- ¼ cup raw pine nuts
- 4 cups leftover vegetables
- 2 garlic cloves, minced
- 1 tablespoon extra-virgin olive oil
- 4 medium zucchinis, cut into long strips resembling noodles

**DIRECTIONS**

1. Heat oil in a large skillet over medium heat and sauté the garlic for 2 minutes.
2. Add the leftover vegetables and place the zucchini noodles on top.
3. Let it cook for 5 minutes.
4. Garnish with pine nuts.

CALORIES: 288 Kcal     FAT: 19.2 g     PROTEIN: 8.2 g     CARBOHYDRATES: 23.6 g

---

*Preparation: 10 min*     *Cooking: 50 min*     *Servings: 2*

## 245. SAUTÉED COLLARD GREENS

**INGREDIENTS**

- 1-pound fresh collard greens, cut into 2-inch pieces
- 1 pinch red pepper flakes
- 3 cups chicken broth
- 1 teaspoon pepper
- 1 teaspoon salt
- 2 cloves garlic, minced
- 1 large onion, chopped
- 3 slices bacon
- 1 tablespoon olive oil

**DIRECTIONS**

1. Using a large skillet, heat oil on medium-high heat. Sauté bacon until crisp. Remove it from the pan and crumble it once cooled. Set it aside.
2. Using the same pan, sauté onion and cook until tender. Add garlic until fragrant. Add the collard greens and cook until they start to wilt.
3. Pour in the chicken broth and season with pepper, salt and red pepper flakes. Reduce the heat to low and simmer for 45 minutes.
4. Serve warm and enjoy.

CALORIES: 80 Kcal     FAT: 1 g     PROTEIN: 1 g     CARBOHYDRATES: 3 g

*Preparation: 20 min*  |  Cooking: 1 hour and 30 min  |  Servings: 6

# 246. ROASTED ROOTS

## INGREDIENTS

- 2 tablespoon olive oil
- 1 head garlic, cloves separated and peeled
- 1 large turnip, peeled and cut into ½-inch pieces
- 1 medium sized red onion, cut into ½-inch pieces
- 1 ½ lbs. beets, trimmed but not peeled, scrubbed and cut into ½-inch pieces
- 1 ½ lbs. Yukon gold potatoes, unpeeled, cut into ½-inch pieces
- 2 ½ lbs. butternut squash, peeled, seeded, cut into ½-inch pieces
- 5 carrots, peeled and cut into slices

## DIRECTIONS

1. Grease 2 rimmed and large baking sheets. Preheat oven to 425oF.
2. In a large bowl, mix all ingredients thoroughly.
3. Into the two baking sheets, evenly divide the root vegetables, spread in one layer.
4. Season generously with pepper and salt.
5. Pop into the oven and roast for 1 hour and 15 minute or until golden brown and tender.
6. Remove from oven and let it cool for at least 15 minutes.
7. Serve with vinegar if you like.

CALORIES: 298 Kcal  |  FAT: 5 g  |  PROTEIN: 7.4 g  |  CARBOHYDRATES: 61.1 g

*Preparation: 5 min*     *Cooking: 20 min*     *Servings: 4*

## 247. CABBAGE WITH COCONUT CREAM SAUCE

### INGREDIENTS

- 3 tablespoons olive oil
- 1 onion, chopped
- 4 cloves of garlic, minced
- 1 head savoy cabbage, chopped finely
- 2 cups bone broth
- 1 cup coconut milk, freshly squeezed
- 1 bay leaf
- Salt and pepper to taste
- 2 tablespoons chopped parsley

### DIRECTIONS

1. Heat the oil in a pot for 2 minutes.
2. Stir in the onions, bay leaf, and garlic until fragrant, for around 3 minutes.
3. Add the rest of the ingredients, except for the parsley and mix well.
4. Cover the pot, bring to boil, and let it simmer for 5 minutes or until cabbage is tender to taste.
5. Stir in the parsley and serve.

CALORIES: 195 Kcal     FAT: 19.7 g     PROTEIN: 2.7 g     CARBOHYDRATES: 12.3 g

---

*Preparation: 20 min*     *Cooking: 40 min*     *Servings: 4*

## 248. STEAMED SQUASH CHOWDER

### INGREDIENTS

- 3 cups chicken broth
- 2 tablespoon ghee
- 1 teaspoon chili powder
- ½ teaspoon cumin
- 1 ½ teaspoon salt
- 2 teaspoon cinnamon
- 3 tablespoon olive oil
- 2 carrots, chopped
- 1 small yellow onion, chopped
- 1 green apple, sliced and cored
- 1 large butternut squash, peeled, seeded, and chopped to ½-inch cubes

### DIRECTIONS

1. In a large pot on medium high fire, melt ghee.
2. Once ghee is hot, sauté onions for 5 minutes or until soft and translucent.
3. Add olive oil, chili powder, cumin, salt, and cinnamon. Sauté for half a minute.
4. Add chopped squash and apples.
5. Sauté for 10 minutes while stirring once in a while.
6. Add broth, cover and cook on medium fire for twenty minutes or until apples and squash are tender.
7. With an immersion blender, puree chowder. Adjust consistency by adding more water.
8. Add more salt or pepper depending on desire.
9. Serve and enjoy.

CALORIES: 228 Kcal     FAT: 18 g     PROTEIN: 2.2 g     CARBOHYDRATES: 17.9 g

Preparation: 10 min Cooking: 10 min Servings: 2

## 249. SLOW COOKED BUTTERY MUSHROOMS

### INGREDIENTS

- 2 tablespoons butter
- 2 tablespoons olive oil
- 3 cloves of garlic, minced
- 16 ounces fresh brown mushrooms, sliced
- 7 ounces fresh shiitake mushrooms, sliced
- A dash of thyme
- Salt and pepper to taste

### DIRECTIONS

1. Heat the butter and oil in a pot.
2. Sauté the garlic until fragrant, around 1 minute.
3. Stir in the rest of the ingredients and cook until soft, around 9 minutes
4. *If you want a delicious sauce to cook your pasta, you can also use this recipe as a sauce. Just chop the mushrooms a little more!

CALORIES: 192 Kcal FAT: 15.5 g PROTEIN: 3.8 g CARBOHYDRATES: 12.7 g

*Preparation: 15 min*  *Cooking: 15 min*  *Servings: 2*

# 250. STEAMED ZUCCHINI-PAPRIKA

## INGREDIENTS

- 4 tablespoons olive oil
- 3 cloves of garlic, minced
- 1 onion, chopped
- 3 medium-sized zucchinis, sliced thinly
- A dash of paprika
- Salt and pepper to taste

## DIRECTIONS

1. Place all the ingredients into a pot.
2. Give a good stir to combine all the ingredients.
3. Close the lid and cook on low flame for 15 minutes.
4. Halfway through the cooking time, open the lid and give a good stir.
5. Serve and enjoy.

CALORIES: 93 Kcal    FAT: 10.2 g    PROTEIN: 0.6 g    CARBOHYDRATES: 3.1 g

---

*Preparation: 10 min*  *Cooking: 15 min*  *Servings: 4*

# 251. FRIED BRUSSELS SPROUTS AND CARROTS

## INGREDIENTS

- 1 tablespoon cider vinegar
- ⅓ cup water
- 1 lb. Brussels sprouts, halved lengthwise
- 1 lb. carrots cut diagonally into ½-inch thick lengths
- 3 tablespoon unsalted butter, divided
- 2 tablespoon chopped shallot
- ½ teaspoon pepper
- ¾ teaspoon salt

## DIRECTIONS

1. On medium high fire, place a nonstick medium fry pan and heat 2 tablespoon butter.
2. Add shallots and cook until softened, around one to two minutes while occasionally stirring.
3. Add pepper salt, Brussels sprouts and carrots. Stir fry until vegetables starts to brown on the edges, around 3 to 4 minutes.
4. Add water, continue to cook and cover.
5. After 5 to 8 minutes, or when veggies are already soft, add remaining butter.
6. If needed season with more pepper and salt to taste.
7. Turn off fire, transfer to a platter, serve and enjoy.

CALORIES: 98 Kcal    FAT: 4.2 g    PROTEIN: 3.5 g    CARBOHYDRATES: 13.9 g

Preparation: 10 min  Cooking: 30 min  Servings: 2

## 252. SUMPTUOUS TOMATO SOUP

### INGREDIENTS

- Pepper and salt to taste
- 2 tablespoon tomato paste
- 1 ½ cups vegetable broth
- 1 tablespoon chopped parsley
- 1 tablespoon olive oil
- 5 garlic cloves
- ½ medium yellow onion
- 4 large ripe tomatoes

### DIRECTIONS

1. Preheat the oven to 350°F.
2. Chop onion and tomatoes into thin wedges. Place on a rimmed baking sheet. Season with parsley, pepper, salt, and olive oil. Toss to combine well. Hide the garlic cloves inside tomatoes to keep it from burning.
3. Pop in the oven and bake for 30 minutes.
4. On medium pot, bring vegetable stock to a simmer. Add tomato paste.
5. Pour baked tomato mixture into the pot. Continue simmering for another 10 minutes.
6. With an immersion blender, puree soup.
7. Adjust salt and pepper to taste before serving.

CALORIES: 179 Kcal   FAT: 7.7 g   PROTEIN: 5.2 g   CARBOHYDRATES: 26.7 g

Preparation: 10 min  Cooking: 30 min  Servings: 2

# 253. STIR-FRIED EGGPLANTS

## INGREDIENTS

- 1 teaspoon cornstarch + 2 tablespoon water, mixed
- 1 teaspoon brown sugar
- 2 tablespoon oyster sauce
- 1 tablespoon fish sauce
- 2 tablespoon soy sauce
- ½ cup fresh basil
- 2 tablespoon oil
- ¼ cup water
- 2 cups Chinese eggplant, spiral
- 1 red chili
- 6 cloves garlic, minced
- ½ purple onion, sliced thinly
- 1 3-oz package medium firm tofu, cut into slivers

## DIRECTIONS

1. Prepare sauce by mixing cornstarch and water in a small bowl. In another bowl mix brown sugar, oyster sauce and fish sauce and set aside.
2. On medium high fire, place a large nonstick saucepan and heat 2 tablespoon oil. Sauté chili, garlic and onion for 4 minutes. Add tofu, stir and fry for 4 minutes.
3. Add eggplant noodles and stir fry for 10 minutes. If pan dries up, add water in small amounts to moisten pan and cook noodles.
4. Pour in sauce and mix well. Once simmering, slowly add cornstarch mixer while continuing to mix vigorously. Once sauce thickens add fresh basil and cook for a minute.
5. Remove from fire, transfer to a serving plate and enjoy.

CALORIES: 369 Kcal  FAT: 25.3 g  PROTEIN: 11.4 g  CARBOHYDRATES: 28.4 g

---

Preparation: 20 min  Cooking: 30 min  Servings: 6

# 254. SUMMER VEGETABLES

## INGREDIENTS

- 1 teaspoon dried marjoram
- 1/3 cup Parmesan cheese
- 1 small eggplant, sliced into ¼-inch thick circles
- 1 small summer squash, peeled and sliced diagonally into ¼-inch thickness
- 3 large tomatoes, sliced into ¼-inch thick circles
- ½ cup dry white wine
- ½ teaspoon freshly ground pepper, divided
- ½ teaspoon salt, divided
- 5 cloves garlic, sliced thinly
- 2 cups leeks, sliced thinly
- 4 tablespoons extra virgin olive oil

## DIRECTIONS

1. On medium fire, place a large nonstick saucepan and heat 2 tablespoon oil.
2. Sauté garlic and leeks for 5 minutes or until garlic is starting to brown. Season with pepper and salt, ¼ teaspoon each.
3. Pour in wine and cook for another minute. Transfer to a 2-quart baking dish.
4. In baking dish, layer in alternating pattern the eggplant, summer squash, and tomatoes. Do this until dish is covered with vegetables. If there are excess vegetables, store for future use.
5. Season with remaining pepper and salt. Drizzle with remaining olive oil and pop in a preheated 425oF oven.
6. Bake for 10 minutes. Remove from oven and top with marjoram and cheese.
7. Return to oven and bake for 15 minutes more or until veggies are soft and edges are browned.

CALORIES: 150 Kcal  FAT: 10.8 g  PROTEIN: 3.3 g  CARBOHYDRATES: 11.8 g

*Preparation: 10 min*     *Cooking: 8 min*     *Servings: 2*

## 255. SUPERFAST CAJUN ASPARAGUS

### INGREDIENTS

- 1 teaspoon Cajun seasoning
- 1-pound asparagus
- 1 teaspoon Olive oil

### DIRECTIONS

1. Snap the asparagus and make sure that you use the tender part of the vegetable.
2. Place a large skillet on stovetop and heat on high flame for a minute.
3. Then grease the skillet with cooking spray, spread asparagus in one layer and season with cajun.
4. Cover the skillet and continue cooking on high flame for 5 to 8 minutes.
5. Halfway through cooking time stir the asparagus, then cover again and continue to cook.
6. Once done cooking, transfer to plates, serve, and enjoy!

CALORIES: 81 Kcal     FAT: 9 g     PROTEIN: 0 g     CARBOHYDRATES: 0 g

*Preparation: 5 min*  *Cooking: 13 min*  *Servings: 4*

## 256. STIR-FRIED BOK CHOY

### INGREDIENTS

- 3 tablespoons coconut oil
- 4 cloves of garlic, minced
- 1 onion, chopped
- 2 heads bok choy, rinsed and chopped
- 2 teaspoons coconut aminos
- Salt and pepper to taste
- 2 tablespoons sesame oil
- 2 tablespoons sesame seeds, toasted

### DIRECTIONS

1. Heat the oil in a pot for 2 minutes.
2. Sauté the garlic and onions until fragrant, around 3 minutes.
3. Stir in the bok choy, coconut aminos, salt and pepper.
4. Cover pan and cook for 5 minutes.
5. Stir and continue cooking for another 3 minutes.
6. Drizzle with sesame oil and sesame seeds on top before serving.

CALORIES: 358 Kcal    FAT: 28.4 g    PROTEIN: 21.5 g    CARBOHYDRATES: 5.2 g

---

*Preparation: 10 min*  *Cooking: 20 min*  *Servings: 6*

## 257. SUMMER VEGGIES IN A POT

### INGREDIENTS

- 2 cups okra, sliced
- 1 cup grape tomatoes
- 1 cup mushroom, sliced
- 1 ½ cups onion, sliced
- 2 cups bell pepper, sliced
- 2 ½ cups zucchini, sliced
- 2 tablespoons basil, chopped
- 1 tablespoon thyme, chopped
- ½ cups balsamic vinegar
- ½ cups olive oil
- Salt and pepper

### DIRECTIONS

1. Place all the ingredients into a pot.
2. Stir the content and close the lid.
3. Cook on low flame for 20 minutes, then let it cool for 5 minutes.
4. Once cooled, evenly divide into serving size, keep in your preferred container, and refrigerate until ready to eat.

CALORIES: 233 Kcal    FAT: 18 g    PROTEIN: 3 g    CARBOHYDRATES: 7 g

*Preparation:* 20 min     *Cooking:* 40 min     Servings: 4

## 258. SWEET AND NUTRITIOUS PUMPKIN SOUP

### INGREDIENTS

- 1 teaspoon chopped fresh basil or parsley
- ½ cup half and half or sour cream
- ½ teaspoon chopped fresh thyme
- 1 teaspoon salt
- 4 cups pumpkin puree
- 6 cups vegetable stock, divided
- 1 clove garlic, minced
- 1 1-inch piece gingerroot, peeled and minced
- 1 cup chopped onion

### DIRECTIONS

1. On medium high fire, place a heavy bottomed pot and for 5 minutes heat ½ cup vegetable stock, ginger, garlic and onions or until veggies are tender.
2. Add the remaining stock and cook for 30 minutes.
3. Season with thyme and salt.
4. With an immersion blender, puree soup until smooth.
5. Turn off the fire and mix in half and half.
6. Transfer pumpkin soup into bowls, garnish with basil, serve and enjoy.

CALORIES: 108 Kcal     FAT: 7.7 g     PROTEIN: 5.1 g     CARBOHYDRATES: 6.6 g

*Preparation: 10 min*     *Cooking: 15 min*     *Servings: 6*

# 259. SWEET POTATO PUREE

## INGREDIENTS

- 2 pounds sweet potatoes, peeled
- 1 ½ cups water
- 5 Medjool dates, pitted and chopped

## DIRECTIONS

1. Get out a melon baller and scoop out balls of cantaloupe, Place all the ingredients into a pot.
2. Close the lid and allow to boil for 15 minutes until the potatoes are soft.
3. Drain the potatoes and place in a food processor together with the dates.
4. Pulse until smooth.
5. Place in individual containers to store in the fridge or serve warm.

CALORIES: 619 Kcal     FAT: 24.3 g     PROTEIN: 4.8 g     CARBOHYDRATES: 97.8 g

---

*Preparation: 10 min*     *Cooking: 30 min*     *Servings: 6*

# 260. SWEET POTATOES OVEN FRIED

## INGREDIENTS

- 1 small garlic clove, minced
- 1 teaspoon grated orange rind
- 1 tablespoon fresh parsley, chopped finely
- ¼ teaspoon pepper
- ¼ teaspoon salt
- 1 tablespoon olive oil
- 4 medium sweet potatoes, peeled and sliced to ¼-inch thickness

## DIRECTIONS

1. In a large bowl mix well pepper, salt, olive oil and sweet potatoes.
2. In a greased baking sheet, in a single layer arrange sweet potatoes.
3. Pop in a preheated 400oF oven and bake for 15 minutes, turnover potato slices and return to oven. Bake for another 15 minutes or until tender.
4. Meanwhile, mix well in a small bowl garlic, orange rind and parsley, sprinkle over cooked potato slices and serve.
5. You can store baked sweet potatoes in a lidded container and just microwave whenever you want to eat it. Consume within 3 days.

CALORIES: 176 Kcal     FAT: 2.5 g     PROTEIN: 2.5 g     CARBOHYDRATES: 36.6 g

Preparation: 10 min — Cooking: 30 min — Servings: 4

## 261. SWEET POTATO SOUP

### INGREDIENTS

- Pepper and salt to taste
- 2 tablespoon thyme leaves
- Juice of half a lemon
- 1 teaspoon ground cumin
- 2 cups mashed sweet potato
- 4 cups chicken stock
- 4 bell pepper, diced
- 1 onion, diced
- 1 tablespoon coconut oil

### DIRECTIONS

1. On medium low fire, place a heavy bottomed pot and heat coconut oil.
2. Sauté peppers and onions for 5 minutes or until slightly soft.
3. Meanwhile, in a blender puree mashed sweet potatoes with 2 cups chicken stock. Pour into pot.
4. Add cumin and remaining chicken stock. Cover and bring to a boil.
5. Lower fire to a simmer and cook for 20 minutes or until peppers are tender.
6. Season with pepper, salt, thyme and lemon juice.
7. Serve while hot.

CALORIES: 112 Kcal — FAT: 4.6 g — PROTEIN: 3.5 g — CARBOHYDRATES: 17.5 g

*Preparation: 10 min*     *Cooking: 10 min*     *Servings: 2*

## 262. TASTY AVOCADO SAUCE OVER ZOODLES

### INGREDIENTS

- 1 zucchini peeled and spiralized into noodles
- 4 tablespoon pine nuts
- 2 tablespoon lemon juice
- 1 avocado peeled and pitted
- 12 sliced cherry tomatoes
- 1/3 cup water
- 1 1/4 cup basil
- Pepper and salt to taste

### DIRECTIONS

1. Make the sauce in a blender by adding pine nuts, lemon juice, avocado, water, and basil. Pulse until smooth and creamy. Season with pepper and salt to taste. Mix well.
2. Place zoodles in salad bowl. Pour over avocado sauce and toss well to coat.
3. Add cherry tomatoes, serve, and enjoy.

CALORIES: 313 Kcal     FAT: 26.8 g     PROTEIN: 6.8 g     CARBOHYDRATES: 18.7 g

---

*Preparation: 5 min*     *Cooking: 10 min*     *Servings: 4*

## 263. TOMATO BASIL CALIFLOWER RICE

### INGREDIENTS

- Salt and pepper to taste
- Dried parsley for garnish
- ¼ cup tomato paste
- ½ teaspoon garlic, minced
- ½ teaspoon onion powder
- ½ teaspoon marjoram
- 1 ½ teaspoon dried basil
- 1 teaspoon dried oregano
- 1 large head of cauliflower
- 1 teaspoon oil

### DIRECTIONS

1. Cut the cauliflower into florets and place in the food processor.
2. Pulse until it has a coarse consistency similar with rice. Set aside.
3. In a skillet, heat the oil and sauté the garlic and onion for three minutes.
4. Add the rest of the ingredients. Cook for 8 minutes.
5. Serve warm and enjoy.

CALORIES: 106 Kcal     FAT: 5 g     PROTEIN: 3.3 g     CARBOHYDRATES: 15.1 g

*Preparation: 10 min*  *Cooking: 15 min*  *Servings: 4*

## 264. LO MEIN

### INGREDIENTS

- 8 ounces egg noodles
- 2 tablespoons olive oil
- 5 cloves of garlic, minced
- 2-inch knob of ginger, grated
- 8 ounces mushrooms, sliced
- ½ pounds zucchini, spiralized
- 1 carrot, julienned
- 1 spring green onions, chopped
- 3 tablespoons coconut aminos
- Salt and pepper to taste
- 1 tablespoon sesame oil

### DIRECTIONS

1. Put a pot of water to boil.
2. In the meantime, heat the oil in a skillet and sauté the garlic and ginger until fragrant.
3. Stir in the mushrooms, zucchini, carrot, and green onions.
4. Season with coconut aminos, salt and pepper.
5. Close the lid and allow to simmer for 5 minutes.
6. Cook the noodles in the boiling water, according to the package instruction.
7. Drain well the noodles, stir in every other ingredient and toss to combine.
8. Drizzle with sesame oil, then serve warm.

CALORIES: 488 Kcal  FAT: 11 g  PROTEIN: 7.6 g  CARBOHYDRATES: 48.7 g

Preparation: 10 min  Cooking: 20 min  Servings: 4

## 265. VEGAN SESAME TOFU AND EGGPLANTS

### INGREDIENTS

- 5 tablespoons olive oil
- 1-pound firm tofu, sliced
- 3 tablespoons rice vinegar
- 2 teaspoons Swerve sweetener
- 2 whole eggplants, sliced
- ¼ cup soy sauce
- Salt and pepper to taste
- 4 tablespoons toasted sesame oil
- ¼ cup sesame seeds
- 1 cup fresh cilantro, chopped

### DIRECTIONS

1. Heat the oil in a pan for 2 minutes.
2. Pan fry the tofu for 3 minutes on each side.
3. Stir in the rice vinegar, sweetener, eggplants, and soy sauce. Season with salt and pepper to taste.
4. Cover and cook for 5 minutes on medium fire. Stir and continue cooking for another 5 minutes.
5. Toss in the sesame oil, sesame seeds, and cilantro.
6. Serve and enjoy.

CALORIES: 616 Kcal  FAT: 49.2 g  PROTEIN: 23.9 g  CARBOHYDRATES: 27.4 g

---

Preparation: 10 min  Cooking: 30 min  Servings: 4

## 266. COCONUT CURRY VEGETABLES

### INGREDIENTS

- 4 tablespoons coconut oil
- 1 medium onion, chopped
- 1 teaspoon minced garlic
- 1 teaspoon minced ginger
- 1 cup broccoli florets
- 2 cups fresh spinach leaves
- 2 teaspoons fish sauce
- 1 tablespoon garam masala
- ½ cup coconut milk
- Salt and pepper to taste

### DIRECTIONS

1. Heat oil in a pot.
2. Sauté the onion and garlic until fragrant, around 3 minutes.
3. Stir in the rest of the ingredients, except for spinach leaves.
4. Season with salt and pepper to taste.
5. Cover and cook on medium fire for 5 minutes.
6. Stir and add spinach leaves. Cover and cook for another 2 minutes.
7. Turn off fire and let it sit for two more minutes before serving.

CALORIES: 210 Kcal  FAT: 20.9 g  PROTEIN: 2.1 g  CARBOHYDRATES: 6.5 g

Preparation: 15 min | Cooking: 30 min | Servings: 4

## 267. JAMAICAN STEW

### INGREDIENTS

- 1 tablespoon cilantro, chopped
- 1 tablespoon lime juice
- 2 cups collard greens, sliced
- 3 cups carrots, cut into cubes
- ½ yellow plantain, cut into cubes
- 1 cup okra, halved
- 2 cups potatoes, cut into cubes
- 2 cups taro, cut into cubes
- 2 cups pumpkin, cut into cubes
- 2 cups water
- 2 cups coconut milk
- 2 bay leaves
- 3 green onions, chopped
- ½ teaspoon dried thyme
- ½ teaspoon ground allspice
- 4 garlic cloves, minced
- 1 tablespoon olive oil
- Salt and pepper to taste

### DIRECTIONS

1. On medium fire, place a stockpot and heat oil. Sauté onions for 4 minutes or until translucent and soft. Add thyme, all spice and garlic. Sauté for a minute.
2. Pour in water and coconut milk and bring to a simmer. Add bay leaves and green onions.
3. Once simmering, slow fire to keep broth at a simmer and add taro and pumpkin. Cook for 5 minutes.
4. Add potatoes and cook for three minutes.
5. Add carrots, plantain and okra. Mix and cook for five minutes.
6. Then remove and fish for thyme sprigs, bay leaves and green onions and discard.
7. Add collard greens and cook for four minutes or until bright green and darker in color.
8. Turn off fire, add pepper, salt and lime juice to taste.
9. Once it tastes good, mix well, transfer to a serving bowl, serve and enjoy.

CALORIES: 531 Kcal | FAT: 32.7 g | PROTEIN: 8.3 g | CARBOHYDRATES: 59.7 g

Preparation: 10 min    Cooking: 30 min    Servings: 6

## 268. MOROCCAN STYLE SOUP

### INGREDIENTS

- 2 oz whole wheat orzo
- 1 large zucchini, cut into cubes
- 8 sprigs fresh cilantro
- 12 sprigs flat leaf parsley
- A pinch of saffron threads
- 2 stalks celery, sliced
- 2 carrots, diced
- 2 small turnips, peeled and diced
- 1 14-oz can tomato, sliced
- 6 cups water
- 1 lb. lamb stew meat, trimmed and cut into ½-inch cubes
- 2 teaspoon ground turmeric
- 1 medium onion, diced finely
- 2 tablespoon olive oil
- Salt and pepper to taste

### DIRECTIONS

1. On medium high fire, place a large Dutch oven and heat oil.
2. Add turmeric and onion, stir fry for two minutes.
3. Add meat and sauté for 5 minutes.
4. Add saffron, celery, carrots, turnips, tomatoes and juice, and water.
5. With a kitchen string, tie cilantro and parsley sprigs together and into pot.
6. Cover and bring to a boil. Once boiling reduce fire to a simmer and continue to cook for 45 to 50 minutes or until meat is tender.
7. Once meat is tender, stir in zucchini. Cover and cook for 8 minutes.
8. Add orzo; cook for 10 minutes or until soft.
9. Remove and discard cilantro and parsley sprigs.
10. Season with pepper and salt.
11. Serve warm in a bowl.

CALORIES: 268 Kcal    FAT: 11.7 g    PROTEIN: 28.1 g    CARBOHYDRATES: 12.9 g

---

Preparation: 10 min    Cooking: 15 min    Servings: 6

## 269. YUMMY CALIFLOWER FRITTERS

### INGREDIENTS

- 1 large cauliflower head, cut into florets
- 2 eggs, beaten
- ½ teaspoon turmeric
- ½ teaspoon salt
- ¼ teaspoon black pepper
- 6 tablespoons coconut oil

### DIRECTIONS

1. Place the cauliflower florets in a pot with water.
2. Bring to a boil and drain once cooked.
3. Place the cauliflowers, eggs, turmeric, salt, and pepper into the food processor.
4. Pulse until the mixture becomes coarse.
5. Transfer into a bowl. Using your hands, form six small flattened balls and place in the fridge for at least 1 hour until the mixture hardens.
6. Heat the oil in a skillet and fry the cauliflower patties for 3 minutes on each side.
7. Serve warm and enjoy.

CALORIES: 157 Kcal    FAT: 15.3 g    PROTEIN: 3.9 g    CARBOHYDRATES: 2.8 g

*Preparation: 5 min*     *Cooking: 20 min*     *Servings: 1*

## 270. RAMEN MISO SOUP

### INGREDIENTS

- 2 teaspoons thinly sliced green onion
- A pinch of salt
- ½ teaspoon shoyu
- 2 tablespoon mellow white miso
- 1 cup zucchini, cut into angel hair spirals
- ½ cup thinly sliced cremini mushrooms
- ½ medium carrot, cut into angel hair spirals
- 1/2 cup baby spinach leaves – optional
- 2 ¼ cups water
- ½ box of medium firm tofu, cut into ¼-inch cubes
- 1 hardboiled egg
- 1 teaspoon chia seeds

### DIRECTIONS

1. In a small bowl, mix ¼ cup of water and miso. Set aside.
2. In a small saucepan on medium high fire, bring to a boil 2 cups water, mushrooms, tofu and carrots.
3. Add salt, shoyu and miso mixture.
4. Allow to boil for 5 minutes.
5. Remove from fire and add green onion, zucchini and baby spinach leaves if using.
6. Let soup stand for 5 minutes before transferring to individual bowls.
7. Garnish with ½ of hardboiled egg per bowl and some chia seeds, serve and enjoy.

CALORIES: 335 Kcal     FAT: 17.6 g     PROTEIN: 30.6 g     CARBOHYDRATES: 19 g

*Preparation: 15 min*      *Cooking: 20 min*      *Servings: 4*

## 271. ZUCCHINI GARLIC FRIES

### INGREDIENTS

- ¼ teaspoon garlic powder
- ½ cup almond flour
- 2 large egg whites, beaten
- 3 medium zucchinis, sliced into fry sticks
- Salt and pepper to taste

### DIRECTIONS

1. Preheat oven to 400°F.
2. Mix all ingredients in a bowl until the zucchini fries are well coated.
3. Place fries on cookie sheet and spread evenly.
4. Put in oven and cook for 20 minutes.
5. Halfway through cooking time, stir the fries.
6. Serve warm and enjoy.

CALORIES: 11 Kcal      FAT: 0.1 g      PROTEIN: 1.5 g      CARBOHYDRATES: 1.1 g

---

*Preparation: 5 min*      *Cooking: 20 min*      *Servings: 2*

## 272. ZUCCHINI PASTA WITH MANGO-KIWI SAUCE

### INGREDIENTS

- 1 teaspoon dried herbs – optional
- ½ Cup Raw Kale leaves, shredded
- 2 small dried figs
- 3 medjool dates
- 4 medium kiwis
- 2 big mangos, seed discarded
- 2 cup zucchini, spiralized
- ¼ cup roasted cashew

### DIRECTIONS

1. On a salad bowl, place kale then topped with zucchini noodles and sprinkle with dried herbs. Set aside.
2. In a food processor, grind to a powder the cashews.
3. Add figs, dates, kiwis and mangoes then puree to a smooth consistency.
4. Pour over zucchini pasta, serve and enjoy.

CALORIES: 330 Kcal      FAT: 8.5 g      PROTEIN: 4 g      CARBOHYDRATES: 35.4 g

*Preparation: 15 min*  *Cooking: 40 min*  *Servings: 6*

# 273. MEDITERRANEAN BAKED CHICKPEAS

## INGREDIENTS

- 1 tablespoon extra-virgin olive oil
- 2 medium onion, chopped
- 3 garlic cloves, chopped
- 2 teaspoons smoked paprika
- 1 teaspoon ground cumin
- 4 cups halved cherry tomatoes
- 2 (15-ounce) cans chickpeas, drained and rinsed
- ½ cup plain, unsweetened, full-fat Greek yogurt, for serving
- 1 cup crumbled feta, for serving

## DIRECTIONS

1. Preheat the oven to 425°F.
2. In an oven-safe sauté pan or skillet, heat the oil over medium heat and sauté the onion and garlic.
3. Cook for about 5 minutes, until softened and fragrant.
4. Stir in the paprika and cumin and cook for 2 minutes.
5. Stir in the tomatoes and chickpeas.
6. Bring to a simmer for 5 to 10 minutes before placing in the oven.
7. Roast in oven for 25 to 30 minutes, until bubbling and thickened.
8. To serve, top with Greek yogurt and feta.

CALORIES: 330 Kcal    FAT: 18.5 g    PROTEIN: 9 g    CARBOHYDRATES: 55.4 g

*Preparation: 10 min*  *Cooking: 15 min*  *Servings: 4*

# 274. QUINOA WITH ALMONDS AND CRANBERRIES

## INGREDIENTS

- 2 cups cooked quinoa
- ⅓ teaspoon cranberries or currants
- ¼ cup sliced almonds
- 2 garlic cloves, minced
- 1¼ teaspoons salt
- ½ teaspoon ground cumin
- ½ teaspoon turmeric
- ¼ teaspoon ground cinnamon
- ¼ teaspoon freshly ground black pepper

## DIRECTIONS

1. In a large bowl, toss the quinoa, cranberries, almonds, garlic, salt, cumin, turmeric, cinnamon, and pepper and stir to combine.
2. Enjoy alone or with roasted cauliflower.

CALORIES: 430 Kcal    FAT: 15.5 g    PROTEIN: 8 g    CARBOHYDRATES: 65.4 g

---

*Preparation: 10 min*  *Cooking: 15 min*  *Servings: 4*

# 275. FELAFEL BITES

## INGREDIENTS

- 1⅔ cups falafel mix
- 1¼ cups water
- Extra-virgin olive oil spray
- 1 tablespoon Pickled Onions (optional)
- 1 tablespoon Pickled Turnips (optional)
- 2 tablespoons Tzatziki Sauce (optional)

## DIRECTIONS

1. In a large bowl, carefully stir the falafel mix into the water. Mix well. Let stand 15 minutes to absorb the water. Form mix into 1-inch balls and arrange on a baking sheet.
2. Preheat the broiler to high.
3. Take the balls and flatten slightly with your thumb (so they won't roll around on the baking sheet).
4. Spray with olive oil, and then broil for 2 to 3 minutes on each side, until crispy and brown.
5. To fry the falafel, fill a pot with ½ inch of cooking oil and heat over medium-high heat to 375°F.
6. Fry the balls for about 3 minutes, until brown and crisp.
7. Drain on paper towels and serve with pickled onions, pickled turnips, and tzatziki sauce (if using).

CALORIES: 530 Kcal    FAT: 18.5 g    PROTEIN: 8 g    CARBOHYDRATES: 35.4 g

*Preparation: 15 min*  *Cooking: 20 min*  *Servings: 6*

## 276. QUICK VEGETABLE KEBABS

### INGREDIENTS

- 4 medium red onions, peeled and sliced into 6 wedges
- 4 medium zucchini, cut into 1-inch-thick slices
- 4 bell peppers, cut into 2-inch squares
- 2 yellow bell peppers, cut into 2-inch squares
- 2 orange bell peppers, cut into 2-inch squares
- 2 beefsteak tomatoes, cut into quarters
- 3 tablespoons Herbed Oil

### DIRECTIONS

1. Preheat the oven or grill to medium-high or 350°F.
2. Thread 1 piece red onion, zucchini, different colored bell peppers, and tomatoes onto a skewer.
3. Repeat until the skewer is full of vegetables, up to 2 inches away from the skewer end, and continue until all skewers are complete.
4. Put the skewers on a baking sheet and cook in the oven for 10 minutes or grill for 5 minutes on each side.
5. The vegetables will be done with they reach your desired crunch or softness.
6. Remove the skewers from heat and drizzle with Herbed Oil.

CALORIES: 235 Kcal  FAT: 14.5 g  PROTEIN: 8 g  CARBOHYDRATES: 30.4 g

---

*Preparation: 15 min*  *Cooking: 10 min*  *Servings: 4*

## 277. TORTELLINI IN RED PEPPER SAUCE

### INGREDIENTS

- 1 (16-ounce) container fresh cheese tortellini (usually green and white pasta)
- 1 (16-ounce) jar roasted red peppers, drained
- 1 teaspoon garlic powder
- ¼ cup tahini
- 1 tablespoon red pepper oil (optional)

### DIRECTIONS

1. Bring a large pot of water to a boil and cook the tortellini according to package directions.
2. In a blender, combine the red peppers with the garlic powder and process until smooth. Once blended, add the tahini until the sauce is thickened. If the sauce gets too thick, add up to 1 tablespoon red pepper oil (if using).
3. Once tortellini are cooked, drain and leave pasta in colander. Add the sauce to the bottom of the empty pot and heat for 2 minutes.
4. Add the tortellini back into the pot and cook for 2 more minutes. Serve and enjoy!

CALORIES: 530 Kcal  FAT: 18.5 g  PROTEIN: 3 g  CARBOHYDRATES: 75.4 g

Preparation: 15 min  Cooking: 10 min  Servings: 6

## 278. FREKEH, CHICKPEA, AND HERB SALAD

### INGREDIENTS

- 1 (15-ounce) can chickpeas, rinsed and drained
- 1 cup cooked freekeh
- 1 cup thinly sliced celery
- 1 bunch scallions, both white and green parts, finely chopped
- ½ cup chopped fresh flat-leaf parsley
- ¼ cup chopped fresh mint
- 3 tablespoons chopped celery leaves
- ½ teaspoon kosher salt
- ⅓ cup extra-virgin olive oil
- ¼ cup lemon juice
- ¼ teaspoon cumin seeds
- 1 teaspoon garlic powder

### DIRECTIONS

1. In a large bowl, combine the chickpeas, freekeh, celery, scallions, parsley, mint, celery leaves, and salt and toss lightly.
2. In a small bowl, whisk together the olive oil, lemon juice, cumin seeds, and garlic powder.
3. Once combined, add to freekeh salad.

CALORIES: 230 Kcal  FAT: 18.5 g  PROTEIN: 2.3 g  CARBOHYDRATES: 8.4 g

---

Preparation: 15 min  Cooking: 10 min  Servings: 4

## 279. WARM MEDITERRANEAN FARRO BOWL

### INGREDIENTS

- ⅓ cup extra-virgin olive oil
- ½ cup chopped red bell pepper
- ⅓ cup chopped red onions
- 2 garlic cloves, minced
- 1 cup zucchini, cut in ½-inch slices
- ½ cup canned chickpeas, drained and rinsed
- ½ cup chopped artichokes
- 3 cups cooked farro
- Salt
- Freshly ground black pepper
- ¼ cup sliced olives, for serving
- ½ cup crumbled feta cheese
- 2 tablespoons fresh basil
- 3 tablespoons balsamic reduction, for serving

### DIRECTIONS

1. In a large sauté pan or skillet, heat the oil over medium heat and sauté the pepper, onions, and garlic for about 5 minutes, until tender.
2. Add the zucchini, chickpeas, and artichokes, then stir and continue to sauté vegetables, approximately 5 more minutes, until just soft.
3. Stir in the cooked farro, tossing to combine and cooking enough to heat through. Season with salt and pepper and remove from the heat.
4. Transfer the contents of the pan into the serving vessels or bowls.
5. Top with olives, feta, and basil (if using). Drizzle with balsamic reduction (if using) to finish.

CALORIES: 430 Kcal  FAT: 11.5 g  PROTEIN: 6.1 g  CARBOHYDRATES: 15.4 g

Preparation: 15 min  Cooking: 20 min  Servings: 4

## 280. CREAMY CHICKPEA SAUCE WITH FUSILLI

### INGREDIENTS

- ¼ cup extra-virgin olive oil
- ½ large shallot, chopped
- 5 garlic cloves, thinly sliced
- 1 (15-ounce) can chickpeas, drained and rinsed, reserving ½ cup canning liquid
- Pinch red pepper flakes
- 1 cup whole-grain fusilli pasta
- ¼ teaspoon salt
- ⅛ teaspoon freshly ground black pepper
- ¼ cup Parmesan cheese
- ¼ cup chopped fresh basil
- 2 teaspoons dried parsley
- 1 teaspoon dried oregano
- Red pepper flakes

### DIRECTIONS

1. In a medium pan, heat the oil over medium heat, and sauté the shallot and garlic for 3 to 5 minutes, until the garlic is golden. Add ¾ of the chickpeas plus 2 tablespoons of liquid from the can, and bring to a simmer.
2. Remove from the heat, transfer into a standard blender, and blend until smooth. At this point, add the remaining chickpeas. Add more reserved chickpea liquid if it becomes thick.
3. Bring a large pot of salted water to a boil and cook pasta until al dente, about 8 minutes. Reserve ½ cup of the pasta water, drain the pasta, and return it to the pot.
4. Add the chickpea sauce to the hot pasta and add up to ¼ cup of the pasta water.
5. Place the pasta pot over medium heat and mix occasionally until the sauce thickens. Season with salt and pepper.
6. Serve, garnished with Parmesan, basil, parsley, oregano, and red pepper flakes.

CALORIES: 230 Kcal  FAT: 18.5 g  PROTEIN: 9.5 g  CARBOHYDRATES: 20.4 g

---

Preparation: 10 min  Cooking: 25 min  Servings: 4

## 281. LINGUINE AND BRUSSELS SPROUTS

### INGREDIENTS

- 8 ounces whole-wheat linguine
- ⅓ cup, plus 2 tablespoons extra-virgin olive oil, divided
- 1 medium sweet onion, diced
- 2 to 3 garlic cloves, smashed
- 8 ounces Brussels sprouts, chopped
- ½ cup chicken stock, as needed
- ⅓ cup dry white wine
- ½ cup shredded Parmesan cheese
- 1 lemon, cut in quarters

### DIRECTIONS

1. Bring a large pot of water to a boil and cook the pasta according to package directions. Drain, reserving 1 cup of the pasta water. Mix the cooked pasta with 2 tablespoons of olive oil, then set aside.
2. In a large sauté pan or skillet, heat the remaining ⅓ cup of olive oil on medium heat. Add the onion to the pan and cook for about 5 minutes, until softened. Add the smashed garlic cloves and cook for 1 minute, until fragrant.
3. Add the Brussels sprouts and cook covered for 15 minutes. Add chicken stock as needed to prevent burning. Once Brussels sprouts have wilted and are fork-tender, add white wine and cook down for about 7 minutes, until reduced.
4. Add the pasta to the skillet and add the pasta water as needed.
5. Serve with the Parmesan cheese and lemon for squeezing over the dish right before eating.

CALORIES: 530 Kcal  FAT: 7.8 g  PROTEIN: 5 g  CARBOHYDRATES: 95.4 g

# 20 Desserts

Preparation: 5 min    Cooking: 0 min    Servings: 4

## 282. BANANA SHAKE BOWLS

### INGREDIENTS

- 4 medium bananas, peeled
- 1 avocado, peeled, pitted and mashed
- ¾ cup almond milk
- ½ teaspoon vanilla extract

### DIRECTIONS

1. In a blender, combine the bananas with the avocado and the other ingredients.
2. Pulse, then divide into bowls.
3. Keep in the fridge until serving.

CALORIES: 185 Kcal    FAT: 4.3 g    PROTEIN: 6.45 g    CARBOHYDRATES: 6 g

*Preparation: 30 min* — *Cooking: 0 min* — *Servings: 4*

## 283. COLD LEMON SQUARES

### INGREDIENTS

- 1 cup avocado oil+ a drizzle
- 2 bananas, peeled and chopped
- 1 tablespoon honey
- ¼ cup lemon juice
- A pinch of lemon zest, grated

### DIRECTIONS

1. In your food processor, mix the bananas with the rest of the ingredients.
2. Pulse well and spread on the bottom of a pan greased with a drizzle of oil.
3. Slice into squares and serve.

CALORIES: 136 Kcal — FAT: 11.2 g — PROTEIN: 1.1 g — CARBOHYDRATES: 7 g

*Preparation: 10 min* — *Cooking: 0 min \ Refrigerating: 2 hours* — *Servings: 4*

## 284. GREEN TEA AND VANILLA CREAM

### INGREDIENTS

- 14 ounces almond milk, hot
- 2 tablespoons green tea powder
- 14 ounces heavy cream
- 3 tablespoons stevia
- 1 teaspoon vanilla extract
- 1 teaspoon gelatin powder

### DIRECTIONS

1. In a bowl, combine the almond milk with the green tea powder and the rest of the ingredient.
2. Whisk well, cool down, divide into cups.
3. Keep in the fridge for 2 hours before serving.

CALORIES: 120 Kcal — FAT: 3 g — PROTEIN: 4 g — CARBOHYDRATES: 7 g

*Preparation: 10 min*  *Cooking: 30 min*  *Servings: 6*

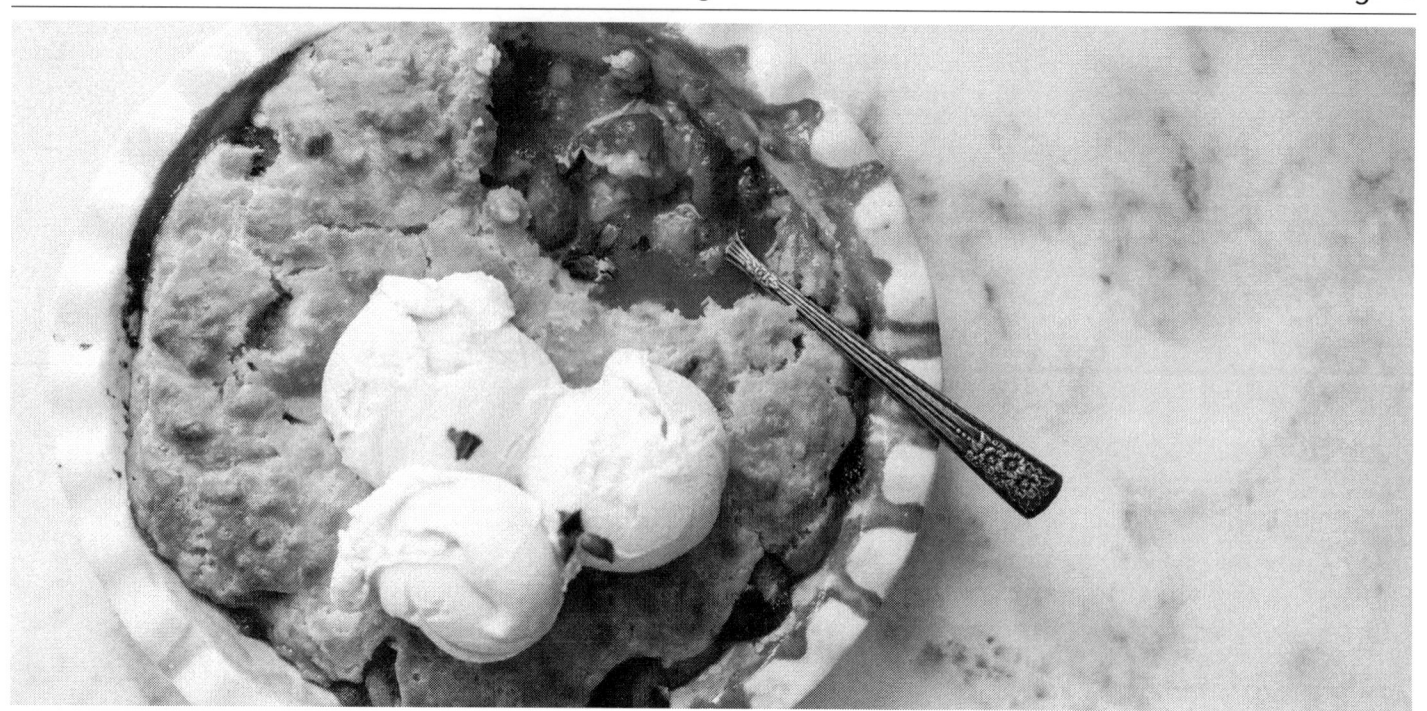

## 285. BLACKBERRIES AND STRAWBERRIES COBBLER

### INGREDIENTS

- ¾ cup stevia
- 6 cups blackberries
- ¼ cup strawberries, cubed
- ¼ teaspoon baking powder
- 1 tablespoon lime juice
- ½ cup almond flour
- ½ cup water
- 3 and ½ tablespoon avocado oil
- Cooking spray

### DIRECTIONS

1. In a bowl, mix the berries with half of the stevia and lemon juice, sprinkle some flour all over, whisk and pour into a baking dish greased with cooking spray.
2. In another bowl, mix flour with the rest of the sugar, baking powder, the water and the oil, and stir the whole thing with your hands.
3. Spread over the berries, introduce in the oven at 375 degrees F and bake for 30 minutes.
4. Serve warm.

CALORIES: 221 Kcal     FAT: 6.3 g     PROTEIN: 9 g     CARBOHYDRATES: 6 g

*Preparation: 10 min*     *Cooking: 1 hour*     *Servings: 6*

## 286. FIGS PIE

### INGREDIENTS

- ½ cup stevia
- 6 figs, cut into quarters
- ½ teaspoon vanilla extract
- 1 cup almond flour
- 4 eggs, whisked

### DIRECTIONS

1. Spread the figs on the bottom of a springform pan lined with parchment paper.
2. In a bowl, combine the other ingredients, whisk and pour over the figs,
3. Bake at 375 digress F for 1 hour, flip the pie upside down when it's cooked.
4. Serve warm or wait until cooled.

CALORIES: 200 Kcal     FAT: 9.4 g     PROTEIN: 8 g     CARBOHYDRATES: 7.6 g

---

*Preparation: 10 min*     *Cooking: 0 min \ Refrigerating: 2 hours*     *Servings: 4*

## 287. CHERRY CREAM

### INGREDIENTS

- 2 cups cherries, pitted and chopped
- 1 cup almond milk
- ½ cup whipping cream
- 3 eggs, whisked
- 1/3 cup stevia
- 1 teaspoon lemon juice
- ½ teaspoon vanilla extract

### DIRECTIONS

1. In a food processor, combine the cherries with the milk and the rest of the ingredients.
2. Pulse well, then divide into cups.
3. Keep in the fridge for 2 hours before serving.

CALORIES: 200 Kcal     FAT: 4.5 g     PROTEIN: 3.4 g     CARBOHYDRATES: 5.6 g

Preparation: 10 min  Cooking: 35 min  Servings: 8

## 288. BLACK TEA CAKE

### INGREDIENTS

- 6 tablespoons black tea powder
- 2 cups almond milk, warmed up
- 1 cup avocado oil
- 2 cups stevia
- 4 eggs
- 2 teaspoons vanilla extract
- 3 and ½ cups almond flour
- 1 teaspoon baking soda
- 3 teaspoons baking powder

### DIRECTIONS

1. In a bowl, combine the almond milk with the oil, stevia and the rest of the ingredients and whisk well.
2. Pour the mixture into a cake pan lined with parchment paper.
3. Introduce in the oven at 350 degrees F and bake for 35 minutes.
4. Leave the cake to cool down, slice and serve with a cup of tea.

CALORIES: 200 Kcal  FAT: 6.4 g  PROTEIN: 5.4 g  CARBOHYDRATES: 6.5 g

Preparation: 10 min  Cooking: 20 min  Servings: 4

## 289. STRAWBERRIES CREAM

**INGREDIENTS**

- ½ cup stevia
- 2 pounds strawberries, chopped
- 1 cup almond milk
- Zest of 1 lemon, grated
- ½ cup heavy cream
- 3 egg yolks, whisked

**DIRECTIONS**

1. Heat up a pan with the milk over medium-high heat.
2. Add the stevia and the rest of the ingredients, whisk well and simmer for 20 minutes.
3. Divide into cups and serve cold.

CALORIES: 152 Kcal  FAT: 4.4 g  PROTEIN: 0.8 g  CARBOHYDRATES: 5.1 g

---

Preparation: 10 min  Cooking: 20 min  Servings: 8

## 290. CINNAMON CHICKPEAS COOKIES

**INGREDIENTS**

- 1 cup canned chickpeas, drained, rinsed and mashed
- 2 cups almond flour
- 1 teaspoon cinnamon powder
- 1 teaspoon baking powder
- 1 cup avocado oil
- ½ cup stevia
- 1 egg, whisked
- 2 teaspoons almond extract
- 1 cup raisins
- 1 cup coconut, unsweetened and shredded

**DIRECTIONS**

1. In a bowl, combine the chickpeas with the flour, cinnamon and the other ingredients, and whisk well until you obtain a dough.
2. Scoop tablespoons of dough on a baking sheet lined with parchment paper, introduce them in the oven at 350 degrees F and bake for 20 minutes.
3. Leave them to cool down for a few minutes and serve.

CALORIES: 200 Kcal  FAT: 4.5 g  PROTEIN: 2.4 g  CARBOHYDRATES: 9.5 g

Preparation: 10 min    Cooking: 40 min    Servings: 4

## 291. APPLES AND PLUMS CAKE

### INGREDIENTS

- 7 ounces almond flour
- 1 egg, whisked
- 5 tablespoons stevia
- 3 ounces warm almond milk
- 2 pounds plums, pitted and cut into quarters
- 2 apples, cored and chopped
- Zest of 1 lemon, grated
- 1 teaspoon baking powder

### DIRECTIONS

1. In a bowl, mix the almond milk with the egg, stevia, and the rest of the ingredients except the cooking spray and whisk well.
2. Grease a cake pan with the oil.
3. Pour the cake mix inside then introduce in the oven.
4. Bake at 350 degrees F for 40 minutes.
5. Let the cake cool down, slice and serve.

CALORIES: 209 Kcal    FAT: 6.4 g    PROTEIN: 6.6 g    CARBOHYDRATES: 8 g

*Preparation: 5 min*  *Cooking: 0 min \ Refrigerating: 30 min*  *Servings: 4*

## 292. CARDAMOM ALMOND CREAM

### INGREDIENTS

- Juice of 1 lime
- ½ cup stevia
- 1 and ½ cups water
- 3 cups almond milk
- ½ cup honey
- 2 teaspoons cardamom, ground
- 1 teaspoon rose water
- 1 teaspoon vanilla extract

### DIRECTIONS

1. In a blender, combine the almond milk with the cardamom and the rest of the ingredients.
2. Pulse well, then divide into cups.
3. Keep in the fridge for 30 minutes before serving.

CALORIES: 283 Kcal    FAT: 11.8 g    PROTEIN: 7.1 g    CARBOHYDRATES: 4.7 g

---

*Preparation: 10 min*  *Cooking: 20 min*  *Servings: 4*

## 293. BANANA CINNAMON CUPCAKES

### INGREDIENTS

- 4 tablespoons avocado oil
- 4 eggs
- ½ cup orange juice
- 2 teaspoons cinnamon powder
- 1 teaspoon vanilla extract
- 2 bananas, peeled and chopped
- ¾ cup almond flour
- ½ teaspoon baking powder
- Cooking spray

### DIRECTIONS

1. In a bowl, combine the oil with the eggs, orange juice and the other ingredients except the cooking spray.
2. Whisk well, pour in a cupcake pan greased with the cooking spray.
3. Introduce in the oven at 350 degrees F and bake for 20 minutes.
4. Cool the cupcakes down and serve.

CALORIES: 142 Kcal    FAT: 5.8 g    PROTEIN: 1.6 g    CARBOHYDRATES: 5.7 g

Preparation: 10 min  Cooking: 20 min  Servings: 8

## 294. COCOA LENTILS BROWNIES

### INGREDIENTS

- 30 ounces canned lentils, rinsed and drained
- 1 tablespoon honey
- 1 banana, peeled and chopped
- ½ teaspoon baking soda
- 4 tablespoons almond butter
- 2 tablespoons cocoa powder
- Cooking spray

### DIRECTIONS

1. In a food processor, combine the lentils with the honey and the other ingredients except the cooking spray and pulse well.
2. Pour this into a pan greased with cooking spray, spread evenly, introduce in the oven at 375 degrees F.
3. Bake for 20 minutes.
4. Cut the brownies and serve cold.

CALORIES: 300 Kcal  FAT: 7.5 g  PROTEIN: 4.3 g  CARBOHYDRATES: 8.7 g

Preparation: 10 min   Cooking: 0 min   Servings: 6

## 295. RHUBARB AND APPLES CREAM

### INGREDIENTS

- 3 cups rhubarb, chopped
- 1 and ½ cups stevia
- 2 eggs, whisked
- ½ teaspoon nutmeg, ground
- 1 tablespoon avocado oil
- ⅓ cup almond milk

### DIRECTIONS

1. In a blender, combine the rhubarb with the stevia and the rest of the ingredients.
2. Pulse well, then divide into cups.
3. Serve cold and enjoy.

CALORIES: 200 Kcal   FAT: 5.2 g   PROTEIN: 2.5 g   CARBOHYDRATES: 7.6 g

Preparation: 10 min   Cooking: 40 min   Servings: 4

## 296. CRANBERRIES AND PEARS PIE

### INGREDIENTS

- 2 cups cranberries
- 3 cups pears, cubed
- A drizzle of olive oil
- 1 cup stevia
- ⅓ cup almond flour
- 1 cup rolled oats
- ¼ avocado oil

### DIRECTIONS

1. In a bowl, mix the cranberries with the pears and the other ingredients except the olive oil and the oats and stir well.
2. Grease a cake pan with a drizzle of olive oil, pour the pears mix inside, sprinkle the oats all over.
3. Bake at 350 degrees F for 40 minutes.
4. Cool the cake and serve.

CALORIES: 172 Kcal   FAT: 3.4 g   PROTEIN: 4.5 g   CARBOHYDRATES: 11.5 g

*Preparation: 5 min*   *Cooking: 10 min\ Refrigerating: 2 hours*   *Servings: 4*

## 297. PEACH SORBET

### INGREDIENTS

- 2 cups apple juice
- 1 cup stevia
- 2 tablespoons lemon zest, grated
- 2 pounds peaches, pitted and quartered

### DIRECTIONS

1. Heat up a pan over medium heat.
2. Add the apple juice and the rest of the ingredients.
3. Simmer for 10 minutes, then transfer to a blender.
4. Pulse, then divide into cups and keep in the freezer for 2 hours.
5. Serve cold and enjoy.

CALORIES: 182 Kcal   FAT: 5.4 g   PROTEIN: 5.4 g   CARBOHYDRATES: 2 g

*Preparation: 5 min*     *Cooking: 10 min \ Refrigerating: 1 hour*     *Servings: 6*

# 298. LEMON CREAM

## INGREDIENTS

- 2 eggs, whisked
- 1 and ¼ cup stevia
- 10 tablespoons avocado oil
- 1 cup heavy cream
- Juice of 2 lemons
- Zest of 2 lemons, grated

## DIRECTIONS

1. In a pan, combine the cream with the lemon juice and the other ingredients and whisk well.
2. Cook for 10 minutes at low flame.
3. Divide into cups and keep in the fridge for 1 hour before serving.

CALORIES: 150 Kcal     FAT: 8.5 g     PROTEIN: 4.5 g     CARBOHYDRATES: 8.6 g

---

*Preparation: 10 min*     *Cooking: 20 min*     *Servings: 4*

# 299. ALMOND RICE DESSERT

## INGREDIENTS

- 1 cup white rice
- 2 cups almond milk
- 1 cup almonds, chopped
- ½ cup stevia
- 1 tablespoon cinnamon powder
- ½ cup pomegranate seeds

## DIRECTIONS

1. In a pot, mix the rice with the milk and stevia.
2. Bring to a simmer and cook for 20 minutes, stirring often.
3. Add the rest of the ingredients, stir, divide into bowls and serve.

CALORIES: 234 Kcal     FAT: 9.5 g     PROTEIN: 6.5 g     CARBOHYDRATES: 12.4 g

Preparation: 10 min     Cooking: 10 min     Servings: 4

## 300. BLUEBERRIES STEW

### INGREDIENTS

- 2 cups blueberries
- 3 tablespoons stevia
- 1 and ½ cups pure apple juice
- 1 teaspoon vanilla extract

### DIRECTIONS

1. In a pan, combine the blueberries with stevia and the other ingredients.
2. Bring to a simmer and cook over medium-low heat for 10 minutes.
3. Divide into cups and serve cold.

CALORIES: 192 Kcal     FAT: 5.4 g     PROTEIN: 4.5 g     CARBOHYDRATES: 9.4 g

*Preparation: 20 min*  *Cooking: 0 min \ Refrigerating: 20 min*  *Servings: 8*

## 301. MANDARIN CREAM

### INGREDIENTS

- 2 mandarins, peeled and cut into segments
- Juice of 2 mandarins
- 2 tablespoons stevia
- 4 eggs, whisked
- ¾ cup stevia
- ¾ cup almonds, ground

### DIRECTIONS

1. In a blender, combine the mandarins with the mandarin's juice and the other ingredients.
2. Whisk well, then divide into cups.
3. Keep in the fridge for 20 minutes before serving.

CALORIES: 106 Kcal    FAT: 3.4 g    PROTEIN: 4 g    CARBOHYDRATES: 2.4 g

---

*Preparation: 10 min*  *Cooking: 30 min*  *Servings: 6*

## 302. CREAMY MINT STRAWBERRY MIX

### INGREDIENTS

- Cooking spray
- ¼ cup stevia
- 1 and ½ cup almond flour
- 1 teaspoon baking powder
- 1 cup almond milk
- 1 egg, whisked
- 2 cups strawberries, sliced
- 1 tablespoon mint, chopped
- 1 teaspoon lime zest, grated
- ½ cup whipping cream

### DIRECTIONS

1. In a bowl, combine the almond with the strawberries, mint and the other ingredients except the cooking spray and whisk well.
2. Grease 6 ramekins with the cooking spray, pour the strawberry mix inside, introduce in the oven and bake at 350 degrees F for 30 minutes.
3. Cool down and serve.

CALORIES: 185 Kcal    FAT: 6.3 g    PROTEIN: 4.5 g    CARBOHYDRATES: 6.5 g

Preparation: 10 min    Cooking: 25 min    Servings: 8

## 303. VANILLA CAKE

### INGREDIENTS

- 3 cups almond flour
- 3 teaspoons baking powder
- 1 cup olive oil
- 1 and ½ cup almond milk
- 1 and 2/3 cup stevia
- 2 cups water
- 1 tablespoon lime juice
- 2 teaspoons vanilla extract
- Cooking spray

### DIRECTIONS

1. In a bowl, mix the almond flour with the baking powder, the oil and the rest of the ingredients except the cooking spray and whisk well.
2. Pour the mix into a cake pan greased with the cooking spray, introduce in the oven.
3. Bake at 370 degrees F for 25 minutes.
4. Leave the cake to cool down, cut and serve.

CALORIES: 200 Kcal    FAT: 7.6 g    PROTEIN: 4.5 g    CARBOHYDRATES: 5.5 g

*Preparation: 5 min*  *Cooking: 5 min*  *Servings: 2*

## 304. PUMPKIN CREAM

### INGREDIENTS

- 2 cups canned pumpkin flesh
- 2 tablespoons stevia
- 1 teaspoon vanilla extract
- 2 tablespoons water
- A pinch of pumpkin spice

### DIRECTIONS

1. In a pan, combine the pumpkin flesh with the other ingredients.
2. Simmer for 5 minutes.
3. Divide into cups and serve cold.

CALORIES: 192 Kcal  FAT: 3.4 g  PROTEIN: 3.5 g  CARBOHYDRATES: 7.6 g

---

*Preparation: 5 min*  *Cooking: 0 min*  *Servings: 2*

## 305. MINTY COCONUT CREAM

### INGREDIENTS

- 1 banana, peeled
- 2 cups coconut flesh, shredded
- 3 tablespoons mint, chopped
- 1 and ½ cups coconut water
- 2 tablespoons stevia
- ½ avocado, pitted and peeled

### DIRECTIONS

1. In a blender, combine the coconut with the banana and the rest of the ingredients.
2. Pulse well.
3. Divide into cups and serve cold.

CALORIES: 193 Kcal  FAT: 5. g  PROTEIN: 3 g  CARBOHYDRATES: 7.6 g

*Preparation: 5 min*  *Cooking: 0 min*  *Servings: 2*

## 306. CHIA AND BERRIES SMOOTHIE BOWL

### INGREDIENTS

- 1 and ½ cup almond milk
- 1 cup blackberries
- ¼ cup strawberries, chopped
- 1 and ½ tablespoons chia seeds
- 1 teaspoon cinnamon powder

### DIRECTIONS

1. In a blender, combine the blackberries with the strawberries and the rest of the ingredients.
2. Pulse well.
3. Divide into small glasses and garnish with some blackberries.
4. Serve cold and enjoy.

CALORIES: 92 Kcal    FAT: 3.4 g    PROTEIN: 3 g    CARBOHYDRATES: 8.4 g

*Preparation: 5 min*     *Cooking: 0 min \ Refrigerating: 20 min*     *Servings: 2*

## 307. WATERMELON CREAM

### INGREDIENTS

- 1-pound watermelon, peeled and chopped
- 1 teaspoon vanilla extract
- 1 cup heavy cream
- 1 teaspoon lime juice
- 2 tablespoons sugar

### DIRECTIONS

1. In a blender, combine the watermelon with the cream and the rest of the ingredients.
2. Pulse well, then divide into cups.
3. Keep in the fridge for 20 minutes before serving.

CALORIES: 122 Kcal     FAT: 5.7 g     PROTEIN: 0.4 g     CARBOHYDRATES: 5.3 g

---

*Preparation: 10 min*     *Cooking: 10 min*     *Servings: 4*

## 308. GRAPES STEW

### INGREDIENTS

- ⅔ cup stevia
- 1 tablespoon olive oil
- ⅓ cup coconut water
- 1 teaspoon vanilla extract
- 1 teaspoon lemon zest, grated
- 2 cup red grapes, halved

### DIRECTIONS

1. Heat up a pan with the water over medium heat.
2. Add the oil, stevia and the rest of the ingredients and toss.
3. Simmer for 10 minutes.
4. Divide into cups and serve.

CALORIES: 122 Kcal     FAT: 3.7 g     PROTEIN: 0.4 g     CARBOHYDRATES: 2.3 g

*Preparation: 5 min*     *Cooking: 0 min \ Refrigerating: 2 hours*     *Servings: 2*

# 309. COCOA SWEET CHERRY CREAM

## INGREDIENTS

- ½ cup cocoa powder
- ¾ cup red cherry jam
- ¼ cup sugar
- 2 cups milk
- 1-pound cherries, pitted and halved

## DIRECTIONS

1. In a blender, mix the cherries with the water and the rest of the ingredients.
2. Pulse well.
3. Divide into glasses and keep in the fridge for 2 hours.
4. Serve garnishing as you like.

CALORIES: 162 Kcal     FAT: 3.4 g     PROTEIN: 1 g     CARBOHYDRATES: 5 g

*Preparation: 10 min*     *Cooking: 25 min*     *Servings: 4*

## 310. APPLE COUSCOUS PUDDING

### INGREDIENTS

- ½ cup couscous
- 1 and ½ cups milk
- ¼ cup apple, cored and chopped
- 3 tablespoons stevia
- ½ teaspoon rose water
- 1 tablespoon orange zest, grated

### DIRECTIONS

1. Heat up a pan with the milk over medium heat.
2. Add the couscous and the rest of the ingredients then whisk.
3. Simmer for 25 minutes.
4. Divide into bowls and serve.

CALORIES: 150 Kcal     FAT: 4.5 g     PROTEIN: 4 g     CARBOHYDRATES: 7.5 g

---

*Preparation: 10 min*     *Cooking: 1 hour*     *Servings: 4*

## 311. RICOTTA RAMEKINS

### INGREDIENTS

- 6 eggs, whisked
- 1 and ½ pounds ricotta cheese, soft
- ½ pound stevia
- 1 teaspoon vanilla extract
- ½ teaspoon baking powder
- Cooking spray

### DIRECTIONS

1. In a bowl, mix the eggs with the ricotta and the other ingredients except the cooking spray and whisk well.
2. Grease 4 ramekins with the cooking spray, pour the ricotta cream in each.
3. Bake at 360 degrees F for 1 hour.
4. Serve cold.

CALORIES: 180 Kcal     FAT: 5.3 g     PROTEIN: 4 g     CARBOHYDRATES: 11.5 g

Preparation: 10 min    Cooking: 0 min    Servings: 2

## 312. PAPAYA CREAMY SMOOTHIE

### INGREDIENTS

- 1 cup papaya, peeled and chopped
- 2 cups milk
- 1 tablespoon sugar
- ½ teaspoon vanilla extract
- 1 cup ice

### DIRECTIONS

1. In a blender, combine the milk, the papaya and the other ingredients.
2. Pulse well.
3. Divide into glasses and serve.

CALORIES: 92 Kcal    FAT: 3.1 g    PROTEIN: 2 g    CARBOHYDRATES: 3.5 g

*Preparation: 10 min*     *Cooking: 15 min*     *Servings: 4*

## 313. ALMONDS AND OATS PUDDING

### INGREDIENTS

- 1 tablespoon lemon juice
- Zest of 1 lime
- 1 and ½ cups almond milk
- 1 teaspoon almond extract
- ½ cup oats
- 2 tablespoons stevia
- ½ cup silver almonds, chopped

### DIRECTIONS

1. In a pan, combine the almond milk with the lime zest and the other ingredients.
2. Whisk, bring to a simmer and cook over medium heat for 15 minutes.
3. Divide the mix into bowls and serve cold.

CALORIES: 174 Kcal     FAT: 12.1 g     PROTEIN: 4.8 g     CARBOHYDRATES: 3.9 g

---

*Preparation: 10 min*     *Cooking: 5 min \ Refrigerating: 20 min*     *Servings: 4*

## 314. STRAWBERRY SORBET

### INGREDIENTS

- 1 cup strawberries, chopped
- 1 tablespoon of liquid honey
- 2 tablespoons water
- 1 tablespoon lemon juice

### DIRECTIONS

1. Preheat the water and liquid honey until you get homogenous liquid.
2. Blend the strawberries until smooth and combine them with honey liquid and lemon juice.
3. Transfer the strawberry mixture in the ice cream maker and churn it for 20 minutes or until the sorbet is thick.
4. Scoop the cooked sorbet in the ice cream cups.

CALORIES: 30 Kcal     FAT: 0.4 g     PROTEIN: 0.9 g     CARBOHYDRATES: 14.9 g

*Preparation:* 10 min    *Cooking:* 25 min    *Servings:* 6

## 315. CINNAMON PEARS

### INGREDIENTS

- 2 pears
- 1 teaspoon ground cinnamon
- 1 tablespoon sugar
- 4 teaspoons butter
- 1 lemon

### DIRECTIONS

1. Cut the pears into slices.
2. Cut a lemon into slices.
3. Sprinkle every pear half with cinnamon and drizzle with sugar.
4. Add butter and place the bears in a baking sheet together with the lemon slices.
5. Bake the pears for 25 minutes at 365F.
6. Remove the pears from the baking sheet and transfer in the serving plates.

CALORIES: 96 Kcal     FAT: 4.4 g     PROTEIN: 0.9 g     CARBOHYDRATES: 3.9 g

*Preparation: 15 min*  *Cooking: 50 min*  *Servings: 8*

## 316. VANILLA APPLE PIE

### INGREDIENTS

- 3 apples, sliced
- ½ teaspoon ground cinnamon
- 1 teaspoon vanilla extract
- 1 tablespoon sugar
- 7 oz yeast roll dough
- 1 egg, beaten

### DIRECTIONS

1. Roll up the dough and cut it on 2 parts.
2. Line the springform pan with baking paper.
3. Place the first dough part in the springform pan.
4. Then arrange the apples over the dough and sprinkle it with sugar, vanilla extract, and ground cinnamon.
5. Then cover the apples with remaining dough and secure the edges of the pie with the help of the fork.
6. Make the small cuts in the surface of the pie.
7. Brush the pie with beaten egg and bake it for 50 minutes at 375F.
8. Cool the cooked pie well and then remove from the springform pan.
9. Cut it on the servings.

CALORIES: 140 Kcal   FAT: 3.4 g   PROTEIN: 2.9 g   CARBOHYDRATES: 23.9 g

---

*Preparation: 15 min*  *Cooking: 10 min*  *Servings: 6*

## 317. GINGER ICE CREAM

### INGREDIENTS

- 1 mango, peeled
- 1 cup Greek yogurt
- 1 tablespoon sugar
- ¼ cup milk
- 1 teaspoon vanilla extract
- ¼ teaspoon ground ginger

### DIRECTIONS

1. Blend the mango until you get puree and combine it with sugar, milk, vanilla extract, and ground ginger.
2. Then mix up together Greek yogurt and mango puree mixture.
3. Transfer it in the plastic vessel.
4. Freeze the ice cream for 35 minutes.

CALORIES: 90 Kcal   FAT: 1.4 g   PROTEIN: 4.9 g   CARBOHYDRATES: 21.9 g

Preparation: 5 min  Cooking: 0 min  Servings: 2

# 318. YOGURT PARFAIT

## INGREDIENTS

- ½ cup blueberries
- 1 cup Plain yogurt
- ½ teaspoon vanilla extract
- ½ cup strawberries
- ½ cup oat flakes
- 1 tablespoon raisins

## DIRECTIONS

1. Slice the strawberries.
2. Mix up together Plain yogurt and vanilla extract.
3. Put around 1/3 of the strawberries, the blueberries, the oat flakes and the raisins in the bottom of a glass.
4. Cover the layer with half of the yogurt.
5. Add another layer made with 1/3 of the fruits and flakes.
6. Make another layer with the remaining plain yogurt.
7. Top with the remaining fruits and oat flakes.
8. Serve cold.
9. Slice the strawberries.
10. Mix up together Plain yogurt and vanilla extract.
11. Put around 1/3 of the strawberries, the blueberries, the oat flakes and the raisins in the bottom of a glass.
12. Cover the layer with half of the yogurt.
13. Add another layer made with 1/3 of the fruits and flakes.
14. Make another layer with the remaining plain yogurt.
15. Top with the remaining fruits and oat flakes.
16. Serve cold.

CALORIES: 64 Kcal  FAT: 0.4 g  PROTEIN: 1.9 g  CARBOHYDRATES: 6.9 g

*Preparation: 50 min*  *Cooking: 20 min*  *Servings: 6*

## 319. CHERRY COMPOTE

**INGREDIENTS**

- 2 peaches, pitted, halved
- 1 cup cherries, pitted
- ½ cup grape juice
- ½ cup strawberries
- 1 tablespoon liquid honey
- 1 teaspoon vanilla extract
- 1 teaspoon ground cinnamon

**DIRECTIONS**

1. Pour grape juice in the saucepan.
2. Add vanilla extract and ground cinnamon. Bring the liquid to boil.
3. After this, put peaches, cherries, and strawberries in the hot grape juice and bring to boil, then cook for other 15 minutes.
4. Remove the mixture from heat, add liquid honey, and close the lid.
5. Let the compote rest for 40 minutes.
6. Carefully mix up the compote and transfer in the serving plate.

CALORIES: 80 Kcal    FAT: 0.4 g    PROTEIN: 0.9 g    CARBOHYDRATES: 19.9 g

---

*Preparation: 15 min*  *Cooking: 10 min*  *Servings: 6*

## 320. CREAMY STRAWBERRIES

**INGREDIENTS**

- 6 tablespoons almond butter
- 1 tablespoon sugar
- 1 cup milk
- 1 teaspoon vanilla extract
- 1 cup strawberries, sliced

**DIRECTIONS**

1. Pour milk in the saucepan.
2. Add sugar, vanilla extract, and almond butter.
3. With the help of the hand mixer mix up the liquid until smooth and bring it to boil.
4. Then remove the mixture from the heat and let it cool.
5. The cooled mixture will be thick.
6. Put the strawberries in the serving glasses and top with the thick almond butter dip.

CALORIES: 192 Kcal    FAT: 14.4 g    PROTEIN: 1.9 g    CARBOHYDRATES: 10.9 g

*Preparation: 15 min*     *Cooking: 10 min*     Servings: 6

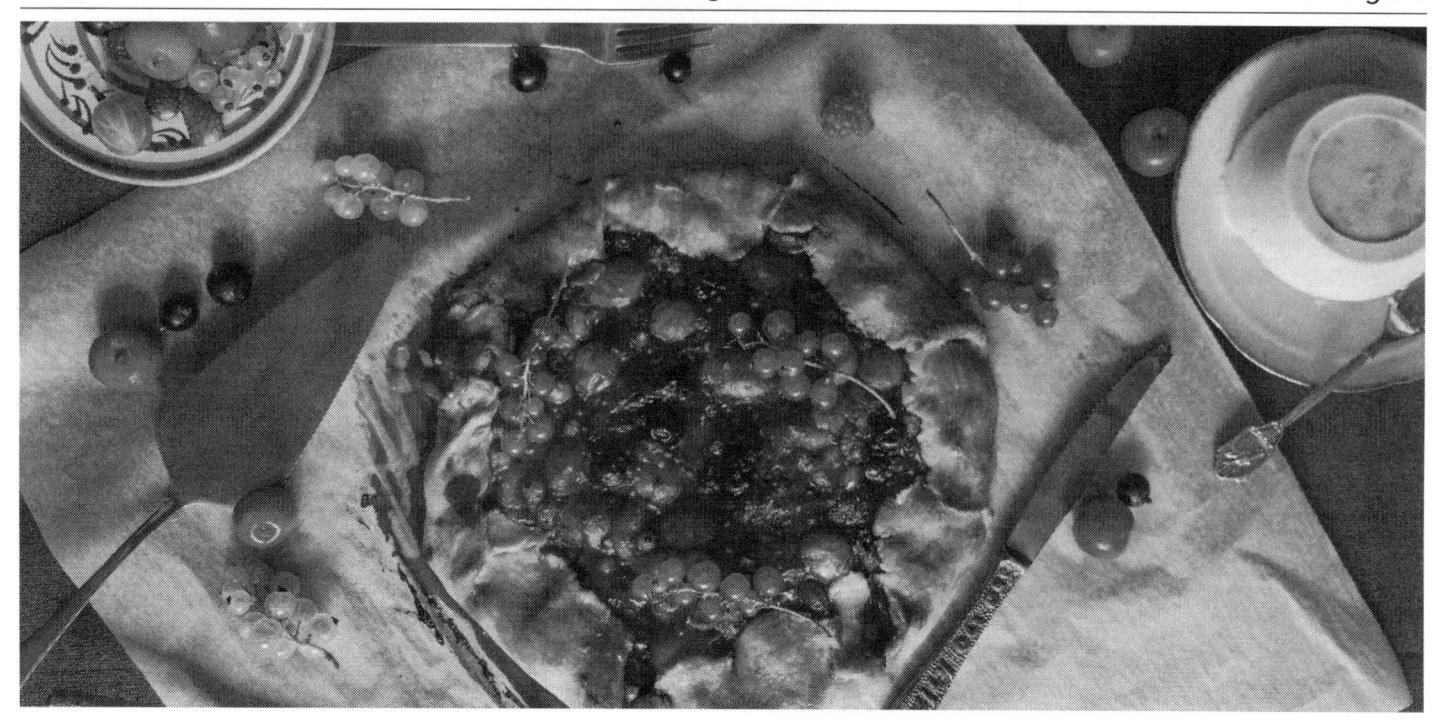

# 321. BERRIES TART

## INGREDIENTS

- 3 tablespoons butter, softened
- 1 cup wheat flour, whole wheat
- 1 teaspoon baking powder
- 1 egg, beaten
- 4 tablespoons pistachio paste
- 2 tablespoons raspberry jam
- 1 cup of various types of berries
- 1 bunch of small grapes

## DIRECTIONS

1. Knead the dough: combine together softened butter, flour, baking powder, and egg. You should get the non-sticky and very soft dough.
2. Put the dough in the springform pan and flatten it with the help of the fingertips until you get pie crust.
3. Bake it for 10 minutes at 365F.
4. After this, spread the pie crust with raspberry jam and then with pistachio paste.
5. Bake the tart at 365F for another 10 minutes.
6. Cool the cooked tart, then garnish with the various types of berries and the grapes.
7. Cut the tart and serve.

CALORIES: 311 Kcal     FAT: 11.4 g     PROTEIN: 1.9 g     CARBOHYDRATES: 14.9 g

Preparation: 5 min  Cooking: 0 min \ Refrigerating: 2 hours  Servings: 6

## 322. CHOCOLATE CUPS

### INGREDIENTS

- ½ cup avocado oil
- 1 cup, chocolate, melted
- 1 teaspoon matcha powder
- 3 tablespoons sugar

### DIRECTIONS

1. In a bowl, mix the chocolate with the oil and the rest of the ingredients and whisk well.
2. Divide into cups.
3. Keep in the freezer for 2 hours before serving.

CALORIES: 174 Kcal  FAT: 9.1 g  PROTEIN: 2.8 g  CARBOHYDRATES: 3.9 g

---

Preparation: 20 min  Cooking: 30 min  Servings: 8

## 323. HONEY WALNUT BARS

### INGREDIENTS

- 5 oz puff pastry
- ½ cup of water
- 3 tablespoons of liquid honey
- 1 teaspoon sugar
- ⅓ cup butter, softened
- ½ cup walnuts, chopped
- 1 teaspoon olive oil

### DIRECTIONS

1. Roll up the puff pastry and cut it on 6 sheets.
2. Then brush the tray with olive oil and arrange the first puff pastry sheet inside.
3. Grease it with butter gently and sprinkle with walnuts.
4. Repeat the same steps with 4 puff pastry sheets.
5. Then sprinkle the last layer with walnuts and sugar and cover with the sixth puff pastry sheet.
6. Cut the baklava on the servings.
7. Bake the baklava for 30 minutes.
8. Meanwhile, bring to boil liquid honey and water.
9. When the baklava is cooked, remove it from the oven.
10. Pour hot honey liquid over baklava and let it cool till the room temperature.

CALORIES: 243 Kcal  FAT: 4.4 g  PROTEIN: 1.9 g  CARBOHYDRATES: 15.9 g

Preparation: 15 min  Cooking: 25 min  Servings: 4

## 324. BLUEBERRY MUFFINS

### INGREDIENTS

- 1 cup whole wheat flour
- 1 teaspoon baking powder
- ¼ cup blueberries
- 1 teaspoon vanilla extract
- 1 tablespoon butter, softened
- ¾ cup sour cream
- 1 tablespoon sugar
- Cooking spray

### DIRECTIONS

1. In the mixing bowl combine together wheat, flour and baking powder.
2. Then add sour cream, vanilla extract, butter and sugar.
3. Stir the mixture well until smooth. You should get a thick batter. Add more sour cream if needed.
4. After this, add blueberries and carefully stir the batter.
5. Spray the muffin molds with the cooking spray.
6. Fill ½ part of every muffin mold with batter.
7. Preheat the oven to 365F.
8. Place the muffins in the prepared oven and cook them for 25 minutes.
9. The cooked muffins will have a golden color surface.

CALORIES: 241 Kcal   FAT: 12.4 g   PROTEIN: 1.9 g   CARBOHYDRATES: 24.9 g

*Preparation: 20 min*     *Cooking: 15 min*     *Servings: 8*

## 325. QUINOA ENERGY BARS

### INGREDIENTS

- ½ cup puffed quinoa
- ¼ cup oats
- 2 oz dark chocolate
- 2 tablespoons almond butter
- ¾ cup maple syrup
- 1 tablespoon butter
- 1 tablespoon coconut flakes

### DIRECTIONS

1. Place dark chocolate, butter, maple syrup, and almond butter in the saucepan.
2. Melt the mixture and add oats, puffed quinoa, and coconut flakes.
3. Mix up well and remove it from the heat.
4. After this, line the baking tray with baking paper and transfer the quinoa mixture in it.
5. Flatten it well with the help of the spatula and cut on the bars (8 pieces).
6. Bake the quinoa bars for 10 minutes at 365F.
7. After this, remove the tray with quinoa bars from the oven and cool well.

CALORIES: 240 Kcal     FAT: 6.4 g     PROTEIN: 1.9 g     CARBOHYDRATES: 29.9 g

---

*Preparation: 10 min*     *Cooking: 15 min*     *Servings: 4*

## 326. CINNAMON STUFFED PEACHES

### INGREDIENTS

- 4 peaches, pitted, halved
- 2 tablespoons ricotta cheese
- 2 tablespoons of liquid honey
- ¾ cup of water
- ½ teaspoon vanilla extract
- ¾ teaspoon ground cinnamon
- 1 tablespoon almonds, sliced
- ¾ teaspoon saffron

### DIRECTIONS

1. Pour water in the saucepan and bring to boil.
2. Add vanilla extract, saffron, ground cinnamon, and liquid honey.
3. Cook the liquid until the honey is melted.
4. Then remove it from the heat.
5. Put the halved peaches in the hot honey liquid.
6. Meanwhile, make the filling: mix up together ricotta cheese, vanilla extract, and sliced almonds.
7. Remove the peaches from honey liquid and arrange in the plate. Fill 4 peach halves with ricotta filling and cover them with remaining peach halves.
8. Sprinkle the cooked dessert with liquid honey mixture gently.

CALORIES: 213 Kcal     FAT: 1.4 g     PROTEIN: 1.9 g     CARBOHYDRATES: 23.9 g

*Preparation:* 10 min  *Cooking:* 30 min  *Servings:* 6

## 327. ALMOND CITRUS MUFFINS

### INGREDIENTS

- 2 eggs, beaten
- 1 ½ cup whole wheat flour
- ½ cup almond meal
- 1 teaspoon vanilla extract
- 1 tablespoon butter, softened
- 1 teaspoon orange zest, grated
- 1 tablespoon orange juice
- ¾ cup sugar
- 1 oz orange pulp
- 1 teaspoon baking powder
- ½ teaspoon lime zest, grated

### DIRECTIONS

1. Make the muffin batter: combine together almond meal, eggs, whole wheat flour, vanilla extract, butter, orange zest, orange juice, and orange pulp.
2. Add lime zest and baking powder, then add sugar.
3. With the help of the hand mixer mix up the ingredients.
4. When the mixture is soft and smooth, it is done.
5. Spray the muffin molds with cooking spray from inside and preheat the oven to 365F.
6. Fill ½ part of every muffin mold with muffin batter and transfer them in the oven.
7. Cook the muffins for 30 minutes.
8. Check if the muffins are cooked by piercing them with a toothpick (if it is dry, the muffins are cooked; if it is not dry, bake the muffins for 5-7 minutes more.)

CALORIES: 204 Kcal  FAT: 7.4 g  PROTEIN: 1.9 g  CARBOHYDRATES: 57.9 g

*Preparation: 10 min*  *Cooking: 25 min*  *Servings: 2*

# 328. SPECIAL LIME, GRAPES AND APPLES

## INGREDIENTS

- ½ cup red grapes
- 2 apples
- 1 teaspoon lime juice
- 1 teaspoon sugar
- 3 tablespoons water

## DIRECTIONS

1. Line the baking tray with baking paper.
2. Then cut the apples on the halves and remove the seeds with the help of the scooper.
3. Cut the apple halves on 2 parts more.
4. Arrange all fruits in the tray in one layer, drizzle with water, and bake for 20 minutes at 375F.
5. Flip the fruits on another side after 10 minutes of cooking.
6. Then remove them from the oven and sprinkle with lime juice and sugar.
7. Return the fruits back in the oven and bake for 5 minutes more.
8. Serve the cooked dessert hot or warm.

CALORIES: 142 Kcal    FAT: 4.4 g    PROTEIN: 2.4 g    CARBOHYDRATES: 40.9 g

---

*Preparation: 20 min*  *Cooking: 45 min*  *Servings: 4*

# 329. LEMON ALMOND CAKE

## INGREDIENTS

- 1 ¼ cup almonds, sliced
- 5 tablespoons whole wheat flour
- ¼ teaspoon salt
- 1 teaspoon baking soda
- 1 tablespoon apple cider vinegar
- 2 eggs, beaten
- 1 teaspoon vanilla extract
- 1 teaspoon almond extract
- 3 tablespoons olive oil
- ¼ cup sugar
- 1 teaspoon lemon zest, grated

## DIRECTIONS

1. Put the almonds and the wheat flour in the food processor and blend the ingredients until smooth.
2. After this, add salt, baking soda, apple cider vinegar, eggs, vanilla extract and almond extract, and sugar.
3. Blend the mixture until smooth.
4. Add lemon zest and olive oil. Blend it for 3 minutes more.
5. Line the springform pan with baking paper and transfer the blended almond batter inside.
6. Flatten the surface of the batter with the help of the spatula.
7. Bake the cake at 350F for 35 minutes.
8. Then cook the cake for 10 minutes more at 365F (for crunchy crust).
9. Chill the cooked cake well and cut on the servings.

CALORIES: 82 Kcal    FAT: 4.4 g    PROTEIN: 1.9 g    CARBOHYDRATES: 19.9 g

*Preparation: 15 min*  *Cooking: 15 min*  *Servings: 6*

## 330. BUTTER COOKIES

### INGREDIENTS

- ⅓ cup wheat flour
- ¼ cup coconut flour
- 2 egg whites
- 3 tablespoons butter, softened
- ½ teaspoon vanilla extract
- 1 tablespoon sugar

### DIRECTIONS

1. In the mixing bowl combine together sugar, wheat flour and coconut flour.
2. Whisk the eggs whites in the separated bowl till you get soft peaks.
3. After this, combine together the wheat mixture and egg whites.
4. Add vanilla extract and softened butter.
5. Carefully mix up the cookies mixture with the help of the fork/spoon.
6. After this, line the baking tray with baking paper.
7. Make six balls from the coconut mixture, press them little with the help of the palm and arrange in the tray. Make enough space for every cookie in the tray.
8. Bake the cookies for 15 minutes at 375F.
9. When the cookies are lightly golden but not brown, they are cooked.
10. Chill them well and store in a glass jar.

CALORIES: 103 Kcal   FAT: 7.4 g   PROTEIN: 3.4 g   CARBOHYDRATES: 11.9 g

*Preparation: 20 min*     *Cooking: 30 min*     *Servings: 6*

# 331. MINTY TART

## INGREDIENTS

- 1 cup tart cherries, pitted
- 1 cup wheat flour, whole grain
- ⅓ cup butter, softened
- ½ teaspoon baking powder
- 1 tablespoon sugar
- ¼ teaspoon dried mint
- ¾ teaspoon salt

## DIRECTIONS

1. Mix up together the wheat flour and butter.
2. Add baking powder and salt. Knead the soft dough.
3. Then place the dough in the freezer for 10 minutes.
4. When the dough is solid, remove it from the freezer and grate with the help of the grater. Place ¼ part of the grated dough in the freezer.
5. Sprinkle the spring form pan with remaining dough and place tart cherries on it.
6. Sprinkle the berries with sugar and dried mint and cover with ¼ part of dough from the freezer.
7. Bake the cake for 30 minutes at 365F. The cooked tart will have a golden-brown surface.

CALORIES: 177 Kcal     FAT: 8.4 g     PROTEIN: 1.1 g     CARBOHYDRATES: 21.9 g

*Preparation: 10 min*     *Cooking: 30 min*     *Servings: 2*

# 332. MANGO OATS MIX

## INGREDIENTS

- ½ cup rolled oats
- 1 mango, peeled, chopped
- ¼ teaspoon ground cinnamon
- ¾ teaspoon salt
- 1 oz coconut, shredded
- 2 tablespoons butter, softened
- 1 tablespoon almond flour
- ½ teaspoon ground nutmeg
- 1 teaspoon maple syrup
- ¼ cup of water

## DIRECTIONS

1. In the mixing bowl combine together rolled oats, ground cinnamon, salt, coconut, butter, almond flour, ground nutmeg, and maple syrup. Add water.
2. When you get a homogenous mixture, add chopped mango. Stir gently.
3. Transfer the crumble mixture in the baking mold and flatten the surface of the mixture well.
4. Cover it with foil and put in the oven.
5. Bake the crumble for 30 minutes at 350F.
6. Cool the cooked dessert well and put in the serving plates.

CALORIES: 189 Kcal     FAT: 9.4 g     PROTEIN: 2.9 g     CARBOHYDRATES: 39.8 g

Preparation: 15 min — Cooking: 18 min — Servings: 6

# 333. LEMON CHOCOLATE COOKIES

## INGREDIENTS

- 4 tablespoons olive oil
- ½ teaspoon almond extract
- 1 egg, beaten
- 1/3 cup sugar
- ½ teaspoon baking soda
- ½ teaspoon lemon juice
- 3 oz dark chocolate, chopped
- 1 cup flour, whole grain

## DIRECTIONS

1. Put olive oil, almond extract, egg, and sugar in the food processor.
2. Blend the mixture until smooth and add baking soda, lemon juice, and flour.
3. Blend the mixture. You should get a soft but non-sticky dough. Add more flour if needed.
4. Then add chopped dark chocolate and mix up the dough with the help of the fingertips.
5. Line the baking tray with baking paper.
6. Scoop the dough into the balls with the help of the scooper and place them in the tray.
7. Bake the cookies at 365F for 18 minutes.
8. Let the cookies cool, then serve.

CALORIES: 146 Kcal — FAT: 10.2 g — PROTEIN: 3.1 g — CARBOHYDRATES: 15.9 g

*Preparation: 30 min*     *Cooking: 0 min*     *Servings: 6*

## 334. FAST BERRY CREAM

**INGREDIENTS**

- 1 cup coconut cream
- ½ cup raspberries
- 1 tablespoon liquid honey
- 1 teaspoon coconut flakes
- ¼ teaspoon lemon zest, grated

**DIRECTIONS**

1. Whip the coconut cream.
2. Blend the raspberries until smooth.
3. Combine the raspberries with coconut flakes, liquid honey, and lemon zest.
4. Fill the serving glasses with whipped coconut cream and top with the raspberries blend.

CALORIES: 128 Kcal     FAT: 4.7 g     PROTEIN: 2.3 g     CARBOHYDRATES: 9.9 g

---

*Preparation: 20 min*     *Cooking: 20 min*     *Servings: 4*

## 335. NUTS AND YOGURT BROWNIES

**INGREDIENTS**

- ½ cup all-purpose flour
- 1 teaspoon baking powder
- 1 oz nuts, chopped
- 1 tablespoon cocoa powder
- 3 tablespoons sugar
- 1 teaspoon vanilla extract
- 1 tablespoon honey
- 3 eggs, beaten
- 2 tablespoons Plain yogurt
- Cooking spray

**DIRECTIONS**

1. Mix up together cocoa powder, sugar, baking powder, flour, vanilla extract, honey, eggs, and Plain Yogurt.
2. When the mixture is smooth, add chopped nuts and stir it with the help of the fork.
3. Spray the baking tray or brownie mold with cooking spray from inside.
4. Pour the brownie batter in the tray and flatten it with the help of the plastic spatula.
5. Bake brownies at 375F for 20 minutes.
6. When the brownie is baked, remove it from the oven and chill well, then serve.

CALORIES: 90 Kcal     FAT: 10.4 g     PROTEIN: 1.2 g     CARBOHYDRATES: 12.9 g

Preparation: 15 min    Cooking: 25 min    Servings: 6

# 336. HONEY FIGS PIE

## INGREDIENTS

- 6 oz puff pastry
- 1 tablespoon honey
- 1 tablespoon butter, softened
- 6 oz figs, sliced
- 1 teaspoon ground ginger
- Cooking spray

## DIRECTIONS

1. Roll up the puff pastry.
2. Spray the baking tray with cooking spray from inside and arrange puff pastry.
3. Brush the surface of puff pastry with butter and sprinkle with ground ginger.
4. Place the sliced figs on the puff pastry and sprinkle them with honey.
5. Bake the pie for 25 minutes at 375F.
6. Slice the pie and place in the serving plates hot.

CALORIES: 255 Kcal    FAT: 13 g    PROTEIN: 4.9 g    CARBOHYDRATES: 35.9 g

*Preparation: 5 min*  *Cooking: 5 min*  *Servings: 4*

## 337. HONEY CARAMEL

### INGREDIENTS

- 1 cup sugar
- 2 tablespoons of liquid honey
- 1 tablespoon lemon juice
- ¼ teaspoon kosher salt
- ¾ cup cream

### DIRECTIONS

1. Place the sugar in the skillet. Add liquid honey.
2. Heat up the mixture until it is melted.
3. Then add cream and lemon juice.
4. Stir well and bring it to boil.
5. Remove the cooked caramel from the heat and pour it in the mason jar.
6. Sprinkle the dessert with salt.

CALORIES: 85 Kcal    FAT: 9.4 g    PROTEIN: 0.9 g    CARBOHYDRATES: 40.9 g

---

*Preparation: 10 min*  *Cooking: 15 min*  *Servings: 4*

## 338. RICE PUDDING

### INGREDIENTS

- 1 teaspoon vanilla extract
- ½ teaspoon ground cinnamon
- 1 cup of grain rice
- 2 cups organic almond milk
- 1 teaspoon butter
- 1 tablespoon pistachio, chopped
- ⅓ cup water
- 4 teaspoons honey

### DIRECTIONS

1. Pour water and organic almond milk in the saucepan and bring to boil.
2. Add rice, ground cinnamon, and vanilla extract. Stir the ingredients with the help of the spoon.
3. Close the lid and simmer the rice for 7 minutes.
4. Then add butter and pistachios. Mix up well.
5. Close the lid and remove the pudding from the heat.
6. Let it rest for 10 minutes.
7. Put the cooked pudding in the serving bowls and drizzle with honey.

CALORIES: 122 Kcal    FAT: 12.4 g    PROTEIN: 4.1 g    CARBOHYDRATES: 21.9 g

*Preparation: 15 min*     Cooking: *1 hour and 30 min*     Servings: *4*

# 339. LEMON MERINGUES

## INGREDIENTS

- 2 egg whites
- 1 cup sugar
- 1 teaspoon lemon juice

## DIRECTIONS

1. Whisk the egg whites till the strong peaks and gradually add sugar and lemon juice.
2. Mix up the egg white mixture until homogenous.
3. Line the baking tray with baking paper.
4. With the help of the spoon place the egg white mixture in the tray in the shape of clouds.
5. Bake the meringues for 1.5 hours at 194°F.
6. Let the meringues cool down, then serve.
7. *if you want to make colorful meringues, you can use some food coloring, adding it in the egg white mixture before cooking.

CALORIES: 9 Kcal     FAT: 0.4 g     PROTEIN: 1.3 g     CARBOHYDRATES: 60.9 g

*Preparation: 15 min*      *Cooking: 45 min*      *Servings: 6*

## 340. CHERRY PIE

### INGREDIENTS

- 1 cup cream
- 1 cup cherries, pitted
- ½ cup all-purpose flour
- 2 eggs, beaten
- 2 tablespoons sugar
- 1 teaspoon butter, softened
- ½ teaspoon vanilla extract

### DIRECTIONS

1. Mix up together flour and cream.
2. Add eggs, sugar, vanilla extract, and stir the mixture until smooth.
3. Grease the round springform pan with butter and arrange cherries inside.
4. Pour the cream mixture over the cherries. Flatten the surface of the clafoutis with the help of the spatula.
5. Preheat the oven to 375F.
6. Place the pie in the oven and bake it for 45 minutes or until it is firm.
7. Chill the cooked clafoutis to the room temperature and cut into the servings.

CALORIES: 101 Kcal      FAT: 7.4 g      PROTEIN: 1.3 g      CARBOHYDRATES: 16.9 g

---

*Preparation: 10 min*      *Cooking: 60 min*      *Servings: 2*

## 341. CREAMY STRAWBERRY MERINGUES

### INGREDIENTS

- 2 teaspoons cream cheese
- 1 cup sugar
- 2 egg whites
- ½ teaspoon lemon juice
- ½ teaspoon vanilla extract
- 2 strawberries, sliced

### DIRECTIONS

1. Whisk the egg whites until you get soft peaks.
2. Keep whisking and gradually add sugar and lemon juice.
3. Whisk the egg whites till you get strong peak mass. After this, mix up together cream cheese and vanilla extract.
4. Line the baking tray with baking paper.
5. With the help of the spoon make egg white nests in the tray.
6. Bake the egg white nests for 60 minutes at 205°F.
7. When the "nests' are cooked, fill them with vanilla cream cheese and top with sliced strawberries.

CALORIES: 36 Kcal      FAT: 13.4 g      PROTEIN: 1.9 g      CARBOHYDRATES: 98.9 g

Preparation: 15 min  Cooking: 7 min  Servings: 4

## 342. COFFEE AND COCONUT TIRAMISU

### INGREDIENTS

- 4 oz ladyfingers
- 1 cup brewed coffee
- 1 tablespoon cocoa powder
- 1 egg yolk, whisked
- 1 cup coconut cream
- ¼ cup sugar
- 1 teaspoon vanilla extract

### DIRECTIONS

1. Mix up together a ¼ cup of sugar, egg yolk, and a ¼ cup of coconut cream.
2. Bring the mixture to boil. Stir it constantly to avoid burning.
3. Whip the remaining coconut cream.
4. Remove the egg yolk mixture from the heat and add whipped coconut cream. Stir the mass carefully with the help of the spatula.
5. After this, mix up together brewed coffee and vanilla extract.
6. Dip every ladyfinger cookie in the brewed coffee.
7. Make the layer of ½ part of all dipped finger ladies in the casserole mold and spread it with ½ of whipped coconut cream mass.
8. Sprinkle the layer with 1 tablespoon of cocoa powder.
9. Then top it with the remaining finger ladies and coconut cream mass.
10. Top the last layer with remaining cocoa powder.
11. Serve cold.
12. If needed, store tiramisu in the fridge up to 3 days.

CALORIES: 262 Kcal  FAT: 18.4 g  PROTEIN: 1.8 g  CARBOHYDRATES: 39.2 g

*Preparation: 5 min*      *Cooking: 5 min \ Refrigerating: 30 min*      *Servings: 2*

## 343. HONEY CREAM

### INGREDIENTS

- ½ cup cream
- ¼ cup milk
- 2 teaspoons honey
- 1 teaspoon vanilla extract
- 1 tablespoons gelatin
- 2 tablespoons orange juice

### DIRECTIONS

1. Mix up together milk and gelatin and leave it for 5 minutes.
2. Meanwhile, pour cream in the saucepan and bring it to boil.
3. Add honey and vanilla extract.
4. Remove the cream from the heat and stir well until honey is dissolved.
5. After this, add gelatin mixture (milk+gelatin) and mix it up until gelatin is dissolved.
6. After this, place 1 tablespoon of orange juice in every serving glass.
7. Add the cream mixture over the orange juice.
8. Refrigerate the mixture for 30-50 minutes in the fridge or until it is solid.

CALORIES: 100 Kcal      FAT: 8.4 g      PROTEIN: 4.9 g      CARBOHYDRATES: 11.9 g

---

*Preparation: 15 min*      *Cooking: 50 min*      *Servings: 2*

## 344. WALNUTS KATAIFI

### INGREDIENTS

- 7 oz kataifi dough
- ⅓ cup walnuts, chopped
- ½ teaspoon ground cinnamon
- ¾ teaspoon vanilla extract
- 4 tablespoons butter, melted
- ¼ teaspoon ground clove
- ⅓ cup water
- 3 tablespoons honey

### DIRECTIONS

1. Mix up together walnuts, ground cinnamon, and vanilla extract. Add ground clove and blend the mixture until smooth.
2. Make the kataifi dough: grease the casserole mold with butter and place ½ part of kataifi dough.
3. Then sprinkle the filling over the kataifi dough.
4. Sprinkle the filling with 1 tablespoon of melted butter.
5. Sprinkle the filling with remaining kataifi dough.
6. Make the roll from ½ part of kataifi dough and cut it.
7. Gently arrange the kataifi roll in the tray.
8. Repeat the same steps with remaining dough.
9. Preheat the oven to 355F and place the tray with kataifi rolls inside, then bake the dessert for 50 minutes.
10. Meanwhile, make the syrup: bring the water to boil.
11. Add honey and heat it up until the honey is dissolved.
12. Pour the hot syrup over the hot kataifi rolls.
13. Cut each kataifi roll, then serve with the remaining syrup.

CALORIES: 120 Kcal      FAT: 6.2 g      PROTEIN: 3.7 g      CARBOHYDRATES: 27.9 g

*Preparation:* 20 min    *Cooking:* 40 min    Servings: 6

## 345. GRAPES TART

### INGREDIENTS

- ½ cup sugar
- ⅓ cup butter, softened
- 1 cup wheat flour
- ½ cup grapes, sliced in half
- 1 teaspoon baking powder
- 1 teaspoon ground cinnamon
- 1 tablespoon almond meal

### DIRECTIONS

1. Sprinkle the round springform pan with almond meal.
2. Place the sliced grapes in a baking dish and sprinkle them with the sugar.
3. Make the dough: mix up together butter, wheat flour, baking powder, and cinnamon.
4. With the help of the cooking machine knead the dough.
5. Put the dough over the grapes and flatten it carefully with the help of the fingertips.
6. Bake the tart for 40 minutes at 365F.
7. When the tart is cooked, remove it from the heat and turn it over to get the grapes on the tart surface.
8. Cut it into the servings.
9. We recommend serving the tart while still hot.

CALORIES: 179 Kcal    FAT: 000 g6.3    PROTEIN: 3.9 g    CARBOHYDRATES: 38.9 g

*Preparation: 15 min* — *Cooking: 20 min* — *Servings: 4*

## 346. BAKED APPLES

### INGREDIENTS

- 4 teaspoon pistachios, chopped
- 4 teaspoon sugar
- 1 teaspoon ground cinnamon
- 4 Granny Smith apples
- 2 teaspoons butter, softened
- ¼ teaspoon ground nutmeg

### DIRECTIONS

1. Make the medium wholes in every apple.
2. In the mixing bowl, churn together ground cinnamon, butter, ground nutmeg, and pistachios.
3. Fill every apple with pistachio mixture.
4. After this, sprinkle every apple whole with 1 teaspoon of sugar.
5. Place the prepared apples in the tray.
6. Bake the apples for 20 minutes at 385°F.
7. Cool the cooked apples for 5 minutes before serving.

CALORIES: 72 Kcal    FAT: 9.3 g    PROTEIN: 1.5 g    CARBOHYDRATES: 22.9 g

---

*Preparation: 25 min* — *Cooking: 15 min* — *Servings: 6*

## 347. SWEET SPINACH PANCAKE

### INGREDIENTS

- 1 cup heavy cream
- ¼ cup sugar
- 1 cup fresh spinach, chopped
- ½ cup skim milk
- 1 teaspoon vanilla extract
- 1 cup all-purpose flour
- ½ cup of rice flour
- 1 teaspoon baking powder
- 1 teaspoon olive oil
- 1 egg, beaten
- ¼ teaspoon ground clove
- 1 teaspoon butter

### DIRECTIONS

1. Blend the spinach until you get puree mixture.
2. Add skim milk, vanilla extract, all-purpose flour, and rice flour.
3. Add baking powder, egg, and ground clove.
4. Blend the ingredients until you get a smooth and thick batter.
5. Add olive oil and pulse the batter for 30 seconds more. Heat up butter in the skillet.
6. Lay 1 ladle of the crepe mixture batter in the skillet and flatten it in the shape of a crepe.
7. Cook it for 1.5 minutes from one side and them flip into another side and cook for 20 seconds more.
8. Place the cooked crepe in the plate.
9. Repeat the same steps will all crepe batter.
10. Make the cake filling: whip the heavy cream with sugar.
11. Spread every crepe with sweet whipped cream, then serve.

CALORIES: 204 Kcal    FAT: 6.2 g    PROTEIN: 1.7 g    CARBOHYDRATES: 38.9 g

Preparation: 20 min         Cooking: 35 min         Servings: 6

## 348. BLACKBERRY PIE

### INGREDIENTS

- 1 cup wheat flour, whole grain
- 1 cup blackberries
- ⅓ cup sugar
- ½ teaspoon ground clove
- ½ cup rolled oats
- ⅓ cup butter, softened

### DIRECTIONS

1. In the mixing bowl combine together blackberries, sugar, and ground clove.
2. Take another bowl and put rolled oats, butter, and wheat flour inside.
3. Mix up the ingredients until it is crumbly.
4. Line the round springform pan with baking paper.
5. Put the blackberry mixture inside the springform pan and flatten it with the help of the spoon.
6. After this, top the berries with all crumbly mixture.
7. Bake the crumble for 35 minutes at 365F.
8. Slice the cake, then serve.

CALORIES: 203 Kcal         FAT: 7.4 g         PROTEIN: 4.1 g         CARBOHYDRATES: 36.9 g

Preparation: 25 min  Cooking: 25 min  Servings: 8

## 349. STEVIA COOKIES

**INGREDIENTS**

- 1 cup almond flour
- ½ cup wheat flour
- 1 teaspoon ground clove
- 5 teaspoons almond flakes
- ⅓ cup butter, softened
- ½ teaspoon vanilla extract
- 3 tablespoon liquid stevia
- 1 tablespoon sugar
- 1 egg white, whisked
- 1 egg, beaten

**DIRECTIONS**

1. Make the dough: in the mixing bowl combine together almond flour, wheat flour, ground clove, 3 tablespoons of almond flakes, butter, vanilla extract, liquid stevia, sugar and the egg.
2. Knead the soft and non-sticky dough.
3. Make the balls from the dough and press them gently with the help of the hand palm.
4. Lime the baking tray with baking paper.
5. Place the cookies in the tray and brush their surface with egg white.
6. Sprinkle every cookie with remaining almond flakes.
7. Bake the cookies for 25 minutes at 365F.
8. Chill the cooked cookies well and store in a glass jar if needed.

CALORIES: 223 Kcal  FAT: 5.4 g  PROTEIN: 2.9 g  CARBOHYDRATES: 10.9 g

---

Preparation: 15 min  Cooking: 5 min \ Rest: 15 min  Servings: 4

## 350. BANANA AND BERRIES TRIFLE

**INGREDIENTS**

- 8 oz biscuits, chopped
- ¼ cup strawberries, chopped
- 1 banana, chopped
- 1 peach, chopped
- ½ mango, chopped
- 1 cup grapes, chopped
- 1 tablespoon liquid honey
- 1 cup of orange juice
- ½ cup Plain yogurt
- ¼ cup cream cheese
- 1 teaspoon coconut flakes

**DIRECTIONS**

1. Bring the orange juice to boil and remove it from the heat.
2. Add liquid honey and stir until it is dissolved.
3. Cool the liquid to the room temperature.
4. Add chopped banana, peach, mango, grapes, and strawberries. Shake the fruits gently and leave to soak the orange juice for 15 minutes.
5. Meanwhile, with the help of the hand mixer mix up together Plain yogurt and cream cheese.
6. Then separate the chopped biscuits, yogurt mixture, and fruits on 4 parts.
7. Place the first part of biscuits in the big serving glass in one layer.
8. Spread it with yogurt mixture and add fruits.
9. Repeat the same steps till you use all ingredients.
10. Top the trifle with coconut flakes.

CALORIES: 164 Kcal  FAT: 6.4 g  PROTEIN: 1.4 g  CARBOHYDRATES: 24.9 g

Preparation: 20 min    Cooking: 30 min \ Refrigerating: 25 min    Servings: 6

## 351. CREAMY CAKE

### INGREDIENTS

- ¼ cup lemon juice
- 1 cup cream
- 4 egg yolks
- 4 tablespoons sugar
- 1 tablespoon cornstarch
- 1 teaspoon vanilla extract
- 3 tablespoons butter
- 6 oz wheat flour, whole grain
- 1 cup of fresh berries or other fruits

### DIRECTIONS

1. Mix up together wheat flour and butter and knead the soft dough.
2. Put the dough in the round cake mold and flatten it in the shape of pie crust. If you like, you can make some little pies instead of a big one.
3. Bake it for 15 minutes at 365°F.
4. Meanwhile, make the lemon filling: Mix up together cream, egg yolks, and lemon juice. When the liquid is smooth, start to heat it up over the medium heat. Stir it constantly.
5. When the liquid is hot, add vanilla extract, cornstarch and sugar. Whisk well until smooth.
6. Bring the lemon filling to boil and remove it from the heat.
7. Cool it to the room temperature.
8. Pour the lemon filling over the pie crust, flatten it well and leave to cool in the fridge for 25 minutes.
9. If you like, decorate the cake with fresh fruits before serving.

CALORIES: 225 Kcal    FAT: 11.4 g    PROTEIN: 2.1 g    CARBOHYDRATES: 34.9 g

*Preparation: 40 min*     *Cooking: 10 min \ Refrigerating: 1 hour*     *Servings: 6*

## 352. PISTACHIO CHEESECAKE

### INGREDIENTS

- ½ cup pistachio, chopped
- 4 teaspoons butter, softened
- 4 teaspoon sugar
- 2 cups cream cheese
- ½ cup cream, whipped

### DIRECTIONS

1. Mix up together pistachios, butter, and sugar.
2. Put the mixture in the baking mold and bake for 10 minutes at 355F.
3. Meanwhile, whisk together cream cheese and whipped cream.
4. When the pistachio mixture is baked, chill it well.
5. After this, transfer the pistachio mixture in the round cake mold and flatten in one layer.
6. Put the cream cheese mixture over the pistachio mixture, flatten the surface until smooth.
7. Cool the cheesecake in the fridge for 1 hour before serving.

CALORIES: 333 Kcal     FAT: 33.4 g     PROTEIN: 1.5 g     CARBOHYDRATES: 10.9 g

---

*Preparation: 20 min*     *Cooking: 1 hour*     *Servings: 6*

## 353. GALAKTOBOUREKO PIE

### INGREDIENTS

- ½ cup milk
- 3 tablespoons semolina
- ½ cup butter, softened
- 8 Phyllo sheets
- 2 eggs, beaten
- 3 tablespoons sugar
- 1 teaspoon lemon rind
- 1 tablespoon lemon juice
- 1 teaspoon vanilla extract
- 2 tablespoons liquid honey
- 1 teaspoon ground cinnamon
- ¼ cup of water

### DIRECTIONS

1. Melt ½ of the butter, then brush the casserole glass mold with the butter and place 1 Phyllo sheet inside.
2. Brush the Phyllo sheet with butter and cover it with second Phyllo sheet.
3. Make the filling: heat up milk and add semolina.
4. Add the remaining softened butter, sugar and vanilla extract.
5. Bring the mixture to boil and simmer it for 2 minutes.
6. Remove it from the heat and cool to the room temperature.
7. Add the beaten eggs and mix, then pour the semolina mixture in the mold over the Phyllo sheets, flatten it if needed.
8. Cover the semolina mixtur with remaining Phyllo sheets and brush with remaining melted butter.
9. Bake the cake for 1 hour at 365°F.
10. Make the syrup: bring to boil lemon juice, honey, and water and remove the liquid from the heat.
11. Pour the syrup over the hot dessert and let it chill well.

CALORIES: 304 Kcal     FAT: 18.4 g     PROTEIN: 6.1 g     CARBOHYDRATES: 31.9 g

Preparation: 15 min   Cooking: 20 min   Servings: 6

## 354. LEMON AND SEMOLINA COOKIES

### INGREDIENTS

- ½ teaspoon lemon zest, grated
- 4 tablespoons sugar
- 4 tablespoons semolina
- 2 tablespoons olive oil
- 8 tablespoons wheat flour, whole grain
- 1 teaspoon vanilla extract
- ½ teaspoon ground clove
- 3 tablespoons coconut oil
- ¼ teaspoon baking powder
- ¼ cup of water

### DIRECTIONS

1. Make the dough: in the mixing bowl combine together lemon zest, semolina, olive oil, wheat flour, vanilla extract, ground clove, coconut oil and baking powder.
2. Knead the soft dough.
3. Make the small cookies in the shape of walnuts and press them gently with the help of the fork.
4. Line the baking tray with the baking paper.
5. Place the cookies in the tray and bake them for 20 minutes at 375F.
6. Meanwhile, bring the water to boil.
7. Add sugar and simmer the liquid for 2 minutes over the medium heat. Cool it.
8. Pour the cooled sweet water over the hot baked cookies and leave them for 10 minutes.
9. When the cookies soaked all the liquid, transfer them into serving plates.

CALORIES: 167 Kcal   FAT: 9.4 g   PROTEIN: 1.8 g   CARBOHYDRATES: 23.9 g

*Preparation: 15 min*      *Cooking: 30 min*      *Servings: 6*

# 355. SEMOLINA CAKE

## INGREDIENTS

- ½ cup wheat flour, whole grain
- ½ cup semolina
- 1 teaspoon baking powder
- ½ cup Plain yogurt
- 1 teaspoon vanilla extract
- 4 tablespoons sugar
- 1 teaspoon lemon rind
- 2 tablespoons olive oil
- 1 tablespoon almond flakes
- 4 teaspoons liquid honey
- ½ cup of orange juice

## DIRECTIONS

1. Mix up together wheat flour, semolina, baking powder, Plain yogurt, vanilla extract, Erythritol, and olive oil.
2. Add the lemon rind and mix up the ingredients until smooth.
3. Transfer the mixture in the non-sticky cake mold, sprinkle with almond flakes, and bake for 30 minutes at 365F.
4. Meanwhile, bring the orange juice to boil.
5. Add liquid honey and stir until dissolved.
6. When the cake is cooked, pour the hot orange juice mixture over it and let it rest for at least 10 minutes.
7. Cut the cake into the servings.

CALORIES: 179 Kcal      FAT: 6.4 g      PROTEIN: 1.8 g      CARBOHYDRATES: 36.9 g

---

*Preparation: 20 min*      *Cooking: 40 min*      *Servings: 2*

# 356. ALMOND PIE

## INGREDIENTS

- 1 egg
- 3 tablespoons butter, softened
- 1 teaspoon baking powder
- 1/3 cup sugar
- 1 teaspoon vanilla extract
- ½ cup almond meal
- ½ cup wheat flour, whole grain
- 1 teaspoon orange zest, grated
- ¼ cup milk
- 1 tablespoon almond flakes

## DIRECTIONS

1. Mix up together butter and sugar and start to mix it with the help of a cooking machine for 4 minutes over the medium speed.
2. Crack the egg and separate it into the egg yolk and egg white.
3. Add the egg yolk in the butter mixture and keep mixing it for 2 minutes more.
4. Whisk the egg white till the strong peaks.
5. Add the egg white in the butter mixture.
6. Add vanilla extract and orange zest, then, when the mixture is homogenous, switch off the cooking machine.
7. Add almond meal, wheat meal, and milk.
8. Mix up the dough until smooth and transfer it in the non-sticky round cake mold.
9. Flatten the surface of the cake with the help of the spatula and sprinkle with almond flakes.
10. Bake the cake for 40 minutes at 345°F.

CALORIES: 245 Kcal      FAT: 13.4 g      PROTEIN: 2.3 g      CARBOHYDRATES: 36.9 g

*Preparation: 20 min* — Cooking: 1 hour — Servings: 8

## 357. ORANGE CAKE

### INGREDIENTS

- 4 oranges
- 1/3 cup water
- ½ cup sugar
- ½ teaspoon ground cinnamon
- 4 eggs, beaten
- 3 tablespoons stevia powder
- 10 oz Phyllo pastry
- ½ teaspoon baking powder
- ½ cup Plain yogurt
- 3 tablespoons olive oil

### DIRECTIONS

1. Squeeze the juice from 1 orange and pour it in the saucepan.
2. Add water, squeezed oranges, water, ground cinnamon and sugar.
3. Bring the liquid to boil.
4. Simmer the liquid for 5 minutes over the medium heat. When the time is over, cool it.
5. Grease the baking mold with 1 tablespoon of olive oil.
6. Chop the phyllo dough and place it in the baking mold.
7. Slice ½ of orange for decorating the cake. Slice it.
8. Squeeze juice from remaining oranges.
9. Mix up together the squeezed orange juice, plain yogurt, baking powder, stevia powder, the remaining oil and eggs.
10. Mix up the mixture with the help of the hand mixer.
11. Pour the liquid over the chopped Phyllo dough.
12. Stir to evenly distribute.
13. Top the cake with sliced orange.
14. Bake for 50 minutes at 370°F.
15. Pour the baked cake with cooled orange juice syrup.

CALORIES: 237 Kcal — FAT: 10.4 g — PROTEIN: 3.6 g — CARBOHYDRATES: 28.9 g

*Preparation: 15 min*  *Cooking: 40 min*  *Servings: 6*

## 358. VANILLA AND COCONUT COOKIES

### INGREDIENTS

- 5 eggs
- ½ cup coconut flour
- ½ cup wheat flour
- 1/3 cup sugar
- 1 teaspoon vanilla extract
- Cooking spray

### DIRECTIONS

1. Crack the eggs in the mixing bowl and mix it up with the help of the hand mixer.
2. Add sugar and keep mixing the egg mixture until it will be changed into the lemon color.
3. Add wheat flour, coconut flour, and vanilla extract.
4. Mix it up for 30 seconds more.
5. Spray the baking tray with cooking spray.
6. Pour the biscuit mixture in the tray and flatten it.
7. Bake the biscuits for 40 minutes at 350°F, then serve.

CALORIES: 132 Kcal    FAT: 8.3 g    PROTEIN: 2.6 g    CARBOHYDRATES: 21.3 g

---

*Preparation: 15 min*  *Cooking: 7 min*  *Servings: 2*

## 359. ALMOND PUDDING

### INGREDIENTS

- ½ cup organic almond milk
- ½ cup milk
- 1/3 cup semolina
- 1 tablespoon butter
- ¼ teaspoon cornstarch
- ½ teaspoon almond extract

### DIRECTIONS

1. Pour almond milk and milk in the saucepan.
2. Bring it to boil and add semolina and cornstarch.
3. Mix up the ingredients until homogenous and simmer them for 1 minute.
4. After this, add almond extract and butter. Stir well and close the lid.
5. Remove the pudding from the heat and leave for 10 minutes.
6. Mix it up again and transfer in the serving ramekins.

CALORIES: 208 Kcal    FAT: 5.4 g    PROTEIN: 1 g    CARBOHYDRATES: 33.9 g

Preparation: 10 min  Cooking: 12 min  Servings: 3

## 360. YOGURT MUFFINS

### INGREDIENTS

- 4 tablespoons wheat flour
- 2 bananas, peeled
- 1 tablespoon Plain yogurt
- ½ teaspoon baking powder
- ¼ teaspoon lemon juice
- 1 teaspoon vanilla extract

### DIRECTIONS

1. Mash the bananas with the help of the fork.
2. Combine the mashed bananas with flour, yogurt, baking powder, and lemon juice.
3. Add vanilla extract and stir the batter until smooth.
4. Fill ½ part of every muffin mold with banana batter and bake them for 12 minutes at 365F.
5. Chill the muffins and remove them from the muffin molds, then serve.

CALORIES: 81 Kcal  FAT: 10.4 g  PROTEIN: 6.1 g  CARBOHYDRATES: 20.9 g

*Preparation: 5 min*  *Cooking: 5min \ Refrigerating: 30 min*  *Servings: 2*

## 361. WATERMELON ICE CREAM

**INGREDIENTS**

- 8 oz watermelon
- 1 tablespoon gelatin powder

**DIRECTIONS**

1. Make the juice from the watermelon with the help of the fruit juicer.
2. Combine together 5 tablespoons of watermelon juice and 1 tablespoon of gelatin powder. Stir it and leave for 5 minutes.
3. Preheat the watermelon juice until warm, add gelatin mixture and heat it up over the medium heat until gelatin is dissolved.
4. Remove the liquid from the heat and put it in the silicone molds.
5. Freeze the jelly for 30 minutes in the freezer or for 4 hours in the fridge.

CALORIES: 46 Kcal    FAT: 0.4 g    PROTEIN: 1.5 g    CARBOHYDRATES: 5.9 g

---

*Preparation: 20 min*  *Cooking: 75 min*  *Servings: 2*

## 362. YOGURT AND HONEY COOKIES

**INGREDIENTS**

- ½ cup plain yogurt
- ½ teaspoon baking powder
- 2 tablespoons sugar
- 1 teaspoon almond extract
- ½ teaspoon ground clove
- ½ teaspoon orange zest, grated
- 3 tablespoons walnuts, chopped
- 1 cup wheat flour
- 1 teaspoon butter, softened
- 1 tablespoon honey
- 3 tablespoons water

**DIRECTIONS**

1. In a mixing bowl, mix up together Plain yogurt, baking powder, sugar, almond extract, ground cloves orange zest, flour and butter.
2. Knead the non-sticky dough. Add olive oil if the dough is very sticky and knead it well.
3. Make a log from the dough and cut it into small pieces.
4. Roll every piece of dough into the balls and transfer in the lined with baking paper tray.
5. Press the balls gently and bake for 25 minutes at 350F.
6. Meanwhile, heat up together honey and water. Simmer the liquid for 1 minute and remove from the heat.
7. When the cookies are cooked, remove them from the oven and let them cool for 5 minutes.
8. Pour the cookies with sweet honey water and sprinkle with walnuts.
9. Let the cookies cool down, then serve.

CALORIES: 134 Kcal    FAT: 8.3 g    PROTEIN: 2.9 g    CARBOHYDRATES: 29 g

*Preparation: 5 min*     *Cooking: 30 min*     *Servings: 6*

# 363. SWEET POTATOES AND COCOA BROWNIES

## INGREDIENTS

- 1 tablespoon cocoa powder
- 1 sweet potato, peeled, boiled
- ½ cup wheat flour
- 1 teaspoon baking powder
- 1 tablespoon butter
- 1 tablespoon olive oil
- 2 tablespoons sugar

## DIRECTIONS

1. In a mixing bowl combine together all ingredients.
2. Mix well, until you get a smooth batter.
3. Pour the batter in the brownie mold and flatten it.
4. Bake the batter for 30 minutes at 365°F.
5. Cut the brownies, then serve while still hot.

CALORIES: 90 Kcal     FAT: 8.1 g     PROTEIN: 1.5 g     CARBOHYDRATES: 17.9 g

*Preparation: 10 min*     *Cooking: 15 min*     *Servings: 2*

# 364. BAKED FIGS

## INGREDIENTS

- 4 figs
- 4 teaspoons honey
- 1 oz Blue cheese, chopped

## DIRECTIONS

1. Make the cross cuts in the figs and fill them with chopped Blue cheese.
2. Sprinkle the figs with honey and wrap in the foil.
3. Bake the figs for 15 minutes at 355°F.
4. Remove the figs from the foil and transfer in the serving plates.

CALORIES: 90 Kcal     FAT: 0.6 g     PROTEIN: 3.9 g     CARBOHYDRATES: 12.9 g

---

*Preparation: 20 min*     *Cooking: 15 min*     *Servings: 2*

# 365. NUTMEG STRAWBERRY PIE

## INGREDIENTS

- 1 cup strawberries
- 7 oz puff pastry
- 3 teaspoons butter, softened
- 3 teaspoons sugar
- ¼ teaspoon ground nutmeg
- 4 teaspoons cream

## DIRECTIONS

1. Roll up the puff pastry and cut it on 6 squares.
2. Slice the strawberries.
3. Grease every puff pastry square with butter and then place the sliced strawberries on it.
4. Sprinkle every strawberry square with cream, ground nutmeg and sugar.
5. Secure the edges of every puff pastry square in the shape of a pie.
6. Line the baking tray with baking paper.
7. Transfer the pies in the tray and place the tray in the oven.
8. Bake the pies for 15 minutes at 375°F.
9. Serve hot.

CALORIES: 90 Kcal     FAT: 9.9 g     PROTEIN: 3.1 g     CARBOHYDRATES: 12.9 g

Preparation: 10 min    Cooking: 30 min    Servings: 6

## 366. SPICED COOKIES

### INGREDIENTS

- 1 egg, beaten
- 1 teaspoon vanilla extract
- ½ teaspoon ground cinnamon
- 1 teaspoon ground turmeric
- 1 tablespoon butter, softened
- 1 cup wheat flour
- 1 teaspoon baking powder
- 4 tablespoons pumpkin puree
- 1 tablespoon sugar

### DIRECTIONS

1. Put all the ingredients in a mixing bowl and knead the soft and non-sticky dough.
2. Line the baking tray with baking paper.
3. Make 6 balls from the dough and press them gently with the help of the spoon.
4. Arrange the dough balls in the tray.
5. Bake the cookies for 30 minutes at 355°F.
6. Let the cookies cool down, then serve.
7. If needed, store them in glass jar.

CALORIES: 111 Kcal    FAT: 9 g    PROTEIN: 2 g    CARBOHYDRATES: 21.1 g

*Preparation: 7 min*     *Cooking: 5 min*     *Servings: 4*

## 367. GINGER PINEAPPLE

**INGREDIENTS**

- 10 oz fresh pineapple
- ½ teaspoon ground ginger
- 1 tablespoon almond butter, softened

**DIRECTIONS**

1. Slice the pineapple into the serving pieces and brush with almond butter.
2. Sprinkle every pineapple piece with ground ginger.
3. Preheat the grill to 400°F.
4. Grill the pineapple for 2 minutes from each side.
5. The cooked fruit should have a light brown surface of both sides.

CALORIES: 61 Kcal     FAT: 10 g     PROTEIN: 2 g     CARBOHYDRATES: 10.9 g

---

*Preparation: 10 min*     *Cooking: 1 min \ Refrigerating: 30 min*     *Servings: 6*

## 368. MINTY COCOA BARS

**INGREDIENTS**

- 3 tablespoons coconut butter
- ½ cup coconut flakes
- 1 egg, beaten
- 1 tablespoon cocoa powder
- 3 oz graham crackers, crushed
- 2 tablespoons sugar
- 3 tablespoons butter
- 1 teaspoon mint extract
- 1 teaspoon stevia powder
- 1 teaspoon of cocoa powder
- 1 tablespoon almond butter, melted

**DIRECTIONS**

1. Churn together coconut butter, coconut flakes, and 1 tablespoon of cocoa powder.
2. Microwave the mixture for 1 minute or until it is melted.
3. Chill the liquid for 1 minute and fast add egg. Whisk it until homogenous and smooth.
4. Stir the liquid in the graham crackers and transfer in the mold. Flatten it well with the help of the spoon.
5. Blend together sugar, butter, mint extract and stevia powder.
6. When the mixture is fluffy, place it over the graham crackers layer.
7. Mix up together 1 teaspoon of cocoa powder and almond butter.
8. Sprinkle the cooked mixture with cocoa liquid and flatten it.
9. Refrigerate the dessert for 30 minutes, then serve.

CALORIES: 213 Kcal     FAT: 9.1 g     PROTEIN: 2.1 g     CARBOHYDRATES: 20.9 g

*Preparation: 20 min* — *Cooking: 30 min* — *Servings: 8*

## 369. PINEAPPLE CAKE

**INGREDIENTS**

- 1 cup of rice flour
- 1 cup coconut flour
- ½ cup wheat flour
- ½ cup sugar
- ½ teaspoon baking powder
- ¾ teaspoon salt
- 1/3 teaspoon ground cinnamon
- ½ cup olive oil
- 2 eggs, beaten
- 3 oz pineapple, chopped
- 1 banana, chopped
- 3 tablespoons walnuts, chopped
- 6 tablespoons cream cheese

**DIRECTIONS**

1. In a mixing bowl, combine together the first 9 ingredients from the list above.
2. When the mixture is smooth add pineapple and bananas, then mix. If you want to decorate the top of the cake with some pineapple and bananas slices, put a few pieces aside.
3. Add walnuts and mix up the dough well.
4. Put the dough into a baking dish, then decorate the top of the cake if you want.
5. Bake for 30 minutes at 355°F.
6. Remove the cooked cake from the oven and let it cool down.
7. Spread the cake with cream cheese, then serve.

CALORIES: 248 Kcal — FAT: 6 g — PROTEIN: 3.1 g — CARBOHYDRATES: 41.9 g

*Preparation: 5 min* — *Cooking: 0 min \ Refrigerating: 30 min* — *Servings: 2*

## 370. MANGO AND HONEY CREAM

**INGREDIENTS**

- 2 cups coconut cream
- 6 teaspoons honey
- 2 mangoes, chopped

**DIRECTIONS**

1. Blend together honey and mango.
2. When the mixture is smooth, combine it with whipped coconut cream and stir carefully.
3. Put the mango-cream mixture in the serving glasses and refrigerate for 30 minutes.

CALORIES: 106 Kcal — FAT: 5.4 g — PROTEIN: 3.5 g — CARBOHYDRATES: 27.9 g

*Preparation: 5 min*  *Cooking: 15 min*  *Servings: 6*

## 371. STUFFED PLUMS

### INGREDIENTS

- 4 plums, pitted, halved, not soft
- 1 tablespoon peanuts, chopped
- 1 tablespoon honey
- ½ teaspoon lemon juice
- 1 teaspoon coconut oil

### DIRECTIONS

1. Make the packet from the foil and place the plum halves in it.
2. Sprinkle the plums with honey, lemon juice, coconut oil, and peanuts.
3. Bake the plums for 15 minutes at 350F.
4. Let the plums cool down a little, then serve.

CALORIES: 69 Kcal    FAT: 4.1 g    PROTEIN: 5.3 g    CARBOHYDRATES: 9.4 g

---

*Preparation: 10 min*  *Cooking: 20 min*  *Servings: 4*

## 372. BLACKBERRIES AND POMEGRANATE PARFAIT

### INGREDIENTS

- 1 cup plain yogurt
- 1 tablespoon coconut flakes
- 1 tablespoon liquid honey
- 4 teaspoons peanuts, chopped
- 1 cup blackberries
- 1 tablespoon pomegranate seeds

### DIRECTIONS

1. Mix up together plain yogurt and coconut flakes.
2. Put the mixture in the freezer.
3. Meanwhile, combine together liquid honey and blackberries.
4. Place ½ part of the blackberry mixture in the serving glasses.
5. Add ¼ part of the cooled yogurt mixture.
6. Sprinkle the yogurt mixture with all peanuts and cover with ½ part of the remaining yogurt mixture.
7. Add the remaining blackberries and top the dessert with yogurt.
8. Garnish the parfait with pomegranate seeds and cool in the fridge for 20 minutes, then serve.

CALORIES: 115 Kcal    FAT: 7.1 g    PROTEIN: 2.4 g    CARBOHYDRATES: 12.9 g

*Preparation: 10 min*     *Cooking: 0 min \ Refrigerating: 2 hours*     *Servings: 4*

## 373. MELON POPSICLES

**INGREDIENTS**

- 9 oz melon, peeled, chopped
- 1 tablespoon sugar
- ½ cup of orange juice

**DIRECTIONS**

1. Blend the melon until smooth and combine it with sugar and orange juice.
2. Mix up the liquid until the sugar is dissolved.
3. Pour the liquid into the popsicles molds.
4. Freeze the popsicles for 2 hours in the freezer.

CALORIES: 36 Kcal     FAT: 0.1 g     PROTEIN: 2.1 g     CARBOHYDRATES: 10.9 g

---

*Preparation: 10 min*     *Cooking: 0 min*     *Servings: 6*

## 374. WATERMELON SALAD

**INGREDIENTS**

- 14 oz watermelon
- 1 oz dark chocolate
- 3 tablespoons coconut cream
- 1 teaspoon sugar
- 2 kiwis, chopped
- 1 oz Feta cheese, crumbled

**DIRECTIONS**

1. Peel the watermelon and remove the seeds from it.
2. Chop the fruit and place in the salad bowl.
3. Add chopped kiwi and crumbled Feta. Stir the salad well.
4. Mix up together the coconut cream and sugar.
5. Pour the cream mixture over the salad.
6. Shave the chocolate over the salad with the help of the potato peeler.
7. Serve immediately.

CALORIES: 90 Kcal     FAT: 4.4 g     PROTEIN: 1.9 g     CARBOHYDRATES: 9.1 g

# 21 Eggs

*Preparation: 10 min*     *Cooking: 15 min*     *Servings: 3*

## 375. EGGS AND AVOCADO

### INGREDIENTS

- 1 teaspoon garlic powder
- ½ teaspoon sea salt
- ¼ cup Parmesan cheese (grated or shredded)
- ¼ teaspoon black pepper
- 3 medium avocados (cut in half, pitted, skin on)
- 6 medium eggs

### DIRECTIONS

1. Prepare some muffin tins and preheat the oven to 350°F.
2. To ensure that the egg would fit inside the cavity of the avocado, lightly scrape off ⅓ of the meat.
3. Place the avocado on a muffin tin to ensure that it faces with the top up.
4. Evenly season each avocado with pepper, salt, and garlic powder.
5. Add one egg on each avocado cavity and garnish tops with cheese.
6. Pop in the oven and bake until the egg white is set, about 15 minutes.
7. Serve and enjoy.

CALORIES: 252 Kcal     FAT: 20 g     PROTEIN: 14 g     CARBOHYDRATES: 4 g

---

*Preparation: 10 min*     *Cooking: 20 min*     *Servings: 8*

## 376. EGG-ARTICHOKE CASSEROLE

### INGREDIENTS

- 16 large eggs
- 14 ounce can artichoke hearts, drained
- 10-ounce box frozen chopped spinach, thawed and drained well
- 1 cup shredded white cheddar
- 1 garlic clove, minced
- 1 teaspoon salt
- ½ cup parmesan cheese
- ½ cup ricotta cheese
- ½ teaspoon dried thyme
- ½ teaspoon crushed red pepper
- ¼ cup milk
- ¼ cup shaved onion

### DIRECTIONS

1. Lightly grease a 9x13-inch baking dish with cooking spray and preheat the oven to 350oF.
2. In a large mixing bowl, add eggs and milk. Mix thoroughly.
3. With a paper towel, squeeze out the excess moisture from the spinach leaves and add to the bowl of eggs.
4. Beak the artichoke hearts into small pieces and separate the leaves. Add to the bowl of eggs.
5. Except for the ricotta cheese, add remaining ingredients in the bowl of eggs and mix thoroughly.
6. Pour the egg mixture into the prepared dish.
7. Evenly add dollops of ricotta cheese on top of the eggs and then pop in the oven.
8. Bake until the eggs are set and doesn't jiggle when shook, about 20 minutes.
9. Remove from the oven and evenly divide into suggested servings.

CALORIES: 302 Kcal     FAT: 18.7 g     PROTEIN: 22.6 g     CARBOHYDRATES: 10.8 g

*Preparation: 10 min*  *Cooking: 25 min*  *Servings: 2*

## 377. EGG-POTATO HASH

**INGREDIENTS**

- 1 zucchini, diced
- ½ cup chicken broth
- ½ pound cooked chicken
- 1 tablespoon olive oil
- 4 ounces shrimp
- Salt and ground black pepper to taste
- 1 large sweet potato, diced
- 2 eggs
- ¼ teaspoon cayenne pepper
- 2 teaspoons garlic powder
- 1 cup fresh spinach (optional)

**DIRECTIONS**

1. In a skillet, add the olive oil.
2. Fry the shrimp, cooked chicken and sweet potato for 2 minutes.
3. Add the cayenne pepper, garlic powder and salt, and toss for 4 minutes.
4. Add the zucchini and toss for another 3 minutes.
5. Whisk the eggs in a bowl and add to the skillet.
6. Season using salt and pepper. Cover with the lid.
7. Cook for 1 minute and add the chicken broth.
8. Cover and cook for another 8 minutes on high heat.
9. Add the spinach and toss for 2 more minutes.
10. Serve immediately.

CALORIES: 190 Kcal   FAT: 12.3 g   PROTEIN: 11.7 g   CARBOHYDRATES: 2.9 g

*Preparation: 10 min*  *Cooking: 35 min*  *Servings: 6*

## 378. DILL AND TOMATO FRITTATA

**INGREDIENTS**

- Pepper and salt to taste
- 1 teaspoon red pepper flakes
- 2 garlic cloves, minced
- ½ cup crumbled goat cheese – optional
- 2 tablespoon fresh chives, chopped
- 2 tablespoon fresh dill, chopped
- 4 tomatoes, diced
- 8 eggs, whisked
- 1 teaspoon coconut oil

**DIRECTIONS**

1. Grease a 9-inch round baking pan and preheat oven to 325oF.
2. In a large bowl, mix well all ingredients and pour into prepped pan.
3. Pop into the oven and bake until middle is cooked through around 30-35 minutes.
4. Remove from oven and garnish with more chives and dill.

CALORIES: 149 Kcal   FAT: 10.3 g   PROTEIN: 13.6 g   CARBOHYDRATES: 9.9 g

*Preparation: 5 min*     *Cooking: 40 min*     *Servings: 4*

## 379. CREAMY SPINACH WITH POLENTA AND EGGS

**INGREDIENTS**

- 2 tablespoons olive oil
- 2 garlic cloves, minced
- 1 red pepper, chopped
- 4 cups baby spinach
- ½ cup heavy cream
- 1 tablespoon all-purpose flour
- Salt and pepper to taste
- ½ cup polenta flour
- 1 ½ cups water
- 1 tablespoon olive oil
- 3 cups water
- 1 tablespoon white wine vinegar
- 4 eggs

**DIRECTIONS**

1. For the creamy spinach, heat the oil in a skillet and add the garlic and red pepper. Cook on high heat for 1 minute then add the spinach and continue cooking for 5-7 minutes until the spinach is softened.
2. Mix the cream with the flour and pour it over the spinach.
3. Cook for 5 more minutes until thickened and creamy.
4. Adjust the taste with salt and pepper and remove off heat.
5. For the polenta, heat the water with salt in a saucepan.
6. When it starts to boil, stir in the oil and polenta flour.
7. Cook on low heat for 10 minutes.
8. For the poached eggs, bring the water, vinegar and a pinch of salt to a boil in a saucepan, then crack open the eggs and drop them in the boiling liquid, one by one, cooking them for 1-2 minutes just until set, but still soft in the center.
9. To serve, spoon the polenta on serving plates. Top with creamy spinach and finish with a poached egg.

CALORIES: 231 Kcal     FAT: 20.7 g     PROTEIN: 7.3 g     CARBOHYDRATES: 5.7 g

---

*Preparation: 10 min*     *Cooking: 10 min*     *Servings: 3*

## 380. PALEO ALMOND BANANA PANCAKES

**INGREDIENTS**

- ¼ cup almond flour
- ½ teaspoon ground cinnamon
- 3 eggs
- 1 banana, mashed
- 1 tablespoon almond butter
- 1 teaspoon vanilla extract
- 1 teaspoon olive oil
- Sliced banana to serve

**DIRECTIONS**

1. Whisk the eggs in a mixing bowl until they become fluffy.
2. In another bowl, mash the banana using a fork and add to the egg mixture.
3. Add the vanilla, almond butter, cinnamon and almond flour.
4. Mix into a smooth batter.
5. Heat the olive oil in a skillet.
6. Add one spoonful of the batter and fry them on both sides.
7. Keep doing these steps until you are done with all the batter.
8. Add some sliced banana on top before serving.

CALORIES: 306 Kcal     FAT: 26 g     PROTEIN: 14.4 g     CARBOHYDRATES: 3.6 g

# 22 Seafood

*Preparation:* 30 min  *Cooking:* 1 hour and 5 min  Servings: 2

## 381. CRISPY TROUT

### INGREDIENTS

- 1 Tablespoon Olive Oil
- 1 Small Shallot, Minced
- 2 Lady Apples, Halved
- 4 Trout Fillets, 3 Ounces Each
- 1 ½ Tablespoons Bread Crumbs, Plain & Fine
- ½ Teaspoon Thyme, Fresh & Chopped
- ½ Tablespoon Butter, Melted & Unsalted
- ½ Cup Apple Cider
- 1 Teaspoon Light Brown Sugar
- ½ Tablespoon Dijon Mustard
- ½ Tablespoon Capers, Rinsed
- Sea Salt & Black Pepper to Taste

### DIRECTIONS

1. Start by heating your oven to 375°F and then get out a small bowl. Combine your bread crumbs, shallot and thyme before seasoning with salt and pepper. Add in the butter and mix.
2. Put the apples cut side up in a baking dish, and then sprinkle with sugar. Top with bread crumbs, and then pour half of your cider around the apples, covering the dish. Bake for a half an hour.
3. Uncover, and then bake for twenty more minutes. The apples should be tender but your crumbs should be crisp. Remove the apples from the oven.
4. Turn the broiler on, and then put the rack four inches away. Pat your trout down, and then season with salt and pepper. Brush your oil on a baking sheet, and then put your trout with the skin side up. Brush your remaining oil over the skin, and broil for six minutes. It should be cooked all the way through. Repeat the apples on the shelf right below the trout. This will keep the crumbs from burning, and it should only take two minutes to heat up.
5. Get out a saucepan and whisk your remaining cider, capers, and mustard together. Add more cider if necessary to thin, and cook for five minutes on medium-high. It should have a sauce like consistency. Spoon the juices over the fish. Serve.

CALORIES: 265 Kcal  FAT: 6.9 g  PROTEIN: 6.6 g  CARBOHYDRATES: 1.2 g

*Preparation: 10 min*     *Cooking: 5 min*     *Servings: 4*

## 382. BERRIES AND GRILLED CALAMARI

### INGREDIENTS

- ¼ cup dried cranberries
- ¼ cup extra virgin olive oil
- ¼ cup olive oil
- ¼ cup sliced almonds
- ½ lemon, juiced
- ¾ cup blueberries
- 1 ½ pounds calamari tube, cleaned
- 1 granny smith apple, sliced thinly
- 1 tablespoon fresh lemon juice
- 2 tablespoons apple cider vinegar
- 6 cups fresh spinach
- Freshly grated pepper to taste
- Sea salt to taste

### DIRECTIONS

1. In a small bowl, make the vinaigrette by mixing well the tablespoon of lemon juice, apple cider vinegar, and extra virgin olive oil. Season with pepper and salt to taste. Set aside.
2. Turn on the grill to medium fire and let the grates heat up for a minute or two.
3. In a large bowl, add olive oil and the calamari tube. Season calamari generously with pepper and salt.
4. Place the seasoned and oiled calamari onto the heated grate and grill until cooked or opaque (around 2 min per side).
5. As you wait for the calamari to cook, you can combine almonds, cranberries, blueberries, spinach, and the thinly sliced apple in a large salad bowl. Toss to mix.
6. Remove cooked calamari from grill and transfer on a chopping board. Cut into ¼-inch thick rings and throw into the salad bowl.
7. Drizzle with vinaigrette and toss well to coat salad.

CALORIES: 567 Kcal     FAT: 24.5 g     PROTEIN: 54.8 g     CARBOHYDRATES: 30.6 g

---

*Preparation: 5 min*     *Cooking: 40 min*     *Servings: 4*

## 383. SEA BASS IN A POCKET

### INGREDIENTS

- 4 sea bass fillets
- 4 garlic cloves, sliced
- 1 celery stalk, sliced
- 1 zucchini, sliced
- 1 cup cherry tomatoes, halved
- 1 shallot, sliced
- 1 teaspoon dried oregano
- Salt and pepper to taste

### DIRECTIONS

1. Mix the garlic, celery, zucchini, tomatoes, shallot and oregano in a bowl. Add salt and pepper to taste.
2. Take 4 sheets of baking paper and arrange them on your working surface.
3. Spoon the vegetable mixture in the center of each sheet.
4. Top with a fish fillet then wrap the paper well so it resembles a pocket.
5. Place the wrapped fish in a baking tray and cook in the preheated oven at 350F for 15 minutes. Serve the fish warm and fresh.

CALORIES: 149 Kcal     FAT: 2.8 g     PROTEIN: 25.2 g     CARBOHYDRATES: 5.2 g

*Preparation: 15 min*     *Cooking: 15 min*     *Servings: 2*

## 384. CAJUN GARLIC SHRIMP NOODLE BOWL

### INGREDIENTS

- ½ teaspoon salt
- 1 onion, sliced
- 1 red pepper, sliced
- 1 tablespoon butter
- 1 teaspoon garlic granules
- 1 teaspoon onion powder
- 1 teaspoon paprika
- 4 oz noodles
- 20 jumbo shrimps, shells removed and deveined
- 3 cloves garlic, minced
- 3 tablespoon ghee
- A dash of cayenne pepper
- A dash of red pepper flakes

### DIRECTIONS

1. Prepare the Cajun seasoning by mixing the onion powder, garlic granules, pepper flakes, cayenne pepper, paprika and salt. Toss in the shrimp to coat in the seasoning.
2. In a skillet, heat the ghee and sauté the garlic. Add in the red pepper and onions and continue sautéing for 4 minutes.
3. Add the Cajun shrimp and cook until opaque. Set aside.
4. In another pan, heat the butter and sauté the noodles for three minutes.
5. Assemble by the placing the Cajun shrimps on top of the noodles.

CALORIES: 612 Kcal     FAT: 30 g     PROTEIN: 17.8 g     CARBOHYDRATES: 41 g

Preparation: 5 min  |  Cooking: 1 hour  |  Servings: 6

## 385. CREAMY FISH GRATIN

### INGREDIENTS

- 1 cup heavy cream
- 2 salmon fillets, cubed
- 2 cod fillets, cubed
- 2 sea bass fillets, cubed
- 1 celery stalk, sliced
- Salt and pepper to taste
- ½ cup grated Parmesan
- ½ cup feta cheese, crumbled

### DIRECTIONS

1. Combine the cream with the fish fillets and celery in a deep-dish baking pan.
2. Add salt and pepper to taste then top with the Parmesan and feta cheese.
3. Cook in the preheated oven at 350°F for 20 minutes.
4. Serve the gratin right away.

CALORIES: 301 Kcal  |  FAT: 16.1 g  |  PROTEIN: 36.9 g  |  CARBOHYDRATES: 1.3 g

---

Preparation: 15 min  |  Cooking: 30 min  |  Servings: 8

## 386. CREAMY BACON-FISH CHOWDER

### INGREDIENTS

- 1 ½ lbs. cod
- 1 ½ teaspoon dried thyme
- 1 large onion, chopped
- 1 medium carrot, coarsely chopped
- 1 tablespoon butter, cut into small pieces
- 1 teaspoon salt, divided
- 3 ½ cups baking potato, peeled and cubed
- 3 slices uncooked bacon
- ¾ teaspoon freshly ground black pepper, divided
- 4 ½ cups water
- 4 bay leaves
- 4 cups 2% reduced-fat milk

### DIRECTIONS

1. In a large skillet, add the water and bay leaves and let it simmer. Add the fish. Cover and let it simmer some more until the flesh flakes easily with fork. Remove the fish from the skillet and cut into large pieces. Set aside the cooking liquid.
2. Place Dutch oven in medium heat and cook the bacon until crisp. Remove the bacon and reserve the bacon drippings. Crush the bacon and set aside.
3. Stir potato, onion and carrot in the pan with the bacon drippings, cook over medium heat for 10 minutes. Add the cooking liquid, bay leaves, 1/2 teaspoon salt, 1/4 teaspoon pepper and thyme, let it boil. Lower the heat and let simmer for 10 minutes. Add the milk and butter, simmer until the potatoes becomes tender, but do not boil. Add the fish, 1/2 teaspoon salt, 1/2 teaspoon pepper. Remove the bay leaves.
4. Serve sprinkled with the crushed bacon.

CALORIES: 400 Kcal  |  FAT: 19.7 g  |  PROTEIN: 20.8 g  |  CARBOHYDRATES: 34.5 g

Preparation: 10 min  Cooking: 15 min  Servings: 2

## 387. BAKED COD FILLETS WITH GHEE SAUCE

### INGREDIENTS

- Pepper and salt to taste
- 2 tablespoons minced parsley
- 1 lemon, sliced into ¼-inch thick circles
- 1 lemon, juiced and zested
- 4 garlic cloves, crushed, peeled, and minced
- ¼ cup melted ghee
- 4 Cod fillets

### DIRECTIONS

1. Preheat the oven to 425°F.
2. Mix parsley, lemon juice, lemon zest, garlic, and melted ghee in a small bowl. Mix well and then season with pepper and salt to taste.
3. Prepare a large baking dish by greasing it with cooking spray.
4. Evenly lay the cod fillets on the greased dish. Season generously with pepper and salt.
5. Pour the bowl of garlic-ghee sauce from step 2 on top of cod fillets. Top the cod fillets with the thinly sliced lemon.
6. Pop in the preheated oven and bake until flaky, around 13 to 15 minutes. Remove from oven, transfer to dishes, serve and enjoy.

CALORIES: 200 Kcal  FAT: 12 g  PROTEIN: 21 g  CARBOHYDRATES: 2 g

Preparation: 15 min        Cooking: 17 min        Servings: 4

## 388. HALIBUT IN SPECIAL SAUCE

### INGREDIENTS

- 1 lime, thinly sliced into 8 pieces
- 2 cups mustard greens, stems removed
- 2 teaspoon olive oil
- 4 – 5 radishes trimmed and quartered
- 4 oz skinless halibut filets
- 4 large fresh basil leaves
- Cayenne pepper to taste – optional
- Pepper and salt to taste
- 1 ½ cups diced cucumber
- 1 ½ finely chopped fresh basil leaves
- 2 teaspoon fresh lime juice
- Pepper and salt to taste

### DIRECTIONS

1. Preheat the oven to 400°F, then prepare parchment papers by making 4 pieces of 15 x 12-inch rectangles. Lengthwise, fold in half and unfold pieces on the table.
2. Season the halibut fillets with pepper and salt.
3. To the right of the fold going lengthwise, place ½ cup of mustard greens. Add a basil leaf, mustard greens, 1 lime slice, ¼ of the radishes and drizzle with ½ teaspoon of oil. Top with a slice of halibut.
4. Fold parchment paper over your filling and crimp the edges of the parchment paper. Repeat the process to remaining ingredients until you have 4 pieces of parchment papers filled with halibut and greens.
5. Place pouches in a baking pan and bake in the oven around 15 to 17 minutes. Meanwhile, make your salsa by mixing all salsa ingredients in a medium bowl.
6. Once the halibut is cooked, remove from the oven and serve.

CALORIES: 335 Kcal        FAT: 16.3 g        PROTEIN: 20.2 g        CARBOHYDRATES: 22.1 g

---

Preparation: 15 min        Cooking: 12 min        Servings: 2

## 389. AVOCADO PEACH SALSA ON SWORDFISH

### INGREDIENTS

- 1 garlic clove, minced
- 1 lemon juice
- 1 tablespoon apple cider vinegar
- 1 tablespoon coconut oil
- 1 teaspoon honey
- 2 swordfish fillets (around 4oz each)
- Pinch cayenne pepper
- Pinch of pepper and salt
- ¼ red onion, finely chopped
- ½ cup cilantro, finely chopped
- 1 avocado, halved and diced
- 1 garlic clove, minced
- 2 peaches, seeded and diced
- Juice of 1 lime
- Salt to taste

### DIRECTIONS

1. In a shallow dish, mix all swordfish marinade ingredients except fillet. Mix well then add fillets to marinate. Place in refrigerator for at least an hour.
2. Meanwhile create salsa by mixing all salsa ingredients in a medium bowl. Put in the refrigerator to cool.
3. Preheat grill and grill fish on medium fire after marinating until cooked around 4 minutes per side.
4. Place each cooked fillet on one serving plate, top with half of salsa, serve and enjoy.

CALORIES: 416 Kcal        FAT: 23.5 g        PROTEIN: 30 g        CARBOHYDRATES: 21 g

*Preparation: 10 min* — *Cooking: 5 min* — *Servings: 4*

## 390. GRILLED CALAMARI

### INGREDIENTS

- ¼ cup extra virgin olive oil
- ¼ cup olive oil
- ¼ cup sliced almonds
- ½ lemon, juiced
- 1 ½ pounds calamari tube, cleaned
- 1 granny smith apple, sliced thinly
- 1 tablespoon fresh lemon juice
- 2 tablespoons apple cider vinegar
- 6 cups fresh spinach
- Freshly grated pepper to taste
- Sea salt to taste

### DIRECTIONS

1. In a small bowl, make the vinaigrette by mixing well the tablespoon of lemon juice, apple cider vinegar, and extra virgin olive oil. Season with pepper and salt to taste. Set aside.
2. Turn on the grill to medium fire and let the grates heat up for a minute or two.
3. In a large bowl, add olive oil and the calamari tube. Season calamari generously with pepper and salt.
4. Place seasoned and oiled calamari onto heated grate and grill until cooked or opaque. This is around two minutes per side.
5. As you wait for the calamari to cook, you can combine almonds, spinach, and the thinly sliced apple in a large salad bowl. Toss to mix.
6. Remove cooked calamari from grill and transfer on a chopping board. Cut into ¼-inch thick rings and throw into the salad bowl.
7. Drizzle with vinaigrette and toss well to coat salad.
8. Serve and enjoy!

CALORIES: 567 Kcal — FAT: 24.5 g — PROTEIN: 54.8 g — CARBOHYDRATES: 30.6 g

*Preparation: 10 min*     *Cooking: 15 min*     *Servings: 4*

# 391. BREADED AND SPICED HALIBUT

## INGREDIENTS

- ¼ cup chopped fresh chives
- ¼ cup chopped fresh dill
- ¼ teaspoon ground black pepper
- ¾ cup panko breadcrumbs
- 1 tablespoon extra-virgin olive oil
- 1 teaspoon finely grated lemon zest
- 1 teaspoon sea salt
- ⅓ cup chopped fresh parsley
- 4 pieces of 6-oz halibut fillets

## DIRECTIONS

1. Line a baking sheet with foil, grease with cooking spray and preheat the oven to 400°F.
2. In a small bowl, mix black pepper, sea salt, lemon zest, olive oil, chives, dill, parsley and breadcrumbs. If needed add more salt to taste. Set aside.
3. Meanwhile, wash halibut fillets on cold tap water. Dry with paper towels and place on prepared baking sheet.
4. Generously spoon crumb mixture onto halibut fillets. Ensure that fillets are covered with crumb mixture. Press down on crumb mixture onto each fillet.
5. Pop into the oven and bake for 10-15 minutes or until fish is flaky and crumb topping are already lightly browned.

CALORIES: 336 Kcal     FAT: 25.3 g     PROTEIN: 25.3 g     CARBOHYDRATES: 4.1 g

---

*Preparation: 5 min*     *Cooking: 10 min*     *Servings: 4*

# 392. BAKED COD CRUSTED WITH HERBS

## INGREDIENTS

- ¼ cup honey
- ¼ teaspoon salt
- ½ cup panko
- ½ teaspoon pepper
- 1 tablespoon extra virgin olive oil
- 1 tablespoon lemon juice
- 1 teaspoon dried basil
- 1 teaspoon dried parsley
- 1 teaspoon rosemary
- 4 pieces of 4-oz cod fillets

## DIRECTIONS

1. With olive oil, grease a 9 x 13-inch baking pan and preheat oven to 375oF.
2. In a zip top bag mix panko, rosemary, salt, pepper, parsley and basil.
3. Evenly spread cod fillets in prepped dish and drizzle with lemon juice.
4. Then brush the fillets with honey on all sides. Discard remaining honey if any.
5. Then evenly divide the panko mixture on top of cod fillets.
6. Pop in the oven and bake for ten minutes or until fish is cooked.

CALORIES: 137 Kcal     FAT: 2 g     PROTEIN: 5 g     CARBOHYDRATES: 21 g

*Preparation: 10 min*  *Cooking: 10 min*  *Servings: 4*

## 393. COCONUT SALSA ON CHIPOTLE FISH TACOS

### INGREDIENTS

- ¼ cup chopped fresh cilantro
- ½ cup seeded and finely chopped plum tomato
- 1 cup peeled and finely chopped mango
- 1 lime cut into wedges
- 1 tablespoon chipotle Chile powder
- 1 tablespoon safflower oil
- 1/3 cup finely chopped red onion
- 10 tablespoon fresh lime juice, divided
- 4 6-oz boneless, skinless cod fillets
- 5 tablespoon dried unsweetened shredded coconut
- 8 pcs of 6-inch tortillas, heated

### DIRECTIONS

1. Whisk well Chile powder, oil, and 4 tablespoon lime juice in a glass baking dish. Add cod and marinate for 12 – 15 minutes. Turning once halfway through the marinating time.
2. Make the salsa by mixing coconut, 6 tablespoon lime juice, cilantro, onions, tomatoes and mangoes in a medium bowl. Set aside.
3. On high, heat a grill pan. Place cod and grill for four minutes per side turning only once.
4. Once cooked, slice cod into large flakes and evenly divide onto tortilla.
5. Evenly divide salsa on top of cod and serve with a side of lime wedges.

CALORIES: 477 Kcal    FAT: 12.4 g    PROTEIN: 35 g    CARBOHYDRATES: 57.4 g

*Preparation: 10 min*  *Cooking: 15 min*  *Servings: 2*

## 394. ONION AND SHRIMPS NOODLES

**INGREDIENTS**

- ½ teaspoon salt
- 4 onions, sliced
- 2 tablespoons olive oil
- 1 teaspoon garlic granules
- 1 teaspoon onion powder
- 1 teaspoon paprika
- 5 oz noodles
- 20 jumbo shrimps, shells removed and deveined

**DIRECTIONS**

1. Prepare seasoning mixing the onions, garlic granules, paprika and onion powder. Toss in the shrimp to coat in the seasoning.
2. In a skillet, heat the ghee and sauté the onion for 10 minutes.
3. Add the Cajun shrimp and cook 2 minutes, then set aside.
4. In another pan, heat 2 tablespoons of oil and sauté the noodles for three minutes.
5. Mix the Shrimp mixture with the noodles, then serve while still hot.

CALORIES: 512 Kcal  FAT: 10 g  PROTEIN: 17.8 g  CARBOHYDRATES: 41 g

*Preparation: 10 min*  *Cooking: 10 min*  *Servings: 4*

## 395. CRAZY SAGANAKI SHRIMP

**INGREDIENTS**

- ¼ teaspoon salt
- ½ cup Chardonnay
- ½ cup crumbled Greek feta cheese
- 1 medium bulb. fennel, cored and finely chopped
- 1 small Chile pepper, seeded and minced
- 1 tablespoon extra virgin olive oil
- 12 jumbo shrimps, peeled and deveined with tails left on
- 2 tablespoon lemon juice, divided
- 5 scallions sliced thinly
- Pepper to taste

**DIRECTIONS**

1. In medium bowl mix salt, lemon juice and shrimp.
2. On medium fire, place a saganaki pan (or large nonstick saucepan) and heat oil.
3. Sauté Chile pepper, scallions, and fennel for 4 minutes or until starting to brown and is already soft.
4. Add wine and sauté for another minute.
5. Place shrimps on top of fennel, cover and cook for 4 minutes or until shrimps are pink.
6. Remove just the shrimp and transfer to a plate.
7. Add pepper, feta and 1 tablespoon lemon juice to pan and cook for a minute or until cheese begins to melt.
8. To serve, place cheese and fennel mixture on a serving plate and top with shrimps.

CALORIES: 310 Kcal  FAT: 6.8 g  PROTEIN: 19.7 g  CARBOHYDRATES: 8.4 g

*Preparation: 000 min*  *Cooking: 1 hour*  *Servings: 6*

## 396. SUMMER FISH STEW

### INGREDIENTS

- 3 tablespoons olive oil
- 4 garlic cloves, minced
- 1 red onion, chopped
- 1 celery stalk, sliced
- 2 red bell peppers, cored and diced
- 2 tablespoons tomato paste
- 2 cups cherry tomatoes
- 1 cup mussels
- 5 shrimps
- 1 cup vegetable stock
- Salt and pepper to taste
- 4 cod fillets, cubed
- 4 sea bass fillets, cubed
- 2 tablespoons all-purpose flour

### DIRECTIONS

1. Season the fish with salt and pepper then sprinkle it with flour.
2. Heat the oil in a skillet then place the fish fillets and cook it on all sides until golden brown. It just must be golden brown, not cooked through just yet.
3. Remove the fish on a platter.
4. Add the garlic, the corn cob, onion and celery in the same skillet as the fish was in and cook for 2 minutes until fragrant.
5. Stir in the remaining ingredients and season with salt and pepper.
6. Cook for 10 minutes on low heat then add every fish and cook for another 10 minutes.
7. Serve the stew warm and fresh.

CALORIES: 318 Kcal   FAT: 10.1 g   PROTEIN: 45.1 g   CARBOHYDRATES: 10.3 g

*Preparation: 10 min*     *Cooking: 6 min*     *Servings: 3*

# 397. SEAFOOD WRAPS WITH AVOCADO

## INGREDIENTS

- 3 corn tortillas
- 5 oz shrimps, peeled
- 3 oz crab meat, chopped
- 1 avocado, peeled, pitted
- 2 tablespoons Greek yogurt
- ¼ teaspoon minced garlic
- ½ teaspoon cayenne pepper
- ¾ teaspoon ground coriander
- 1 teaspoon butter
- ¼ cup heavy cream
- 1 cucumber, trimmed

## DIRECTIONS

1. Pour heavy cream in the saucepan.
2. Add crab meat, shrimps, minced garlic, cayenne pepper, butter, and ground coriander.
3. Boil the seafood for 6 minutes.
4. After this, spread the tortillas with Greek yogurt from one side.
5. Cut avocado and cucumber into the wedges.
6. Arrange them on the tortillas.
7. Then add the seafood mixture.
8. Wrap the tortillas carefully and secure with the toothpicks.

CALORIES: 340 Kcal     FAT: 20.4 g     PROTEIN: 18.8 g     CARBOHYDRATES: 22.3 g

---

*Preparation: 10 min*     *Cooking: 30 min*     *Servings: 8*

# 398. FISH CHOWDER

## INGREDIENTS

- 1 1/2 lbs. cod
- 1 1/2 teaspoon dried pepper
- 3 large potatoes, peeled and chopped
- 1 carrot, chopped
- 1 tablespoon oil
- 1 teaspoon salt, divided
- 4 cups mussels
- 3/4 teaspoon freshly ground black pepper, divided
- 4 1/2 cups water
- 4 bay leaves
- 3 medium tomatoes

## DIRECTIONS

1. In a large skillet, add the water and bay leaves and let it simmer. Add the cod. Cover and let it simmer some more until the flesh flakes easily with fork. Remove the fish from the skillet and cut into large pieces. Set aside the cooking liquid.
2. Stir the potato, the tomatoes, onion and carrot a pan and cook over medium heat for 10 minutes.
3. Add the cooking liquid, bay leaves, 1/2 teaspoon salt, 1/4 teaspoon pepper and thyme, let it boil for around 10 minutes.
4. Lower the heat, then add the mussels.
5. Let simmer for 5 minutes or until the potatoes becomes tender and the mussels are opened.
6. Add the cod, 1/2 teaspoon salt, 1/2 teaspoon pepper.
7. Remove the bay leaves and serve.

CALORIES: 320 Kcal     FAT: 11.7 g     PROTEIN: 20.8 g     CARBOHYDRATES: 34.5 g

*Preparation: 15 min*      *Cooking: 21 min*      *Servings: 4*

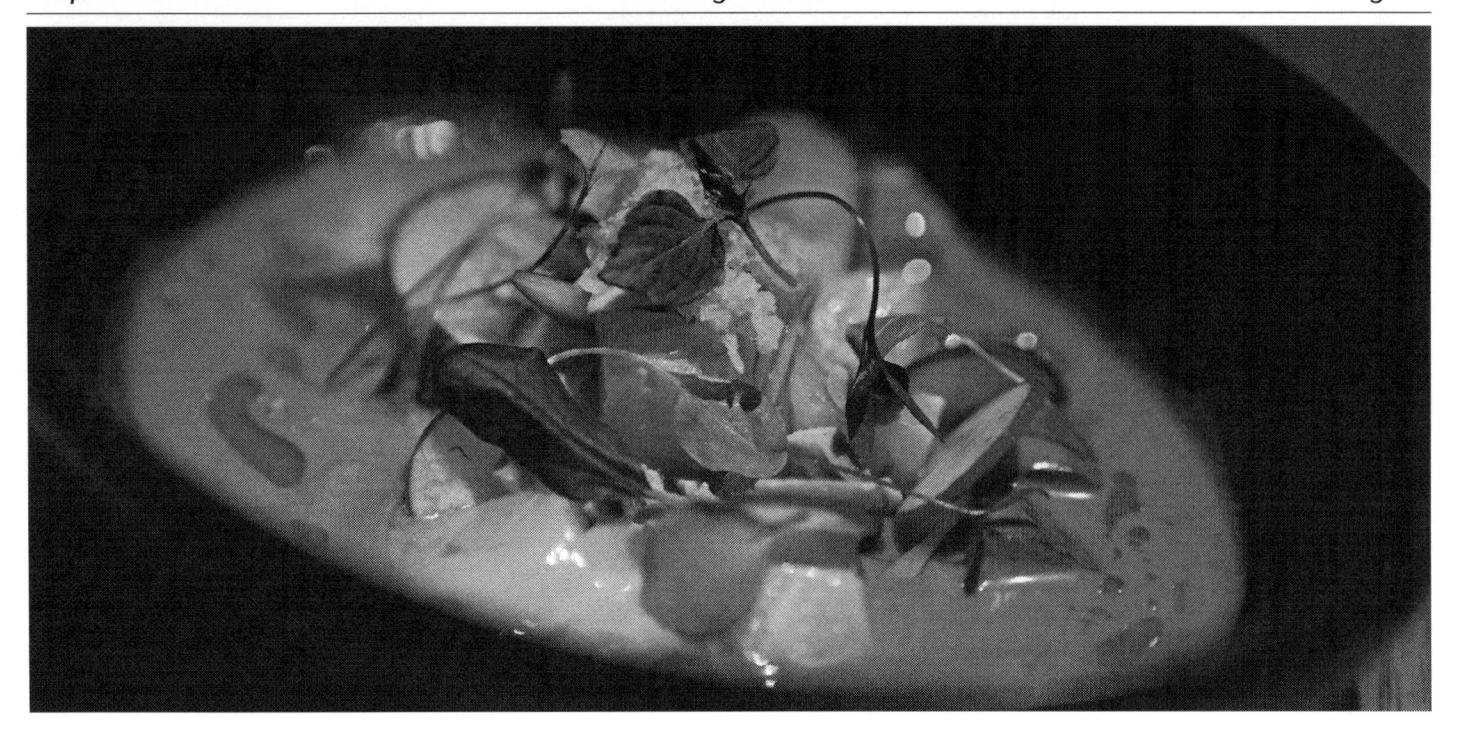

## 399. TOMATO SALSA HALIBUT

### INGREDIENTS

- 1 lime, thinly sliced into 8 pieces
- 2 tablespoons olive oil
- 4 4-oz skinless halibut filets
- 4 large fresh basil leaves
- Pepper and salt to taste
- 1 ½ finely chopped fresh basil leaves
- Pepper and salt to taste
- 1 onion, chopped
- 1 garlic clove
- 1 cup olives
- 6 large tomatoes, chopped
- 1 sliced radish

### DIRECTIONS

1. In a pot, heat the oil with the garlic and the onion.
2. Cook for 1 minute at medium flame, then add the tomatoes, the olives, the salt and the pepper.
3. Add 1 tablespoon of water and cook for around 10 minutes at medium flame.
4. Add the halibut fillets and cook for another 10 minutes with the pot crocked.
5. Turn off the heat, then add the basil leaves.
6. Serve with some lime and sliced radish to decorate.

CALORIES: 315 Kcal      FAT: 9.8 g      PROTEIN: 18.1 g      CARBOHYDRATES: 14 g

*Preparation: 10 min*     *Cooking: 5 min*     *Servings: 4*

## 400. SPECIAL ONION COD WRAPS

### INGREDIENTS

- 4 corn tortillas
- 4 cod fillets
- 4 sea bass fillets, chopped
- 2 onions, sliced
- ½ teaspoon cayenne pepper
- 1 teaspoon thyme
- 1 tablespoon olive oil
- 1 teaspoon red pepper, finely chopped

### DIRECTIONS

1. In a pot add the oil, the red pepper and the onions.
2. Cook at medium heat for 5 minutes, stirring often.
3. Add the water, then the fish fillets.
4. Cook for 10 minutes, with the pot corked.
5. Take a tortilla and heat it in a pan if you like, cooking at high flame 1 minute per side.
6. Arrange the cooked fish and his cooking sauce on the tortillas.
7. Serve and enjoy.

CALORIES: 310 Kcal     FAT: 10.3 g     PROTEIN: 15 g     CARBOHYDRATES: 21 g

---

*Preparation: 10 min*     *Cooking: 20 min*     *Servings: 4*

## 401. CRISPED COCO-SHRIMP WITH MANGO DIP

### INGREDIENTS

- 1 cup shredded coconut
- 1 lb. raw shrimp, peeled and deveined
- 2 egg whites
- 4 tablespoon tapioca starch
- Pepper and salt to taste
- 1 cup mango, chopped
- 1 jalapeño, thinly minced
- 1 teaspoon lime juice
- ⅓ cup coconut milk
- 3 teaspoon raw honey

### DIRECTIONS

1. Preheat oven to 400°F.
2. Ready a pan with wire rack on top.
3. In a medium bowl, add tapioca starch and season with pepper and salt.
4. In a second medium bowl, add egg whites and whisk.
5. In a third medium bowl, add coconut.
6. To ready shrimps, dip first in tapioca starch, then egg whites, and then coconut. Place dredged shrimp on wire rack. Repeat until all shrimps are covered.
7. Pop shrimps in the oven and roast for 10 minutes per side.
8. Meanwhile make the dip by adding all ingredients in a blender. Puree until smooth and creamy. Transfer to a dipping bowl.
9. Once shrimps are golden brown, serve with the mango dip.

CALORIES: 294 Kcal     FAT: 7 g     PROTEIN: 26.6 g     CARBOHYDRATES: 31.2 g

*Preparation: 10 min*     Cooking: 8 min     *Servings: 4*

## 402. CURRY SALMON WITH MUSTARD

### INGREDIENTS

- ¼ teaspoon ground red pepper or chili powder
- ¼ teaspoon ground turmeric
- ¼ teaspoon salt
- 1 teaspoon honey
- 1/8 teaspoon garlic powder or 1 clove garlic minced
- 2 teaspoon. whole grain mustard
- 4 pcs 6-oz salmon fillets

### DIRECTIONS

1. In a small bowl mix well salt, garlic powder, red pepper, turmeric, honey and mustard.
2. Preheat oven to broil and grease a baking dish with cooking spray.
3. Place salmon on baking dish with skin side down and spread evenly mustard mixture on top of salmon.
4. Pop in the oven and broil until flaky around 8 minutes.
5. Serve with some fresh vegetables to enjoy a super healthy meal.

CALORIES: 324 Kcal     FAT: 18.9 g     PROTEIN: 34 g     CARBOHYDRATES: 2.9 g

*Preparation: 10 min*  *Cooking: 10 min*  *Servings: 2*

## 403. MARINATED SHRIMPS

### INGREDIENTS

- ½ cup fresh lime juice, plus lime zest as garnish
- ½ cup rice vinegar
- ½ teaspoon hot sauce
- 1 bay leaf
- 1 cup water
- 1 lb. uncooked shrimp, peeled and deveined
- 1 medium red onion, chopped
- 2 tablespoon capers
- 2 tablespoon Dijon mustard
- 3 whole cloves

### DIRECTIONS

1. Mix the hot sauce, mustard, capers, lime juice and onion in a shallow baking dish and set aside.
2. Bring to a boil in a large saucepan bay leaf, cloves, vinegar and water.
3. Once boiling, add shrimps and cook for a minute while stirring continuously.
4. Drain the shrimps and pour them into the onion mixture.
5. Serve garnished with some lime zests.

CALORIES: 232 Kcal     FAT: 3 g     PROTEIN: 17.8 g     CARBOHYDRATES: 15 g

*Preparation: 5 min*  *Cooking: 45 min*  *Servings: 4*

## 404. ASPARAGUS BAKED PLAICE

### INGREDIENTS

- 4 plaice fillets
- 2 cups cherry tomatoes
- 1 bunch asparagus, trimmed and halved
- ½ lemon, juiced
- 2 tablespoons olive oil
- Salt and pepper to taste

### DIRECTIONS

1. Combine the tomatoes, asparagus, lemon juice and oil in a deep-dish baking pan. Season with salt and pepper.
2. Place the fillets on top and cook in the preheated oven at 350°F for 15 minutes.
3. Serve the plaice and the veggies warm and fresh.

CALORIES: 113 Kcal     FAT: 1.6 g     PROTEIN: 8.1 g     CARBOHYDRATES: 19.4 g

*Preparation: 10 min*     *Cooking: 45 min*     *Servings: 6*

## 405. FRENCH SEAFOOD STEW

### INGREDIENTS

- Pepper and Salt
- ½ lb. littleneck clams
- ½ lb. mussels
- 1 lb. shrimp, peeled and deveined
- 1 large lobster
- 2 lbs. assorted small whole fresh fish, scaled and cleaned
- 2 tablespoons parsley, chopped
- 2 tablespoons garlic, chopped
- Juice and zest of one orange
- 3 cups tomatoes, chopped
- 1 cup leeks, julienned
- 1 cup white wine
- Water
- 1 lb. fish bones
- 2 sprigs thyme
- ½ cup chopped celery
- 2 tablespoon olive oil

### DIRECTIONS

1. Do the stew: Heat oil in a large saucepan. Sauté the celery and onions for 3 minutes. Season with pepper and salt. Stir in the garlic and cook for about a minute.
2. Add the thyme. Stir in the wine, water and fish bones.
3. Let it boil then before reducing to a simmer.
4. Take the pan off the fire and strain broth into another container.
5. Bring the strained broth to a simmer and stir in the parsley, leeks, orange juice, orange zest, garlic and tomatoes.
6. Sprinkle with pepper and salt. Stir in the lobsters and fish.
7. Let it simmer for eight minutes before stirring in the clams, mussels and shrimps.
8. For six minutes, allow to cook while covered before seasoning again with pepper and salt.
9. Assemble in a dish all the seafood and pour the broth over it.

CALORIES: 348 Kcal     FAT: 15.2 g     PROTEIN: 31.8 g     CARBOHYDRATES: 20 g

*Preparation: 10 min*  *Cooking: 12 min*  *Servings: 2*

## 406. DILL RELISH ON WHITE SEA BASS

### INGREDIENTS

- 1 ½ tablespoon chopped white onion
- 1 ½ teaspoon chopped fresh dill
- 1 lemon, quartered
- 1 teaspoon Dijon mustard
- 1 teaspoon lemon juice
- 1 teaspoon pickled baby capers, drained
- 4 pieces of 4-oz white sea bass fillets

### DIRECTIONS

1. Preheat the oven at 375°F.
2. Mix lemon juice, mustard, dill, capers and onions in a small bowl.
3. Prepare four aluminum foil squares and place 1 fillet per foil.
4. Squeeze a lemon wedge per fish.
5. Evenly divide into 4 the dill spread and drizzle over fillet.
6. Close the foil over the fish securely and pop in the oven.
7. Bake for 10 to 12 minutes or until fish is cooked through.
8. Remove from foil and transfer to a serving platter, serve and enjoy.

CALORIES: 315 Kcal    FAT: 3 g    PROTEIN: 10 g    CARBOHYDRATES: 12 g

---

*Preparation: 10 min*  *Cooking: 10 min*  *Servings: 2*

## 407. ROASTED SHRIMPS WITH ZUCCHINI PASTA

### INGREDIENTS

- 2 medium-sized zucchinis, cut into thin strips or spaghetti noodles
- Salt and pepper to taste
- 1 lemon, zested and juiced
- 2 garlic cloves, minced
- 2 tablespoon ghee, melted
- 2 tablespoon olive oil
- 8 ounces shrimps, cleaned and deveined

### DIRECTIONS

1. Preheat the oven to 400°F.
2. In a mixing bowl, mix all the ingredients except the zucchini noodles. Toss to coat the shrimp.
3. Bake for 10 minutes until the shrimps turn pink.
4. Add the zucchini pasta, then toss.
5. Serve and enjoy.

CALORIES: 250 Kcal    FAT: 7 g    PROTEIN: 14.3 g    CARBOHYDRATES: 10.9 g

Preparation: 10 min    Cooking: 5 min    Servings: 4

## 408. FRESH OYSTERS

### INGREDIENTS

- 2 lemons
- 24 medium oysters
- tabasco sauce

### DIRECTIONS

1. If you are a newbie when it comes to eating oysters, then I suggest that you blanch the oysters before eating. If you want to eat the oysters raw, just skip to the last step.
2. For some, eating oysters raw is a great way to enjoy this dish because of the consistency and juiciness of raw oysters. Plus, adding lemon juice prior to eating the raw oysters cooks it a bit.
3. To blanch oysters, bring a big pot of water to a rolling boil. Add oysters in batches of 6-10 pieces. Leave on boiling pot of water between 3-5 minutes and remove oysters right away.
4. To eat oysters, squeeze lemon juice on oyster on shell, add tabasco as desired and eat.

CALORIES: 247 Kcal    FAT: 7 g    PROTEIN: 21 g    CARBOHYDRATES: 4 g

*Preparation: 10 min*  *Cooking: 6 min*  *Servings: 4*

## 409. GINGER SCALLION SAUCE OVER SEARED AHI

### INGREDIENTS

- 1 bunch scallions, bottoms removed, finely chopped
- 1 tablespoon rice wine vinegar
- 1 tablespoon. Bragg's liquid amino
- 16-oz ahi tuna steaks
- 2 tablespoon. fresh ginger, peeled and grated
- 3 tablespoon. coconut oil, melted
- Pepper and salt to taste

### DIRECTIONS

1. In a small bowl mix together vinegar, 2 tablespoon. oil, soy sauce, ginger and scallions. Put aside.
2. On medium fire, place a large saucepan and heat remaining oil. Once oil is hot and starts to smoke, sear tuna until deeply browned or for two minutes per side.
3. Place seared tuna on a serving platter and let it stand for 5 minutes before slicing into 1-inch thick strips.
4. Drizzle ginger-scallion mixture over seared tuna, serve and enjoy.

CALORIES: 247 Kcal   FAT: 1 g   PROTEIN: 29 g   CARBOHYDRATES: 8 g

---

*Preparation: 10 min*  *Cooking: 10 min*  *Servings: 2*

## 410. HEALTHY POACHED TROUT

### INGREDIENTS

- 1 8-oz boneless, skin on trout fillet
- 2 cups chicken broth or water
- 2 leeks, halved
- 6-8 slices lemon
- salt and pepper to taste

### DIRECTIONS

1. On medium fire, place a large nonstick skillet and arrange leeks and lemons on pan in a layer.
2. Cover with soup stock or water and bring to a simmer.
3. Meanwhile, season trout on both sides with pepper and salt. Place trout on simmering pan of water.
4. Cover and cook until trout is flaky, around 8 minutes.
5. In a serving platter, spoon leek and lemons on bottom of plate, top with trout and spoon sauce into plate.
6. Serve and enjoy.

CALORIES: 360 Kcal   FAT: 7.5 g   PROTEIN: 13.8 g   CARBOHYDRATES: 11.5 g

Preparation: 10 min  Cooking: 10 min  Servings: 2

# 411. BROILED LOBSTERS

## INGREDIENTS

- 2 6-oz frozen lobsters
- 1 tablespoon olive oil
- 1 teaspoon pepper seasoning
- 1 lemon, sliced

## DIRECTIONS

1. Preheat the oven broiler or, if you don't have one, preheat some water into a pot, to steam cook the lobster.
2. With the help of a knife cut the lobster lengthwise, but let the back remain intact. The cut should not be complete, but something like a pocket.
3. Add some olive oil into the cut you made.
4. Season the outside and the cut with lemon and pepper.
5. Place the lobster in a baking sheet.
6. Place on top broiler rack and broil for 10 minutes until lobster meat is lightly browned on the sides and center meat is opaque.
7. Serve and enjoy.

CALORIES: 175.6 Kcal   FAT: 10 g   PROTEIN: 9 g   CARBOHYDRATES: 10.2 g

*Preparation: 10 min*     *Cooking: 7 min*     *Servings: 4*

## 412. YOGURT TOPPED GRILLED FISH

**INGREDIENTS**

- ¼ cup 2% plain Greek yogurt
- ¼ teaspoon + 1/8 teaspoon salt
- ¼ teaspoon black pepper
- ½ green onion, finely chopped
- ½ teaspoon dried oregano
- 1 tablespoon finely chopped fresh mint leaves
- 3 tablespoon finely chopped English cucumber
- 4 5-oz cod fillets

**DIRECTIONS**

1. Brush a grill grate with oil and preheat the grill with a medium flame or in the oven.
2. Season the cod fillets on both sides with pepper, ¼ teaspoon salt and oregano.
3. Grill the cod for 3 minutes per side or until cooked as you like it.
4. Mix ⅛ teaspoon salt, onion, mint, cucumber and yogurt in a small bowl.
5. Serve the cod with a dollop of the dressing.
6. This dish can be served with salad greens or brown rice.

CALORIES: 253 Kcal     FAT: 7 g     PROTEIN: 25.5 g     CARBOHYDRATES: 5 g

---

*Preparation: 10 min*     *Cooking: 10 min*     *Servings: 2*

## 413. ONE-POT SEAFOOD CHOWDER

**INGREDIENTS**

- 3 cans milk
- 1 tablespoon garlic, minced
- Salt and pepper to taste
- 3 cans clams, chopped
- 2 cans shrimps, canned
- 1 package fresh shrimps, shelled and deveined
- 1 can corn, drained
- 4 large potatoes, diced
- 2 carrots, peeled and chopped
- 2 celery stalks, chopped

**DIRECTIONS**

1. Place every ingredient into a pot and give a good stir to mix everything.
2. Close the lid and turn on the heat to medium.
3. Bring to boil and allow to simmer for 15 minutes.
4. Serve hot and enjoy with some bread or white rice.

CALORIES: 532 Kcal     FAT: 8.7 g     PROTEIN: 20.3 g     CARBOHYDRATES: 22.5 g

*Preparation: 10 min*     *Cooking: 10 min*     *Servings: 4*

## 414. LEFTOVER SALMON SALAD POWER BOWLS

### INGREDIENTS

- 1 cup zucchini, sliced
- 1 lemon, juice squeezed
- 1 tablespoon balsamic glaze
- 2 sprigs of thyme, chopped
- 2 tablespoon olive oil
- 6 cups seasonal greens
- 9 ounces leftover grilled salmon
- Salt and pepper to taste
- 1 cup tomatoes, sliced

### DIRECTIONS

1. Heat oil in a skillet over medium flame and sauté the greens if they aren't some that you can eat raw.
2. Season with salt and pepper to taste.
3. In a mixing bowl, mix all the ingredients together with the leftover salmon.
4. Toss to combine everything.
5. Sprinkle with lemon juice if you like, then serve.

CALORIES: 410 Kcal     FAT: 25.5 g     PROTEIN: 23.4 g     CARBOHYDRATES: 9.3 g

Preparation: 10 min — Cooking: 33 min — Servings: 4

## 415. ORANGE HERBED SAUCED WHITE BASS

### INGREDIENTS

- ¼ cup thinly sliced green onions
- ½ cup orange juice
- 1 ½ tablespoon fresh lemon juice
- 1 ½ tablespoon olive oil
- 1 large onion, halved, thinly sliced
- 1 large orange, unpeeled, sliced
- 3 tablespoon chopped fresh dill
- 6 3-oz skinless white bass fillets
- Additional unpeeled orange slices

### DIRECTIONS

1. Grease a 13 x 9-inch glass baking dish and preheat the oven to 400°F.
2. Arrange the orange slices in single layer on baking dish, top with onion slices, salt, pepper and oil.
3. Pop in the oven and roast for 25 minutes or until onions are tender and browned.
4. Remove from the oven and increase the oven temperature to 450°F.
5. Push onion and orange slices on sides of dish and place bass fillets in middle of dish. Season with 1 ½ tablespoon dill, pepper and salt. Arrange the onions and orange slices on top of the fish and pop into the oven, the roast for 8 minutes.
6. In a small bowl, mix 1 ½ tablespoon dill, lemon juice, green onions and orange juice.
7. Transfer the salmon to a serving plate, drizzle with the orange sauce and garnish with orange slices.

CALORIES: 312 Kcal — FAT: 23.1 g — PROTEIN: 24.2 g — CARBOHYDRATES: 33.9 g

---

Preparation: 10 min — Cooking: 20 min — Servings: 2

## 416. PAPRIKA SALMON AND GREEN BEANS

### INGREDIENTS

- ¼ cup olive oil
- ½ tablespoon onion powder
- ½ teaspoon bouillon powder
- ½ teaspoon cayenne pepper
- 1 tablespoon smoked paprika
- 1-pound green beans
- 2 teaspoon minced garlic
- 3 tablespoon fresh herbs
- 8 ounces of salmon steak
- Salt and pepper to taste

### DIRECTIONS

1. Preheat the oven to 400°F.
2. Grease a baking sheet and set aside.
3. Heat a skillet over medium low heat and add the olive oil. Sauté the garlic, smoked paprika, fresh herbs, cayenne pepper and onion powder. Stir for a minute then let the mixture sit for 5 minutes. Set aside.
4. Put the salmon steaks in a bowl and add salt and the paprika spice mixture. Rub to coat the salmon well.
5. Place the salmon on the baking sheet and cook for 18 minutes.
6. Meanwhile, blanch the green beans in boiling water with salt.
7. Serve the beans with the salmon.

CALORIES: 545 Kcal — FAT: 26.6 g — PROTEIN: 33.5 g — CARBOHYDRATES: 13.1 g

Preparation: 10 min   Cooking: 15 min   Servings: 4

## 417. LEMON-GARLIC BAKED HALIBUT

### INGREDIENTS

- 1 large garlic clove, minced
- 1 tablespoon chopped flat leaf parsley
- 1 teaspoon olive oil
- 4 5-oz boneless, skin-on halibut fillets
- 2 teaspoon lemon zest
- Juice of ½ lemon, divided
- Salt and pepper to taste

### DIRECTIONS

1. Grease a baking dish with cooking spray and preheat oven to 400°F.
2. Place halibut with skin touching the dish and drizzle with olive oil.
3. Season with pepper and salt.
4. Pop into the oven and bake until flaky around 12-15 minutes.
5. Remove from oven and drizzle with remaining lemon juice, serve and enjoy with a side of salad greens.

CALORIES: 315 Kcal   FAT: 10.5 g   PROTEIN: 14.1 g   CARBOHYDRATES: 36.6 g

*Preparation: 10 min*  *Cooking: 12 min*  *Servings: 4*

## 418. PECAN CRUSTED TROUT

### INGREDIENTS

- ½ cup crushed pecans
- ½ teaspoon grated fresh ginger
- 1 egg, beaten
- 1 teaspoon crush dried rosemary
- 1 teaspoon salt
- 4 4-oz trout fillets
- Black pepper to taste
- Cooking spray
- Whole wheat flour, as needed

### DIRECTIONS

1. Grease a baking sheet lightly with cooking spray and preheat the oven to 400°F.
2. In a shallow bowl, combine black pepper, salt, rosemary and pecans. In another shallow bowl, add whole wheat flour. In a third bowl, add beaten egg.
3. To prepare the fish, dip it in the flour until covered well. Shake off excess flour. Then dip it into the beaten egg, until coated well. Let the excess egg drip off before dipping trout fillet into pecan crumbs. Press the trout lightly onto pecan crumbs to make it stick to the fish.
4. Place the breaded fish onto the prepared pan. Repeat this process for every remaining fillet.
5. Pop into the oven and bake for 10 to 12 minutes or until fish is flaky, then serve.

CALORIES: 329 Kcal  FAT: 19 g  PROTEIN: 26.9 g  CARBOHYDRATES: 7 g

---

*Preparation: 10 min*  *Cooking: 10 min*  *Servings: 4*

## 419. PESTO AND LEMON HALIBUT

### INGREDIENTS

- 1 tablespoon fresh lemon juice
- 1 tablespoon lemon rind, grated
- 2 garlic cloves, peeled
- 2 tablespoon olive oil
- ¼ cup Parmesan Cheese, freshly grated
- 2/3 cups firmly packed basil leaves
- ⅛ teaspoon freshly ground black pepper
- ¼ teaspoon salt, divided
- 4 pcs 6-oz halibut fillets

### DIRECTIONS

1. Preheat a grill to medium fire and grease his grate with cooking spray.
2. Season the fish fillets with pepper and 1/8 teaspoon salt.
3. Place the fillets on the grill and cook until halibut is flaky, around 4 minutes per side.
4. Meanwhile, make your lemon pesto by combining lemon juice, lemon rind, garlic, olive oil, Parmesan cheese, basil leaves and the remaining salt in a blender. Pulse the mixture until finely minced, but not pureed.
5. Once the Halibut is cooked transfer it to a serving platter, pour over the lemon pesto sauce, serve and enjoy.

CALORIES: 277 Kcal  FAT: 13 g  PROTEIN: 18.7 g  CARBOHYDRATES: 2.9 g

Preparation: 10 min  Cooking: 10 min  Servings: 4

## 420. ORANGE ROSEMARY SEARED SALMON

### INGREDIENTS

- ½ cup chicken stock
- 1 cup fresh orange juice
- 1 tablespoon olive oil
- 1 tablespoon tapioca starch
- 2 garlic cloves, minced
- 2 tablespoon fresh lemon juice
- 2 teaspoon fresh rosemary, minced
- 2 teaspoon orange zest
- 4 salmon fillets, skins removed
- Salt and pepper to taste

### DIRECTIONS

1. Season the salmon fillet on both sides.
2. In a skillet, heat the olive oil over medium high heat. Cook the salmon fillets for 5 minutes on each side. Set aside.
3. In a mixing bowl, combine the orange juice, chicken stock, lemon juice and orange zest.
4. In the skillet, sauté the garlic and rosemary for 2 minutes and pour the orange juice mixture. Bring to a boil. Lower the heat to medium low and simmer. Season with salt and pepper to taste.
5. Pour the sauce all over the salmon fillets, then serve.

CALORIES: 493 Kcal    FAT: 17.9 g    PROTEIN: 27.1 g    CARBOHYDRATES: 12.8 g

Preparation: 10 min  Cooking: 30 min  Servings: 4

## 421. PEPPERS & PINEAPPLE TOPPED MAHI-MAHI

### INGREDIENTS

- ¼ teaspoon black pepper
- ¼ teaspoon salt
- 1 cup whole wheat couscous
- 1 red bell pepper, diced
- 2 1/3 cups low sodium chicken broth
- 2 cups chopped fresh pineapple
- 2 tablespoon. chopped fresh chives
- 2 teaspoon. olive oil
- 4 pieces of skinless, boneless mahi mahi (dolphin fish) fillets (around 4-oz each)

### DIRECTIONS

1. On high fire, add 1 1/3 cups broth to a small saucepan and heat until boiling. Once boiling, add couscous. Turn off fire, cover and set aside to allow liquid to be fully absorbed around 5 minutes.
2. On medium high fire, place a large nonstick saucepan and heat oil.
3. Season fish on both sides with pepper and salt. Add mahi mahi to hot pan and pan fry until golden around one minute each side. Once cooked, transfer to plate.
4. On same pan, sauté bell pepper and pineapples until soft, around 2 minutes on medium high fire.
5. Add couscous to pan along with chives, and remaining broth.
6. On top of the mixture in pan, place fish. With foil, cover pan and continue cooking until fish is steaming and tender underneath the foil, around 3-5 minutes.

CALORIES: 302 Kcal  FAT: 4.8 g  PROTEIN: 33.1 g  CARBOHYDRATES: 22 g

---

Preparation: 10 min  Cooking: 12 min  Servings: 4

## 422. ROASTED HALIBUT WITH BANANA RELISH

### INGREDIENTS

- ¼ cup cilantro
- ½ teaspoon freshly grated orange zest
- ½ teaspoon kosher salt, divided
- 1 lb. halibut or any deep-water fish
- 1 teaspoon ground coriander, divided into half
- 2 oranges (peeled, segmented and chopped)
- 2 ripe bananas, diced
- 2 tablespoon lime juice

### DIRECTIONS

1. In a pan, prepare the fish by rubbing ½ teaspoon coriander and ¼ teaspoon kosher salt.
2. Place in a baking sheet with cooking spray and bake for 8 to 12 minutes inside a 450-degree Fahrenheit preheated oven.
3. Prepare the relish by stirring the orange zest, bananas, chopped oranges, lime juice, cilantro and the rest of the salt and coriander in a medium bowl.
4. Spoon the relish over the roasted fish.

CALORIES: 245 Kcal  FAT: 6 g  PROTEIN: 15.3 g  CARBOHYDRATES: 21 g

*Preparation: 10 min*     Cooking: 5 min     *Servings: 4*

# 423. PAN FRIED TUNA WITH HERBS

## INGREDIENTS

- ¼ cup almonds, chopped finely
- ¼ cup fresh tangerine juice
- ½ teaspoon fennel seeds, chopped finely
- ½ teaspoon ground pepper, divided
- ½ teaspoon sea salt, divided
- 1 tablespoon olive oil
- 2 tablespoon. fresh mint, chopped finely
- 2 tablespoon. red onion, chopped finely
- 4 pieces of 6-oz Tuna steak cut in half

## DIRECTIONS

1. Mix fennel seeds, olive oil, mint, onion, tangerine juice and almonds in small bowl. Season with ¼ each of pepper and salt.
2. Season the fish with the remaining pepper and salt.
3. On medium high fire, place a large nonstick fry pan and grease with cooking spray.
4. Pan fry the tuna until the desired cooking is reached or for two minutes per side.
5. Transfer the cooked tuna into a serving plate, drizzle with the dressing and serve.

CALORIES: 272 Kcal     FAT: 9.7 g     PROTEIN: 32 g     CARBOHYDRATES: 4.2 g

*Preparation: 10 min*  *Cooking: 30 min*  *Servings: 2*

## 424. ROASTED POLLOCK FILLET WITH BACON

### INGREDIENTS

- ¼ cup olive oil
- ½ cup white wine
- 1 ½ lbs. Pollock fillets
- 1 sprig fresh thyme
- 1 tablespoon chopped fresh thyme
- 2 tablespoon. olive oil
- 4 leeks, sliced

### DIRECTIONS

1. Grease a 9x13 baking dish and preheat oven to 400°F.
2. In baking pan, add the olive oil and leeks, then toss to combine.
3. Pop into the oven and roast for 10 minutes.
4. Remove from the oven; add white wine and 1 tablespoon chopped thyme. Insert again in the oven and roast for another 10 minutes.
5. Remove pan from oven and add fish on top. With a spoon, spoon olive oil mixture onto fish until coated fully. Return to oven and roast for another ten minutes.
6. Remove from the oven, garnish with a sprig of thyme and serve.

CALORIES: 442 Kcal   FAT: 20 g   PROTEIN: 22.9 g   CARBOHYDRATES: 13.6 g

---

*Preparation: 10 min*  *Cooking: 8 min*  *Servings: 4*

## 425. SCALLOPS IN WINE AND OLIVE OIL

### INGREDIENTS

- ¼ teaspoon salt
- ½ cup dry white wine
- 1 ½ lbs. large sea scallops
- 1 ½ teaspoon chopped fresh tarragon
- 2 tablespoon olive oil
- Black pepper – optional

### DIRECTIONS

1. On medium high fire, place a large nonstick fry pan and heat oil.
2. Add scallops and fry for 3 minutes per side or until edges are lightly browned. Transfer to a serving plate.
3. On same pan, add salt, tarragon and wine while scraping pan to loosen browned bits.
4. Turn off fire.
5. Pour the sauce over the scallops and serve.

CALORIES: 205 Kcal   FAT: 8 g   PROTEIN: 18.6 g   CARBOHYDRATES: 4.7 g

*Preparation: 10 min*     Cooking: 40 min     Servings: 6

## 426. SEAFOOD STEW CIOPPINO

### INGREDIENTS

- ¼ cup Italian parsley, chopped
- ¼ teaspoon dried basil
- ¼ teaspoon dried thyme
- ½ cup dry white wine
- ½ lb. King crab legs, cut at each joint
- ½ onion, chopped
- ½ teaspoon red pepper flakes (adjust to desired spiciness)
- 1 28-oz can crushed tomatoes
- 1 lb. mahi mahi, cut into cubes
- 1 lb. raw shrimp
- 1 tablespoon olive oil
- 2 bay leaves
- 2 cups clam juice
- 50 live clams, washed
- 6 cloves garlic, minced
- Pepper and salt to taste

### DIRECTIONS

1. On medium fire, place a stockpot and heat oil.
2. Add onion and for 4 minutes sauté until soft.
3. Add bay leaves, thyme, basil, red pepper flakes and garlic. Cook for a minute while stirring a bit.
4. Add clam juice and tomatoes. Once simmering, place fire to medium low and cook for 20 minutes uncovered.
5. Add white wine and clams. Cover and cook for 5 minutes or until clams have slightly opened.
6. Stir pot then add fish pieces, crab legs and shrimps. Do not stir soup to maintain the fish's shape. Cook while covered for 4 minutes or until clams are fully opened; fish and shrimps are opaque and cooked.
7. Season with pepper and salt to taste.
8. Transfer Cioppino to serving bowls and garnish with parsley before serving.

CALORIES: 371 Kcal     FAT: 6.8 g     PROTEIN: 18 g     CARBOHYDRATES: 15.5 g

Preparation: 10 min  Cooking: 15 min  Servings: 3

## 427. SIMPLE COD PICCATA

### INGREDIENTS

- ¼ cup capers, drained
- ½ teaspoon salt
- ¾ cup chicken stock
- 1/3 cup almond flour
- 1-pound cod fillets, patted dry
- 2 tablespoon fresh parsley, chopped
- 2 tablespoon grapeseed oil
- 3 tablespoon extra-virgin oil
- 3 tablespoon lemon juice

### DIRECTIONS

1. In a bowl, combine the almond flour and salt.
2. Dredge the fish in the almond flour to coat. Set aside.
3. Heat a little bit of olive oil to coat a large skillet. Heat the skillet over medium high heat. Add grapeseed oil. Cook the cod for 3 minutes on each side to brown. Remove from the plate and place on a paper towel-lined plate.
4. In a saucepan, mix together the chicken stock, capers and lemon juice. Simmer to reduce the sauce to half. Add the remaining grapeseed oil.
5. Drizzle the fried cod with the sauce and sprinkle with parsley.

CALORIES: 277 Kcal   FAT: 15.3 g   PROTEIN: 11.9 g   CARBOHYDRATES: 3.7 g

Preparation: 10 min  Cooking: 0 min  Servings: 4

## 428. SMOKED TROUT TARTINE

### INGREDIENTS

- ½ 15-oz can cannellini beans
- ½ cup diced roasted red peppers
- ¾ lb. smoked trout, flaked into bite-sized pieces
- 1 stalk celery, finely chopped
- 1 tablespoon extra virgin olive oil
- 1 teaspoon chopped fresh dill
- 1 teaspoon Dijon mustard
- 2 tablespoon capers, rinsed and drained
- 2 tablespoon freshly squeezed lemon juice
- 2 teaspoon minced onion
- 4 large whole grain bread, toasted
- Dill sprigs – for garnish
- A pinch of sugar

### DIRECTIONS

1. Mix the sugar, mustard, olive oil and lemon juice in a big bowl.
2. Add the rest of the ingredients, except for the toasted bread.
3. Toss to mix well.
4. Evenly divide fish mixture on top of bread slices and garnish with dill sprigs.
5. Serve and enjoy.

CALORIES: 348 Kcal   FAT: 10.1 g   PROTEIN: 21.2 g   CARBOHYDRATES: 36.1 g

*Preparation: 10 min*     *Cooking: 15 min*     *Servings: 4*

## 429. STEAMED MUSSELS THAI STYLE

### INGREDIENTS

- ¼ cup minced shallots
- ½ teaspoon Madras curry
- 1 cup dry white wine
- 1 small bay leaf
- 1 tablespoon chopped fresh basil
- 1 tablespoon chopped fresh cilantro
- 1 tablespoon chopped fresh mint
- 2 lbs. mussel, cleaned and debearded
- 2 tablespoon butter
- 4 medium garlic cloves, minced

### DIRECTIONS

1. Place a large heavy bottomed pot over medium-high fire.
2. Add the curry powder, bay leaf, wine plus the minced garlic and shallots.
3. Bring to boil and simmer for 3 minutes.
4. Add the cleaned mussels, stir, cover, and cook for 3 minutes.
5. Stir mussels again, cover, and cook for another 2 or 3 minutes. Cooking is done when majority of shells have opened.
6. With a slotted spoon, transfer cooked mussels in a large bowl. Discard any unopened mussel.
7. Continue heating the pot with the sauce. Add the butter and the chopped herbs.
8. Season with pepper and salt to taste.
9. Once good, pour over the mussels, serve and enjoy.

CALORIES: 407 Kcal     FAT: 15.2 g     PROTEIN: 12.4 g     CARBOHYDRATES: 10.8 g

*Preparation: 10 min*     *Cooking: 10 min*     *Servings: 4*

# 430. TASTY TUNA SCALOPPINE

## INGREDIENTS

- ¼ cup chopped almonds
- ¼ cup fresh tangerine juice
- ½ teaspoon fennel seeds
- ½ teaspoon ground black pepper, divided
- ½ teaspoon salt
- 1 tablespoon extra virgin olive oil
- 2 tablespoon chopped fresh mint
- 2 tablespoon chopped red onion
- 4 6-oz sushi-grade Yellowfin tuna steaks, each split in half horizontally
- Cooking spray

## DIRECTIONS

1. In a small bowl mix fennel seeds, olive oil, mint, onion, tangerine juice, almonds, ¼ teaspoon pepper and ¼ teaspoon salt. Combine thoroughly.
2. Season fish with remaining salt and pepper.
3. On medium high fire, place a large nonstick pan and grease with cooking spray. Pan fry fish in two batches cooking each side for a minute.
4. Fish is best served with a side of salad greens or a half cup of cooked brown rice.

CALORIES: 405 Kcal     FAT: 11.9 g     PROTEIN: 18.5 g     CARBOHYDRATES: 20.1 g

---

*Preparation: 10 min*     *Cooking: 25 min*     *Servings: 2*

# 431. THYME AND LEMON ON BAKED SALMON

## INGREDIENTS

- 1/2 Cup Water
- 1 1/4 lb. Lamb Loin Chops, Trimmed
- 1/2 Tablespoon Garlic, Minced
- 1/4 Cup Couscous, Whole Wheat
- 1 Pinch Sea Salt
- 1/2 Tablespoon Parsley, Fresh & Chopped Fine
- 1 Tomato, Chopped
- 1 Teaspoon Olive Oil

## DIRECTIONS

1. In a foil line baking sheet, place a parchment paper on top.
2. Place salmon with skin side down on parchment paper.
3. Season generously with pepper and salt.
4. Place capers on top of fillet. Cover with thinly sliced lemon.
5. Garnish with thyme.
6. Pop in cold oven and bake for 25 minutes at 400oF settings.
7. Serve right away and enjoy.

CALORIES: 484 Kcal     FAT: 19.7 g     PROTEIN: 20.3 g     CARBOHYDRATES: 4.3 g

Preparation: 10 min    Cooking: 30 min    Servings: 2

## 432. WARM CAPER TAPENADE ON COD

**INGREDIENTS**

- ¼ cup chopped cured olives
- ¼ teaspoon freshly ground pepper
- 1 ½ teaspoon chopped fresh oregano
- 1 cup halved cherry tomatoes
- 1 lb. cod fillet
- 1 tablespoon capers, rinsed and chopped
- 1 tablespoon minced shallot
- 1 teaspoon balsamic vinegar
- 3 teaspoon extra virgin olive oil, divided

**DIRECTIONS**

1. Grease baking sheet with cooking spray and preheat oven to 450oF.
2. Place cod on prepared baking sheet. Rub with 2 teaspoon oil and season with pepper.
3. Roast in oven for 15 to 20 minutes or until cod is flaky.
4. While waiting for cod to cook, on medium fire, place a small fry pan and heat 1 teaspoon oil.
5. Sauté shallots for a minute.
6. Add tomatoes and cook for two minutes or until soft.
7. Add capers and olives. Sauté for another minute.
8. Add vinegar and oregano. Turn off fire and stir to mix well.
9. Evenly divide cod into 4 serving and place on a plate.
10. To serve, top cod with Caper-Olive-Tomato Tapenade and enjoy.

CALORIES: 241 Kcal    FAT: 8.9 g    PROTEIN: 12.6 g    CARBOHYDRATES: 10 g

---

Preparation: 10 min    Cooking: 10 min    Servings: 4

## 433. YUMMY SALMON PANZANELLA

**INGREDIENTS**

- ¼ cup thinly sliced fresh basil
- ¼ cup thinly sliced red onion
- ¼ teaspoon pepper
- ½ teaspoon salt
- 1 lb. center cut salmon, skinned and cut into 4 equal portions
- 1 medium cucumber, peeled, seeded, and cut into 1-inch slices
- 1 tablespoon capers, rinsed and chopped
- 2 large tomatoes, cubed
- 2 thick slices day old whole grain bread, sliced into 1-inch cubes
- 3 tablespoon extra virgin olive oil
- 3 tablespoon red wine vinegar
- 8 Kalamata olives, chopped

**DIRECTIONS**

1. Grease a grill grate and preheat it at high flame or in the oven at 400°F.
2. In a large bowl, whisk 1/8 teaspoon pepper, capers, vinegar, and olives. Add oil and whisk well.
3. Stir in basil, onion, cucumber, tomatoes, and bread.
4. Season both sides of salmon with the remaining pepper and salt.
5. Grill the salmon for 4 minutes per side.
6. Into 4 plates, evenly divide the salad, top with grilled salmon, and serve.

CALORIES: 383 Kcal    FAT: 20.6 g    PROTEIN: 21.4 g    CARBOHYDRATES: 13.6 g

# 23 Beans

Preparation: 10 min  Cooking: 10 min  Servings: 4

## 434. BEAN AND TOASTED PITA SALAD

### INGREDIENTS

- 3 tablespoon chopped fresh mint
- 3 tablespoon chopped fresh parsley
- 1 cup crumbled feta cheese
- 1 cup sliced romaine lettuce
- ½ cucumber, peeled and sliced
- 1 cup diced plum tomatoes
- 2 cups cooked pinto beans, well drained and slightly warmed
- Pepper to taste
- 3 tablespoon extra virgin olive oil
- 2 tablespoon ground toasted cumin seeds
- 2 tablespoon fresh lemon juice
- ⅛ teaspoon salt
- 2 cloves garlic, peeled
- 2 6-inch whole wheat pita bread, cut or torn into bite-sized pieces

### DIRECTIONS

1. In large baking sheet, spread torn pita bread and bake in a preheated 400oF oven for 6 minutes.
2. With the back of a knife, mash garlic and salt until paste like. Add into a medium bowl.
3. Whisk in ground cumin and lemon juice. In a steady and slow stream, pour oil as you whisk continuously. Season with pepper.
4. In a large salad bowl, mix cucumber, tomatoes and beans. Pour in dressing, toss to coat well.
5. Add mint, parsley, feta, lettuce and toasted pita, toss to mix once again and serve.

CALORIES: 427 Kcal  FAT: 20.4 g  PROTEIN: 17.7 g  CARBOHYDRATES: 47.3 g

*Preparation: 10 min*  *Cooking: 20 min*  *Servings: 4*

# 435. BLACK EYED PEAS STEW

## INGREDIENTS

- ½ cup extra virgin olive oil, divided
- 1 cup fresh dill, stems removed, chopped
- 1 cup fresh parsley, stems removed, chopped
- 1 cup water
- 2 bay leaves
- 2 carrots, peeled and sliced
- 2 cups black eyed beans, drained and rinsed
- 2 slices orange with peel and flesh
- 2 Tablespoons tomato paste
- 4 green onions, thinly sliced
- Salt and pepper, to taste

## DIRECTIONS

1. Place a pot on medium high fire and heat. Add ¼ cup oil and heat for 3 minutes.
2. Stir in bay leaves and tomato paste. Sauté for 2 minutes.
3. Stir in carrots and a cup of water. Cover and simmer for 5 minutes.
4. Stir in dill, parsley, beans, and orange. Cover and cook for 3 minutes or until heated through.
5. Season with pepper and salt to taste.
6. Stir in remaining oil and green onions cook for 2 minutes.
7. Serve and enjoy.

CALORIES: 376 Kcal   FAT: 17.8 g   PROTEIN: 8.8 g   CARBOHYDRATES: 25.6 g

---

*Preparation: 10 min*  *Cooking: 15 min*  *Servings: 4*

# 436. BRUSSELS SPROUTS AND WHITE BEAN MEDLEY

## INGREDIENTS

- 1 teaspoon salt
- 2 tablespoon olive oil
- 3 cans white beans, drained and rinsed
- 3 medium onions, peeled and sliced
- 3 tablespoon lemon juice
- 4 ½ cups Brussels sprouts, cleaned and sliced in half
- 6 garlic cloves, smashed, peeled, and minced
- Pepper to taste

## DIRECTIONS

1. Place a saucepan on medium high fire and heat for 2 minutes.
2. Add oil and heat for a minute.
3. Sauté garlic and onions for 3 minutes.
4. Stir in Brussels sprouts and sauté for 5 minutes.
5. Stir in white beans and sauté for 5 minutes.
6. Season with pepper and salt.

CALORIES: 371 Kcal   FAT: 8.1 g   PROTEIN: 21.4 g   CARBOHYDRATES: 27.8 g

Preparation: 10 min  Cooking: 30 min  Servings: 4

## 437. BEANS AND SPINACH MEDITERRANEAN SALAD

### INGREDIENTS

- 1 can (14 ounces) water-packed artichoke hearts, rinsed, drained and quartered
- 1 can (14 ½ ounces) no-salt-added diced tomatoes, undrained
- 1 can (15 ounces) cannellini beans, rinsed and drained
- 1 small onion, chopped
- 1 tablespoon olive oil
- ¼ teaspoon pepper
- ¼ teaspoon salt
- ⅛ teaspoon crushed red pepper flakes
- 2 garlic cloves, minced
- 2 tablespoons Worcestershire sauce
- 6 ounces fresh baby spinach (about 8 cups)

### DIRECTIONS

1. Place a saucepan on medium high fire and heat for a minute.
2. Add oil and heat for 2 minutes. Stir in onion and sauté for 4 minutes. Add garlic and sauté for another minute.
3. Stir in seasonings, Worcestershire sauce, and tomatoes. Cook for 5 minutes while stirring continuously until sauce is reduced.
4. Stir in spinach, artichoke hearts, and beans. Sauté for 3 minutes until spinach is wilted and other ingredients are heated through.
5. Serve and enjoy.

CALORIES: 187 Kcal  FAT: 4 g  PROTEIN: 8 g  CARBOHYDRATES: 30 g

*Preparation: 10 min*     *Cooking: 0 min*     *Servings: 4*

# 438. CHICKPEA ALFREDO SAUCE

## INGREDIENTS

- ¼ teaspoon ground nutmeg
- ¼ teaspoon sea salt or to taste
- 1 clove garlic minced
- 2 cups chickpeas, rinsed and drained
- 1 tablespoon white miso paste
- 1-½ cups water
- 2 tablespoons lemon juice
- 3 tablespoons nutritional yeast

## DIRECTIONS

1. Add every ingredient in a blender.
2. Puree until smooth and creamy.
3. Add some other oil if you like, then serve with some fresh vegetable and some bread.

CALORIES: 123 Kcal     FAT: 2.4 g     PROTEIN: 6.2 g     CARBOHYDRATES: 20.2 g

---

*Preparation: 10 min*     *Cooking: 10 min*     *Servings: 4*

# 439. CHICKPEA FRIED EGGPLANT SALAD

## INGREDIENTS

- 1 cup chopped dill
- 1 cup chopped parsley
- 1 cup cooked or canned chickpeas, drained
- 1 large eggplant, thinly sliced (no more than 1/4 inch in thickness)
- 1 small red onion, sliced
- 1/2 English cucumber, diced
- 3 tomatoes, diced
- 3 tablespoon Za'atar spice
- oil for frying
- 1 tablespoon of lime juice
- 1/3 cup extra virgin olive oil
- 1–2 garlic cloves, minced
- Salt & Pepper to taste

## DIRECTIONS

1. On a baking sheet, spread out sliced eggplant and season with salt generously. Let it sit for 30 minutes. Then pat dry with paper towel.
2. Place a small pot on medium high fire and fill halfway with oil. Heat oil for 5 minutes. Fry eggplant in batches until golden brown, around 3 minutes per side. Place cooked eggplants on a paper towel lined plate.
3. Once eggplants have cooled, assemble the eggplant on a serving dish. Sprinkle with 1 tablespoon of Za'atar.
4. Mix dill, parsley, red onions, chickpeas, cucumbers, and tomatoes in a large salad bowl. Sprinkle remaining Za'atar and gently toss to mix.
5. Whisk well the vinaigrette ingredients in a small bowl. Drizzle 2 tablespoon of the dressing over the fried eggplant. Add remaining dressing over the chickpea salad and mix.
6. Add the chickpea salad to the serving dish with the eggplant.

CALORIES: 642 Kcal     FAT: 35.1 g     PROTEIN: 16.6 g     CARBOHYDRATES: 25.9 g

*Preparation: 10 min*  *Cooking: 0 min*  *Servings: 4*

## 440. BLACK BEANS HUMMUS

### INGREDIENTS

- 10 Greek olives
- ¼ teaspoon paprika
- ¼ teaspoon cayenne pepper
- ½ teaspoon salt
- ¾ teaspoon ground cumin
- 1 ½ tablespoon tahini
- 2 tablespoon lemon juice
- 1 15-oz can black beans, drain and reserve liquid
- 1 clove garlic

### DIRECTIONS

1. In food processor, mince garlic.
2. Add cayenne pepper, salt, cumin, tahini, lemon juice, 2 tablespoon reserved black beans liquid, and black beans.
3. Process until smooth and creamy. Scrape the side of processor as needed and continue pureeing.
4. To serve, garnish with Greek olives and paprika.
5. Best eaten as a dip for pita bread or chips.

CALORIES: 205 Kcal   FAT: 2.9 g   PROTEIN: 12.1 g   CARBOHYDRATES: 34.4 g

*Preparation: 7 min*     *Cooking: 40 min*     *Servings: 4*

## 441. MERJIMEK

**INGREDIENTS**

- 1 cup red lentils
- 3 tablespoons sunflower oil
- 1 teaspoon pepper paste
- ½ teaspoon chili pepper
- ½ teaspoon chili flakes
- ½ teaspoon salt
- 1 teaspoon butter
- ½ teaspoon paprika
- ½ teaspoon ground black pepper
- 4 cups of water
- 1 green pepper, chopped
- 2 potatoes, finely chopped

**DIRECTIONS**

1. Put the butter in the pan and melt it.
2. Add chopped pepper and potatoes and roast the vegetables for 5 minutes over the medium heat. Stir them occasionally.
3. After this, add water, lentils, ground black pepper, paprika, salt, chili flakes, chili pepper, pepper paste, and oil. Stir the ingredients with the help of the spoon.
4. Close the lid and cook soup for 35 minutes over the medium heat.
5. The cooked soup should have tender puree texture.

CALORIES: 354 Kcal     FAT: 12.2 g     PROTEIN: 18 g     CARBOHYDRATES: 47.7 g

---

*Preparation: 5 min*     *Cooking: 1 hour*     *Servings: 6*

## 442. CHORIZO WHITE BEAN STEW

**INGREDIENTS**

- 3 tablespoons olive oil
- 4 chorizo links, sliced
- 2 sweet onions, chopped
- 4 garlic cloves, minced
- 2 celery stalks, sliced
- 2 carrots, sliced
- 2 red bell peppers, cored and diced
- 2 tablespoons tomato paste
- 1 can diced tomatoes
- 2 cans white beans, drained
- 1 bay leaf
- 1 teaspoon sherry vinegar
- ½ teaspoon dried oregano
- 1 cup chicken stock
- Salt and pepper to taste

**DIRECTIONS**

1. Heat the oil in a deep saucepan and stir in the chorizo. Cook for 5 minutes then add the onions and garlic, as well as celery and carrots.
2. Cook for another 10 minutes to soften.
3. Add the rest of the ingredients then season with salt and pepper to taste.
4. Cook on low heat for 35-40 minutes.
5. Serve the stew right away or freeze it into individual portions for later serving.

CALORIES: 386 Kcal     FAT: 17.4 g     PROTEIN: 20.2 g     CARBOHYDRATES: 38.8 g

*Preparation: 10 min*  *Cooking: 1 hour and 10 min*  *Servings: 6*

## 443. CHICKEN AND BLACK EYED PEAS

### INGREDIENTS

- 2 tablespoon fresh cilantro, chopped
- 2 cups grated Monterey Jack cheese
- 3 cups water
- 1/8 teaspoon cayenne pepper
- 2 teaspoon pure chile powder
- 2 teaspoon ground cumin
- 1 4-oz can chopped green chiles
- 1 cup corn kernels
- 2 15-oz cans black eyed peas, drained and rinsed
- 2 garlic cloves
- 1 medium onion, diced
- 2 tablespoon extra virgin olive oil
- 2 lb. chicken

### DIRECTIONS

1. Slice the chicken into ½-inch cubes and with pepper and salt, season it.
2. On high fire, place a large nonstick fry pan and heat oil.
3. Sauté the chicken pieces for three to four minutes or until lightly browned.
4. Reduce the fire to medium and add garlic and onion.
5. Cook for 5 to 6 minutes or until onions are translucent.
6. Add water, spices, chilies, corn and beans. Bring to a boil.
7. Once boiling, slow fire to a simmer and continue simmering for an hour, uncovered.
8. To serve, garnish with a sprinkling of cilantro and a tablespoon of cheese.

CALORIES: 433 Kcal    FAT: 21.8 g    PROTEIN: 30.6 g    CARBOHYDRATES: 29.5 g

Preparation: 10 min    Cooking: 35 min    Servings: 4

## 444. CHORIZO-KIDNEY BEANS QUINOA PILAF

### INGREDIENTS

- ¼ pound dried Spanish chorizo diced (about 2/3 cup)
- ¼ teaspoon red pepper flakes
- ¼ teaspoon smoked paprika
- ½ teaspoon cumin
- ½ teaspoon sea salt
- 1 3/4 cups water
- 1 cup quinoa
- 1 large clove garlic minced
- 1 small red bell pepper finely diced
- 1 small red onion finely diced
- 1 tablespoon tomato paste
- 1 15-ounce can kidney beans rinsed and drained

### DIRECTIONS

1. Place a nonstick pot on medium high fire and heat for 2 minutes. Add chorizo and sauté for 5 minutes until lightly browned.
2. Stir in peppers and onion. Sauté for 5 minutes.
3. Add tomato paste, red pepper flakes, salt, paprika, cumin, and garlic. Sauté for 2 minutes.
4. Stir in quinoa and mix well. Sauté for 2 minutes.
5. Add water and beans. Mix well. Cover and simmer for 20 minutes or until liquid is fully absorbed.
6. Turn off fire and fluff quinoa. Let it sit for 5 minutes more while uncovered.
7. Serve and enjoy.

CALORIES: 260 Kcal    FAT: 6.8 g    PROTEIN: 9.6 g    CARBOHYDRATES: 409 g

---

Preparation: 10 min    Cooking: 0 min    Servings: 4

## 445. CILANTRO VINAIGRETTE ON KIDNEY BEANS

### INGREDIENTS

- 1 15-oz. can kidney beans, drained and rinsed
- 1/2 English cucumber, chopped
- 1 Medium-sized tomato, chopped
- 1 bunch fresh cilantro, chopped
- 1 red onion, chopped
- 1 tablespoon of lemon or lime juice
- 3 tablespoon extra-virgin olive oil
- 1 teaspoon Dijon mustard
- ½ teaspoon chopped garlic
- 1 teaspoon sumac
- Salt and pepper to taste

### DIRECTIONS

1. In a small bowl, whisk well all vinaigrette ingredients.
2. In a salad bowl, combine cilantro chopped veggies, and kidney beans.
3. Add vinaigrette to salad and toss well to mix.
4. If you have the time, place the salad in the fridge for 30 minutes to allow the flavors to settle.
5. Mix and adjust seasoning if needed before serving.

CALORIES: 154 Kcal    FAT: 7.4 g    PROTEIN: 5.5 g    CARBOHYDRATES: 18.3 g

*Preparation: 10 min*  *Cooking: 0 min*  *Servings: 6*

## 446. CHICKPEA SALAD MOROCCAN STYLE

### INGREDIENTS

- ⅓ cup crumbled low-fat feta cheese
- ¼ cup fresh mint, chopped
- ¼ cup fresh cilantro, chopped
- 1 red bell pepper, diced
- 2 plum tomatoes, diced
- 3 green onions, sliced thinly
- 1 large carrot, peeled and julienned
- 3 cups canned chickpeas or garbanzo beans
- A pinch of cayenne pepper
- ¼ teaspoon salt
- ¼ teaspoon pepper
- 2 teaspoon ground cumin
- 3 tablespoon fresh lemon juice
- 3 tablespoon olive oil

### DIRECTIONS

1. Make the dressing by whisking cayenne, black pepper, salt, cumin, lemon juice and oil in a small bowl and set aside.
2. Mix together feta, mint, cilantro, red pepper, tomatoes, onions, carrots and chickpeas in a large salad bowl.
3. Pour the dressing over salad and toss to coat well.
4. Serve and enjoy.

CALORIES: 300 Kcal    FAT: 12.8 g    PROTEIN: 13.2 g    CARBOHYDRATES: 35.4 g

*Preparation: 10 min*     *Cooking: 0 min*     *Servings: 6*

## 447. EXTRAORDINARY GREEN HUMMUS

### INGREDIENTS

- ¼ cup fresh lemon juice
- ¼ cup chopped tarragon or basil
- ¼ cup tahini
- ½ cup roughly chopped, loosely packed fresh parsley
- ½ teaspoon salt, more to taste
- 1 large garlic clove, roughly chopped
- 2 tablespoons water, optional
- 2 tablespoons olive oil, plus more for serving
- 3 tablespoons chopped fresh chives or green onion
- 1 tablespoon chopped fresh herbs
- One (15-ounce) can of chickpeas, drained and rinsed

### DIRECTIONS

1. Place all the ingredients in a blender and puree until smooth and creamy.
2. Transfer to a bowl and adjust seasoning if needed.
3. Serve with pita chips.

CALORIES: 98 Kcal     FAT: 8.3 g     PROTEIN: 3.8 g     CARBOHYDRATES: 13 g

---

*Preparation: 10 min*     *Cooking: 25 min*     *Servings: 4*

## 448. POTATOES & GREEN BEANS IN OLIVE OIL

### INGREDIENTS

- 1 1/2 onion, sliced thin
- 1 bunch of dill, chopped
- 1 cup water
- 1 large zucchini, quartered
- 1 lb. green beans, frozen
- 1 teaspoon dried oregano
- 1/2 bunch parsley, chopped
- 1/2 cup extra virgin olive oil
- 15 oz can diced tomatoes
- 2 potatoes, quartered
- salt and pepper, to taste

### DIRECTIONS

1. Place a pot on medium high fire and heat pot for 2 minutes.
2. Add oil and heat for 3 minutes.
3. Stir in onions and sauté for 2 minutes. Stir in dill, oregano, and potatoes. Cook for 3 minutes. Season with pepper and salt.
4. Add dice tomatoes and water. Cover and simmer for 10 minutes.
5. Stir in zucchini and green beans. Cook for 5 minutes.
6. Adjust seasoning to taste, turn off fire, and stir in parsley.
7. Serve and enjoy.

CALORIES: 384 Kcal     FAT: 27.9 g     PROTEIN: 5.9 g     CARBOHYDRATES: 30.6 g

Preparation: 10 min  Cooking: 10 min  Servings: 4

## 449. GARBANZO AND KIDNEY BEANS SALAD

### INGREDIENTS

- 1 (15 ounce) can kidney beans, drained
- 1 (15.5 ounce) can garbanzo beans, drained
- 1 lemon, zested and juiced
- 2 medium tomatoes, chopped
- 1 teaspoon capers, rinsed and drained
- 1/2 cup chopped fresh parsley
- 1/2 teaspoon salt, or to taste
- 1/4 cup chopped red onion
- 3 tablespoons extra virgin olive oil
- 1 teaspoon paprika

### DIRECTIONS

1. In a pot, cook the tomatoes with 1 tablespoon of oil for 10 minutes, until it becomes sauce.
2. In a salad bowl, whisk well lemon juice, olive oil and salt until dissolved.
3. Stir in garbanzo, kidney beans, cooked tomatoes, red onion, parsley, and capers. Toss well to coat.
4. Allow flavors to mix for 30 minutes by setting in the fridge, if you have time. Mix again and sprinkle with paprika before serving.
5. Serve with some white rice, if you like.

CALORIES: 329 Kcal  FAT: 12 g  PROTEIN: 12.1 g  CARBOHYDRATES: 29.6 g

*Preparation: 10 min*  *Cooking: 0 min*  *Servings: 4*

## 450. FETA ON TOMATO-BLACK BEAN

**INGREDIENTS**

- 1/2 red onion, sliced
- 1/4 cup crumbled feta cheese
- 1/4 cup fresh dill, chopped
- 2 14.5-ounce cans black beans, drained and rinsed
- 2 tablespoons extra-virgin olive oil
- 4 Roma or plum tomatoes, diced
- Juice of 1 lemon
- Salt to taste

**DIRECTIONS**

1. Except for feta, mix well all the ingredients in a salad bowl.
2. Sprinkle with feta.
3. Serve and enjoy.

CALORIES: 121 Kcal    FAT: 5 g    PROTEIN: 6 g    CARBOHYDRATES: 15 g

---

*Preparation: 10 min*  *Cooking: 1 hour and 30 min*  *Servings: 6*

## 451. GARBANZO AND LENTILS SOUP

**INGREDIENTS**

- 1 14.5-oz can petite diced tomatoes, undrained
- 2 15-oz cans Garbanzo beans, rinsed and drained
- 1 cup lentils
- 6 cups vegetable broth
- ¼ teaspoon ground cayenne pepper
- ½ teaspoon ground cumin
- 1 teaspoon turmeric
- 1 teaspoon garam masala
- 1 teaspoon minced garlic
- 2 teaspoon grated fresh ginger
- 1 cup diced carrots
- 1 cup chopped celery
- 2 onions, chopped

**DIRECTIONS**

1. On medium high fire, place a heavy bottomed large pot and grease with cooking spray.
2. Add onions and sauté until tender, around three to four minutes.
3. Add celery and carrots. Cook for another five minutes.
4. Add cayenne pepper, cumin, turmeric, ginger, garam masala and garlic, cook for half a minute.
5. Add diced tomatoes, garbanzo beans, lentils and vegetable broth. Bring to a boil.
6. Once boiling, slow fire to a simmer and cook while covered for 90 minutes. Occasionally stir soup.
7. If you want a thicker and creamier soup, you can puree ½ of the pot's content and mix in.
8. Once lentils are soft, turn off fire and serve.

CALORIES: 196 Kcal    FAT: 3.6 g    PROTEIN: 10.1 g    CARBOHYDRATES: 33.3 g

*Preparation: 10 min*     *Cooking: 10 min*     *Servings: 2*

## 452. TORTILLA WRAPS WITH HUMMUS

### INGREDIENTS

- 2 corn tortillas
- 1 cup Romaine lettuce, chopped
- 4 teaspoons hummus
- 1 tablespoon lemon juice
- ¼ teaspoon cayenne pepper
- 8 oz chicken fillet
- ½ teaspoon olive oil
- ½ teaspoon salt

### DIRECTIONS

1. Slice the chicken fillet onto 2 fillets.
2. Rub every chicken fillet with cayenne pepper, olive oil, and salt.
3. Heat up the skillet well.
4. Place the chicken fillets in the skillet and roast them for 4 minutes from each side over the medium heat.
5. Meanwhile, spread one side of the corn tortillas with hummus.
6. Arrange the chopped lettuce on hummus and sprinkle with lemon juice.
7. Add hot roasted chicken fillet and roll the tortillas (wrap). Secure every wrap with a toothpick.

CALORIES: 300 Kcal     FAT: 11.3 g     PROTEIN: 15.1 g     CARBOHYDRATES: 13.2 g

*Preparation: 10 min*     *Cooking: 0 min*     *Servings: 6*

## 453. GOAT CHEESE AND RED BEANS SALAD

### INGREDIENTS

- 2 cans of Red Kidney Beans, drained and rinsed well
- Water or vegetable broth to cover beans
- 1 bunch parsley, chopped
- 1 1/2 cups red grape tomatoes, halved
- 3 cloves garlic, minced
- 3 tablespoons olive oil
- 3 tablespoons lemon juice
- 1/2 teaspoon salt
- 1/2 teaspoon white pepper
- 6 ounces goat cheese, crumbled

### DIRECTIONS

1. In a large bowl combine beans, parsley, tomatoes and garlic.
2. Add olive oil, lemon juice, salt and pepper.
3. Mix well and refrigerate until ready to serve.
4. Spoon into individual dishes topped with crumbled goat cheese.

CALORIES: 385 Kcal     FAT: 15 g     PROTEIN: 22.5 g     CARBOHYDRATES: 27.1 g

---

*Preparation: 10 min*     *Cooking: 15 min*     *Servings: 4*

## 454. GREEK SPELT SALAD

### INGREDIENTS

- ½ teaspoon salt
- 1 cup spelt, rinsed
- 2 tablespoons olive oil
- 2 garlic cloves, pressed or minced
- ½ small red onion, sliced
- 1 avocado, sliced
- 1 cucumber, sliced
- 15 pitted Kalamata olives, sliced
- 1-pint cherry tomatoes, sliced
- 2 cups cooked chickpeas (or one 14-ounce can, rinsed and drained)
- 5 ounces mixed greens
- 1 ¼ cups plain Greek yogurt
- 1 ½ tablespoon fresh dill
- 1 ½ tablespoon fresh mint
- 1 tablespoon lemon juice

### DIRECTIONS

1. Add in a blender the Greek yogurt, fresh dill, fresh mint, lemon juice and 1 tablespoon of olive oil.
2. Blend and puree, then set aside.
3. Cook the spelt by placing in a pot filled halfway with water. Bring to a boil, reduce the fire to simmer and cook for 15 minutes or until the spelt is tender.
4. Drain well, mix in salt, garlic and olive oil, then stir.
5. Evenly divide the cooled spelt into 4 bowls.
6. Evenly divide the sliced onion, avocado, cucumber, olives, tomatoes, chickpeas and greens between the bowls.
7. Top with the yogurt dressing, then serve.

CALORIES: 328 Kcal     FAT: 14.5 g     PROTEIN: 11.7 g     CARBOHYDRATES: 17.6 g

Preparation: 000 min        Cooking: 1 hour and 10 min        Servings: 6

## 455. GARLICKY LEMON HUMMUS

### INGREDIENTS

- ¼ cup tahini
- ¼ teaspoon fine grain sea salt
- ⅓ cup fresh lemon juice
- ¾ cup chopped parsley
- 1 tablespoon olive oil, plus more for drizzling
- 1 ½ cans (15 ounces each) chickpeas, rinsed and drained
- 5 cloves garlic, peeled and roughly chopped
- a dash of freshly ground black pepper
- 1 teaspoon paprika

### DIRECTIONS

1. Place all the ingredients in a blender and puree until smooth and creamy.
2. Transfer to a bowl and adjust seasoning if needed.
3. If the dip dries up, just add more olive oil and mix well.
4. Sprinkle with paprika.
5. Serve and enjoy with carrot sticks or some crispy bread.

CALORIES: 131 Kcal        FAT: 7 g        PROTEIN: 4.9 g        CARBOHYDRATES: 13.8 g

*Preparation: 10 min*  *Cooking: 0 min*  *Servings: 6*

## 456. RED BEANS AND CHICKPEAS HUMMUS

**INGREDIENTS**

- ¼ teaspoon cumin
- 1 bunch parsley
- 1 teaspoon sea salt
- 1 ½ cups cooked red beans
- 1 cup cooked chickpeas
- 2 garlic cloves, peeled and crushed
- 2 lemons, juiced
- 3 tablespoon extra-virgin olive oil
- 3 tablespoon tahini

**DIRECTIONS**

1. Add olive oil, lemon juice, tahini, salt, ang garlic cloves in a blender. Puree until smooth and creamy.
2. Add the chickpeas and the red beans. Puree until smooth and creamy.
3. Transfer to a bowl.
4. Drizzle with more olive oil. Sprinkle with parsley.
5. Serve and enjoy as a dip.

CALORIES: 215 Kcal    FAT: 8 g    PROTEIN: 9.4 g    CARBOHYDRATES: 28.2 g

*Preparation: 10 min*  *Cooking: 15 min*  *Servings: 4*

## 457. KIDNEY BEANS AND BEET SALAD

**INGREDIENTS**

- 1 14.5-ounce can kidney beans, drained and rinsed
- 1 tablespoon pomegranate syrup or juice
- 2 tablespoons olive oil
- 4 beets, scrubbed and stems removed
- 4 green onions, chopped
- Juice of 1 lemon
- Salt and pepper to taste

**DIRECTIONS**

1. Bring a pot of water to boil and add beets. Simmer for 10 minutes or until tender. Drain beets and place in ice bath for 5 minutes.
2. Peel bets and slice in halves.
3. Toss to mix the pomegranate syrup, olive oil, lemon juice, green onions, and kidney beans in a salad bowl.
4. Stir in the beets. Season with pepper and salt to taste.
5. Serve and enjoy.

CALORIES: 175 Kcal    FAT: 7 g    PROTEIN: 6 g    CARBOHYDRATES: 22 g

*Preparation: 10 min*     *Cooking: 30 min*     *Servings: 4*

# 458. ITALIAN WHITE BEANS SOUP

## INGREDIENTS

- 1 (14 ounce) can chicken broth
- 1 bunch fresh spinach, rinsed and thinly sliced
- 1 clove garlic, minced
- 1 stalk celery, chopped
- 1 tablespoon lemon juice
- 1 tablespoon vegetable oil
- 1 onion, chopped
- 1 carrot, peeled and chopped
- ¼ teaspoon ground black pepper
- ⅛ teaspoon dried thyme
- 2 (16 ounce) cans white kidney beans, rinsed and drained
- 2 cups water

## DIRECTIONS

1. Place a pot on medium high fire and heat it for a minute. Add the oil and heat for another minute.
2. Stir in the celery, the onion and the carrot. Sauté for 7 minutes.
3. Stir in the garlic and cook for another minute.
4. Add water, thyme, pepper, chicken broth, and beans. Cover and simmer for 15 minutes.
5. Remove 2 cups of the bean and celery mixture with a slotted spoon and set aside.
6. With an immersion blender, puree remaining soup in pot until smooth and creamy.
7. Return the 2 cups of bean mixture. Stir in spinach and lemon juice. Cook for 2 minutes until heated through and spinach is wilted.
8. Serve and enjoy.

CALORIES: 245 Kcal     FAT: 7.9 g     PROTEIN: 12 g     CARBOHYDRATES: 28.1 g

*Preparation: 10 min*  *Cooking: 0 min*  *Servings: 6*

## 459. KIDNEY BEANS AND PARSLEY-LEMON SALAD

### INGREDIENTS

- ¼ cup lemon juice
- ¼ cup olive oil
- ¾ cup chopped fresh parsley
- ¾ teaspoon salt
- 1 can (15 ounces) chickpeas, rinsed and drained, or 1 ½ cups cooked chickpeas
- 1 medium cucumber, diced
- 1 small red onion, diced
- 2 cans (15 ounces each) red kidney beans, rinsed and drained, or 3 cups cooked kidney beans
- 2 stalks celery, chopped
- 2 tablespoons chopped dill
- 3 cloves garlic, minced
- A pinch of red pepper flakes

### DIRECTIONS

1. Whisk well in a small bowl the pepper flakes, salt, garlic, and lemon juice until emulsified.
2. In a serving bowl, combine the prepared kidney beans, chickpeas, onion, celery, cucumber, parsley and dill.
3. Drizzle the salad with the dressing and toss well to coat.
4. Serve and enjoy.

CALORIES: 228 Kcal  FAT: 7.4 g  PROTEIN: 8.5 g  CARBOHYDRATES: 26.2 g

---

*Preparation: 10 min*  *Cooking: 0 min*  *Servings: 6*

## 460. WHITE BEANS AND CHICKPEA SALAD

### INGREDIENTS

- ¼ cup lemon juice
- ¼ teaspoon ground cinnamon
- ½ cup chopped fresh mint
- ½ cup extra-virgin olive oil
- 1 15-ounce can chickpeas, rinsed
- 1 cup finely diced carrot
- 1 small clove garlic, peeled and minced
- 1 teaspoon kosher salt, divided
- 1½ cups chopped fresh parsley
- 2 15-ounce cans white beans, rinsed
- 2 tablespoons ground cumin

### DIRECTIONS

1. In a salad bowl, whisk well lemon juice, cinnamon, olive oil, garlic, salt, parsley, and cumin.
2. Stir in remaining ingredients and toss well to coat in the dressing.
3. Serve and enjoy.

CALORIES: 221 Kcal  FAT: 12 g  PROTEIN: 6 g  CARBOHYDRATES: 22 g

*Preparation:* **10 min**  *Cooking:* **1 hour and 15 min**  Servings: **6**

## 461. KIDNEY AND BLACK BEANS CHICKEN SOUP

### INGREDIENTS

- 2 chicken breasts fillets, chopped
- ½ cup chopped cilantro
- Salt to taste
- ½ teaspoon black pepper
- 1 tablespoon chili powder
- The juice of 1 lime
- 2 ½ cups water
- 1 cup tomatoes, sliced
- 1 cup green peppers, sliced
- 1 cup kidney beans, rinsed and drained
- 1 cup black beans, rinsed and drained
- 1 garlic clove, minced
- 1 onion, diced

### DIRECTIONS

1. Add all the ingredients into a pot, then cover with the lid.
2. Heat the pot on medium fire.
3. Once the mixture is boiling, lower the flame and let it simmer for 1 hour more.
4. Once soup is cooked, serve into bowls and enjoy with some crispy bread.

CALORIES: 392 Kcal    FAT: 12.8 g    PROTEIN: 12 g    CARBOHYDRATES: 21 g

Preparation: 10 min  Cooking: 20 min  Servings: 4

## 462. MUSHROOM CHICKPEA MARSALA

### INGREDIENTS

- 2 tablespoon olive oil
- 8 oz. baby portobello mushrooms, sliced
- 2 garlic cloves, minced
- 1 cup dry Marsala wine
- 2 tablespoon lemon juice, or to taste
- 1 teaspoon rubbed sage
- ½ teaspoon black pepper
- ¼ teaspoon salt
- 2 tablespoon chopped fresh parsley
- 1-14 oz. can or 1 3/4 cups cooked chickpeas, rinsed and drained

### DIRECTIONS

1. On medium fire, place a large saucepan and heat oil.
2. Add mushrooms, cover and cook for 5 minutes.
3. Stir in garlic and cook for 2 minutes.
4. Add wine, lemon juice, sage, salt and pepper. Deglaze the pot.
5. Simmer for 10 minutes while covered.
6. Add chickpeas and mix well. Cook for 3 minutes.
7. Remove pot from fire and stir in parsley.
8. Serve and enjoy.

CALORIES: 159 Kcal  FAT: 8.5 g  PROTEIN: 6.1 g  CARBOHYDRATES: 16.8 g

---

Preparation: 10 min  Cooking: 50 min  Servings: 6

## 463. ROASTED CHICKPEA-CAULIFLOWER STEW

### INGREDIENTS

- 1 teaspoon ground coriander
- 1 teaspoon Sweet paprika
- 1 cauliflower, chopped
- Salt and pepper
- 1 tablespoon olive oil
- 1 onion, chopped
- 6 garlic cloves, chopped
- 1 ½ teaspoon turmeric
- 1 ½ teaspoon cumin
- 1 ½ teaspoon cinnamon
- ½ teaspoon cardamom
- 5 carrots, peeled and sliced
- ½ cup parsley, chopped
- 1 28-oz can diced tomatoes
- 2 14-oz cans chickpeas, drained and rinsed

### DIRECTIONS

1. Preheat the oven to 475°F.
2. Mix well all the spices in a small bowl.
3. Lightly oil a baking sheet and spread carrots and cauliflower. Season with salt and pepper. Add a little more than ½ of the spice mixture. Drizzle generously with olive oil, then toss.
4. Pop in the oven and bake until soft, around 20 minutes.
5. Heat 2 tablespoon olive oil in a large cast iron pan on medium high fire.
6. Sauté onion for 3 minutes. Stir in garlic and the remaining spices. Sauté for 2-3 more minutes.
7. Stir in canned tomatoes and chickpeas. Season with salt and pepper. Bring to a boil, then reduce heat to medium-low. Cover and simmer for 5 minutes.
8. Stir in the cauliflower and carrots. Cover and cook for other 15-20 minutes. Stir occasionally. Add water if needed.
9. Garnish with fresh parsley, serve and enjoy.

CALORIES: 407 Kcal  FAT: 15.3 g  PROTEIN: 12.1 g  CARBOHYDRATES: 28.9 g

Preparation: 10 min  Cooking: 1 hour  Servings: 6

## 464. RICE AND CHICKPEA STEW

### INGREDIENTS

- ½ cup chopped fresh cilantro
- ¼ teaspoon freshly ground pepper
- ¼ teaspoon salt
- ⅔ cup brown basmati rice
- 3 cups peeled and diced sweet potato
- 2 15-oz cans chickpeas, rinsed
- 4 cups chicken broth
- 1 cup orange juice
- 2 teaspoon ground coriander
- 2 teaspoon ground cumin
- 3 medium onions, halved and thinly sliced
- 1 tablespoon extra-virgin olive oil

### DIRECTIONS

1. On medium fire, place a large nonstick fry pan and heat oil.
2. Sauté onions for 8 minutes or until soft and translucent.
3. Add coriander and cumin, sauté for half a minute.
4. Add broth and orange juice.
5. Add salt, rice, sweet potato, and chickpeas.
6. Bring to a boil, once boiling lower fire to a simmer, cover and cook.
7. Stir occasionally, cook for 45 minutes or until potatoes and rice are tender.
8. Season with pepper.
9. Stew will be thick, if you want a less thick soup, just add water and adjust salt and pepper to taste.
10. To serve, garnish with cilantro.

CALORIES: 332 Kcal    FAT: 7.5 g    PROTEIN: 13 g    CARBOHYDRATES: 35.5 g

*Preparation: 10 min*     *Cooking: 20 min*     *Servings: 6*

## 465. SAFFRON GREEN BEAN-QUINOA SOUP

### INGREDIENTS

- 2 tablespoons extra virgin olive oil
- 1 large leek, sliced
- 2 cloves garlic, minced
- 8 ounces fresh green beans, chopped
- 2 large pinches saffron
- 15 ounces chickpeas and liquid
- 1 large tomato, chopped
- salt and freshly ground pepper
- freshly chopped basil, for serving
- 1 large carrot, chopped
- 1 large celery stalk, chopped
- 1 large zucchini, chopped
- ½ cup quinoa, rinsed
- 4-5 cups vegetable stock

### DIRECTIONS

1. Place a large pot on medium fire and heat olive oil for 2 minutes.
2. Stir in celery and carrots. Cook for 6 minutes or until soft.
3. Mix in garlic and leek. Sauté for 3 minutes.
4. Add the zucchini and green beans, and sauté 1 minute more.
5. Pour in broth and saffron. Bring to a boil. Stir in chickpeas and quinoa. Cook until quinoa is soft, around 11 minutes while covered.
6. Stir in the diced tomato and salt and pepper, to taste, and remove from heat.
7. Serve the soup with the freshly chopped basil and enjoy!

CALORIES: 196 Kcal     FAT: 7.5 g     PROTEIN: 7.9 g     CARBOHYDRATES: 26.6 g

---

*Preparation: 10 min*     *Cooking: 0 min*     *Servings: 6*

## 466. SPICY SWEET RED HUMMUS

### INGREDIENTS

- 1 (15 ounce) can garbanzo beans, drained
- 1 (4 ounce) jar roasted red peppers
- 1 ½ tablespoons tahini
- 1 clove garlic, minced
- 1 tablespoon chopped fresh parsley
- ½ teaspoon cayenne pepper
- ½ teaspoon ground cumin
- ¼ teaspoon salt
- 3 tablespoons lemon juice

### DIRECTIONS

1. In a blender, add all the ingredients and process until smooth and creamy.
2. Adjust seasoning to taste if needed.
3. Serve cold or heat it before serving if preferred.
4. Hummus can be stored in fridge for up to 3 days.

CALORIES: 104 Kcal     FAT: 2.2 g     PROTEIN: 2.5 g     CARBOHYDRATES: 9.6 g

*Preparation: 10 min*  *Cooking: 1 hour and 35 min*  *Servings: 6*

## 467. SIMPLY GOOD CHICKPEAS BROTH

### INGREDIENTS

- 1 14.5-oz can of petite diced tomatoes, undrained
- 2 15-oz cans garbanzo beans, rinsed and drained
- 1 cup lentils
- 6 cups vegetable broth or stock
- ¼ teaspoon ground cayenne pepper
- ½ teaspoon ground cumin
- 1 teaspoon turmeric
- 1 teaspoon garam masala
- 1 teaspoon minced garlic
- 2 teaspoon grated fresh ginger
- 1 cup diced carrots
- 1 cup chopped celery
- 2 onions, chopped
- 1 tablespoon olive oil

### DIRECTIONS

1. On medium high fire, set a large soup pot and heat oil.
2. Add onions and cook until tender around 3-4 minutes.
3. Add celery and carrots, continue sautéing for 5 minutes.
4. Add garlic, cayenne pepper, cumin, turmeric and garam masala and cook until heated through.
5. Add tomatoes, garbanzo beans, lentils and broth. Cook while covered for 90 minutes or until the garbanzo beans are tender.
6. If desired, you can puree half of the soup to make a thick broth.
7. Serve while hot.

CALORIES: 211 Kcal   FAT: 5.3 g   PROTEIN: 10.1 g   CARBOHYDRATES: 33.3 g

*Preparation: 10 min*      *Cooking: 22 min*      *Servings: 6*

## 468. SUN-DRIED TOMATOES AND CHICKPEAS

### INGREDIENTS

- 1 red bell pepper
- 1/2 cup parsley, chopped
- 1/4 cup red wine vinegar
- 2 14.5-ounce cans chickpeas, drained and rinsed
- 2 cloves garlic, chopped
- 2 cups water
- 2 tablespoons extra-virgin olive oil
- 4 sun-dried tomatoes
- Salt to taste

### DIRECTIONS

1. Lengthwise, slice bell pepper in half. Place on baking sheet with skin side up. Broil on top rack for 5 minutes until skin is blistered.
2. In a brown paper bag, place the charred bell pepper halves. Fold bag and leave in there for 10 minutes. Remove pepper and peel off skin. Slice into thin strips.
3. Meanwhile, microwave 2 cups of water to boiling. Add the sun-dried tomatoes and leave in to reconstitute for 10 minutes. Drain and slice into thin strips.
4. Whisk well olive oil, garlic, and red wine vinegar.
5. Mix in parsley, sun-dried tomato, bell pepper, and chickpeas.
6. Season with salt to taste and serve.

CALORIES: 195 Kcal      FAT: 7 g      PROTEIN: 8 g      CARBOHYDRATES: 26 g

---

*Preparation: 10 min*      *Cooking: 0 min*      *Servings: 2*

## 469. GREEK-STYLE BEANS AND CUCUMBER SALAD

### INGREDIENTS

- ½ cup cucumber, chopped
- ½ cup black beans, cooked
- ½ cup tomatoes, chopped
- 2 tablespoons organic canola oil
- 1 orange, chopped
- ½ teaspoon ground cumin

### DIRECTIONS

1. Mix black beans and cucumber in the salad bowl.
2. Add tomatoes, organic canola oil, orange, and ground cumin.
3. Stir the salad gently and serve.
4. If needed, store it in the fridge for up to 3 days.

CALORIES: 173 Kcal      FAT: 9.3 g      PROTEIN: 6.3 g      CARBOHYDRATES: 13.4 g

*Preparation: 10 min*      *Cooking: 8 min*      *Servings: 4*

## 470. POTATO CHICKPEAS PATTIES

### INGREDIENTS

- 1 ½ cups old-fashioned rolled oats
- 1 ½ tablespoon Cajun seasoning
- 1 cup cooked and pureed sweet potato
- 1 large egg
- ½ cup diced onion
- ½ cup red bell pepper
- ¼ cup diced celery
- ¼ teaspoon cayenne
- ¼ teaspoon garlic powder
- 1-2 cloves garlic, smashed and minced
- 2 cups chickpeas, rinsed and drained
- 2 teaspoon extra virgin olive oil
- salt and pepper to taste
- 1 salad leaf

### DIRECTIONS

1. Boil the sweet potato until tender. Discard skin and puree in a blender.
2. Place pureed sweet potato in a large bowl.
3. Add chickpeas in blender and pulse to desired texture and not too creamy.
4. Next pulse one and a half cups of oats until flour-like. Add to the sweet potato mixture.
5. On medium high fire, place a saucepan and heat oil for 2 minutes. Sauté celery, bell pepper and onion for 5 minutes. Stir in garlic and cook for another 2 minutes. Transfer to bowl.
6. In a small bowl, whisk egg, salt, cayenne pepper, garlic powder, and Cajun seasoning.
7. With hands, mix well chickpea mixture. Pour eggs and continue mixing well.
8. Evenly divide into 5. Form each into a burger pattie.
9. Cook for 4 minutes per side or until lightly browned.
10. Serve and enjoy with burger buns and desired condiment.

CALORIES: 269 Kcal      FAT: 6 g      PROTEIN: 11 g      CARBOHYDRATES: 33 g

Preparation: 10 min  Cooking: 8 min  Servings: 4

## 471. WHITE BEANS AND TUNA SALAD

### INGREDIENTS

- 1 (12 ounce) can solid white albacore tuna, drained
- 1 (16 ounce) can Great Northern beans, drained and rinsed
- 1 (2.25 ounce) can sliced black olives, drained
- 1 teaspoon dried oregano
- 1/2 teaspoon lemon zest
- 1/4 medium red onion, sliced
- 3 tablespoons lemon juice
- 3/4-pound green beans, trimmed
- 4 large hard-cooked eggs, peeled and quartered
- 6 tablespoons extra-virgin olive oil
- Salt and ground black pepper, to taste

### DIRECTIONS

1. Place a saucepan on medium high fire. Add a cup of water and the green beans. Cover and cook for 8 minutes. Drain immediately once tender.
2. In a salad bowl, whisk well oregano, olive oil, lemon juice, and lemon zest. Season generously with pepper and salt and mix until salt is dissolved.
3. Stir in drained green beans, tuna, beans, olives, and red onion. Mix thoroughly to coat.
4. Adjust seasoning to taste.
5. Spread eggs on top.
6. Serve and enjoy.

CALORIES: 551 Kcal    FAT: 18.3 g    PROTEIN: 16.3 g    CARBOHYDRATES: 33.4 g

---

Preparation: 10 min  Cooking: 15 min  Servings: 4

## 472. LIGHT FAVA BEANS

### INGREDIENTS

- 1 ½ tablespoon avocado oil
- 2 oz tomato, chopped
- ¼ teaspoon garlic powder
- ½ white onion, diced
- ¼ cup cilantro, chopped
- 1 teaspoon ground coriander
- 2 cups fava beans, canned
- 2 tablespoons apple cider vinegar

### DIRECTIONS

1. Heat the avocado oil in the saucepan.
2. Add onion and cook it until light brown.
3. Then add tomato, garlic powder, cilantro, ground coriander, fava beans, and apple cider vinegar.
4. Cook the meal for 5 minutes on medium heat.

CALORIES: 123 Kcal    FAT: 6.1 g    PROTEIN: 12.3 g    CARBOHYDRATES: 33.4 g

Preparation: 10 min  Cooking: 0 min  Servings: 4

## 473. BEAN AND AVOCADO DIP

### INGREDIENTS

- 6 oz white beans, boiled
- 1 avocado, peeled, chopped
- 1 oz Parmesan, grated
- 1 teaspoon chili flakes
- 1 garlic clove, minced
- 1 tablespoon olive oil
- ½ teaspoon sweet paprika
- ½ teaspoon vinegar

### DIRECTIONS

1. Blend the white bean and avocado in the blender until smooth.
2. Transfer the mixture into a bowl, add parmesan, chili flakes, then every other ingredient.
3. Carefully stir the dip with the help of the spoon.
4. Adjust the seasoning if needed.
5. Serve immediately with some bread or low-fat crisps to dip in.
6. If needed, the dip can be stored in fridge for up to 2 days.

CALORIES: 123 Kcal  FAT: 9.3 g  PROTEIN: 9.4 g  CARBOHYDRATES: 8.4 g

*Preparation: 10 min*      *Cooking: 0 min*      *Servings: 2*

## 474. BEAN MIX

**INGREDIENTS**

- ½ cup fava beans, cooked
- 1 cup arugula, chopped
- 1 red onion, diced
- 1 tablespoon apple cider vinegar
- 2 tablespoons olive oil
- ½ teaspoon chili flakes

**DIRECTIONS**

1. Put fava beans in the bowl. Add arugula and diced onion.
2. Shake the vegetables and sprinkle them with apple cider vinegar, olive oil, and chili flakes.
3. Stir the meal and transfer in the serving plates.

CALORIES: 274 Kcal      FAT: 4.1 g      PROTEIN: 10.3 g      CARBOHYDRATES: 10.5 g

---

*Preparation: 15 min*      *Cooking: 7 min*      *Servings: 3*

## 475. TUNISIAN STYLE GREEN BEANS

**INGREDIENTS**

- 2 tablespoons organic canola oil
- 1 cup green beans
- ¼ teaspoon white pepper
- 1 teaspoon sesame seeds
- 1 tablespoon balsamic vinegar
- ¼ teaspoon dried tarragon
- 1 cup of water

**DIRECTIONS**

1. Bring the water to boil and put the green beans inside.
2. Boil the beans for 7 minutes. Then cool the beans in ice water and chop roughly.
3. Put the cooked green beans in the bowl, add white pepper, organic canola oil, sesame seeds, balsamic vinegar, and dried tarragon.
4. Stir the meal well.

CALORIES: 103 Kcal      FAT: 8.5 g      PROTEIN: 9.3 g      CARBOHYDRATES: 3.4 g

*Preparation: 10 min*  *Cooking: 0 min*  *Servings: 3*

## 476. BEAN BURRITO

### INGREDIENTS

- 1 oz scallions, chopped
- 1 tablespoon olive oil
- 1 bell pepper, sliced
- 1 cup pinto beans, canned
- 4 tablespoon parsley, chopped
- 3 corn tortillas
- ½ cup cheddar cheese, shredded
- ½ cup lettuce

### DIRECTIONS

1. Mix scallions with bell pepper and olive oil.
2. Put the mixture on the tortillas.
3. Add pinto beans, parsley, cheddar cheese, and lettuce.
4. Roll the tortillas in the shape of the burrito.

CALORIES: 398 Kcal    FAT: 10.3 g    PROTEIN: 15.3 g    CARBOHYDRATES: 33.4 g

*Preparation: 10 min*      *Cooking: 20 min*      *Servings: 4*

## 477. HERBED BEANS

### INGREDIENTS

- 4 teaspoons olive oil
- ½ teaspoon garlic powder
- ¼ cup chicken stock
- ½ white onion, sliced
- ¼ cup bell pepper, chopped
- 3 cups butter beans, canned
- ½ teaspoon dried thyme
- ¼ teaspoon ground coriander

### DIRECTIONS

1. Heat the oil in a pan, then add the onion.
2. Cook it until light brown and add garlic powder, chicken stock, bell pepper, thyme, and ground coriander.
3. Simmer the ingredients for 5 minutes.
4. Add butter beans, stir the meal, and cook for 5 minutes more.
5. Serve and enjoy with some bread.

CALORIES: 146 Kcal      FAT: 8.3 g      PROTEIN: 13.3 g      CARBOHYDRATES: 24.1 g

---

*Preparation: 10 min*      *Cooking: 25 min*      *Servings: 4*

## 478. BEANS AND CHICKPEAS BOWL

### INGREDIENTS

- 2 tablespoons olive oil
- 2 garlic cloves, diced
- 2 teaspoons cajun spice mix
- 1 cup chickpeas, canned
- ½ cup tomatoes, chopped
- 1 cup green beans, chopped
- 1 cup chicken stock

### DIRECTIONS

1. Pour olive oil in the saucepan and heat it.
2. Add Cajun seasonings, garlic, and tomatoes. Cook them for 10 minutes on medium heat.
3. Then add chicken stock, green beans, and chickpeas.
4. Close the lid and cook the meal for 10 minutes on low heat.
5. Transfer the meal in the serving bowls.

CALORIES: 239 Kcal      FAT: 8.4 g      PROTEIN: 12.3 g      CARBOHYDRATES: 23.4 g

*Preparation: 10 min* — *Cooking: 25 min* — *Servings: 2*

## 479. BAKED BEANS

### INGREDIENTS

- 1 cup cauliflower, chopped
- 1 cup broccoli, thinly chopped
- 1 tablespoon olive oil
- ½ cup celery stalk, roughly chopped
- 1 teaspoon smoked paprika
- 1 cup haricot beans, canned
- 2 tablespoons tomato sauce

### DIRECTIONS

1. Preheat the oven to 375°F.
2. Line the baking pan with baking paper.
3. Then mix all ingredients in the mixing bowl until homogenous.
4. Place the vegetable mixture in the baking tray, flatten, and transfer in the preheated to 375°F oven.
5. Bake the meal for 25 minutes. Stir the vegetables after 10 minutes of cooking.
6. Serve with some bread or meat and enjoy.

CALORIES: 310 Kcal — FAT: 3.8 g — PROTEIN: 12.3 g — CARBOHYDRATES: 30.4 g

*Preparation: 10 min* — *Cooking: 10 min* — *Servings: 4*

## 480. BLACK BEANS RAGOUT

### INGREDIENTS

- 1 cup okra, chopped, cooked
- ½ teaspoon ground black pepper
- 1 cup black beans, cooked
- 2 tomatoes, chopped
- 2 tablespoons avocado oil
- 1 tablespoon apple cider vinegar
- ½ avocado, chopped

### DIRECTIONS

1. Put okra and black beans in the big bowl.
2. Sprinkle the ingredients with avocado oil and ground black pepper.
3. Add tomatoes, apple cider vinegar, and avocado.
4. Stir the meal and bake in the baking pan for 10 minutes at 375°F.
5. Serve and enjoy.

CALORIES: 231 Kcal — FAT: 10.3 g — PROTEIN: 9.3 g — CARBOHYDRATES: 13.4 g

---

*Preparation: 10 min* — *Cooking: 10 min* — *Servings: 2*

## 481. YOGURT GREEN BEANS

### INGREDIENTS

- 2 cups green beans
- 1 cup of water
- 1 teaspoon chili flakes
- ½ teaspoon onion powder
- 1 tablespoon lemon juice
- 1 tablespoon fresh dill, chopped
- ½ cup plain yogurt

### DIRECTIONS

1. Soak tBoil the green beans in water for 10 minutes.
2. Then cool the beans and put them in the mixing bowl.
3. Add chili flakes, onion powder, lemon juice, fresh dill, and plain yogurt.
4. Carefully mix the green beans, then serve.

CALORIES: 143 Kcal — FAT: 8.3 g — PROTEIN: 7.3 g — CARBOHYDRATES: 17.1 g

Preparation: 10 min  Cooking: 5 min  Servings: 4

## 482. CANNELLINI BEANS DIP

### INGREDIENTS

- 2 cups cannellini beans, cooked
- 1 tablespoon olive oil, softened
- 1 teaspoon garlic powder
- 2 tablespoons lemon juice

### DIRECTIONS

1. In a pot, roast the cooked cannellini beans and olive oil for 5 minutes.
2. Sprinkle the beans with lemon juice and garlic powder.
3. Blend the beans with the help of the immersion blender until smooth.
4. Serve as a dip for crispy bread, chips or cheese.

CALORIES: 227 Kcal    FAT: 7.4 g    PROTEIN: 15.1 g    CARBOHYDRATES: 21.2 g

*Preparation: 10 min*     *Cooking: 5 min*     *Servings: 2*

## 483. BEANS AND SCALLOPS SALAD

### INGREDIENTS

- 1 cup red kidney beans, cooked
- 4 oz scallops
- Direction:
- ¼ teaspoon ground coriander
- ½ teaspoon lemon juice
- 1 tablespoon olive oil
- 1 teaspoon sesame seeds
- 1 tablespoon avocado oil

### DIRECTIONS

1. Heat the olive oil in the skillet.
2. Then sprinkle the scallops with ground coriander and put in the hot oil.
3. Roast them for 2 minutes per side.
4. Transfer the cooked scallops in the salad bowl.
5. Add red kidney beans, lemon juice, sesame seeds, and avocado oil.
6. Gently stir the cooked meal.

CALORIES: 119 Kcal     FAT: 4.3 g     PROTEIN: 12.3 g     CARBOHYDRATES: 15.4 g

---

*Preparation: 10 min*     *Cooking: 20 min*     *Servings: 2*

## 484. 5-INGREDIENTS BEAN SOUP

### INGREDIENTS

- 4 cups chicken stock
- 1 cup red kidney beans, cooked
- 1 carrot, chopped
- 1 tablespoon olive oil
- 1 onion, diced

### DIRECTIONS

1. Roast the onion with olive oil in a skillet, until light brown.
2. Bring the chicken stock to boil and add onion, carrot, and red kidney beans.
3. Simmer the soup for 10 minutes.
4. Turn off the heat, then stir well.
5. Serve with some oiled bread and enjoy.

CALORIES: 212 Kcal     FAT: 7.4 g     PROTEIN: 10.1 g     CARBOHYDRATES: 31 g

Preparation: 10 min  Cooking: 5 min  Servings: 2

## 485. ROASTED BEANS BOWL

### INGREDIENTS

- 6 oz green beans, boiled
- 1 tablespoon olive oil
- 1 tablespoon lemon juice
- 1 teaspoon dried thyme
- 3 tomatoes, roughly sliced
- ½ teaspoon dried rosemary
- 1 tablespoon olive oil

### DIRECTIONS

1. Preheat the grill to 400°F.
2. Sprinkle the green beans and tomatoes with olive oil.
3. Grill the boiled green beans and tomatoes for 2 minutes per side.
4. Then transfer the grilled vegetables in the serving bowls.
5. Sprinkle them with thyme, lemon juice, rosemary, and olive oil.
6. Shake the meal gently, then serve.

CALORIES: 92 Kcal   FAT: 1.3 g   PROTEIN: 2.1g   CARBOHYDRATES: 15.4 g

*Preparation: 10 min*  *Cooking: 0 min*  *Servings: 6*

## 486. BEAN PASTE

### INGREDIENTS

- 3 cups white beans, cooked
- 1 tablespoon olive oil, melted
- 1 tablespoon chives, chopped
- ½ teaspoon smoked paprika
- ¼ teaspoon chili powder

### DIRECTIONS

1. Put all ingredients in the blender and blend until smooth.
2. Transfer the paste in the bowl, flatten the surface of it and leave in the fridge for 10 minutes.
3. Use the paste to complete a dish or eat with some wole grain bread.

CALORIES: 267 Kcal   FAT: 7.1 g   PROTEIN: 17.3 g   CARBOHYDRATES: 23.3 g

*Preparation: 5 min*  *Cooking: 55 min*  *Servings: 8*

## 487. BEANS STEW

### INGREDIENTS

- 2 pounds pork shoulder, chopped
- 2 cups red kidney beans, soaked
- 1 cup tomatoes, chopped
- 1 teaspoon cayenne pepper
- 1 teaspoon salt
- 1 cup fresh cilantro, chopped
- 4 cups of water

### DIRECTIONS

1. Put all the ingredients in a pot, except the water.
2. Roast for 5 minutes at high flame.
3. Lower the flame, then add the water.
4. Let the stew simmer for 50 minutes, with the pot covered.
5. Stir the stew well, then serve in a bowl.

CALORIES: 328 Kcal   FAT: 11.1 g   PROTEIN: 10 g   CARBOHYDRATES: 15.1 g

*Preparation: 5 min*  *Cooking: 15 min*  *Servings: 4*

## 488. BEANS AND CHICKEN STOCK SOUP

### INGREDIENTS

- 1 cup red kidney beans, cooked
- ½ cup zucchini, chopped
- 2 tablespoons tomato paste
- 1 teaspoon chili powder
- 1 jalapeno pepper, chopped
- ½ cup chicken stock

### DIRECTIONS

1. Bring the chicken stock to boil and add tomato paste, chili powder, jalapeno pepper, and zucchini.
2. Simmer the ingredients for 5 minutes.
3. Add red kidney beans and cook the stuffing with open lid for 10 minutes.
4. Blend the mixture with the help of a blender, until smooth.
5. Serve in a bowl and enjoy with some bread.

CALORIES: 168 Kcal   FAT: 17.3 g   PROTEIN: 11.3 g   CARBOHYDRATES: 23.4 g

*Preparation: 10 min*  *Cooking: 0 min*  *Servings: 6*

## 489. BEANS DISH

### INGREDIENTS

- 1 cup canned cannellini beans, drained
- 1 cup canned red kidney beans, drained
- 1 cup canned white beans, drained
- 1 red onion, diced
- 3 tablespoons olive oil
- ½ teaspoon dried thyme
- 1 teaspoon lemon juice
- ½ teaspoon lime zest, grated
- 1 carrot, grated

### DIRECTIONS

1. Make the dressing: mix lime zest, lemon juice, dried thyme, and olive oil in the shallow bowl.
2. Mix every remaining ingredient in the mixing bowl.
3. Add dressing, shake well, and transfer the meal in the serving plates.
4. Serve and enjoy.

CALORIES: 154 Kcal   FAT: 6.1 g   PROTEIN: 10 g   CARBOHYDRATES: 25 g

---

*Preparation: 15 min*  *Cooking: 0 min*  *Servings: 6*

## 490. BEANS TOAST SPREAD

### INGREDIENTS

- 10 oz broad beans, cooked
- 2 oz goat cheese, crumbled
- 1 tablespoon olive oil
- 1 teaspoon dried mint
- 1 teaspoon lemon juice

### DIRECTIONS

1. Mash the broad beans with the help of the potato masher.
2. Add olive oil, dried mint and lemon juice.
3. Stir the mashed beans mixture well and add goat cheese.
4. Carefully mix the spread, then serve in a toast.

CALORIES: 221 Kcal   FAT: 15 g   PROTEIN: 10.3 g   CARBOHYDRATES: 24 g

Preparation: 10 min  Cooking: 15 min  Servings: 2

## 491. GARBANZO BEANS WITH MEAT STRIPS

### INGREDIENTS

- 10 oz beef sirloin
- 1 teaspoon Cajun seasonings
- 2 tablespoons olive oil
- 1 cup garbanzo beans, cooked
- 1 cup tomato sauce
- 1 garlic clove, minced
- 1 carrot, peeled and chopped
- 1 teaspoon chopped parsley

### DIRECTIONS

1. Preheat the oven at 400°F.
2. Rub the beef sirloin with Cajun seasonings and brush with 1 tablespoon of olive oil.
3. Grill the meat for 5 minutes per side at 400°F.
4. In the meantime, place the garlic in a pot with 1 tablespoon of oil, the carrot and the tomato sauce, then cook for 10 minutes.
5. Turn off the fire and remove the meat from the oven.
6. Cut the meat into strips, mix with the garbanzo beans and the tomato sauce.
7. Sprinkle with parsley, then serve.

CALORIES: 299 Kcal   FAT: 15.3 g   PROTEIN: 11.1 g   CARBOHYDRATES: 23.1 g

*Preparation: 10 min*     *Cooking: 45 min*     *Servings: 2*

## 492. BEAN BOWL WITH MEAT

**INGREDIENTS**

- 1 tablespoon olive oil
- 1 onion, chopped
- 1 teaspoon garlic powder
- 7 oz beef sirloin, chopped
- 1 cup green beans, chopped, boiled
- 2 tablespoons tomato paste
- ½ cup of water

**DIRECTIONS**

1. Roast the meat with olive oil in the saucepan for 2 minutes per side.
2. Then add onion and garlic powder. Stir the ingredients and cook for 1 minute more.
3. Add green beans, tomato paste and water.
4. Stir gently, close the lid and simmer the meal on low heat for 40 minutes.
5. Stir well, then serve in a bowl.

CALORIES: 201 Kcal     FAT: 17.1 g     PROTEIN: 11.3 g     CARBOHYDRATES: 14.2 g

*Preparation: 10 min*     *Cooking: 0 min*     *Servings: 4*

## 493. VEGAN BEAN MIX

**INGREDIENTS**

- 1 cup pepper, chopped
- 1 cup lettuce, chopped
- 1 cucumber, chopped
- ½ cup corn kernels, cooked
- ½ cup fresh parsley, chopped
- 1 cup black beans, cooked

**DIRECTIONS**

1. Put all ingredients in the mixing bowl and carefully mix.
2. Transfer the mix in the serving bowls.
3. Add olive oil and seasoning if needed.

CALORIES: 227 Kcal     FAT: 7.2 g     PROTEIN: 15.3 g     CARBOHYDRATES: 19 g

*Preparation: 10 min*  *Cooking: 15 min*  *Servings: 2*

## 494. GRILLED SALMON WITH GREEN BEANS

### INGREDIENTS

- 1-pound salmon fillet
- ½ teaspoon thyme
- ½ teaspoon ground coriander
- 1 tablespoon olive oil
- ¼ cup edamame beans, boiled
- 1 tablespoon mustard
- 1 tablespoon various seeds
- 1 cup green beans

### DIRECTIONS

1. Make a horizontal cut in the salmon and fill it with edamame beans.
2. Secure the cut with toothpicks.
3. After this, gently rub the fish with thyme, ground coriander, olive oil, mustard and the various seeds
4. Preheat the grill to 390°F.
5. Put the fish in the preheated grill and cook it for 7 minutes per side.
6. In the meantime, cook the green beans in a pot with some oil, for around 15 minutes.
7. Remove the fish from the oven, then serve with a portion of green beans.

CALORIES: 315 Kcal   FAT: 11.2 g   PROTEIN: 15.2 g   CARBOHYDRATES: 23.1 g

Preparation: 10 min  Cooking: 1 hour and 10 min  Servings: 6

## 495. HOT WHITE BEANS STEW

**INGREDIENTS**

- 1 teaspoon cayenne pepper
- 1 teaspoon curry powder
- 2 cups white beans
- 8 cups of water
- 1 tablespoon olive oil
- 1 bell pepper, diced
- 2 oz tomato paste

**DIRECTIONS**

1. Heat the olive oil in a saucepan.
2. Add the bell pepper and roast it for 3 minutes.
3. Add white beans, curry powder, cayenne pepper, and tomato paste.
4. Add water and close the lid.
5. Simmer the stew for 65 minutes on medium-low heat.
6. Serve in a bowl and enjoy with some bread or chips.

CALORIES: 260 Kcal  FAT: 14.1 g  PROTEIN: 16.3 g  CARBOHYDRATES: 33.4 g

---

Preparation: 10 min  Cooking: 11 min  Servings: 2

## 496. CUMIN BLACK BEANS

**INGREDIENTS**

- 1 cup black beans, boiled
- 1 teaspoon cumin seeds
- 1 teaspoon garlic, diced
- 2 tablespoons avocado oil

**DIRECTIONS**

1. Heat the pan and put cumin seeds inside.
2. Roast them for 3 minutes on medium heat.
3. Add the avocado oil, garlic, and black beans.
4. Roast the ingredients for 8 minutes. Stir the meal every 2 minutes.

CALORIES: 178 Kcal  FAT: 6.3 g  PROTEIN: 12 g  CARBOHYDRATES: 13.4 g

Preparation: 10 min  Cooking: 20 min  Servings: 2

## 497. STIR-FRIED GREEN BEANS

### INGREDIENTS

- 2 pounds green beans
- 1 tablespoon olive oil
- 1 teaspoon allspices
- ¼ cup of water
- 1 teaspoon apple cider vinegar

### DIRECTIONS

1. Chop the green beans roughly and put them in the hot saucepan.
2. Add water and cook the vegetables for 10 minutes on low heat.
3. Add olive oil, allspices, and stir well.
4. Cook the green beans for 10 minutes more.
5. When the vegetables are soft, they are cooked.
6. Sprinkle the beans with apple cider vinegar and transfer in the plates.

CALORIES: 86 Kcal    FAT: 3.3 g    PROTEIN: 8.3 g    CARBOHYDRATES: 7.4 g

*Preparation: 10 min*  *Cooking: 35 min*  *Servings: 6*

## 498. BLACK EYED PEAS WITH ORANGES

### INGREDIENTS

- 3 cans black-eyed peas, drained
- ½ cup fresh dill, chopped
- 3 oz scallions, chopped
- 1 orange, peeled, chopped
- 1 teaspoon ground coriander
- 1 carrot, chopped
- 3 tablespoons avocado oil
- 1 cup of water

### DIRECTIONS

1. Heat avocado oil in the saucepan.
2. Add dill, scallions, orange, ground coriander, and carrot.
3. Roast the ingredients for 10 minutes on low heat.
4. Then add water and black-eyed peas.
5. Cook the meal for 25 minutes on medium heat.
6. Serve and enjoy.

CALORIES: 159 Kcal   FAT: 8.5 g   PROTEIN: 12.1 g   CARBOHYDRATES: 15 g

---

*Preparation: 10 min*  *Cooking: 20 min*  *Servings: 2*

## 499. GREEK STYLE WHITE BEANS SOUP

### INGREDIENTS

- 1 teaspoon dried thyme
- 1 cup Greek yogurt
- ½ teaspoon dried rosemary
- 2 cups white beans, boiled
- 1 carrot, diced
- ½ cup celery stalk, chopped
- 2 tablespoons water

### DIRECTIONS

1. Put all the ingredients into a big saucepan and close the lid.
2. Simmer the soup for 15 minutes on low heat.
3. Remove the lid and roast at high flame for 5 minutes.
4. Add the water, then mix well.
5. Serve the meal and enjoy with some bread or chips.

CALORIES: 307 Kcal   FAT: 14.1 g   PROTEIN: 20.1 g   CARBOHYDRATES: 18 g

Preparation: 10 min  Cooking: 7 min  Servings: 2

## 500. BEANS PORRIDGE

### INGREDIENTS

- 4 oz edamame beans, cooked
- ¼ cup quinoa
- 1 cup chicken stock
- 1 red pepper, diced
- 1 tablespoon olive oil
- ¼ teaspoon garlic powder

### DIRECTIONS

1. Bring the chicken stock to boil and add quinoa.
2. Cook it for 5 minutes.
3. Then add garlic powder, red pepper, and edamame beans.
4. Add olive oil, carefully stir the ingredients, and cook the meal for 1 minute.
5. With the help of a blender, blend well the mixture.
6. Serve with some crispy bread.

CALORIES: 219 Kcal  FAT: 8.3 g  PROTEIN: 10 g  CARBOHYDRATES: 23.4 g

Preparation: 10 min    Cooking: 15 min    Servings: 2

## 501. CELERY BEANS

### INGREDIENTS

- 1 cup red kidney beans, boiled
- 1 cup celery stalk, chopped
- 2 cups fresh spinach, chopped
- 3 cups chicken stock
- 1 teaspoon ground turmeric
- ½ teaspoon smoked paprika
- 1 tablespoon olive oil

### DIRECTIONS

1. Heat the olive oil in the saucepan.
2. Add spinach and celery stalk and roast them for 3 minutes.
3. Then mix the vegetables and add smoked paprika and ground turmeric.
4. Add red kidney beans and chicken stock.
5. Close the lid and simmer the meal for 10 minutes on low heat.
6. Serve and enjoy.

CALORIES: 162 Kcal    FAT: 7.1 g    PROTEIN: 11 g    CARBOHYDRATES: 10.3 g

---

Preparation: 10 min    Cooking: 40 min    Servings: 4

## 502. GREEN BEANS SOUP

### INGREDIENTS

- 1 cup tomatoes, roughly chopped
- 12 oz green beans, roughly chopped
- 1 tablespoon dried dill
- 1 cup potatoes, chopped
- 1 onion, sliced
- 1 teaspoon cayenne pepper
- 4 cups chicken stock

### DIRECTIONS

1. Put all the ingredients into a saucepan except the chicken stock.
2. Roast at high flame for 3 minutes.
3. Add the water and close the lid.
4. Simmer the stew for 35 minutes on medium-low heat.
5. Serve and enjoy.

CALORIES: 80 Kcal    FAT: 2.4 g    PROTEIN: 8.1 g    CARBOHYDRATES: 5 g

*Preparation:* 10 min   *Cooking:* 50 min   Servings: 4

## 503. GREEN BEANS WITH MEAT

### INGREDIENTS

- 7 oz pork shoulder, chopped
- 2 tablespoons tomato paste
- 1 carrot, chopped
- 12 oz green beans, chopped
- 4 cups of water
- 1 tablespoon organic canola oil
- 1 teaspoon dried sage
- 2 cups water
- 2 cups basmati rice

### DIRECTIONS

1. Roast the pork shoulder with organic canola oil in the saucepan for 2 minutes per one side.
2. Then add tomato paste, carrot, green beans, and sage.
3. Add 4 cups of water and gently stir the mixture.
4. Cook the meal for 30 minutes on medium heat.
5. Meanwhile, bring 2 cups of water to boil.
6. After 30 minutes, add the boiling water to the soup.
7. Add the basmati rice.
8. Cook for another 15 minutes, then serve in a bowl.

CALORIES: 256 Kcal   FAT: 10.3 g   PROTEIN: 11.3 g   CARBOHYDRATES: 30.4 g

Preparation: 10 min   Cooking: 0 min   Servings: 4

## 504. FETA AND WHITE BEANS BOWL

### INGREDIENTS

- 1 tomato, diced
- 1 cup white beans, boiled
- 3 oz Feta, crumbled
- 1 cup baby spinach
- 1 tablespoon olive oil
- ¼ teaspoon dried rosemary
- ¼ teaspoon garlic, diced

### DIRECTIONS

1. Make the dressing: whisk the olive oil with garlic and dried rosemary.
2. Then mix tomato, white beans, and baby spinach.
3. Sprinkle the vegetables with dressing and shake.
4. Then add crumbled Feta and gently stir.
5. Transfer the meal in the serving bowls.

CALORIES: 210 Kcal   FAT: 12 g   PROTEIN: 10 g   CARBOHYDRATES: 15.4 g

---

Preparation: 10 min   Cooking: 6 min   Servings: 2

## 505. FRIED BEANS WITH YOGURT DRESSING

### INGREDIENTS

- ½ cup black-eyed peas, canned, drained
- ½ cup fresh cilantro, chopped
- 1 teaspoon cayenne pepper
- ⅓ cup plain yogurt
- 1 teaspoon smoked paprika
- 1 cucumber, chopped
- 1 tablespoon apple cider vinegar

### DIRECTIONS

1. Put black-eyed peas in the hot skillet and roast for 6 minutes. Stir the beans after 3 minutes of cooking.
2. Then mix plain yogurt, smoked paprika, cayenne pepper, and apple cider vinegar.
3. Cool the fried black-eyed peas and mix them with cilantro and cucumber.
4. Add yogurt mixture and mix.

CALORIES: 53 Kcal   FAT: 6.3 g   PROTEIN: 4.3 g   CARBOHYDRATES: 8.4 g

*Preparation: 10 min*  *Cooking: 10 min*  *Servings: 3*

## 506. BEAN PATTIES

### INGREDIENTS

- ½ cup white beans, canned
- 1 egg, beaten
- 2 tablespoons semolina
- 1 teaspoon chili flakes
- 1 tablespoon almond meal
- 1 tablespoon olive oil

### DIRECTIONS

1. With the help of a blender, blend the white beans well.
2. Add the egg, semolina, chili flakes, almond meal and other seeds if you like (pumpink seeds, chia seeds, etc.).
3. Mix the ingredients with the help of a spoon until you get a smooth mass.
4. Make the medium size ball. Press them in the shape of patties.
5. Heat the olive oil in a skillet and add the patties.
6. Roast them for 3 minutes per side or until the patties are light brown.
7. Insert the patty in a bun with tomato slices and salad, if you like.

CALORIES: 189 Kcal   FAT: 4.8 g   PROTEIN: 12.4 g   CARBOHYDRATES: 27 g

*Preparation: 10 min*     *Cooking: 0 min*     *Servings: 2*

# 507. MEDITERRANEAN BEAN SALAD

## INGREDIENTS

- 2 oz red kidney beans, canned
- 2 oz edamame beans, boiled
- 1 cucumber, diced
- 1 tablespoon fresh dill, chopped
- 1 tomato, chopped
- 1 tablespoon avocado oil
- ½ teaspoon ground black pepper

## DIRECTIONS

1. Put red kidney beans and edamame beans in the bowl.
2. Add cucumber, dill, and tomato.
3. Then sprinkle the salad with avocado oil and ground black pepper.
4. Stir the salad well.

CALORIES: 121 Kcal     FAT: 3.3 g     PROTEIN: 8.3 g     CARBOHYDRATES: 7.4 g

---

*Preparation: 10 min*     *Cooking: 0 min*     *Servings: 4*

# 508. SPECIAL BEANS BOWL

## INGREDIENTS

- 1 cup radish, sliced
- 3 cups red kidney beans, cooked
- 1 avocado, sliced
- 1 cup cherry tomatoes, halved
- 4 tablespoons lemon juice
- 2 tablespoons olive oil

## DIRECTIONS

1. Put radish, red kidney beans, avocado, and cherry tomatoes one-by-one in the serving bowls.
2. Sprinkle every serving with lemon juice and olive oil.

CALORIES: 157 Kcal     FAT: 4.2 g     PROTEIN: 9.3 g     CARBOHYDRATES: 12.4 g

*Preparation: 10 min*     *Cooking: 5 min*     *Servings: 2*

## 509. BEANS AND COUSCOUS SALAD

### INGREDIENTS

- ½ cup couscous
- 1 cup chicken stock, hot
- ⅓ cup cannellini beans, canned, drained
- 1 bell pepper, chopped
- 2 tablespoons plain yogurt

### DIRECTIONS

1. Mix couscous with hot chicken stock and leave for 5 minutes or till couscous soaks all liquid.
2. Mix the cooked couscous with cannellini beans, bell pepper, and plain yogurt.
3. Serve in a bowl and enoy.

CALORIES: 150 Kcal     FAT: 3.9 g     PROTEIN: 8 g     CARBOHYDRATES: 26 g

---

*Preparation: 20 min*     *Cooking: 15 min*     *Servings: 4*

## 510. BEANS MEATBALLS

### INGREDIENTS

- 3 cups mung beans, cooked
- 3 tablespoons flax meal
- ¼ cup onion, minced
- 1 teaspoon dried oregano
- 2 oz black olives, chopped
- 1 tablespoon olive oil
- ½ teaspoon cayenne pepper

### DIRECTIONS

1. Mash the mung beans gently and mix with flax meal, minced onion, dried oregano, olives, and cayenne pepper.
2. Make the balls from the mixture.
3. Brush the baking pan with olive oil and put the mung beans balls inside.
4. Cook them for 10 minutes at 355F.
5. Flip the meatballs on another side and cook them for 5 minutes.
6. Serve in a platter with some fresh vegetables.

CALORIES: 243 Kcal     FAT: 8.9 g     PROTEIN: 21 g     CARBOHYDRATES: 13 g

*Preparation: 10 min*     *Cooking: 0 min*     *Servings: 6*

## 511. SPECIAL BEAN BLEND

### INGREDIENTS

- 1 tablespoon tahini
- 5 tablespoons olive oil
- 1 teaspoon garlic powder
- ¼ teaspoon ground cinnamon
- 4 cups cannellini beans, canned

### DIRECTIONS

1. Blend the beans until smooth and transfer the big bowl.
2. Add olive oil, garlic powder, ground cinnamon, and tahini.
3. Carefully stir the blend, then serve with some fresh bread or some crisps.

CALORIES: 103 Kcal     FAT: 3.2 g     PROTEIN: 6.1 g     CARBOHYDRATES: 10 g

---

*Preparation: 10 min*     *Cooking: 15 min*     *Servings: 6*

## 512. BACON GREEN BEANS

### INGREDIENTS

- 3 pounds green beans
- 6 bacon slices, chopped
- 2 cups of water
- 2 oz Parmesan, grated

### DIRECTIONS

1. Bring the water to boil, add green beans and boil them for 8 minutes.
2. Cook the cooked vegetables in ice water and chop roughly.
3. Roast the chopped bacon until crunchy.
4. Top the chopped green beans with bacon and grated Parmesan.

CALORIES: 131 Kcal     FAT: 5.4 g     PROTEIN: 9.1 g     CARBOHYDRATES: 14 g

*Preparation: 10 min*     *Cooking: 15 min*     *Servings: 6*

## 513. GINGER PEAS

### INGREDIENTS

- 1 cup sugar snap peas
- 6 oz tempeh, chopped
- 1 teaspoon fresh ginger, grated
- 2 cups broccoli, chopped
- ½ teaspoon sesame seeds
- 1 tablespoon avocado oil
- 1 cup water, for the steamer

### DIRECTIONS

1. Pour the water in a steamer, insert the steamer rack, and put snap peas and broccoli inside.
2. Steam the vegetables until they are soft.
3. Meanwhile, heat the avocado oil.
4. Add tempeh, ginger, and sesame seeds.
5. Roast the ingredients for 2 minutes. Then stir them and cook for 1 minute more.
6. Add to the mixture the steamed vegetables.

CALORIES: 133 Kcal     FAT: 5.4 g     PROTEIN: 11.1 g     CARBOHYDRATES: 10 g

# 24 Soups

Preparation: 10 min  Cooking: 1 hour  Servings: 6

# 514. MOROCCAN LENTILS SOUP

## INGREDIENTS

- 2 tablespoons extra virgin olive oil
- 1 large onion, chopped
- 2 stalks celery, chopped
- 1 carrot, chopped
- ⅓ cup chopped parsley
- ½ cup chopped cilantro
- 5 garlic cloves, minced
- 1 teaspoon minced ginger
- 1 teaspoon turmeric
- 1 teaspoon cinnamon
- 2 teaspoons sweet paprika
- 1 ¼ cups dry red lentils, rinsed and picked over
- 1 x 15 oz. can garbanzo beans, drained
- 1 x 28 oz. can sieved tomatoes
- 7–8 cups chicken broth
- Salt & pepper to taste

## DIRECTIONS

1. Grab a large saucepan, add the olive oil and place over a medium heat.
2. Add the onion, celery, carrots, garlic, and ginger and cook for 5 minutes until soft.
3. Throw in the turmeric, cinnamon, paprika and pepper and continue to cook for another 5 minutes.
4. Add the tomatoes and broth, stir well then bring to a simmer.
5. Add the lentils, garbanzo beans, cilantro and parsley.
6. Cook uncovered for 35 minutes until the lentils become very soft.
7. Season well, then serve and enjoy.

CALORIES: 551 Kcal  FAT: 25 g  PROTEIN: 20.3 g  CARBOHYDRATES: 30.4 g

*Preparation: 10 min*     *Cooking: 45 min*     *Servings: 4*

# 515. ROASTED RED PEPPER AND TOMATO SOUP

## INGREDIENTS

- 2 red bell peppers
- 3 tomatoes
- ½ medium onion
- 2 cloves garlic, minced
- 1-2 tablespoons olive oil
- ¼ teaspoon salt
- ¼ teaspoon ground black pepper
- 2 cups vegetable broth
- 2 tablespoons tomato paste
- ¼ cup parsley, chopped
- ¼ teaspoon Italian seasoning
- ¼ teaspoon paprika
- ⅛ teaspoon. cayenne pepper

## DIRECTIONS

1. Preheat your oven to 375°F.
2. Grab a medium bowl and add the red peppers, tomatoes, onion, garlic, olive oil and salt and pepper. Toss well to coat.
3. Place onto a baking sheet and pop into the oven for 45 minutes until soft.
4. Next place the veggie broth over a medium heat and add the roasted veggies, tomato paste, parsley, paprika and cayenne.
5. Stir to combine then simmer for 10 minutes.
6. Use an immersion blender to puree the soup then return back to the pan.
7. Reheat if required, add extra seasoning then serve and enjoy.

CALORIES: 531 Kcal     FAT: 19.3 g     PROTEIN: 26.3 g     CARBOHYDRATES: 21.4 g

---

*Preparation: 10 min*     *Cooking: 35 min*     *Servings: 4*

# 516. GREEK SPRING SOUP

## INGREDIENTS

- 6 cups chicken broth
- 1 ½ cups diced or shredded cooked chicken
- 2 tablespoons olive oil
- 1 small onion, diced
- 1 bay leaf
- ⅓ cup arborio rice
- 1 large free-range egg
- 2 tablespoons water
- Juice of half of a lemon
- 1 cup chopped asparagus
- 1 cup diced carrots
- ½ cup fresh chopped dill, divided
- Salt and pepper, to taste

## DIRECTIONS

1. Find a large pan, add the oil and place over a medium heat.
2. Add the onions and cook for five minutes until soft.
3. Next add ¼ cup dill, plus the chicken broth and bay leaf. Bring to a boil.
4. Add the rice and reduce the heat to low. Simmer for 10 minutes.
5. Add the carrots and asparagus and cook for 10 more minutes until the rice and veggies are tender.
6. Add the chicken and simmer.
7. Meanwhile find a medium bowl and add the egg, lemon and water. Whisk well.
8. Add ½ cup of the stock to the egg mixture, stirring constantly then pour it all back into the pot.
9. Heat through and allow the soup to thicken.
10. Add remaining dill, season well then serve and enjoy.

CALORIES: 551 Kcal     FAT: 13.4 g     PROTEIN: 16.3 g     CARBOHYDRATES: 24.1 g

Preparation: 10 min     Cooking: 40 min     Servings: 4

# 517. FAST SEAFOOD GUMBO

## INGREDIENTS

- ¼ cup olive oil
- ¼ cup flour
- 1 medium white onion, chopped
- 1 cup celery, chopped
- 1 red or green bell pepper, chopped and deseeded
- 1 red chili, chopped
- 2 cups okra, chopped
- 1 cup canned crushed tomatoes
- 2 large cloves garlic, crushed
- 1 teaspoon dried thyme
- 2 cups fish stock
- 1 bay leaf
- 1 teaspoon cayenne powder
- 2 x 8 oz. can crab meat with brine
- 1 lb. shrimp, peeled and deveined
- Salt & pepper, to taste
- ¼ cup fresh parsley, chopped

## DIRECTIONS

1. Find a large pan, add the oil and place over a medium heat.
2. Add the flour and stir well until it forms a thick paste.
3. Add the onions, celery, peppers and okra and stir well, cooking for 5 minutes.
4. Add the garlic, tomatoes, thyme, stock, bay leaf and cayenne and stir again.
5. Bring to a boil the reduce the heat and simmer for 15 minutes.
6. Add the shrimp and crab and cook for 8 minutes more.
7. Serve and enjoy.

CALORIES: 510 Kcal     FAT: 14.8 g     PROTEIN: 24.1 g     CARBOHYDRATES: 20 g

*Preparation: 10 min*  *Cooking: 1 hour*  *Servings: 4*

## 518. MINESTRONE SOUP

### INGREDIENTS

- 1 small white onion, minced
- 4 cloves garlic, minced
- 1/2 cup sliced carrots
- 1 medium zucchini, sliced
- 1 medium squash, sliced
- 2 tablespoons minced parsley
- 1/4 cup celery, sliced
- 3 tablespoons olive oil
- 2 x 15 oz. cans cannellini beans
- 2 x 15 oz. cans red kidney beans
- 1 x 14.5 oz. can tomato
- 4 cups vegetable stock
- 2 cups water
- Salt and pepper to taste
- 3/4 cup small pasta
- 4 cups fresh spinach

### DIRECTIONS

1. Grab a stock pot and place over a medium heat.
2. Add the oil then the onions, garlic, carrots, zucchini, squash, parsley and celery.
3. Cook for five minutes until the veggies are getting soft.
4. Pour in the stock, water, beans, tomatoes, salt and pepper. Stir well.
5. Reduce the heat, cover and simmer for 30 minutes.
6. Add the pasta and spinach, stir well then cover and cook for a further 20 minutes until the pasta is cooked through.
7. Stir and add some cheese if you like, then serve and enjoy.

CALORIES: 348Kcal    FAT: 20.5 g    PROTEIN: 26.3 g    CARBOHYDRATES: 33.4 g

---

*Preparation: 10 min*  *Cooking: 20 min*  *Servings: 4*

## 519. PARMESAN TOMATO SOUP

### INGREDIENTS

- ½ cup tomatoes, chopped
- 1 tablespoon tomato paste
- 1 teaspoon garlic, diced
- 2 cups beef broth
- 1 teaspoon chili pepper
- 2 oz Parmesan, grated
- 1/3 cup fresh cilantro, chopped
- 2 potatoes, chopped

### DIRECTIONS

1. Mix up together tomatoes and tomato paste and transfer the mixture in the pan.
2. Add garlic and beef broth.
3. Add chopped potatoes and chili pepper.
4. Boil the ingredients for 15 minutes or until potato is soft.
5. Then blend the mixture with the help of the hand blender or in the food processor.
6. Add chopped cilantro and simmer the soup for 5 minutes.
7. Ladle the cooked soup in the serving bowls and top every bowl with Parmesan generously.

CALORIES: 241 Kcal    FAT: 12.4 g    PROTEIN: 9.8 g    CARBOHYDRATES: 16 g

*Preparation: 10 min*  *Cooking: 20 min*  *Servings: 2*

## 520. MUSHROOM AND CHEESE SOUP

### INGREDIENTS

- 1 cup cremini mushrooms, chopped
- 1 cup Cheddar cheese, shredded
- 2 cups of water
- ½ teaspoon salt
- 1 teaspoon dried thyme
- ½ teaspoon dried oregano
- 1 tablespoon fresh parsley, chopped
- 1 tablespoon olive oil
- 1 bell pepper, chopped

### DIRECTIONS

1. Pour olive oil in the pan.
2. Add mushrooms and bell pepper. Roast the vegetables for 5 minutes over the medium heat.
3. Then sprinkle them with salt, thyme, and dried oregano.
4. Add parsley and water. Stir the soup well.
5. Cook the soup for 10 minutes.
6. After this, blend the soup until it is smooth and simmer it for 5 minutes more.
7. Add cheese and stir until cheese is melted.
8. Ladle the cooked soup into the bowls. It is recommended to serve soup hot.

CALORIES: 320 Kcal    FAT: 26 g    PROTEIN: 15.7 g    CARBOHYDRATES: 15.1 g

*Preparation: 10 min*  *Cooking: 30 min*  *Servings: 4*

## 521. MEATBALL SOUP

### INGREDIENTS

- 1 cup ground beef
- 1 tablespoon semolina
- ½ teaspoon salt
- 1 egg yolk
- ½ teaspoon ground black pepper
- 4 cups chicken stock
- 1 carrot, chopped
- 1 yellow onion, diced
- 1 tablespoon butter
- ½ teaspoon turmeric
- ½ teaspoon garlic powder

### DIRECTIONS

1. Toss butter in the skillet and heat it up until it is melted.
2. Add onion and cook it until light brown.
3. Meanwhile, pour chicken stock in the pan.
4. Add garlic powder and turmeric.
5. Bring the liquid to boil. Add chopped carrot and boil it for 10 minutes.
6. In the mixing bowl, mix up together ground beef, semolina, salt, egg yolk, and ground black pepper.
7. Make the small sized meatballs.
8. Put the meatballs in the chicken stock.
9. Add cooked onion.
10. Cook the soup for 15 minutes over the medium-low heat, then serve.

CALORIES: 190 Kcal    FAT: 18.4 g    PROTEIN: 21 g    CARBOHYDRATES: 24 g

---

*Preparation: 10 min*  *Cooking: 50 min*  *Servings: 8*

## 522. LEMON LAMB SOUP

### INGREDIENTS

- 1 ½-pound lamb bone in
- 4 eggs, beaten
- 2 cups lettuce, chopped
- 1 tablespoon chives, chopped
- ½ cup fresh dill, chopped
- ½ cup lemon juice
- 1 teaspoon salt
- ½ teaspoon white pepper
- 2 tablespoons avocado oil
- 5 cups of water

### DIRECTIONS

1. Chop the lamb roughly and place in the pan.
2. Add avocado oil and roast the meat for 10 minutes over the medium heat. Stir it with the help of spatula from time to time.
3. Then sprinkle the meat with white pepper and salt. Add water and bring the mixture to boil.
4. In the mixing bowl, whisk together eggs and lemon juice.
5. Add a ½ cup of boiling water from the pan and whisk the egg mixture until smooth.
6. Add dill, chives, and lettuce in the soup. Stir well.
7. Cook the soup for 30 minutes over the medium-high heat.
8. Then add egg mixture and stir it fast to make the homogenous texture of the soup.
9. Cook it for 3 minutes more.

CALORIES: 360 Kcal    FAT: 22.9 g    PROTEIN: 33.6 g    CARBOHYDRATES: 8.9 g

Preparation: 10 min  Cooking: 30 min  Servings: 4

## 523. EGGPLANT SOUP

### INGREDIENTS

- ½ cup tomatoes, chopped
- 2 eggplants, trimmed
- ¼ cup fresh parsley, chopped
- ¼ cup fresh cilantro, chopped
- 1 yellow onion, diced
- ½ teaspoon ground cumin
- ½ teaspoon cayenne pepper
- 1 celery stalk, chopped
- 1 tablespoon olive oil
- 1 teaspoon salt
- 1 garlic clove, peeled
- 1 teaspoon butter
- 4 cups chicken stock

### DIRECTIONS

1. Peel eggplants and sprinkle them with olive oil and salt.
2. Preheat the oven to 360°F.
3. Put the eggplants in the tray and transfer it in the preheated oven.
4. Bake the vegetables for 25 minutes.
5. Meanwhile, pour chicken stock in the pan.
6. Add chopped tomatoes, parsley, cilantro, ground cumin, cayenne pepper, celery stalk, and diced garlic clove.
7. Simmer the mixture for 5 minutes.
8. Meanwhile, heat up the butter in the skillet.
9. Add onion and roast it until translucent.
10. Add the onion in the boiled chicken stock mixture.
11. When the eggplants are cooked, transfer them in the food processor and blend until smooth.
12. After this, put the blended eggplants in the chicken stock mixture.
13. Blend the soup with the help of the hand blender until you get a creamy texture, then simmer for 5 minutes more.

CALORIES: 184 Kcal  FAT: 6.1 g  PROTEIN: 12 g  CARBOHYDRATES: 21.1 g

*Preparation: 10 min*     *Cooking: 20 min*     *Servings: 6*

## 524. LEMON CHICKEN SOUP

### INGREDIENTS

- 10 cups chicken broth
- 3 tablespoons olive oil
- 8 cloves garlic, minced
- 1 sweet onion, sliced
- 1 large lemon, zested
- 2 boneless skinless chicken breasts
- 1 cup Israeli couscous
- 1/2 teaspoon crushed red pepper
- 2 oz. crumbled feta
- ⅓ cup chopped chive
- Salt and pepper, to taste

### DIRECTIONS

1. Grab a stock pot, add the oil and place over a medium heat.
2. Add the onion and garlic and cook for five minutes until soft.
3. Add the broth, chicken breasts, lemon zest and crushed pepper.
4. Raise the heat, cover and bring to a boil.
5. Reduce the heat then simmer for 5 minutes.
6. Turn off the heat, remove the lid and remove the chicken from the pot.
7. Pop onto a place and use two forks to shred.
8. Pop back into the pot, add the feta, chives and salt and pepper.
9. Stir well then serve and enjoy.

CALORIES: 251 Kcal     FAT: 30.3 g     PROTEIN: 16.3 g     CARBOHYDRATES: 23.4 g

---

*Preparation: 10 min*     *Cooking: 30 min*     *Servings: 6*

## 525. TUSCAN VEGETABLE PASTA SOUP

### INGREDIENTS

- 2 tablespoons extra virgin olive oil
- 4 cloves garlic, minced
- 1 medium yellow onion, diced
- 1/2 cup carrot, chopped
- 1/2 cup celery, chopped
- 1 medium zucchini, sliced and quartered
- 1 x 15 oz. can diced tomatoes
- 6 cups vegetable stock
- 2 tablespoons tomato paste
- 6-8 oz. whole wheat pasta
- 1 x 15 oz. can white beans
- 2 large handfuls baby spinach
- 6 basil cubes
- Salt and pepper, to taste
- Fresh chopped parsley, for garnish

### DIRECTIONS

1. Grab a stock pot, add the oil and pop over a medium heat.
2. Add the onion and garlic and cook for five minutes until soft.
3. Throw in the carrots, celery and zucchini and cook for an extra 5 minutes, stirring occasionally.
4. Add the tomato and salt and pepper and cook for 1-2 minutes.
5. Add the veggies broth and tomato paste, stir well then bring to the boil.
6. Throw in the pasta, cook for 10 minutes then add the spinach, white beans, basil cubes and seasoning.
7. Stir well then remove from the heat.
8. Divide between large bowls and serve and enjoy.

CALORIES: 151 Kcal     FAT: 22.5 g     PROTEIN: 20 g     CARBOHYDRATES: 30.8 g

*Preparation: 10 min*     *Cooking: 25 min*     Servings: 8

# 526. DAIRY FREE ZUCCHINI SOUP

## INGREDIENTS

- 2½ lb. zucchini
- 1 medium onion, diced
- 2 tablespoons olive oil
- 4 garlic cloves, chopped
- 4 cups chicken stock
- Sea salt and pepper, to taste
- ⅓ cup fresh basil leaves

## DIRECTIONS

1. Grab a pan, add the oil and pop over a medium heat.
2. Add the onion, garlic and zucchini and cook for five minutes until soft.
3. Add the stock and simmer for 15 minutes.
4. Remove from the heat, stir through the basil, add the seasoning and use an immersion blender to whizz until smooth.
5. Serve and enjoy.

CALORIES: 247 Kcal     FAT: 3.5 g     PROTEIN: 9.5 g     CARBOHYDRATES: 10 g

Preparation: 10 min  Cooking: 1 hour  Servings: 4

## 527. FARRO STEW WITH KALE & CANNELLINI BEANS

### INGREDIENTS

- 2 tablespoons olive oil
- 2 medium carrots, diced
- 1 medium onion, chopped
- 2 sticks celery, chopped
- 4 cloves garlic, minced
- 5 cups vegetable broth
- 1 x 14.5 oz. can tomatoes
- 1 cup farro, rinsed
- 1 teaspoon dried oregano
- 1 bay leaf
- Salt to taste
- ½ cup parsley
- 4 cups chopped kale
- 1 x 15 oz. can cannellini beans
- 1 tablespoon fresh lemon juice
- ½ cup feta cheese, crumbled

### DIRECTIONS

1. Grab a stock pot, add the oil and place over a medium heat.
2. Add the onion, carrots and celery and cook for five minutes until becoming soft.
3. Add the garlic and cook for another 30 seconds.
4. Stir through the broth, tomatoes, farro, oregano, bay leaf, parsley and salt.
5. Cover with the lid and bring to the boil. Reduce the heat then simmer for 20 minutes.
6. Remove the lid, add the kale and cook for a further 10-15 minutes.
7. Remove the bay leaf, add the beans, stir through the lemon juice and any additional liquid then stir well to combine.
8. Serve and enjoy.

CALORIES: 210 Kcal   FAT: 6.3 g   PROTEIN: 15.4 g   CARBOHYDRATES: 11.1 g

---

Preparation: 10 min  Cooking: 45 min  Servings: 6

## 528. ITALIAN MEATBALL SOUP

### INGREDIENTS

- 1 egg
- 1 teaspoon dried oregano
- 3 tablespoons olive oil
- 2 quarts chicken broth
- 3 tablespoons tomato paste
- 1 onion, diced
- 2 bay leaves
- 4-5 sprigs fresh thyme
- ½ teaspoon whole black peppercorns
- Fresh parmesan cheese, grated
- 1-2 tablespoons fresh basil leaves, torn
- 4 tablespoons parsley, chopped
- Salt and pepper, to taste

### DIRECTIONS

1. Place all the meatball ingredients except the oil into a medium bowl.
2. Using your hands, mix well and form into meatballs.
3. Place the oil into a stock pot, place over a medium heat and add the meatballs, browning on all sides.
4. Remove the meatballs from the pan.
5. Add more oil to the pan if needed and then add the onion. Cook for five minutes until soft.
6. Add the remaining soup ingredients, stir well then cook for 10 minutes.
7. Return the meatballs to the pan and simmer for a few minutes to warm through.
8. Serve and enjoy.

CALORIES: 331 Kcal   FAT: 20.1 g   PROTEIN: 15.4 g   CARBOHYDRATES: 16 g

Preparation: 10 min  |  Cooking: 40 min  |  Servings: 6

# 529. TUSCAN WHITE BEAN SOUP WITH SAUSAGE

## INGREDIENTS

- ¼ cup extra virgin olive oil
- 1 lb. hot sausage,
- 1 onion, chopped
- 1 carrot, chopped
- 1 stalk celery, chopped
- 2 cloves garlic, chopped
- ½ lb. kale, stems removed and chopped
- 4 cups chicken broth
- 1 x 28 oz. can cannelloni beans, rinsed and drained
- 1 teaspoon rosemary, dried
- 1 bay leaf
- ¼ teaspoon pepper
- Salt, to taste
- ½ cup shredded parmesan

## DIRECTIONS

1. Find a stock pot, pop over a medium heat and add the oil.
2. Cook the sausage until browned on all sides.
3. Throw in the onion, carrot, celery and garlic then cook for a further five minutes.
4. Add the kale and stir through.
5. Next add the broth, beans, rosemary and bay leaf.
6. Stir well, bring to the boil then cover with the lid.
7. Turn down the heat then simmer for 30 minutes.
8. Serve and enjoy.

CALORIES: 530 Kcal  |  FAT: 30 g  |  PROTEIN: 21 g  |  CARBOHYDRATES: 25.5 g

---

Preparation: 10 min  |  Cooking: 45 min  |  Servings: 4

# 530. VEGETABLE SOUP

## INGREDIENTS

- 8 oz. sliced mushrooms
- 2 medium-size zucchinis, sliced
- 1 bunch parsley, chopped
- 1 red onion, chopped
- 2 garlic cloves, chopped
- 2 celery ribs, chopped
- 2 carrots, peeled, chopped
- 2 potatoes, diced
- 1 teaspoon ground coriander
- 1/2 teaspoon turmeric powder
- 1/2 teaspoon sweet paprika
- 1/2 teaspoon thyme
- Salt, pepper, olive oil to taste
- 1 x 32 oz. can peeled tomatoes
- 6 cups vegetable broth
- 1 x 15 oz. can garbanzo beans

## DIRECTIONS

1. Grab a large stockpot, add a tablespoon of olive oil and pop over a medium heat.
2. Add the mushrooms and cook for five minutes, stirring often.
3. Remove from the pan and pop to one side.
4. Add the sliced zucchini and cook for another five minutes. Remove from the pan.
5. Add more oil and add the parsley, onions, garlic, celery, carrots and potatoes. Stir through the spices, salt and pepper.
6. Cook for five minutes until the veggies are softening.
7. Add the tomatoes, bay leaves and broth then bring to a boil.
8. Cover and cook on medium low for 15 minutes.
9. Remove the lid and add the garbanzo beans, mushrooms and zucchini.
10. Heat then serve and enjoy.

CALORIES: 152 Kcal  |  FAT: 6.5 g  |  PROTEIN: 12.5 g  |  CARBOHYDRATES: 4 g

*Preparation: 10 min*  *Cooking: 35 min*  *Servings: 6*

## 531. CARROT SOUP

**INGREDIENTS**

- 5 cups beef broth
- 4 carrots, peeled
- 1 teaspoon dried thyme
- ½ teaspoon ground cumin
- 1 teaspoon salt
- 1 ½ cup potatoes, chopped
- 1 tablespoon olive oil
- ½ teaspoon ground black pepper
- 1 tablespoon lemon juice
- 1/3 cup fresh parsley, chopped
- 1 chili pepper, chopped
- 1 tablespoon tomato paste
- 1 tablespoon sour cream

**DIRECTIONS**

1. Line the baking tray with baking paper.
2. Put sweet potatoes and carrot on the tray and sprinkle with olive oil and salt.
3. Bake the vegetables for 25 minutes at 365F.
4. Meanwhile, pour the beef broth in the pan and bring it to boil.
5. Add dried thyme, ground cumin, chopped chili pepper, and tomato paste.
6. When the vegetables are cooked, add them in the pan.
7. Boil the vegetables until they are soft.
8. Then blend the mixture with the help of the blender until smooth.
9. Simmer it for 2 minutes and add lemon juice. Stir well.
10. Then add sour cream and chopped parsley. Stir well.
11. Simmer the soup for 3 minutes more.

CALORIES: 210 Kcal     FAT: 5.7 g     PROTEIN: 8.8 g     CARBOHYDRATES: 10.5 g

---

*Preparation: 10 min*  *Cooking: 0 min*  *Servings: 4*

## 532. SWEET YOGURT BULGUR BOWL

**INGREDIENTS**

- 1 cup grapes, halved
- ½ cup bulgur, cooked
- ¼ cup celery stalk, chopped
- 2 oz walnuts, chopped
- ¼ cup plain yogurt
- ½ teaspoon ground cinnamon

**DIRECTIONS**

1. Mix grapes with bulgur, celery stalk, and walnut
2. Then add plain yogurt and ground cinnamon.
3. Stir the mixture with the help of the spoon and transfer in the serving bowls.

CALORIES: 120 Kcal     FAT: 8.5 g     PROTEIN: 4.6 g     CARBOHYDRATES: 10.2 g

*Preparation: 15 min*     *Cooking: 0 min*     *Servings: 6*

# 533. SPRING FARRO PLATE

## INGREDIENTS

- 1 cup farro, cooked
- 2 cups baby spinach
- 2 grapefruits, roughly chopped
- 2 tablespoons balsamic vinegar
- ¼ teaspoon white pepper
- 1 tablespoon olive oil

## DIRECTIONS

1. Mix baby spinach and farro in the big bowl.
2. Then add grapefruit and shake the ingredients well.
3. Transfer the mixture in the serving plates and sprinkle with white pepper, olive oil, and balsamic vinegar.

CALORIES: 113 Kcal     FAT: 5.8 g     PROTEIN: 9.6 g     CARBOHYDRATES: 14.2 g

---

*Preparation: 10 min*     *Cooking: 0 min*     *Servings: 2*

# 534. SORGHUM TABOULE

## INGREDIENTS

- 2 oz sorghum, cooked
- 3 oz pumpkin, diced, boiled
- ½ white onion, diced
- 1 date, pitted, chopped
- 1 tablespoon avocado oil
- ½ teaspoon liquid honey
- 2 oz Feta, crumbled

## DIRECTIONS

1. Put sorghum, pumpkin, onion, and date in the big bowl.
2. Then sprinkle the ingredients with avocado oil and liquid honey. Stir well.
3. Transfer the cooked taboule in the serving plates and top with crumbled feta.

CALORIES: 102 Kcal     FAT: 7.2 g     PROTEIN: 6.4 g     CARBOHYDRATES: 13 g

*Preparation: 10 min*  *Cooking: 15 min*  *Servings: 4*

## 535. ROASTED SORGHUM

### INGREDIENTS

- 1 tablespoon avocado oil
- ½ cup sorghum, cooked
- 1 carrot, diced
- 2 tablespoons dried parsley
- ½ teaspoon dried oregano
- 2 tablespoons cream cheese

### DIRECTIONS

1. Heat avocado oil and add the carrot.
2. Roast it for 5 minutes.
3. Then add cooked sorghum, parsley, oregano, and cream cheese.
4. Roast the meal for 10 minutes on low heat. Stir it from time to time to avoid burning.

CALORIES: 145 Kcal   FAT: 8.4 g   PROTEIN: 6.4 g   CARBOHYDRATES: 14 g

---

*Preparation: 10 min*  *Cooking: 25 min*  *Servings: 4*

## 536. SORGHUM STEW

### INGREDIENTS

- 1 cup sorghum
- ½ cup ground sausages
- ½ cup tomatoes
- 1 jalapeno pepper, chopped
- ½ cup bell pepper, chopped
- 4 cups chicken stock

### DIRECTIONS

1. Roast the sausages for 5 minutes in the saucepan.
2. Then add tomatoes, jalapeno, and bell pepper.
3. Cook the ingredients for 10 minutes.
4. After this, add sorghum and chicken stock and boil the stew for 10 minutes more.

CALORIES: 174 Kcal   FAT: 8.9 g   PROTEIN: 10.5 g   CARBOHYDRATES: 17.2 g

*Preparation: 10 min*     *Cooking: 10 min*     *Servings: 3*

## 537. SORGHUM SALAD

**INGREDIENTS**

- 3 oz butternut squash, chopped
- ¼ cup sorghum
- ¼ cup fresh cilantro, chopped
- 1 teaspoon ground cumin
- 2.5 cups water
- 2 tablespoons organic canola oil
- 2 tablespoons apple cider vinegar

**DIRECTIONS**

1. Put sorghum and butternut squash in the saucepan.
2. Add water and cook for 10 minutes.
3. Then cool the ingredients and transfer in the salad bowl.
4. Add cilantro, ground cumin, organic canola oil, and apple cider vinegar.
5. Stir the meal well.

CALORIES: 142 Kcal     FAT: 4.2 g     PROTEIN: 14 g     CARBOHYDRATES: 19.5 g

---

*Preparation: 10 min*     *Cooking: 25 min*     *Servings: 4*

## 538. SORGHUM BAKED

**INGREDIENTS**

- ½ cup sorghum
- 1 apple, chopped
- 1 oz raisins
- 1.5 cup of water

**DIRECTIONS**

1. Put sorghum in the pan. Flatten it.
2. Then top it with raisins, apple, and water.
3. Cover the meal with baking paper and transfer in the preheated to 375F oven.
4. Bake the meal for 25 minutes.
5. Serve and enjoy.

CALORIES: 102 Kcal     FAT: 3.1 g     PROTEIN: 9g     CARBOHYDRATES: 12 g

# 25 Rice and Grains

Preparation: 5 min	Cooking: 17 min	Servings: 6

## 539. FRAGRANT BASMATI RICE

### INGREDIENTS

- 1 cup long-grain rice
- 1 tablespoon olive oil
- 1 teaspoon dried rosemary
- 2 ½ cup water

### DIRECTIONS

1. Heat the olive oil in the saucepan.
2. Add rice and roast it for 2 minutes. Stir it constantly.
3. Then add rosemary and water.
4. Stir the rice and close the lid.
5. Cook it for 15 minutes or until it soaks all water.
6. Serve and enjoy with some sauce or meat.

CALORIES: 150 Kcal	FAT: 2 g	PROTEIN: 6 g	CARBOHYDRATES: 35 g

*Preparation: 5 min*     *Cooking: 20 min*     *Servings: 4*

## 540. CRANBERRY RICE

**INGREDIENTS**

- ¼ cup basmati rice
- 1 cup of organic almond milk
- 2 oz dried cranberries
- ¼ teaspoon ground cinnamon

**DIRECTIONS**

1. Put all the ingredients in the saucepan, stir, and close the lid.
2. Cook the rice on low heat for 20 minutes.
3. Serve hot and enjoy.

CALORIES: 134 Kcal     FAT: 4 g     PROTEIN: 7 g     CARBOHYDRATES: 30 g

---

*Preparation: 8 min*     *Cooking: 15 min*     *Servings: 4*

## 541. PESTO RICE

**INGREDIENTS**

- ½ cup of basmati rice
- 1 ½ cup of water
- 2 tablespoons pesto sauce

**DIRECTIONS**

1. Simmer the rice water for 15 minutes on the low heat or until the rice soaks all liquid.
2. Mix the cooked rice with pesto sauce.

CALORIES: 175 Kcal     FAT: 6 g     PROTEIN: 5 g     CARBOHYDRATES: 32.1 g

Preparation: 5 min    Cooking: 25 min    Servings: 6

## 542. ITALIAN STYLE WILD RICE

### INGREDIENTS

- 1 cup wild rice
- 3 cups chicken stock
- 1 teaspoon Italian seasonings
- 2 oz Feta, crumbled
- 1 tablespoon olive oil

### DIRECTIONS

1. Mix wild rice with olive oil and chicken stock.
2. Close the lid and cook it for 25 minutes over the medium-low heat.
3. Then add Italian seasonings and crumbled feta.
4. Stir the rice.

CALORIES: 253 Kcal    FAT: 7.5 g    PROTEIN: 8 g    CARBOHYDRATES: 33 g

*Preparation: 10 min*     *Cooking: 0 min*     *Servings: 4*

## 543. RICE SALAD

### INGREDIENTS

- ½ cup long-grain rice, cooked
- ½ cup corn kernels, cooked
- 1 tomato, chopped
- 1 teaspoon chili flakes
- ¼ cup plain yogurt
- 1 cucumber pickle

### DIRECTIONS

1. Grate the cucumber pickle and mix it with cooked rice, corn kernels, tomato, chili flakes, and plain yogurt.
2. Serve in a bowl and enjoy cold.

CALORIES: 148 Kcal     FAT: 6.3 g     PROTEIN: 4.5 g     CARBOHYDRATES: 25 g

---

*Preparation: 10 min*     *Cooking: 15 min*     *Servings: 2*

## 544. RICE MEATBALLS

### INGREDIENTS

- ¼ cup Cheddar cheese, shredded
- 1 teaspoon ground black pepper
- 1 cup of basmati rice, cooked
- ¼ cup ground chicken
- 1 teaspoon olive oil

### DIRECTIONS

1. In the mixing bowl, mix Cheddar cheese, ground black pepper, rice, and ground chicken.
2. Then make the balls from the mixture.
3. Heat the olive oil well and put the rice balls in the hot oil.
4. Roast the balls for 1 minute per side on high heat.
5. Then transfer the balls in the oven and bake them for 20 minutes at 360F.

CALORIES: 154 Kcal     FAT: 4.5 g     PROTEIN: 6.4 g     CARBOHYDRATES: 34 g

*Preparation: 5 min*     *Cooking: 20 min*     *Servings: 3*

## 545. BROWN RICE SAUTE

### INGREDIENTS

- 3 oz brown rice
- 9 oz chicken stock
- 1 teaspoon curry powder
- 1 onion, diced
- 4 tablespoons olive oil

### DIRECTIONS

1. Heat olive oil in the saucepan.
2. Add onion and cook it until light brown.
3. Add brown rice, curry powder, and chicken stock.
4. Close the lid and saute the rice for 15 minutes.
5. Serve with some fresh vegetables and enjoy.

CALORIES: 237 Kcal     FAT: 4.5 g     PROTEIN: 7 g     CARBOHYDRATES: 24.8 g

*Preparation: 5 min* — *Cooking: 50 min* — *Servings: 4*

## 546. MUSHROOM PILAF

### INGREDIENTS

- 2 tablespoons olive oil
- 1 shallot, chopped
- 2 garlic cloves, minced
- 1-pound button mushrooms
- 1 cup brown rice
- 2 cups chicken stock
- 1 bay leaf
- 1 thyme sprig
- Salt and pepper to taste

### DIRECTIONS

1. Heat the oil in a skillet and stir in the shallot and garlic. Cook for 2 minutes until softened and fragrant.
2. Add the mushrooms and rice and cook for 5 minutes.
3. Add the stock, bay leaf and thyme, as well as salt and pepper and continue cooking for 20 more minutes on low heat.
4. Serve the pilaf warm and fresh.

CALORIES: 265 Kcal — FAT: 8.9 g — PROTEIN: 7.6 g — CARBOHYDRATES: 32.4 g

---

*Preparation: 5 min* — *Cooking: 30 min* — *Servings: 6*

## 547. RICE JAMBALAYA

### INGREDIENTS

- 1 cup tomatoes, chopped
- 1 cup bell pepper, chopped
- ¼ cup carrot, chopped
- 1 teaspoon cayenne pepper
- 4 cups chicken stock
- 1 cup of basmati rice
- 2 tablespoons olive oil
- ½ cup chickpeas, cooked

### DIRECTIONS

1. Melt the olive oil and add carrot, bell pepper, and tomatoes.
2. Cook the vegetables for 10 minutes on medium heat.
3. Then add chicken stock, chickpeas, and rice.
4. Add cayenne pepper and stir the meal.
5. Close the lid and cook it for 20 minutes on low heat.

CALORIES: 263 Kcal — FAT: 3.8 g — PROTEIN: 6.9 g — CARBOHYDRATES: 37 g

*Preparation: 10 min*     *Cooking: 30 min*     *Servings: 6*

## 548. MEDITERRANEAN PAELLA

### INGREDIENTS

- 1 cup risotto rice
- 2 oz yellow onion, diced
- ½ teaspoon ground paprika
- 1 cup tomatoes, chopped
- 1 cup shrimps, peeled
- 1 teaspoon olive oil
- 3 cups of water

### DIRECTIONS

1. Heat olive oil in the saucepan.
2. Add onion and cook it for 2 minutes.
3. Then stir well, add shrimps, ground paprika, tomatoes, and stir well.
4. Cook the ingredients for 5 minutes.
5. Add water and risotto rice. Stir well, close the lid, and cook the meal for 20 minutes on low heat.

CALORIES: 273 Kcal     FAT: 10.4 g     PROTEIN: 10.5 g     CARBOHYDRATES: 38 g

Preparation: 10 min  Cooking: 10 min  Servings: 6

## 549. JASMINE RICE WITH SCALLIONS

INGREDIENTS

- 3 tablespoons olive oil
- 1 cup jasmine rice
- 2 tablespoons scallions, chopped
- ½ teaspoon ground black pepper
- 2 teaspoons lemon juice

DIRECTIONS

1. Cook the rice according to the directions of the manufacturer.
2. Then add scallions, olive oil, ground black pepper, and lemon juice.
3. Carefully stir the meal.

CALORIES: 197 Kcal  FAT: 4.5 g  PROTEIN: 7.4 g  CARBOHYDRATES: 29 g

---

Preparation: 000 min  Cooking: 000 min  Servings: 6

## 550. CREMINI MUSHROOMS PILAF

INGREDIENTS

- 2 cups of water
- ½ cup white onion, diced
- 1 cup cremini mushrooms, chopped
- 1 cup of basmati rice
- ¼ teaspoon lime zest, grated
- 2 oz goat cheese, crumbled
- 2 tablespoons olive oil

DIRECTIONS

1. Put rice in the saucepan.
2. Add water and cook for 15 minutes over the low heat.
3. Then roast the mushrooms with olive oil, lime zest, and white onion in the skillet until they are light brown.
4. Add the cooked mushrooms in the cooked rice. Stir well.
5. Top the meal with crumbled goat cheese.

CALORIES: 193 Kcal  FAT: 9.7g  PROTEIN: 8.4 g  CARBOHYDRATES: 32.4 g

*Preparation: 10 min* — *Cooking: 20 min* — *Servings: 4*

# 551. FAST CHICKEN RICE

## INGREDIENTS

- 1 cup basmati rice
- 3 tablespoons avocado oil
- 2.5 cups chicken stock
- ½ teaspoon dried dill
- 10 oz chicken breast, skinless, boneless, chopped

## DIRECTIONS

1. Mix oil with rice and roast it in the saucepan for 5 minutes over the low heat.
2. Then add chicken and chicken stock.
3. Add dill, stir the ingredients and cook the meal on medium heat for 15 minutes or until all ingredients are cooked.

CALORIES: 213 Kcal    FAT: 13.4 g    PROTEIN: 14.8 g    CARBOHYDRATES: 32.1 g

*Preparation: 10 min*     *Cooking: 20 min*     *Servings: 6*

## 552. RICE WITH GRILLED TOMATOES

### INGREDIENTS

- 1 cup of basmati rice
- 2.5 cups chicken stock
- 1 teaspoon olive oil
- 2 tomatoes, roughly sliced

### DIRECTIONS

1. Sprinkle the tomatoes with olive oil and grill in the preheated to 400F grill for 1 minute per side.
2. Then cook rice with chicken stock for 15 minutes.
3. Transfer the cooked rice in the bowls and top with grilled tomatoes.

CALORIES: 124 Kcal     FAT: 2.1 g     PROTEIN: 7.8 g     CARBOHYDRATES: 21 g

---

*Preparation: 10 min*     *Cooking: 0 min*     *Servings: 6*

## 553. RICE AND MEAT SALAD

### INGREDIENTS

- 1 cup white cabbage, shredded
- 1 cup long grain rice, cooked
- 8 oz beef steak, cooked, cut into the strips
- 1/3 cup plain yogurt
- 1 teaspoon salt
- 1 teaspoon chives, chopped

### DIRECTIONS

1. Put cabbage and rice in the big bowl.
2. Add white rice and meat strips.
3. Then add plain yogurt, chives, and salt.
4. Stir the salad until homogenous.

CALORIES: 210 Kcal     FAT: 5 g     PROTEIN: 9 g     CARBOHYDRATES: 22 g

Preparation: 10 min  Cooking: 30 min  Servings: 6

## 554. VEGETABLE RICE

### INGREDIENTS

- 2 cups wild rice
- 1 teaspoon Italian seasonings
- 1 tablespoon olive oil
- ¼ cup carrot, sliced
- ¼ cup celery, sliced
- ½ cup snap peas, frozen
- 5 cups of water

### DIRECTIONS

1. Mix 4 cups of water and wild rice in the saucepan.
2. Cook the rice for 15 minutes or until the rice soaks all liquid.
3. Then heat the olive oil in the separated saucepan.
4. Add the carrot and the celery and roast for 5 minutes.
5. Add snap peas, water, and rice.
6. Stir well and close the lid.
7. Cook the rice for 10 minutes.
8. Serve and enjoy.

CALORIES: 209 Kcal   FAT: 4.1 g   PROTEIN: 9.7 g   CARBOHYDRATES: 25.2 g

*Preparation: 10 min*     *Cooking: 0 min*     *Servings: 6*

# 555. RICE BOWL

## INGREDIENTS

- 1 cup of basmati rice, cooked
- 4 oz beef sirloin, grilled
- ½ cup tomatoes, chopped
- 2 tablespoons soy sauce
- 1 teaspoon ground paprika
- 2 oz scallions, sliced

## DIRECTIONS

1. Put the cooked rice in the serving bowls.
2. Add beef sirloin, tomatoes, and scallions.
3. Then sprinkle the meal with soy sauce and ground paprika.

CALORIES: 243 Kcal     FAT: 10.4 g     PROTEIN: 12 g     CARBOHYDRATES: 34 g

---

*Preparation: 10 min*     *Cooking: 20 min*     *Servings: 4*

# 556. SCALLIONS RICE

## INGREDIENTS

- 1 cup basmati rice
- 3 tablespoons olive oil
- 2 cups chicken stock
- ½ teaspoon dried dill
- 1 cup scallions, chopped
- ½ cup of chopped parmesan

## DIRECTIONS

1. Mix oil with rice and roast it in the saucepan for 5 minutes over the low heat.
2. Then add the scallions and chicken stock.
3. Add the dill, stir the ingredients and cook the meal on medium heat for 15 minutes or until all ingredients are cooked.
4. Sprinkle with parmesan, then serve.

CALORIES: 254 Kcal     FAT: 9.8 g     PROTEIN: 12.3 g     CARBOHYDRATES: 28 g

*Preparation: 10 min* — *Cooking: 20 min* — *Servings: 4*

## 557. TOMATO RICE

### INGREDIENTS

- 1 cup basmati rice
- 3 cups chicken stock
- 1 teaspoon ground coriander
- ¼ teaspoon dried thyme
- 2 tablespoons olive oil
- 2 tablespoons tomato paste
- 1 tablespoon chopped parsley

### DIRECTIONS

1. Roast the rice with olive oil in the saucepan for 5 minutes. Stir it.
2. Then add thyme, coriander, and tomato paste.
3. Add water, mix the rice mixture, and close the lid.
4. Cook the rice for 15 minutes over the medium heat.
5. Sprinkle with parsley, then serve.

CALORIES: 206 Kcal — FAT: 6.4 g — PROTEIN: 7.5 g — CARBOHYDRATES: 31 g

*Preparation: 10 min*  *Cooking: 25 min*  *Servings: 2*

## 558. ZUCCHINI RICE

### INGREDIENTS

- ½ cup of long grain rice
- 1.5 cup chicken stock
- 1 zucchini, cubed
- 1 tablespoon olive oil
- 1 teaspoon curry powder
- 1 tablespoon raisins

### DIRECTIONS

1. Mix rice and chicken stock in the saucepan and cook for 15 minutes or until the rice soaks the liquid.
2. Then heat the olive oil.
3. Add zucchini in the oil and roast for 5 minutes.
4. After this, sprinkle the zucchini with curry powder, add raisins and rice.
5. Carefully mix the rice and cook for 5 minutes.

CALORIES: 197 Kcal   FAT: 3.4 g   PROTEIN: 9.1 g   CARBOHYDRATES: 25 g

---

*Preparation: 10 min*  *Cooking: 20 min*  *Servings: 4*

## 559. RICE SOUP

### INGREDIENTS

- 3 cups chicken stock
- ½ pound chicken breast, shredded
- 1 tablespoon chives, chopped
- 1 egg, whisked
- ½ white onion, diced
- 1 bell pepper, chopped
- 1 tablespoon olive oil
- ¼ cup arborio rice
- ½ teaspoon salt
- 1 tablespoon fresh cilantro, chopped

### DIRECTIONS

1. Pour olive oil in the stock pan and preheat it.
2. Add onion and bell pepper. Roast the vegetables for 3-4 minutes. Stir them from time to time.
3. After this, add rice and stir well.
4. Cook the ingredients for 3 minutes over the medium heat.
5. Then add chicken stock and stir the soup well.
6. Add salt and bring the soup to boil.
7. Add shredded chicken breast, cilantro, and chives. Add egg and stir it carefully.
8. Close the lid and simmer the soup for 5 minutes over the medium heat.
9. Remove the cooked soup from the heat.

CALORIES: 263 Kcal   FAT: 9.4 g   PROTEIN: 11 g   CARBOHYDRATES: 31 g

Preparation: 10 min   Cooking: 30 min   Servings: 4

## 560. SEAFOOD RICE

### INGREDIENTS

- ½ cup seafood mix, frozen
- ½ cup of long grain rice
- 3 cups of water
- 1 tablespoon olive oil
- ½ teaspoon ground coriander

### DIRECTIONS

1. Boil the rice with water for 15-18 minutes or until it soaks all water.
2. Then heat olive oil in the saucepan.
3. Add seafood mix and ground coriander. Cook the ingredients for 10 minutes on low heat.
4. Then add rice, stir well, and cook for 5 minutes more.

CALORIES: 173 Kcal   FAT: 6.4 g   PROTEIN: 7.4 g   CARBOHYDRATES: 22.1 g

Preparation: 5 min	Cooking: 20 min	Servings: 6

## 561. RICE WITH PRUNES

### INGREDIENTS

- 1 ½ cups basmati rice
- 3 tablespoons organic canola oil
- 5 prunes, chopped
- ¼ cup cream cheese
- 3 ½ cups water
- ½ teaspoon salt

### DIRECTIONS

1. Mix water and basmati rice in the saucepan and boil for 15 minutes on low heat.
2. Then add cream cheese, salt, and prunes.
3. Stir the rice carefully and bring it to boil.
4. Add organic canola oil and cook for 1 minute more.

CALORIES: 187 Kcal	FAT: 6.1 g	PROTEIN: 5.5 g	CARBOHYDRATES: 30 g

---

Preparation: 10 min	Cooking: 10 min	Servings: 6

## 562. RICE AND FISH CAKES

### INGREDIENTS

- 6 oz salmon, canned, shredded
- 1 egg, beaten
- ¼ cup of basmati rice, cooked
- 1 teaspoon dried cilantro
- ½ teaspoon chili flakes
- 1 tablespoon organic canola oil

### DIRECTIONS

1. Mix salmon with egg, basmati rice, dried cilantro, and chili flakes.
2. Heat the organic canola oil in the skillet.
3. Make small cakes from the salmon mixture and put in the hot oil.
4. Roast the cakes for 2 minutes per side or until they are light brown.

CALORIES: 204 Kcal	FAT: 9.1 g	PROTEIN: 14 g	CARBOHYDRATES: 32.4 g

Preparation: 10 min  Cooking: 30 min  Servings: 6

## 563. VEGETARIAN PILAF

### INGREDIENTS

- 1 cup of long grain rice
- 2 cups of water
- 1 carrot, grated
- 2 tablespoons olive oil
- 1 tablespoon dried dill
- ½ teaspoon dried mint
- ½ teaspoon salt

### DIRECTIONS

1. Boil rice with water for 15 minutes on medium heat.
2. Meanwhile, melt the olive oil and add the carrot.
3. Roast the carrot for 10 minutes or until it is soft.
4. Then add dried dill, mint, and cooked rice.
5. Carefully stir the pilaf and cook for 5 minutes.

CALORIES: 187 Kcal  FAT: 6.4 g  PROTEIN: 8.7 g  CARBOHYDRATES: 34.4 g

*Preparation: 10 min*  *Cooking: 15 min*  *Servings: 6*

## 564. SALSA RICE

### INGREDIENTS

- 9 oz long grain rice
- 4 cups chicken stock
- 1 cup of salsa
- 2 tablespoons avocado oil

### DIRECTIONS

1. Mix chicken stock and rice in the saucepan.
2. Cook the rice for 15 minutes on medium heat.
3. Then cool it to the room temperature and mix with avocado oil and salsa.

CALORIES: 177 Kcal    FAT: 10.5 g    PROTEIN: 15 g    CARBOHYDRATES: 32.1 g

---

*Preparation: 15 min*  *Cooking: 35 min*  *Servings: 6*

## 565. RICE ROLLS

### INGREDIENTS

- 4 white cabbage leaves
- 4 oz ground chicken
- ½ teaspoon garlic powder
- ¼ cup of long grain rice, cooked
- ½ cup chicken stock
- ½ cup tomatoes, chopped

### DIRECTIONS

1. In the bowl, mix ground chicken, garlic powder, and rice.
2. Then put the rice mixture on every cabbage leaf and roll.
3. Arrange the rice rolls in the saucepan.
4. Add chicken stock and tomatoes and close the lid.
5. Cook the rice rolls for 35 minutes on low heat.

CALORIES: 241 Kcal    FAT: 15.4 g    PROTEIN: 12.7 g    CARBOHYDRATES: 32 g

Preparation: 5 min    Cooking: 20 min    Servings: 2

## 566. QUINOA AND PEPPER

### INGREDIENTS

- 1 red bell pepper, cubed
- 1 tablespoon lemon juice
- 1 cup quinoa
- 2 cups of water
- 1 tablespoon chopped mint

### DIRECTIONS

1. Put the red bell pepper in a saucepan.
2. Add lemon juice and water.
3. Cook the pepper for 10 minutes.
4. Add the quinoa and cook the meal for 10 minutes.
5. Remove the cooked meal from the heat, add the mint and stir well.
6. Serve and enjoy.

CALORIES: 237 Kcal    FAT: 5.8 g    PROTEIN: 10.4 g    CARBOHYDRATES: 33 g

*Preparation: 10 min*     *Cooking: 30 min*     *Servings: 6*

## 567. RICE STEW WITH SQUID

### INGREDIENTS

- 5 oz long grain rice
- 4 oz squid, sliced
- 1 jalapeno pepper, chopped
- ½ cup tomatoes, chopped
- 1 onion, diced
- 2 cups chicken stock
- 1 tablespoon avocado oil

### DIRECTIONS

1. Roast the onion with avocado oil in the skillet for 3-4 minutes or until the onion is light brown.
2. Add squid, jalapeno pepper, and tomatoes.
3. Cook the ingredients for 7 minutes.
4. Then cook rice with water for 15 minutes.
5. Add cooked rice in the squid mixture, stir, and cook for 3 minutes more.

CALORIES: 167 Kcal     FAT: 4.8 g     PROTEIN: 5.9 g     CARBOHYDRATES: 29 g

---

*Preparation: 10 min*     *Cooking: 10 min*     *Servings: 6*

## 568. CREAMY MILLET

### INGREDIENTS

- ½ cup millet
- 1 oz cream cheese
- ¼ teaspoon salt
- 1 ½ cups hot water

### DIRECTIONS

1. Mix hot water and millet in the saucepan.
2. Boil it for 8 minutes on low heat.
3. Add cream cheese and salt.
4. Carefully stir the cooked millet.

CALORIES: 208 Kcal     FAT: 2.4 g     PROTEIN: 3.5 g     CARBOHYDRATES: 37 g

*Preparation: 10 min*     *Cooking: 20 min*     *Servings: 6*

## 569. CHICKEN RICE

### INGREDIENTS

- 2 cups chicken stock
- 1-pound chicken breast, shredded
- 1 cup of rice, cooked
- 3 tablespoons lemon juice
- 1/3 cup fresh parsley, chopped
- ½ teaspoon salt
- ¼ teaspoon ground black pepper
- 1 cup black cabbage

### DIRECTIONS

1. Pour the chicken stock in the saucepan and bring to boil.
2. Add the rice, lemon juice, black cabbage and salt.
3. Cook for 20 minutes.
4. Add shredded chicken breast, parsley, and ground black pepper.
5. Boil the for 5 minutes more.
6. Serve and enjoy.

CALORIES: 235 Kcal     FAT: 13.7 g     PROTEIN: 19.4 g     CARBOHYDRATES: 24.7 g

*Preparation: 15 min*        Cooking: 7 min        *Servings: 4*

## 570. OTMEAL CAKES

**INGREDIENTS**

- ½ cup oatmeal
- 1 egg, beaten
- 1 carrot, grated
- 1 tablespoon olive oil
- 1 teaspoon flax meal

**DIRECTIONS**

1. Put oatmeal, egg, grated carrot, and flax meal in the blender. Blend the mixture well.
2. Then heat olive oil in the skillet.
3. Make the medium size cakes from the oatmeal mixture and cook for 3 minutes per side on medium heat.

CALORIES: 157 Kcal      FAT: 6.7 g      PROTEIN: 12.4 g      CARBOHYDRATES: 22 g

---

*Preparation: 5 min*        Cooking: 13 min        *Servings: 2*

## 571. YOGURT BUCKWHEAT

**INGREDIENTS**

- ½ cup buckwheat
- 1 ½ cup chicken stock
- 1 tablespoon plain yogurt

**DIRECTIONS**

1. Put all ingredients in the saucepan and close the lid.
2. Cook the meal for 13 minutes on low heat or until the buckwheat soaks all liquid.
3. Carefully stir the cooked meal.

CALORIES: 154 Kcal      FAT: 13 g      PROTEIN: 9 g      CARBOHYDRATES: 20 g

*Preparation: 10 min*      *Cooking: 15 min*      *Servings: 4*

## 572. HALLOUMI BUCKWHEAT BOWL

**INGREDIENTS**

- 1 cup buckwheat
- 2 ½ cups chicken stock
- 4 oz halloumi cheese
- 1 tablespoon olive oil
- ½ teaspoon dried thyme

**DIRECTIONS**

1. Mix chicken stock and buckwheat in the saucepan, bring to boil and cook for 7 minutes on medium heat.
2. After this, sprinkle the halloumi cheese with olive oil and dried thyme.
3. Grill it for 2 minutes per side or until the cheese is light brown.
4. Then put the cooked buckwheat in the bowls.
5. Chop the cheese roughly and top the buckwheat with it.

CALORIES: 193 Kcal      FAT: 6.6 g      PROTEIN: 9 g      CARBOHYDRATES: 16 g

---

*Preparation: 10 min*      *Cooking: 7 min*      *Servings: 4*

## 573. AROMATIC GREEN MILLET

**INGREDIENTS**

- 1 cup millet
- 2 cups of water
- 4 tablespoons pesto sauce
- ¼ teaspoon cayenne pepper

**DIRECTIONS**

1. Mix water and millet in the saucepan and boil for 7 minutes.
2. Then add cayenne pepper and pesto sauce.
3. Stir the millet until homogenous and green.

CALORIES: 193 Kcal      FAT: 9.7 g      PROTEIN: 12.4 g      CARBOHYDRATES: 24 g

*Preparation: 5 min*  *Cooking: 4 min*  *Servings: 4*

## 574. ALMOND QUINOA

**INGREDIENTS**

- 1 cup quinoa
- 2 cups of water
- 1 cup organic almond milk
- ½ cup strawberries, sliced
- 1 tablespoon honey

**DIRECTIONS**

1. Pour water and milk in the saucepan and bring to boil.
2. Add quinoa and cook it for 12 minutes.
3. Then cool the cooked quinoa and add honey. Stir.
4. Transfer the quinoa in the bowls and top with strawberries.

CALORIES: 252 Kcal  FAT: 6.1 g  PROTEIN: 5.2 g  CARBOHYDRATES: 26 g

---

*Preparation: 10 min*  *Cooking: 1 min*  *Servings: 8*

## 575. SPRING ROLLS WITH QUINOA

**INGREDIENTS**

- 8 rice pepper wraps
- 1 cup quinoa, cooked
- 1 carrot, cut into strips
- 1 cup lettuce leaves
- 1 tablespoon olive oil

**DIRECTIONS**

1. Make the rice pepper wraps wet.
2. Then put the cooked quinoa on every rice pepper wrap.
3. Add carrot and lettuce leaves and wrap them into the rolls.
4. Brush every roll with olive oil and put it in the hot skillet.
5. Roast the spring rolls for 20 seconds per side.

CALORIES: 257 Kcal  FAT: 4.2 g  PROTEIN: 12.4 g  CARBOHYDRATES: 20.1 g

*Preparation: 10 min*  *Cooking: 25 min*  *Servings: 6*

## 576. MUSHROOM QUINOA SKILLET

### INGREDIENTS

- 1 cup mushrooms, sliced
- ½ cup of water
- 1 tablespoon olive oil
- 1 teaspoon Italian seasonings
- ½ cup quinoa
- ½ cup organic almond milk
- ¼ teaspoon dried thyme

### DIRECTIONS

1. Roast mushrooms with olive oil in the saucepan for 10 minutes.
2. Then stir them well, add Italian seasonings, dried thyme, and quinoa.
3. Add almond milk and water.
4. Close the lid and simmer the meal for 15 minutes. Stir it from time to time to avoid burning.

CALORIES: 195 Kcal   FAT: 6.2 g   PROTEIN: 5 g   CARBOHYDRATES: 21 g

---

*Preparation: 10 min*  *Cooking: 15 min*  *Servings: 8*

## 577. STRAWBERRY QUINOA BOWL

### INGREDIENTS

- 2 ½ cups quinoa, cooked
- ¼ cup strawberries, roughly chopped
- ½ cup fresh spinach, chopped
- 2 pecans, chopped
- 1 tablespoon balsamic vinegar
- 1 teaspoon avocado oil

### DIRECTIONS

1. Mix quinoa, fresh spinach, and pecans in the big bowl.
2. Then add strawberries and avocado oil.
3. Gently shake the mixture and transfer in the serving bowls.
4. Sprinkle every serving with a small amount of balsamic vinegar.

CALORIES: 215 Kcal   FAT: 11.4 g   PROTEIN: 14.2 g   CARBOHYDRATES: 24 g

*Preparation: 15 min*     *Cooking: 30 min*     *Servings: 6*

# 578. QUINOA MEATBALLS

## INGREDIENTS

- ½ cup quinoa, cooked
- ½ cup ground pork
- 1 tablespoon chives, chopped
- 1 egg, beaten
- 1 tablespoon sesame seeds
- 1 teaspoon chili flakes
- 1 cup tomato juice

## DIRECTIONS

1. In the bowl mi quinoa, ground pork, chives, egg, sesame seeds, and chili flakes.
2. Then make the small meatballs and put them in the baking pan.
3. Top the meatballs with tomato juice and cook in the preheated to 375°F oven for 30 minutes.

CALORIES: 177 Kcal     FAT: 8.5 g     PROTEIN: 10.2 g     CARBOHYDRATES: 30 g

---

*Preparation: 000 min*     *Cooking: 000 min*     *Servings: 6*

# 579. STIR-FRIED SPELT

## INGREDIENTS

- 1 cup spelt, cooked
- 1 egg, beaten
- 1 tablespoon olive oil
- ½ teaspoon chili flakes
- 

## DIRECTIONS

1. Heat olive oil and egg beaten egg.
2. Cook it for 1 minute and then stir it carefully.
3. Add cooked spelt and chili flakes.
4. Fry the meal for 7 minutes. Stir it from time to time.

CALORIES: 157 Kcal     FAT: 3.4 g     PROTEIN: 9.7 g     CARBOHYDRATES: 24.1 g

*Preparation: 10 min*  *Cooking: 15 min*  *Servings: 6*

## 580. QUICK SPELT SKILLET

**INGREDIENTS**

- 2 oz fresh spinach, chopped
- 2 oz asparagus, chopped
- 1/3 cup spelt, cooked
- 1 tablespoon olive oil
- ½ teaspoon curry powder

**DIRECTIONS**

1. Line the skillet with baking paper.
2. Put all ingredients in the prepared skillet, flatten them gently and transfer in the preheated to 365°F oven.
3. Cook the meal for 15 minutes.

CALORIES: 174 Kcal  FAT: 7.9 g  PROTEIN: 8.2 g  CARBOHYDRATES: 21 g

---

*Preparation: 10 min*  *Cooking: 0 min*  *Servings: 4*

## 581. BULGUR BOWL

**INGREDIENTS**

- 6 oz salmon, boiled, chopped
- ½ cup bulgur, cooked
- 1 cup fresh cilantro, chopped
- 1 cup tomato, chopped
- 3 tablespoons lemon juice
- 1 tablespoon olive oil

**DIRECTIONS**

1. Put salmon, bulgur, cilantro, and tomato in the bowl.
2. Add lemon juice and olive oil.
3. Shake the mixture well and transfer in the serving bowls.

CALORIES: 193 Kcal  FAT: 8.2 g  PROTEIN: 13 g  CARBOHYDRATES: 25 g

# 26 Pasta and Pizza

*Preparation: 20 min*     *Cooking: 20 min / Resting: 2 hours and 30 min*     Servings: 6

# 582. HERB-TOPPED FOCACCIA

## INGREDIENTS

- 1 tablespoon dried rosemary or 3 tablespoons minced fresh rosemary
- 1 tablespoon dried thyme or 3 tablespoons minced fresh thyme leaves
- ½ cup extra-virgin olive oil
- 1 teaspoon sugar
- 1 cup warm water
- 1 (¼-ounce) packet active dry yeast
- 2½ cups flour, divided
- 1 teaspoon salt
- 1 lemon, sliced

## DIRECTIONS

1. In a small bowl, combine the rosemary and thyme with the olive oil.
2. In a large bowl, whisk together the sugar, water, and yeast. Let stand for 5 minutes.
3. Add 1 cup of flour, half of the olive oil mixture, and the salt to the mixture in the large bowl. Stir to combine.
4. Add the remaining 1½ cups flour to the large bowl. Using your hands, combine dough until it starts to pull away from the sides of the bowl.
5. Put the dough on a floured board or countertop and knead 10 to 12 times. Place the dough in a well-oiled bowl and cover with plastic wrap. Put it in a warm, dry space for 2 hours.
6. Oil a baking pan and place the dough into it.
7. Evenly pour the remaining half of the olive oil mixture over the dough. Let the dough rise for another 30 minutes. While you wait, preheat the oven to 450°F.
8. Decorate the dough with lemon slices, then place it into the oven and let cook for 18 to 20 minutes.

CALORIES: 254 Kcal     FAT: 6.3 g     PROTEIN: 10.3 g     CARBOHYDRATES: 29.4 g

Preparation: 10 min  Cooking: 25 min  Servings: 4

## 583. ONION FLATBREAD WITH ARUGULA

### INGREDIENTS

- 4 tablespoons extra-virgin olive oil, divided
- 2 large onions, sliced into ¼-inch-thick slices
- 1 teaspoon salt, divided
- 1 sheet puff pastry
- 1 (5-ounce) package goat cheese
- 8 ounces arugula
- ½ teaspoon freshly ground black pepper

### DIRECTIONS

1. Preheat the oven to 400°F.
2. In a large skillet over medium heat, cook 3 tablespoons olive oil, the onions, and ½ teaspoon of salt, stirring, for 10 to 12 minutes, until the onions are translucent and golden brown.
3. To assemble, line a baking sheet with parchment paper. Lay the puff pastry flat on the parchment paper.
4. Evenly distribute the onions and the goat cheese on the dough.
5. Put the dough in the oven to bake for 10 to 12 minutes.
6. Remove the pastry from the oven, set aside. In a medium bowl, add the arugula, remaining 1 tablespoon of olive oil, remaining ½ teaspoon of salt, and ½ teaspoon black pepper; toss to evenly dress the arugula.
7. Cut the pastry into even squares. Top the pastry with dressed arugula and serve.

CALORIES: 185 Kcal  FAT: 9.5 g  PROTEIN: 10.8 g  CARBOHYDRATES: 29.6 g

---

Preparation: 5 min  Cooking: 20 min  Servings: 4

## 584. SPAGHETTI ALL'OLIO

### INGREDIENTS

- 8 oz. spaghetti
- 3 tablespoons olive oil
- 4 garlic cloves, minced
- 2 red peppers, sliced
- 1 tablespoon lemon juice
- Salt and pepper to taste
- ½ cup grated parmesan cheese

### DIRECTIONS

1. Preheat a pot of salty water.
2. Heat the oil in a skillet and add the garlic. Cook for 30 seconds then stir in the red peppers and cook for 1 more minute on low heat, making sure to only infuse them, not to burn or fry them.
3. Add the lemon juice and remove off heat.
4. Cook the spaghetti in a large pot of boiling salty water for 8 minutes or as stated on the package, just until they become al dente.
5. Drain the spaghetti well and mix them with the garlic and pepper oil.
6. Serve right away.

CALORIES: 297 Kcal  FAT: 6.5 g  PROTEIN: 7.2 g  CARBOHYDRATES: 35.2 g

*Preparation: 10 min*     *Cooking: 20 min*     *Servings: 4*

# 585. QUICK SHRIMP SPAGHETTI

## INGREDIENTS

- 8 ounces spaghetti pasta
- ¼ cup extra-virgin olive oil
- 3 tablespoons garlic, minced
- 1-pound large shrimps (21-25), peeled and deveined
- ⅓ cup lemon juice
- 1 tablespoon lemon zest
- ½ teaspoon salt
- ½ teaspoon freshly ground black pepper
- ½ cup little tomatoes

## DIRECTIONS

1. Bring a large pot of salted water to a boil. Add the fettuccine and cook for 8 minutes.
2. In the meantime, in a large saucepan over medium heat, cook the olive oil, garlic and the tomatoes for 1 minute.
3. Add the shrimp to the saucepan and cook for 3 minutes on each side. Remove the shrimp from the pan and set aside.
4. Add the lemon juice and lemon zest to the saucepan, along with the salt and pepper.
5. Reserve ½ cup of the pasta water and drain the pasta.
6. Add the pasta water to the saucepan with the lemon juice and zest and stir everything together. Add the pasta and toss together to evenly coat the pasta. Transfer the pasta to a serving dish and top with the cooked shrimp. Serve warm.

CALORIES: 391 Kcal     FAT: 9.1 g     PROTEIN: 13.1 g     CARBOHYDRATES: 36.8 g

*Preparation: 5 min*     *Cooking: 45 min*     *Servings: 4*

## 586. SPAGHETTI IN CLAM SAUCE

### INGREDIENTS

- 8 oz. spaghetti
- 2 tablespoons olive oil
- 2 garlic cloves, minced
- 2 tomatoes, peeled and diced
- 1 cup cherry tomatoes, halved
- 1-pound fresh clams, cleaned and rinsed
- 2 tablespoons white wine
- 1 teaspoon sherry vinegar

### DIRECTIONS

1. Heat the oil in a heavy saucepan and add the garlic. Cook for 30 seconds until fragrant then add the tomatoes, wine and vinegar.
2. Bring to a boil and cook for 5 minutes then stir in the clams and continue cooking for 10 more minutes.
3. In the meantime, bring a large pot of water to a boil with a pinch of salt and add the spaghetti.
4. Cook them for 8 minutes just until al dente. Drain well and mix with the clam sauce.
5. Serve the dish right away.

CALORIES: 305 Kcal     FAT: 8.8 g     PROTEIN: 8.1 g     CARBOHYDRATES: 37.1 g

---

*Preparation: 5 min*     *Cooking: 35 min*     *Servings: 4*

## 587. BROCCOLI PESTO SPAGHETTI

### INGREDIENTS

- 8 oz. spaghetti
- 1-pound broccoli, cut into florets
- 2 tablespoons olive oil
- 4 garlic cloves, chopped
- 4 basil leaves
- 2 tablespoons blanched almonds
- 1 lemon, juiced
- Salt and pepper to taste

### DIRECTIONS

1. For the pesto, combine the broccoli, oil, garlic, basil, lemon juice and almonds in a blender and pulse until well mixed and smooth.
2. Cook the spaghetti in a large pot of salty water for 8 minutes or until al dente. Drain well.
3. Mix the warm spaghetti with the broccoli pesto and serve right away.

CALORIES: 310 Kcal     FAT: 10.5 g     PROTEIN: 9.5 g     CARBOHYDRATES: 34.7 g

*Preparation: 5 min*      *Cooking: 15 min*      *Servings: 4*

# 588. TOMATO SPAGHETTI

## INGREDIENTS

- 8 oz. spaghetti
- 3 tablespoons olive oil
- 4 garlic cloves, sliced
- 1 jalapeno, sliced
- 2 cups cherry tomatoes
- Salt and pepper to taste
- 1 teaspoon balsamic vinegar
- ½ cup grated Parmesan
- 1 teaspoon chopped basil

## DIRECTIONS

1. Heat a large pot of water on medium flame. Add a pinch of salt and bring to a boil then add the pasta.
2. Cook for 8 minutes or until al dente.
3. While the pasta cooks, heat the oil in a skillet and add the garlic and jalapeno. Cook for 1 minute then stir in the tomatoes, as well as salt and pepper.
4. Cook for 5-7 minutes until the tomatoes' skins burst.
5. Add the vinegar and remove off heat.
6. Drain the pasta well and mix it with the tomato sauce.
7. Sprinkle with cheese and basil, then serve. away.

CALORIES: 358 Kcal      FAT: 12.2 g      PROTEIN: 9.7 g      CARBOHYDRATES: 36 g

*Preparation: 5 min*  *Cooking: 40 min*  *Servings: 4*

## 589. ROASTED EGGPLANT RED PEPPER PENNE

### INGREDIENTS

- 8 oz. penne
- 2 eggplants
- 4 roasted red bell peppers, sliced
- ½ teaspoon dried oregano
- 2 tablespoons olive oil
- Salt and pepper to taste

### DIRECTIONS

1. Heat a large pot of water on medium flame. Add a pinch of salt and bring it to a boil.
2. Add the penne and cook them until al dente, not more than 8 minutes.
3. Cut the eggplants in half, season them with salt and pepper and place them in a baking tray.
4. Cook in the preheated oven at 400F for 15 minutes.
5. When done, scoop out the flesh and chop it into fine bits. Mix with the sliced bell peppers, oregano and oil then adjust the taste with salt and pepper.
6. Stir in the cooked penne and serve the pasta right away.

CALORIES: 292 Kcal   FAT: 8.8 g   PROTEIN: 9.1 g   CARBOHYDRATES: 37.3 g

---

*Preparation: 7 min*  *Cooking: 25 min*  *Servings: 4*

## 590. GNOCCHI WITH SHRIMP

### INGREDIENTS

- ½ lb. Shrimp, Peeled and Deveined
- ¼ Cup Shallots, Sliced
- ½ Tablespoon + 1 Teaspoon Olive Oil
- 8 Ounces Shelf Stable Gnocchi
- ½ Bunch Asparagus, Cut into Thirds
- 3 Tablespoons Parmesan Cheese
- 1 Tablespoon Lemon Juice, Fresh
- ⅓ Cup Chicken Broth
- Sea Salt & Black Pepper to Taste

### DIRECTIONS

1. Start by heating a half a tablespoon of oil over medium heat, and then add in your gnocchi. Cook while stirring often until they turn plump and golden. This will take from seven to ten minutes. Place them in a bowl.
2. Heat your remaining teaspoon of oil with your shallots, cooking until they begin to brown. Make sure to stir, but this will take two minutes. Stir in the broth before adding your asparagus. Cover, and cook for three to four minutes.
3. Add the shrimp, seasoning with salt and pepper. Cook until they are pink and cooked through, which will take roughly four minutes.
4. Return the gnocchi to the skillet with lemon juice, cooking for another two minutes. Stir well, and then remove it from heat.
5. Sprinkle with parmesan, and let it stand for two minutes. Your cheese should melt. Serve warm.

CALORIES: 350 Kcal   FAT: 13.2 g   PROTEIN: 10.4 g   CARBOHYDRATES: 39 g

*Preparation: 20 min*  *Cooking: 30 min*  *Servings: 2*

## 591. LASAGNA ROLLS

### INGREDIENTS

- 2 zucchini, trimmed
- 1 cup Mozzarella, shredded
- 1 cup ground beef
- ½ teaspoon salt
- ½ teaspoon ground black pepper
- ½ teaspoon ground paprika
- ½ teaspoon dried oregano
- ¼ teaspoon cayenne pepper
- ⅓ cup tomato sauce
- 1 teaspoon olive oil
- ¼ cup Cheddar cheese, shredded
- ⅓ cup chicken stock

### DIRECTIONS

1. Slice the zucchini lengthwise.
2. In the mixing bowl, mix up together salt, ground beef, ground black pepper, ground paprika, and cayenne pepper.
3. Spread every zucchini slice with ground beef mixture and roll them.
4. Brush the casserole mold with olive oil from inside and arrange zucchini rolls.
5. Top every zucchini rolls with Mozzarella and Cheddar cheese.
6. Then mix up together tomato sauce, dried oregano, and chicken stock.
7. Pour the liquid over zucchini.
8. Cover the casserole mold with foil and secure the edges.
9. Bake lasagna rolls for 30 minutes at 355°F.

CALORIES: 357 Kcal    FAT: 18.2 g    PROTEIN: 16 g    CARBOHYDRATES: 10.1 g

---

*Preparation: 10 min*  *Cooking: 10 min*  *Servings: 4*

## 592. SIMPLE PESTO PASTA

### INGREDIENTS

- 1 pound spaghetti
- 4 cups fresh basil leaves, stems removed
- 3 cloves garlic
- 1 teaspoon salt
- ½ teaspoon freshly ground black pepper
- ¼ cup lemon juice
- ½ cup pine nuts, toasted
- ½ cup grated Parmesan cheese
- 1 cup extra-virgin olive oil

### DIRECTIONS

1. Bring a large pot of salted water to a boil. Add the spaghetti to the pot and cook for 8 minutes.
2. Put basil, garlic, salt, pepper, lemon juice, pine nuts, and Parmesan cheese in a food processor bowl with chopping blade and purée.
3. While the processor is running, slowly drizzle the olive oil through the top opening. Process until all the olive oil has been added.
4. Reserve ½ cup of the pasta water. Drain the pasta and put it into a bowl. Immediately add the pesto and pasta water to the pasta and toss everything together. Serve warm.

CALORIES: 310 Kcal    FAT: 8.9 g    PROTEIN: 10.3 g    CARBOHYDRATES: 33.4 g

*Preparation: 5 min*     *Cooking: 20 min*     *Servings: 2*

## 593. GREEK CHICKEN PENNE

### INGREDIENTS

- 1 Clove Garlic, Minced
- 8 Ounces Penne Pasta
- ½ lb. Chicken Breast Halves, Boneless, Skinless & Chopped
- ¼ Cup Red Onion, Chopped
- ¾ Tablespoon Butter
- 8 Ounces Artichoke Hearts, Canned
- 1 Small Tomato, Chopped
- 1 ½ tablespoons Parsley, Fresh & Chopped
- ¼ Cup Feta Cheese, Crumbled
- 1 Tablespoon Lemon Juice, Fresh
- ½ Teaspoon Oregano
- Sea Salt & Black Pepper to Taste

### DIRECTIONS

1. Start by cooking your pasta per package instructions so that it's al dente. Drain your pasta and place it to the side.
2. Get out a skillet and melt your butter over medium-high heat. Cook your onion and garlic for two minutes before adding in your chicken. Cook for six more minutes, making sure to stir occasionally to keep it from burning.
3. Reduce the heat to medium-low before draining and chopping your artichoke hearts. Throw them in the skillet with your parsley, tomato, oregano, lemon juice, feta cheese and drained pasta. Heat the skillet and cook for three minutes.
4. Season with salt and pepper, and serve warm.

CALORIES: 295 Kcal     FAT: 10 g     PROTEIN: 9.4 g     CARBOHYDRATES: 31 g

---

*Preparation: 10 min*     *Cooking: 15 min*     *Servings: 4*

## 594. ZA'ATAR PIZZA

### INGREDIENTS

- 1 sheet puff pastry
- ¼ cup extra-virgin olive oil
- ⅓ cup za'atar seasoning

### DIRECTIONS

1. Preheat the oven to 350°F.
2. Put the puff pastry on a parchment-lined baking sheet. Cut the pastry into desired slices.
3. Brush the pastry with olive oil. Sprinkle with the za'atar.
4. Put the pastry in the oven and bake for 10 to 12 minutes or until edges are lightly browned and puffed up. Serve warm or at room temperature.

CALORIES: 253 Kcal     FAT: 4.2 g     PROTEIN: 5.3 g     CARBOHYDRATES: 36 g

*Preparation: 10 min*  *Cooking: 15 min*  *Servings: 6*

# 595. WHITE PIZZA WITH PROSCIUTTO

## INGREDIENTS

- 1-pound prepared pizza dough
- ½ cup ricotta cheese
- 1 tablespoon garlic, minced
- 1 cup grated mozzarella cheese
- 3 ounces prosciutto, thinly sliced
- ½ cup fresh arugula
- ½ teaspoon freshly ground black pepper

## DIRECTIONS

1. Preheat the oven to 450°F. Roll out the pizza dough on a floured surface.
2. Put the pizza dough on a parchment-lined baking sheet or pizza sheet. Put the dough in the oven and bake for 8 minutes.
3. In a small bowl, mix together the ricotta, garlic, and mozzarella.
4. Remove the pizza dough from the oven and spread the cheese mixture over the top. Bake for another 5 to 6 minutes.
5. Top the pizza with prosciutto, arugula, and pepper; serve warm.

CALORIES: 273 Kcal    FAT: 8.3 g    PROTEIN: 7.3 g    CARBOHYDRATES: 33.4 g

---

*Preparation: 20 min*  *Cooking: 15 min*  *Servings: 4*

# 596. FLAT MEAT PIES

## INGREDIENTS

- ½ pound ground beef
- 1 small onion, finely chopped
- 1 medium tomato, finely diced and strained
- ½ teaspoon salt
- ½ teaspoon freshly ground black pepper
- 2 sheets puff pastry

## DIRECTIONS

1. Preheat the oven to 400°F.
2. In a medium bowl, combine the beef, onion, tomato, salt, and pepper. Set aside.
3. Line 2 baking sheets with parchment paper. Cut the puff pastry dough into 4-inch squares and lay them flat on the baking sheets.
4. Scoop about 2 tablespoons of beef mixture onto each piece of dough. Spread the meat on the dough, leaving a ½-inch edge on each side.
5. Put the meat pies in the oven and bake for 12 to 15 minutes until edges are golden brown.

CALORIES: 305 Kcal    FAT: 10.9 g    PROTEIN: 9.4 g    CARBOHYDRATES: 30 g

*Preparation: 10 min*  *Cooking: 40 min*  *Servings: 6*

## 597. MEATY BAKED PENNE

### INGREDIENTS

- 1-pound penne pasta
- 1-pound ground beef
- 1 teaspoon salt
- 1 (25-ounce) jar marinara sauce
- 1 (1-pound) bag baby spinach, washed
- 3 cups shredded mozzarella cheese, divided

### DIRECTIONS

1. Bring a large pot of salted water to a boil, add the penne, and cook for 7 minutes. Reserve 2 cups of e pasta water and drain the pasta.
2. Preheat the oven to 350°F.
3. In a large saucepan over medium heat, cook the ground beef and salt. Brown the ground beef for about 5 minutes.
4. Stir in marinara sauce, and 2 cups of pasta water. Let simmer for 5 minutes.
5. Add a handful of spinach at a time into the sauce, and cook for another 3 minutes.
6. To assemble, in a 9-by-13-inch baking dish, add the pasta and pour the pasta sauce over it. Stir in 1½ cups of the mozzarella cheese. Cover the dish with foil and bake for 20 minutes.
7. After 20 minutes, remove the foil, top with the rest of the mozzarella, and bake for another 10 minutes. Serve warm.

CALORIES: 273 Kcal  FAT: 9.3 g  PROTEIN: 10 g  CARBOHYDRATES: 32 g

---

*Preparation: 10 min*  *Cooking: 10 min*  *Servings: 4*

## 598. CHEESY SPAGHETTI WITH PINE NUTS

### INGREDIENTS

- 8 ounces spaghetti
- 4 tablespoons (½ stick) unsalted butter
- 1 teaspoon freshly ground black pepper
- ½ cup pine nuts
- 1 cup fresh grated Parmesan cheese, divided

### DIRECTIONS

1. Bring a large pot of salted water to a boil. Add the pasta and cook for 8 minutes.
2. In a large saucepan over medium heat, combine the butter, black pepper, and pine nuts. Cook for 2 to 3 minutes or until the pine nuts are lightly toasted.
3. Reserve ½ cup of the pasta water. Drain the pasta and put it into the pan with the pine nuts.
4. Add ¾ cup of Parmesan cheese and the reserved pasta water to the pasta and toss everything together to evenly coat the pasta.
5. To serve, put the pasta in a serving dish and top with the remaining ¼ cup of Parmesan cheese.

CALORIES: 297 Kcal  FAT: 9 g  PROTEIN: 11 g  CARBOHYDRATES: 35 g

*Preparation: 5 min*      *Cooking: 20 min*      *Servings: 6*

## 599. PROSCIUTTO PITA BREAD PIZZA

**INGREDIENTS**

- 4 pita breads
- 8 figs, quartered
- 8 slices prosciutto
- 8 oz. mozzarella, crumbled

**DIRECTIONS**

1. Place the pita breads on a baking tray.
2. Top with crumbled cheese then figs and prosciutto.
3. Bake in the preheated oven at 350F for 8 minutes.
4. Serve the pizza right away.

CALORIES: 381 Kcal      FAT: 11.7 g      PROTEIN: 13.2 g      CARBOHYDRATES: 37.5 g

---

*Preparation: 5 min*      *Cooking: 25 min*      *Servings: 6*

## 600. CREAMY GARLIC-PARMESAN CHICKEN PASTA

**INGREDIENTS**

- 2 boneless, skinless chicken breasts
- 3 tablespoons extra-virgin olive oil
- 1½ teaspoons salt
- 1 large onion, thinly sliced
- 3 tablespoons garlic, minced
- 1-pound fettuccine pasta
- 1 cup heavy (whipping) cream
- ¾ cup freshly grated Parmesan cheese, divided
- ½ teaspoon freshly ground black pepper

**DIRECTIONS**

1. Bring a large pot of salted water to a simmer.
2. Cut the chicken into thin strips.
3. In a large skillet over medium heat, cook the olive oil and chicken for 3 minutes.
4. Next add the salt, onion, and garlic to the pan with the chicken. Cook for 7 minutes.
5. Bring the pot of salted water to a boil and add the pasta, then let it cook for 7 minutes.
6. While the pasta is cooking, add the cream, ½ cup of Parmesan cheese, and black pepper to the chicken; simmer for 3 minutes.
7. Reserve ½ cup of the pasta water. Drain the pasta and add it to the chicken cream sauce.
8. Add the reserved pasta water to the pasta and toss together. Let simmer for 2 minutes. Top with the remaining ¼ cup Parmesan cheese and serve warm.

CALORIES: 313 Kcal      FAT: 9 g      PROTEIN: 8.1 g      CARBOHYDRATES: 32 g

# 27 7-Days Meal Plan

# Day 1

**Breakfast**

Fig, Balsamic, And Ricotta Toast

Preparation time -> 20 minutes

Cooking time -> 15 minutes

Ingredients:

6 slice of dough bread

Olive oil, preferably extra virgin

½ tablespoon for honey

Balsamic vinegar

6 figs

Tomato juice

Direction:

Heat a pan over medium heat. Sear the bread on both sides with olive oil, put in the pan to cook for 4 minutes while flipping the sides.

While doing that, prepare the ricotta and put it in a bowl with pepper and honey.

Put aside the cooked toast and sprinkle or smear it with the ricotta mixture.

Serve with tomato juice when done and enjoy.

**Midmorning snack**

Plums

Preparation time -> 5 minutes

Direction:

Access 3 plums cut into four sides

Serve and enjoy.

**Lunch**

Mediterranean Salad

Preparation time -> 15 minutes

Cooking time -> 15 minutes

Ingredients:

Salad green mix 3 cups

1 cup of cucumber (sliced)

2 tablespoon of olive oil

3 tablespoon of carrot (grated)

Balsamic vinegar 2 cups

8 dough bread slices

Pepper

½ hummus

Direction:

Put all ingredients together: cucumber, carrot, and greens in a bowl.

Pour vinegar and oil in the bowl, sprinkle with pepper and salt.

Serve with hummus, pita and enjoy!

**Afternoon snack**

Raspberry

Preparation time -> 5 minutes

2 cups of raspberry

**Dinner**

Chicken Chili with Sweet Potatoes

Preparation time -> 10 minutes

Cooking time -> 40 minutes

Ingredients:

Chicken chili with sweet potatoes coupled

¼ diced avocado and 1 tablespoon of non-fat plain yogurt.

Directions:

Heat oil then add the ingredients that are available.

Add the chicken pieces to it then fry it for 4 minutes.

Heat vegetable oil then add spring onions and fry.

Add the ingredients and stir.

Add the fried chicken pieces and stir well. Serve warm with some noodles and yogurt

# Day 2

**Breakfast**

Raspberry with Muesli

Preparation time -> 20 minutes

Cooking time -> 15 minutes

Ingredients:

4 cups apple juice

4 cups rolled oats

3 green apples (grated)

3 tablespoon vanilla

500g raspberry

3 tablespoon honey

3 cups of yogurt (natural)

3 tablespoon vanilla essence

Direction:

Open fire and heat the juice in the pan for at least 3 minutes until warm.

Assemble vanilla and oats to a big bowl and pour your warm juice there.

Place in a freezer for 30 minutes until the juiced is soaked.

Remove it from the freezer, add raspberries and apple on the top and mix.

Add the natural yogurt, honey, and vanilla and stir them well.

Place the oat mixture in a glass and serve.

Enjoy.

**Lunch**

Roasted Quinoa Salad

Preparation time -> 10 minutes

Cooking time -> 25 minutes

Ingredients:

1 red onion

1 cup sweet potato

1 cup zucchini

2 cup tomato (cherry)

1 lemon

5 tablespoons olive oil

Salt, pepper

1 cup fresh parsley

2 tablespoon apple

5 cup quinoa

Direction:

Heat the oven till warm.

Add ingredients: onion, corn, tomatoes, sweet potatoes, and zucchini to the baking sheet in the oven.

Make juice with the lemon.

Pour olive oil to the lemon juice and then add salt and pepper.

Roast the veggie for 25 minutes.

Add quinoa to the transferred bowl of roasted veggie and toss them well.

Mix apple cider with olive oil in another bowl and make sure to toss them, too.

Lastly, access the parsley and garnish, serve and enjoy.

Afternoon snack

10 peanuts will be enough to keep you going until dinner time.

**Dinner**

Carrot and Chickpea Salad

Preparation time -> 5 minutes

Cooking time -> 25 minutes

Ingredients:

Clove garlic

½ cup olive oil

Lemon

2 (15 1/2 –ounce) cans chickpeas rinsed and drained

Ground cumin ½

3 carrots

½ teaspoon salt

Direction:

Make juice from the lemon.

Combine all the ingredients together: lemon juice, salt, olive oil, and chickpeas and place them in a blender.

Stir them a bit, transfer to a bowl, and place them on a freezer for 2 hours.

Cut and peel the carrots.

Serve with hummus and enjoy.

# Day 3

**Breakfast**

Fig and Ricotta Toast

Preparation time -> 5 minutes

Cooking time -> 10 minutes

Ingredients:

2 fig (sliced)

2 teaspoon sesame

2 dash cinnamon

2 teaspoon honey

½ cup skim ricotta

3 slice whole wheat

Direction:

Pick a bowl, combine skim ricotta with cinnamon and honey.

Smear the combination on whole wheat toast.

Spread some sesame seeds and fig.

Serve with tomato juice and enjoy.

**Mid-morning snack**

Preparation time -> 5 minutes

2 plums

**Lunch**

Tomato & Artichoke Gnocchi

Preparation time -> 10 minutes

Cooking time -> 20 minutes

Ingredients:

1 tablespoon salt and garlic

3 Olive oil

Tomatoes

1 jar Artichoke hearts (chopped)

2 tablespoon Basil fresh

6 ounces of cheese

2 tablespoon oregano

Gnocchi 1 package

Direction:

Heat olive oil in a pan.

Add salt and sauté until golden.

Add ingredients: artichokes, tomatoes, basil, and oregano.

Boil for 7 minutes.

Put half-size water in a pan heat, then add gnocchi and boil until you start seeing it float up to the water.

Stir all of them until they fully blend for about 7 minutes.

Serve while hot and enjoy.

**Afternoon snack**

Raspberry and Greek yogurt

Preparation time -> 5 minutes

Ingredients:

2 tablespoon almonds (sliced)

2 cup raspberry

½ cup of Greek yogurt

Direction:

Pick raspberry, mix Greek yogurt and almonds, then top with a raspberry.

Serve and enjoy.

**Dinner**

Fish Fillet

Preparation time -> 10 minutes

Cooking time -> 40 minutes

Ingredients:

Onion (chopped)

Olive oil

Tomatoes

½ cup white wine

Chopped parsley 2 tablespoon

Sugar preferably 1 teaspoon

Salt and pepper ¼ teaspoon

Fish fillet 1 kg

Cream 2 cups

Directions:

Heat the oven and fry chopped and peeled onion until golden brown.

Add tomatoes and stir them all together for 1 minute.

Add other ingredients: parsley, sugar, salt, pepper, and wine.

Continue stirring while boiling then add the fish fillet and continue stirring while flipping on each side.

Cook for 8 minutes.

Set aside. Pick cream and stir well in medium heat while tasting.

Pour your fish fillet when the cream is tasty and cook for another 2 minutes.

Serve with brown rice and side salad while hot and enjoy.

# Day 4

**Breakfast**

Creamy Blueberry and Pecan Oats

Cooking time -> 10 minutes

Ingredients:

Salt, ¼ tablespoon

Water, 1 cup

1 cup Rolled oats

1 cup blueberry

3 maple tablespoons

3 tablespoons of Greek yogurt

Toasted pecans preferably 2 teaspoons

Direction:

Heat the pan.

Boil half full of water. Add salt.

Add oats and stir oats then cook for 5 minutes.

Ensure that water is completely absorbed while stirring.

Remove after 5 minutes and give it time to cool.

Add pecan, blueberries, and yogurt.

Serve and enjoy.

**Midmorning snack**

Orange

Preparation time -> 3 minutes

Direction:

Cut into pieces after peeling the skin off and enjoy.

**Lunch**

Roasted Quinoa Salad

Preparation time -> 10 minutes

Cooking time -> 25 minutes

Ingredients:

1 red onion

1 cup sweet potato

1 cup zucchini

2 cup tomato (cherry)

1 lemon

5 tablespoons olive oil

Salt, pepper

1 cup fresh parsley

2 tablespoon apple

5 cup quinoa

Direction:

Heat the oven till warm.

Add ingredients: onion, corn, tomatoes, sweet potatoes, and zucchini to the baking sheet in the oven.

Make juice with the lemon.

Pour olive oil to the lemon juice and then add salt and pepper.

Roast the veggie for 25 minutes.

Add quinoa to the transferred bowl of roasted veggie and toss them well.

Mix apple cider with olive oil in another bowl and make sure to toss them, too.

Lastly, access the parsley and garnish, serve and enjoy.

**Dinner**

Chicken and White Beans

Preparation time -> 30 minutes

Cooking time -> 1 hour

Ingredients:

½ tablespoon vegetable oil

3 chicken breasts

White beans

3 cups chicken broth

Pepper and salt teaspoon

Peeled and chopped onions

¾ cup of water

Ground cumin

Cooking instructions

Heat oven with less heat.

Place broth and beans and cover them. Cover for two hours.

In another cooker, pour olive oil and boil for 20 seconds then add chicken and salt.

After a minute, add pepper. Flip the chicken on sides while cooking for 6 minutes.

Drain after the minutes are over.

Continue cooking by adding ingredients: chilies, onion mixture, and garlic.

Add water when done and let it cook.

Cook for 30 minutes while stirring.

Remove beans from the other cooker and set in a plate then add chicken.

Serve while hot and enjoy.

# Day 5

**Breakfast**

Raspberry with Muesli

Preparation time -> 20 minutes

Cooking time -> 15 minutes

Ingredients:

4 cups apple juice

4 cups rolled oats

3 green apples (grated)

3 tablespoon vanilla

500g raspberry

3 tablespoon honey

3 cups of yogurt (natural)

3 tablespoon vanilla essence

Direction:

Open fire and heat the juice in the pan for at least 3 minutes until warm.

Assemble vanilla and oats to a big bowl and pour your warm juice there.

Place in a freezer for 30 minutes until the juiced is soaked.

Remove it from the freezer. Add raspberries and apple on the top and mix.

Add the natural yogurt, honey, and vanilla and stir them well.

Place the oat mixture in a glass and serve.

Enjoy.

**Midmorning snack**

Cucumber and Vinaigrette

Preparation time -> 5 minutes

Preparation method

Mix cucumber and vinaigrette together.

Serve and enjoy.

**Lunch**

Tomato & Artichoke Gnocchi

Preparation time -> 10 minutes

Cooking time -> 20 minutes

Ingredients:

1 tablespoon Salt garlic

3 Olive oil

Tomatoes

1 jar Artichoke hearts (chopped)

2 tablespoon Basil fresh

6 ounces of cheese

2 tablespoon oregano

Gnocchi 1 package

Cooking instructions

Heat olive oil in a pan.

Add salt and sauté until golden.

Add ingredients: artichokes, tomatoes, basil, and oregano

Boil for 7 minutes.

Put half-size water in a pan and heat, then add gnocchi and boil until you start seeing it float up in the water.

Stir all of them until they fully blend for about 7 minutes.

Serve while hot and enjoy.

Afternoon snack

Orange (or any seasonal fruit)

Preparation time -> 3 minutes

Preparation method

Cut into pieces after peeling the skin off and enjoy.

**Dinner**

Roasted Root Vegetables with Goat Cheese

Preparation time -> 10 minutes

Cooking time -> 50 minutes

Ingredients:

Fresh thyme

3 peppers green

2 two onions

Salt

Olive oil

Goat cheese ¼ kg

Parsley

Cooking instructions
Heat the oven.
Add olive oil to the pan.
Add the ingredients: onion, pepper.
Add salt and thyme.
Add vegetables and roast for 20 minutes.
Serve with cheese and parsley and enjoy

# Day 6

**Breakfast**
Creamy Blueberry and Pecan Oats
Preparation time -> 5 minutes
Cooking time -> 10 minutes
Ingredients:
Salt, ¼ tablespoon
Water, 1 cup
1 cup Rolled oats
1 cup blueberry
3 maple tablespoon
3 tablespoon of Greek yogurt
Toasted pecans preferably 2 teaspoon
Direction:
Heat the pan.
Boil half full of water. Add salt.
Add oats and stir the oats then cook for 5 minutes.
Ensure that water is completely absorbed while stirring.
Remove after 5 minutes and give it time to cool.
Add pecan, blueberries, and yogurt.
Serve and enjoy.

**Lunch**
Chickpea and Veggie Grain
Cooking time -> 10 minutes
Ingredients:
Lemmon juice
Garlic salt
Parsley
3 Ounces cauliflower
Tamari
Chicken peas ½ sumac teaspoon
½ cup Brown rice

Tahini paste ½ tablespoon
Greek yogurt
Cooking instructions
Boil water.
Slice and peel the ingredients and add them.
Boil for 10 minutes.
Serve with Greek yogurt and enjoy.

**Afternoon Snack**
10 peanuts (0r any dried fruits) will be enough to keep you going until dinner time.

**Dinner**
Mediterranean Chicken and Orzo
Preparation time -> 10 minutes
Cooking time -> 50 minutes
Ingredients:
Lemon juice
Virgin olive oil
3 oregano (dry)
Coriander 2 Tsp
3teaspoons paprika
Pepper and salt
7 garlic
4 cups of Chicken broth
Whole Grain
Tomatoes
Direction:
Heat the oven on medium heat.
Pick a bowl and mix all the ingredient and spices together: coriander, pepper, paprika, salt, and oregano.
Add lemon juice to the coated chicken and set aside for 20 minutes.
Add chicken and cook for 10 minutes while flipping till they turn brown. Add green pepper.
In another oven, add ingredients: pepper, onions and olive oil together and cook while stirring for three minutes. Add chicken broth and salt and continue boiling.
Serve with Mediterranean salad and roasted garlic hummus.

# Day 7

**Breakfast**

Creamy Blueberry and Pecan Oats

Preparation time -> 5 minutes

Cooking time -> 40 minutes

Ingredients:

Pepper

Garlic

Olive oil

Potatoes

Onion

Mixed herbs

Tomatoes

Egg

Cheese

Direction:

Heat the oven.

Boil water and put potatoes, let them boil for 8 minutes.

Prepare ingredients: pepper, cheese, onion, and tomatoes.

Fry the ingredients.

Add orange pepper and cook for a minute.

Cook potatoes with garlic for three minutes. Add cheese.

Beat eggs and drizzle garlic and pepper.

Pour the eggs on a vegetable mixture of cheese and bake for 20 minutes.

Serve while hot and enjoy.

**Midmorning snack**

Raspberry and Greek Yogurt

Preparation time -> 5 minutes

Ingredients:

2 tablespoon almonds (sliced)

2 cup raspberry

½ cup of Greek yogurt

Preparation method

Pick raspberry, mix Greek yogurt, and almonds then top with a raspberry.

Serve and enjoy.

**Lunch**

Tilapia

Ingredients:

Tilapia

Olive oil

Butter

Melon salsa

Direction:

Heat olive oil and cook the tilapia at least 5 minutes while flipping.

Accompany the fish with mango-melon salsa, and a cup of strawberry Jell-O.

Serve and enjoy.

**Dinner**

Quinoa and roasted vegetables

Cooking time -> 20 minutes

Ingredients:

Vegetable and Quinoa

Fudge bar and a side salad with vinaigrette or Italian dressing

Direction:

Roast the vegetable and stir them together with quinoa.

Add fudge and a slide salad. Serve while hot.

# 28 Conversion Tables

## Volume equivalents (liquid)

| US Standard | US Standard (ounces) | Metric (approximate) |
|---|---|---|
| 2 tablespoons | 1 fl. oz. | 30 mL |
| ¼ cup | 2 fl. oz. | 60 mL |
| ½ cup | 4 fl. oz. | 120 mL |
| 1 cup | 8 fl. oz. | 240 mL |
| 1½ cups | 12 fl. oz. | 355 mL |
| 2 cups or 1 pint | 16 fl. oz. | 475 mL |
| 4 cups or 1 quart | 32 fl. oz. | 1 L |
| 1 gallon | 128 fl. oz. | 4 L |

## Oven Temperatures

| Fahrenheit(F) | Celsius (C) (approximate) |
|---|---|
| 250°F | 120°C |
| 300°F | 150°C |
| 325°F | 165°C |
| 350°F | 180°C |
| 375°F | 190°C |
| 400°F | 200°C |
| 425°F | 220°C |
| 450°F | 230°C |

## Volume equivalents (dry)

| US Standard | Metric (approximate) |
| --- | --- |
| ⅛ teaspoon | 0.5 mL |
| ¼ teaspoon | 1 mL |
| ½ teaspoon | 2 mL |
| ¾ teaspoon | 4 mL |
| 1 teaspoon | 5 mL |
| 1 tablespoon | 15 mL |
| ¼ cup | 59 mL |
| ½ cup | 118 mL |
| ¾ cup | 177 mL |
| 1 cup | 235 mL |
| 2 cups or 1 pint | 475 mL |
| 3 cups | 700 mL |
| 4 cups or 1 quart | 1 L |

## Weight equivalents

| US Standard | Metric (approximate) |
| --- | --- |
| ½ ounce | 15 g |
| 1 ounce | 30 g |
| 2 ounces | 60 g |
| 4 ounces | 115 g |
| 8 ounces | 225 g |
| 12 ounces | 340 g |
| 16 ounces or 1 pound | 455 g |

# 29 The Food Pyramid

The Mediterranean lifestyle follows a very specific food pyramid that is probably a little different than the one you're used to. Certain food groups are given priority while others should be consumed in moderation. Studies have shown that these foods are protective against the effects of certain chronic diseases.

In short, plant-based foods make up the largest chunk of this food pyramid so they should be consumed in greater proportions than the rest. You'll notice that all recipes found in this book are mostly comprised of plant-based foods. Here are some of the main takeaways from the Mediterranean food pyramid.

**These Should Be Eaten Every Day**

Your meals should be built around these three elements.

Whole Grains: You should consume at least one full serving of whole grains with every meal. These can be in the form of bread, pasta, rice, and couscous.

Vegetables: You should consume at least two servings of vegetables per meal. Including a variety of different vegetables ensures that you are getting all of the proper antioxidants and protective nutrients.

Fruits: You should consume at least two servings of fruit per day. You'll find that breakfast and late night desserts are your best options for eating fruit.

**Make Sure You Drink Enough Water**

I know it's not exactly a food group, but it's essential that you drink the right amount of water per day. Divide your weight in half to determine how many ounces of water you need to drink per day. Of course, this amount will change slightly depending on your age and the amount of physical activity you take part in every day.

Good hydration is important because it helps maintain balance within the body.

**Consume These Foods in Moderation Daily**

Here are some more important foods to the Mediterranean diet, but they should be eaten in moderation.

Dairy Products: You should consume at least one serving per day. Dairy products possess a lot of essential nutrients that contribute to good bone health and can also be an amazing source of healthy fats.

Olive Oil: There is a reason why olive oil can be found at the center of the Mediterranean food pyramid. This entire way of life revolves around it. Olive oil is highly nutritious, and its unique composition provides a much higher resistance to cooking than other oils. It can also be used to make amazing homemade salad dressings. Just make sure you limit it to one tablespoon per meal.

**Regular Exercise**

Research shows that being physically active is one of the most important things you can do for your health. According to the CDC, physical activity can help control weight; reduce the risk of heart disease, diabetes, and cancers; strengthen bones, muscles, and mobility; improve mental health; and lead to a longer life.

Exercise plays an important role in the 28-day Mediterranean diet plan because it will help you feel more energetic and help burn the calories you are eating more efficiently. Ideally, a regimen of 30 minutes of cardio 4 days a week is optimal. However, if you have never exercised before, feel like you have no time, or are timid about starting, don't fret. Every bit counts, so it's okay to start slowly. Sometimes, 10 minutes a day is all you need to jump-start your motivation to do more.

I always tell my patients that you don't have to run a marathon. Just start somewhere. If walking around the parking lot at work is an option, start there. If you can get to the gym on the weekends, do that. If you have a treadmill at home collecting dust, clean it off and hop on for 15 minutes while making a call or watching your favorite television show. Decide what is best for you and work it into your schedule. To hold yourself accountable, write it on your calendar like any other important date. Over time, you can gradually increase your workouts.

Exercise should include a combination of aerobic (cardio) and muscle-strengthening activities. Both the American Heart Association and World Health Organization recommend 30 minutes of moderate aerobic activity 5 days per week, or 25 minutes of vigorous aerobic activity 3 days per week, or a combination. They also recommend strengthening activities at least 2 days per week for additional health benefits. Individuals who wish to lower their blood pressure or cholesterol should get 40 minutes of aerobic activity at least 3 times a week. Do not let the statistics muddle your brain, though. Every minute spent working your body helps.

**Getting the Most out of Your Workouts**

The key is to find the right exercise for you. It should be one you enjoy.

Cardio workouts are extremely important for any weight-loss and health plan. No matter what type of cardio you do, here are some tips for getting the most out of your workouts:

Mix It Up With Interval Training. You'll burn more calories by alternating between a few minutes at a regular pace and a few minutes going faster. You will also build endurance.

Use Your Arms. Many forms of cardio are all about the legs, so whenever possible, maximize your cardio time by focusing on working your arms as well. While walking or running, raise your arms up and down above your head or swinging them to the side. If you can, try to work your arms while on a treadmill or elliptical.

Go A Little Bit Longer. If you are doing 30 minutes, try doing 5 or 10 minutes more. You'd be surprised how many more calories you burn by pushing yourself a little longer—and you'll feel so empowered!

Incorporate Strength Training. Use inclines whenever possible and carry or wear light weights when walking.

Change It Up. Get more out of your cardio workouts by including three or more different varieties each week. Walk for a few minutes and move to the elliptical or bike. This enables you to work different muscle groups and keep the routine fresh and interesting.

Challenge Yourself. Find other ways to make your cardio workout harder. If you bike, stand instead of resting. If you're in a class, try the more intensive movements.

Getting started is the hardest part of exercise. Once you're going, try to give it all you've got. When you are done with your workout, you will feel great.

**Set a Routine**

Aerobic and strengthening activities work differently, but both are important for weight loss and good health. Aerobic, or cardio, activity increases our heart rate and blood circulation through the body. It also releases endorphins, a feel-good hormone. Walking, jogging, running, biking, swimming, rowing, elliptical use, and stair climbing are some of the more common cardio exercises that raise metabolic rates and burn calories.

Strength training, much like cardio, helps strengthen your heart and improves blood flow. It also strengthens your core, builds muscle, increases bone density, and more. This is good news for dieters, especially because muscle mass burns more calories than body fat, even at rest. It is important to strengthen muscles, but it is even more important to strengthen your core. Push-ups, sit-ups, walking lunges, Pilates exercises, and repetitions using weights are just a few strength exercises you can use to work your core and muscles.

Scheduling both cardio and strength exercises in your workout routine will help you reap optimum results! The following is a four-week sample exercise recommendation table you can follow or fill in with an exercise plan that works for you. This particular plan includes 30 minutes of cardio activity 4 times weekly, along with an increasing buildup of strength-training exercises. After the first 4 weeks, you can maintain a regular pattern of cardio and core exercise.

# Conclusion

If your main goal is to lose weight while eating Mediterranean meals, then you will make a wonderful choice. Slimming with this diet goes steadily and in a healthy way. There is no restriction or starvation, but rather eating foods that are not processed.

Switching to the fresh and whole foods might be challenging if you are used to eating fast food, red and processed meats, sweets, white flour, sugar, and alcohol. The risk of cancer, heart failures, high blood pressure, cholesterol, depression, inflammations, poor immunity, and other health issues is significantly higher when your menu consists mostly of unhealthy food.
This diet is a sure way to purge your blood, improve your general mood and health, boost your immunity, and lower the risk of evil diseases such as type 2 diabetes, breast and colon cancer, or Alzheimer's disease.

Studies have shown that even depression and anxiety are directly connected with the choice of food. Foods that grew naturally and under the sun have a far bigger chance to improve your mood and boost your body with serotonin. One of the greatest things about the Mediterranean way of eating is that you do not have to be an extraordinary cook to prepare your meals. With the right ingredients, you can always make simple and delicious meals that don't require hours in the kitchen.

Prepare your weekly meal plan, buy the groceries, and simply stick to eating the suitable foods. Your energy will be higher, your brain's cognitive functions and memory will improve, and you will never feel bloated. Digestion will become easier, and you will feel happier.

The most important thing for people who want to slim down with this diet is to keep a positive mindset. This is a healthy lifestyle that requires you to pay attention to the food you are eating, spend more time with your loved ones, and do more physical activity. Once you lose weight, you will keep maintaining your figure by simply eating your favorite meals. Since this diet does not feel like a diet, it is super easy to follow. There is no yo-yo effect because you will remain true to your Mediterranean menu.

This diet is a wonderful way for you to get rid of your unhealthy eating habits and kill all the cravings for junk food. At the end of the day, nothing is forbidden in this diet.

There are foods that are recommended to be consumed frequently, and foods that should be eaten every once in a while.

Recipes grasp the precepts of the Mediterranean Diet Pyramid, deciphering its not so much meat-but rather more vegetables approach into dynamic, solid one-dish suppers that remove the mystery from adjusting partitions and various dishes.

When you see that you have lost a couple of pounds within the first week, you will know that you brought the right decision.

Finally, what matters is you feeling content, happy, and good in your skin.

The Mediterranean diet will change the way you look in a matter of days. It will improve your overall health, your metabolism and it will help you lose the extra weight.

Printed in Great Britain
by Amazon